DEALING WITH
CHINA

Also by Henry M. Paulson, Jr.

*On the Brink: Inside the Race to Stop the Collapse of
the Global Financial System*

DEALING WITH
CHINA

AN INSIDER
UNMASKS THE NEW ECONOMIC
SUPERPOWER

HENRY M.
PAULSON, JR.

TWELVE

NEW YORK   BOSTON

Twelve
Hachette Book Group
1290 Avenue of the Americas
New York, NY 10104
twelvebooks.com
twitter.com/twelvebooks

Originally published in hardcover by Hachette Book Group
First Trade Paperback Edition: April 2016

Twelve is an imprint of Grand Central Publishing.
The Twelve name and logo are trademarks of Hachette Book Group, Inc.

The publisher is not responsible for websites (or their content) that are not owned by the publisher.

The Hachette Speakers Bureau provides a wide range of authors for speaking events. To find out more, go to www.hachettespeakersbureau.com or call (866) 376-6591.

Library of Congress Cataloging-in-Publication Data

Paulson, Henry M., 1946–
    Dealing with China: an insider unmasks the new economic superpower / by Henry M. Paulson Jr.—First Edition.
        pages cm
    Summary: "DEALING WITH CHINA takes the reader behind closed doors to witness the creation and evolution of China's state-controlled capitalism" —Provided by publisher.
    Includes bibliographical references and index.
    ISBN 978-1-4555-0421-3 (hardback)—ISBN 978-1-4555-4533-9 (large print)—
ISBN 978-1-4555-7770-5 (international)—ISBN 978-1-61969-626-6 (audio download)—
ISBN 978-1-61113-899-3 (audio book)—ISBN 978-1-4555-0422-0 (ebook)
    1. China—Economic policy—2000– 2. Free enterprise—China. 3. China—Politics and government—21st century. I. Title.
    HC427.95.P38 2015
    330.951—dc23

                                                                2014046269

ISBN: 978-1-4555-0420-6 (trade paperback)

Printed in the United States of America

LSC-C

10 9 8 7 6 5 4 3 2

For Willa, Cassidy, Finn, and Addie
So you will know why Boppa has spent so much time in China

Visiting with future president Xi Jinping at Hangzhou's famed West Lake State Guest House on my first trip to China as Treasury secretary in September 2006 *(AP Photo/Eugene Hoshiko)*

Contents

Map of China   ix

Preface   xi

Part One: Banking on Reform   1

Chapter One: At the Purple Light Pavilion   3

Chapter Two: Chinese Bodies, Foreign Technology   16

Chapter Three: Dealmaking with Chinese Characteristics   29

Chapter Four: Real Gold and Silver   43

Chapter Five: Your Chairman Has Gone to Sleep   66

Chapter Six: Cleaning the Stables in Guangdong   86

Chapter Seven: School for Success   104

Chapter Eight: Saving Shangri-La   115

Chapter Nine: One Bank, Two Systems   132

Chapter Ten: The World's Biggest Mattress   154

Part Two: Breaking New Ground   175

Chapter Eleven: A Call to Serve   177

Chapter Twelve: The Great Patio Debate   203

Chapter Thirteen: Hammering Out a New Framework   223

Chapter Fourteen: A Global Reckoning   239

Part Three: Building Bridges   265

Chapter Fifteen: Darkness at Noon   267

Chapter Sixteen: Skylines and Shorelines   283

Chapter Seventeen: BIT by BIT   309

Chapter Eighteen: The $10 Trillion Reboot   328

Chapter Nineteen: The Party Line   350

Chapter Twenty: The Way Forward   378

Acknowledgments   405

Cast of Characters   407

List of Acronyms   413

Index   417

About the Author   429

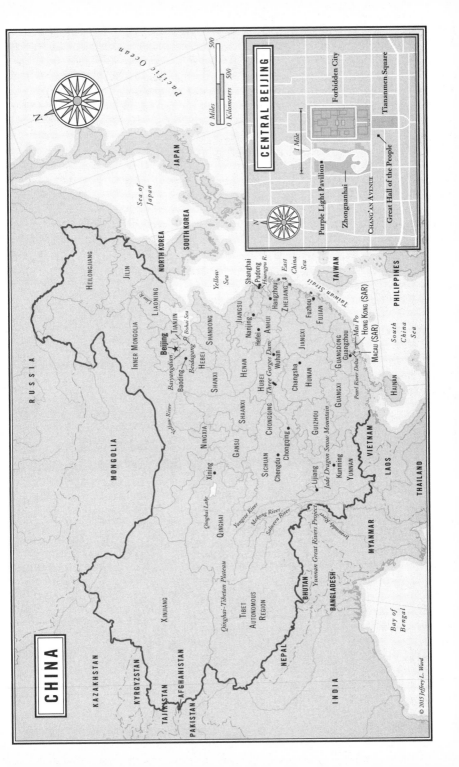

Preface

China's rise to economic superpower surely ranks among the most extraordinary stories in history. In barely three decades, this once backward, insular country has moved hundreds of millions of people out of poverty while turning itself into the world's second-biggest economy. I can think of no country that has grown so much so quickly. The U.S.'s rise to industrial supremacy after the Civil War comes to mind, but the Chinese may have already outstripped our great run, and they're not done yet. In the not-too-distant future, they are likely to surpass us as the world's biggest economy, knocking us off a perch we've occupied for nearly 150 years.

China's transformation has been as spectacular as it has been swift. Its spanking-new skyscrapers, high-speed rail lines, and space-age airports stand in sharp contrast to our own increasingly creaky infrastructure. One day we read of a Chinese entrepreneur's grandiose plans to spend $50 billion to carve a passage through Nicaragua twice the size of the Panama Canal; the next we learn that a Chinese developer wants to buy a chunk of Iceland; then it's a manufacturer turned builder who hopes to erect the world's tallest building, from prefabricated units, in six months.

Today's China is a land of superlatives. It is home to the world's fastest supercomputer, the biggest wind-power base, the longest sea bridge. It produces and uses nearly half of the world's coal, cement, iron ore, and steel; it consumes 40 percent of the aluminum and copper. By one estimate, China will soon account for nearly half of all the new buildings under construction on earth. Forty years ago most Americans wouldn't have imagined owing China one red cent. Now it is the U.S.'s biggest creditor, owning just under $1.3 trillion of our government's debt. It's enough to make the head spin—or for Americans to wonder how the world got turned upside down so fast.

Lately, however, China has become as much a source of concern as a source of awe. We find ourselves increasingly at cross purposes with an ever more competitive China as it flexes its newfound muscles in world markets and in bitter territorial disputes with its neighbors, while it seeks to challenge the U.S.-led order in Asia and in aspects of the system of global governance that has prevailed since World War II. Its government appears unwilling or unable to prevent the cybertheft of intellectual property from U.S. companies, and it is tightening its grip on Chinese society through an authoritarian, one-party system of government that Americans don't understand and don't like.

Suspicion is a two-way street. Support for positive relations with the United States is waning among Chinese, growing numbers of whom believe that the U.S. and other countries want to impede their country's ascent.

These developments threaten to undermine a relationship that, over more than four decades, has made substantial contributions to economic growth, job creation, and prosperity in both countries, while enhancing international security, not least by helping to fashion a peaceful end to the Cold War. Now, no shortage of Americans wonder: What do the Chinese really want? Why are they spending so much money on their military? Are they friends or enemies, trading partners or commercial and geopolitical adversaries? In short, how do we deal with China?

This book is my attempt to address these concerns, through stories of my personal experience in working with the Chinese to get things done. I'm not a scholar or theorist. I don't read, write, or speak Chinese. I'm a businessman who brings a firsthand knowledge of China and its corporate and political leaders. I have gleaned this over more than 100 visits to the country and nearly 25 years of dealing with Chinese officials on commercial matters while at Goldman Sachs, on affairs of state and macroeconomic policy while U.S. secretary of the Treasury, and, nowadays, as head of the Paulson Institute, which promotes sustainable economic growth and a cleaner environment through greater cooperation between the U.S. and China. During that time I've had the opportunity to work closely with the most senior leaders of the last three administrations in China: Jiang Zemin and Zhu Rongji in the 1990s, Hu Jintao and Wen Jiabao in the early years of this century; and Xi Jinping and Li Keqiang today.

I write as an American who is deeply concerned about our country's standing in the world, the health of our economy and our environment, and the long-term prospects of our citizens. I take the view that all of these will benefit from active engagement with China, that clear-eyed, constructive cooperation is the best way to advance our national interest. The Chinese are formidable competitors. But we should not fear competition or shrink from it.

I've held this conviction for a long time. Within weeks of being sworn in as Treasury secretary, I traveled to China to lay the groundwork for a new approach to our most important bilateral relationship. Growth and economic reform were China's dominant concerns, and I believed we could leverage our newly conceived Strategic Economic Dialogue to more effectively manage many other pressing matters as well.

China's rise has spawned a misconception that haunts the way some in both countries view our relationship: namely that the "China model" represents a better form of capitalism that is triumphing even as the U.S. fades into decline. In fact, China's leaders know only too well their country's vulnerabilities. Market reforms first began under Deng Xiaoping in 1978, but expanding their reach and impact is more important than ever to the leadership. For all of its success, China has a long way to go. More than 100 million of its people remain mired in poverty. Its per-capita GDP ranks 80th in the world. That's just one place ahead of Iraq, and roughly one-eighth our level. The pace of China's prodigious growth is slowing down, making market reforms at once more urgent and more difficult to achieve. The country's 7.4 percent increase in GDP in 2014 came in under the official forecast for the first time in 16 years—and many experts expect further declines in the growth rate.

China needs to shift its $10 trillion economy from an overreliance on exports and inefficient government investment in infrastructure, fueled by ominously rising debts at all levels of regional government, toward increased domestic consumption and a greater emphasis on service industries and high-end manufacturing. That's an enormous task, complicated by the fact that much of the economy remains under the thumb of central planners, even after years of reform. Entrenched interests are resisting further changes. Meantime, years of not-so-benign neglect have left the environment a near disaster that has sparked growing restiveness among China's citizens.

And while there's much we must do to fix our own house, the U.S. remains the world's biggest, most advanced, and most dynamic economy. China's leaders understand that to further their economic transformation they need the continued goodwill and cooperation of the U.S. and other countries that, in so many ways, continue to dominate the global economic system. They want greater access to our markets, our knowhow, and our most advanced technologies.

The U.S.-China relationship will become better balanced and more secure and productive for both sides if each country makes some adjustments. We Americans worry about China's increasingly militaristic tone; they view our "pivot to Asia" as a potential effort to contain their country's rise. We want the Chinese to open their markets to our companies, and we want them to abide by the existing rules as they integrate further into the international system. China prefers to modify these rules and be treated with greater respect and deference in the global arena.

There are some who believe that an immutable law of history holds that conflict is inevitable when a rising power begins to bump up against an established one. But this law is not immutable. Choices matter. Lessons can be learned. And statesmen and stateswomen can, and do, make a difference.

I do not believe that anything is "inevitable" about the U.S.-China relationship, but there are real risks that could lead to intensified competition, or even conflict. The key to avoiding a hostile relationship is to get tangible things done that benefit both of us. For all the potential flashpoints between our countries, we share far more interests—spurring global growth, combating climate change, maintaining peace and stability. Yet this fact won't matter a whit unless we are able to turn common concerns into complementary policies and actions. We need to broaden and deepen our economic ties, especially. And it is my hope that *Dealing with China* will shed some light on how to do just that.

One thing I will not do is to try to predict the future. I won't hesitate, however, to make recommendations about a range of topics including economic reform, financial markets, urbanization, the environment, and ways to strengthen U.S.-China relations. Prescriptions, after all, are easier to make than predictions. My prescriptions are rooted in the personal experiences I share in these pages. I hope they will help those working with China, whether in business, government, or philanthropy, to get concrete and productive results. That can't help but bring our two countries closer together.

We face daunting challenges in today's increasingly complex and interconnected world. Almost all of them, from cybersecurity to opening up big markets for American exports, will be easier to meet if the United States and China can work together or in complementary ways. Our task will be much more difficult, if not impossible, to solve if the world's two most important economic powers work against each other.

PART ONE

Banking on Reform

CHAPTER ONE

At the Purple Light Pavilion

The streets were quiet, the concrete vastness of Tiananmen Square mostly empty, as our car sped through central Beijing toward Zhongnanhai, the secluded compound of the Chinese leadership. It was the 25th of February 1997, a crisp, late winter day, near dusk. The globes of the square's streetlamps had just come on. In my frequent trips to China, I had become used to the din and press of great throngs everywhere, not least on the roads with their ever-increasing ranks of cars, trucks, and buses. But today's was an eerie quiet such as I had never encountered before. Deng Xiaoping, the paramount leader of China, had died the previous week, and the nation was in mourning. I was on my way, with colleagues from Goldman Sachs, to a private meeting with one of Deng's protégés.

Deng had been the chief architect of the extraordinary changes sweeping China. With savvy, willpower, and relentless pragmatism, he had shucked ideological chains to devise a unique brand of "socialism with Chinese characteristics," introduced market principles, and encouraged individual enterprise throughout the economy, starting with agriculture and extending into industrial and financial areas. The results of his "Reform and Opening Up" initiatives, begun in 1978, had been nothing short of spectacular. After the political and economic chaos of Mao's last years, China's gross domestic product had soared by near double-digit average annual increases for two decades, lifting hundreds of millions of people out of poverty. Once scarce food staples were plentiful. Previously unavailable, or unaffordable, consumer goods could be bought at rapidly proliferating retail outlets, and China was quickly becoming a global manufacturing and export powerhouse.

Deng's death, though, raised questions of how far, and how fast, the country would pursue his vision. That morning Jiang Zemin, general secretary of the Communist Party and the nation's most senior leader, had sought to reassure the country and the world that he would stay the course. In a teary eulogy delivered before 10,000 handpicked Party and military leaders in the Great Hall of the People—and an estimated 400 million on live television—Jiang had condemned the "grave mistake" of the Cultural Revolution and pledged to continue Deng's policies of economic reform and international engagement. But, as I knew, certain hard-liners in the Communist Party and in the apparatus of the state were pressing to slow down or even halt reform. They feared that China would abandon Marxism or that the disruptions caused by the changes might destabilize the nation.

It was an altogether crucial juncture for the country. In July, a little more than four months away, Hong Kong was to be returned to China after more than 150 years under British rule. From this distance in time, it can be easy, especially for Americans, to forget just how momentous—and nerve-wracking—an occasion this was for all sides. Deng had devised a formula of "one country, two systems" to guarantee that Hong Kong could continue its capitalist ways, with some political autonomy, for at least 50 years after its return to China. But many in Hong Kong remained skeptical: a good number had fled China after the Communists came to power, and painful memories had been reawakened by Beijing's harsh crackdown on protesters, mostly students, in Tiananmen Square in June 1989, nearly eight years before. Some 700,000 Hong Kong citizens, more than one in ten, had obtained foreign passports as a precaution, and a number of companies had changed their corporate domiciles.

I had flown up from Hong Kong that morning, eager and a little on edge. I was scheduled to meet with Vice Premier Zhu Rongji, the country's economic czar. I knew that any matters involving reform or Hong Kong held the highest of priorities for China's senior leaders and had to be dealt with just right. There was simply no margin for error. At the time, I was president and chief operating officer of Goldman Sachs, the investment bank, and, as it happened, I would be discussing with Zhu a matter that touched closely on both issues—restructuring China's telecommunications system through an offering of shares in a newly formed Hong Kong–listed company. As part of its rapid modernization, China had been investing heavily in the area, keenly aware of how crucial state-of-the-art telecommunications were to a modern economy.

Western bankers were Promethean figures in this process: we jetted in and competed to show the Chinese how to kindle the fire of capital markets. Goldman had been discussing aspects of a listing for months with representatives of China International Capital Corporation (CICC), an investment bank that was a joint venture between one of the country's four biggest commercial banks and Morgan Stanley. It was one of the many oddities of doing business in China that we found ourselves working closely with the most senior Chinese banker at the partner of our most intense U.S. rival. It was even odder that Morgan Stanley did not know what we were doing—and we had no interest in letting them find out.

Our team that day included John Thornton, a superb dealmaker who had helped establish our investment banking presence in Europe and had just been named chairman of Asia; Mike Evans, the head of our equity capital markets, who had worked on transforming state-owned industries into private companies across Europe; Hsueh-ming Wang, a seasoned relationship banker from the Hong Kong office; and Cherry Li, a native Chinese, who was our first representative in Beijing, where we had opened an office in 1994. John and Hsueh-ming had been working assiduously for months to cultivate the senior Chinese executives of CICC.

We drove in two cars past the Forbidden City, the immense former imperial palace, and then past the Xinhua Gate, the ornate, imposing southern entrance to Zhongnanhai. We turned north onto Fuyou Street, which traced the red walls, topped with traditional cylindrical tiling, of the leadership compound, before being admitted through the northwest entrance. Guards had already been informed of the license plate numbers of our cars, and after a quick head count, they waved us into the grounds with smart salutes.

For the center of power in China, where members of the leadership have worked, and sometimes lived, since the revolution, the compound itself was unprepossessing and understated. It resembled nothing so much as the campus of a small college during winter break, with traditional Chinese structures scattered among small-scale beige and gray buildings, perhaps three or four stories high, that were bland and uninspired from the outside, what an architectural historian might call Soviet-style. Originally an imperial park and garden, Zhongnanhai had housed several palaces alongside its lakes. Following the fall of the Qing dynasty, it served as the headquarters for the government of the Republic of China until 1928, then became a public park until the Communists came to power in 1949.

Zhu Rongji had chosen to see us at the Purple Light Pavilion, set near the edge of a lake. It was a striking, pagodalike structure, with vermilion walls and green roof tiles; it dated to the Ming dynasty and had long been used by the leadership to meet foreign guests in a more private manner. Chinese aides informed us that Zhu Rongji had not yet arrived and we had a few minutes to wait, so we hopped out of the cars into the brisk late afternoon air.

We strolled across a grass verge dotted with sycamores and conifers, mostly pines and cedars. I heard the rasp of a magpie but saw nothing when I peered into the branches of the trees. Across a small lake I could see the outlines of the palace tops behind the immense walls of the Forbidden City, ghostly in the fading light. A military guard unit quickstepped past, their arms swinging in that stiff, elbows-locked way favored by the People's Liberation Army.

I did a last-minute run-through in my mind of the points that I wanted to make. My approach by necessity would have to be a bit circuitous. I wanted to be careful not to presume that any specific deal might be done, or to drag Zhu Rongji too deeply into the details, or worse, to give the impression that I might somehow be asking him to make a decision in favor of us, right then and there. But I wanted to make it clear that we understood how important reforming the economy was to China's future and how crucial modernizing and overhauling state-owned enterprises (SOEs) like China's telecom business were to that process. And I wanted to make clear that Goldman Sachs was the best bank in the world to get done all these things that we were not going to specifically speak about.

I asked Mike Evans if I was forgetting anything.

"You're set," he said. "Just remember how much reform matters to Zhu."

I had met Zhu Rongji a few years before, when China was planning to raise money in the international bond markets and we had advised the country on how to work with the credit agencies. He was a formidable figure. Tall and erect, he had been plucked by Deng from his post as mayor of Shanghai and installed as vice premier in 1991. Though officially the country's economic portfolio fell under Premier Li Peng, Zhu ran the economy day to day and was expected to succeed Li when the new leaders of the government were selected over the coming year.

Zhu had done a first-rate job. When the economy overheated in 1993, he had taken direct charge of the central bank and put in place a series of tough austerity measures and smart administrative fixes, battling inflation, which would rise to more than 20 percent before he guided China to a soft landing. Privatization efforts, which had begun in a modest way in 1992 and 1993, had been shelved temporarily, but now as the economy recovered, these had come to the forefront again in discussions with individual ministries and the State Council, China's equivalent of the U.S. Cabinet.

Selling shares in the telecommunications system to the public was meant to be a showcase and the cornerstone of the next ambitious phase of reform, the restructuring of the giant state-owned enterprises that dominated Chinese commercial life. In anticipation of membership in the World Trade Organization, Zhu Rongji had in mind a thorough revamping that would modernize these lumbering money-losing behemoths and make Chinese businesses more efficient and more competitive. He would accomplish this in part by bringing in foreign know-how and investors that he believed would push for global standards of management, controls, operations, and governance.

If Deng was the architect of reform, and Jiang Zemin the general contractor carrying out his vision, then, to borrow a term often used to describe me, Zhu Rongji was the hammer. He had no shortage of big ideas himself, but above all he got things done. He was frank, practical, and to the point. I never doubted for a second what he wanted, nor did his subordinates. Known as the Boss, he was tough, demanding, fond of imposing unrealistically tight deadlines: in short, a man after my own heart.

To get a meeting in China with an important government figure requires a sponsor. Our meeting with Zhu had been suggested and arranged by Wang Qishan, the head of China Construction Bank (CCB), the bank partnering with Morgan Stanley in CICC. Wang was a warm, dynamic leader who exuded charisma and intellectual curiosity and had an uncanny ability to connect with people, Chinese or Western. I could see he was gifted and going places. Today, after several years as a vice premier overseeing finance and trade, Wang Qishan serves on the Party's seven-member Politburo Standing Committee, China's most powerful body, and heads its Central Commission for Discipline Inspection, tasked with rooting out corruption.

The previous summer Wang Qishan had stopped by my office at Goldman Sachs in New York to gauge our interest in helping to take China Telecom public. China Construction Bank was unhappy with Morgan Stanley and looking for an alternative. My colleagues and I were eager to work on a groundbreaking transaction of such importance to the future of China, but we were also wary. Taking China Telecom public would involve an immense amount of work, because, to begin with, there was no such thing as a company as we understood it in conventional terms. There were customers, there were phones, there were exchanges, there was a small but rapidly growing mobile telephony business, but it was all scattered throughout the country in the village, township, city, county, and provincial outposts and headquarters of the Ministry of Posts and Telecommunications.

The MPT was a creaky bureaucratic holdover of the Maoist era that had under its purview more than a million employees and thousands of local bureaus. It had little in the way of modern management systems or controls, much less a sound capital structure. Building and upgrading the communications infrastructure had been a focal point of one national five-year plan after another. China had spent $35 billion since 1992 and was adding more than 16 million lines a year. But phone access was still minimal, and coverage was spotty. In a country of 1.2 billion, there were just 55 million landline subscribers, concentrated in coastal cities and special economic zones.

Several Chinese aides escorted us inside the pavilion, up a set of steps flanked by traditional stone lions, and around an imposing, intricately carved wooden door screen. We entered a bright, airy wood-framed room that soared to coffered ceilings perhaps 20 feet high; these were painted in pastels—salmon pink, green, and blue—and trimmed in gold. Zhu Rongji greeted us warmly, shaking our hands and inviting us to take our seats.

I sat to Zhu's right. Cherry Li, acting as my interpreter, was behind me and to my side, while Zhu's interpreter was behind him. Wang Qishan sat to Zhu's left, flanked by additional executives from China Construction Bank. Chinese meetings have a definite choreography and ceremony to them, and it is within this context that you look for the signals being sent and the messages being given. In general, everyone sits in chairs set out in a horseshoe or U-shaped arrangement, with the most senior Chinese official at the closed end of the U and the most important visitor to his right; other Chinese officials and members of the visiting delegation are arrayed in descending rank on the flanks of the horseshoe, facing one another. In the old days the chair backs were quaintly covered with antimacassars; you see fewer of these Victorian artifacts today.

Meetings are anything but free-form. The host and his guest take turns speaking, followed by their interpreters, who usually sit behind the leaders. The rest of the attendees do not speak unless spoken to—which often means not at all. There is no interchange or dialogue in the conventional sense. There can be a stilted, scripted feel to the proceedings. On the Chinese side, a bevy of officials and aides, young and old, junior and senior in rank, assiduously take notes. Note taking is de rigueur, a ubiquitous element of Chinese official life—even today when so many more sophisticated recording methods are available. Indeed, when I met with the now-disgraced Chongqing Party secretary Bo Xilai in Chongqing in December 2011, I was amused to see a handful of note takers diligently copying down everything we said, even though I had noticed the lights of recording devices blinking away under our tented name cards on the broad conference table.

Note taking allows Party and government officials to get quick reads on what went on at meetings they didn't attend. Senior officials can disseminate information internally as well as keep a close eye on what's being said by others in the hierarchy so that messages don't deviate from expectations. I can recall only a few times I went to a meeting in China where I was not reminded, one way or another, by a senior official of something that had come up in an earlier meeting with one of his colleagues. It does tend to keep you on your toes. Private meetings with senior government officials without recording devices or note takers are rare and highly sought after.

Zhu apologized for his tardiness; he had just come from another meeting. Then he invited me to speak first, and I began by expressing my condolences and those of my colleagues at Goldman on the passing of Deng Xiaoping. And while commending Zhu's success in reducing inflation and guiding the economy to a soft landing, I expressed confidence that under his leadership, "the pace of reform [would] speed up a notch."

The competition to work with the government would be intense, so I reviewed Goldman's extensive experience in advising governments. And I reminded Zhu of our senior executives whom he knew personally—men like Brian Griffiths, Baron Griffiths of Fforestfach, who had run the Thatcher government's privatization efforts, and Peter Sutherland, the former head of the General Agreement on Tariffs and Trade and subsequently the first director-general of the World Trade Organization. Zhu was spearheading China's effort to join the WTO, which would not only bring economic benefits but serve as a welcome outside source of pressure to promote his program of domestic reform.

I spoke for several minutes, stopping after every couple of sentences for Zhu's translator to pick up the thread and repeat it in Chinese. I watched as Zhu nodded both at my words as I said them and at the translation. He spoke English fairly well and understood it even better, and later, as I got to know him, he would frequently slip in a sentence or two of English.

Following a suggestion from Wang Qishan, I focused on our work with Deutsche Telekom. I explained how Goldman had led the German company to its successful IPO the previous November. That had come after nearly eight years of our advising the Germans on how to revamp a bloated government department, akin to China's Ministry of Posts and Telecommunications, with posts and telecom business mixed together, which was plagued by low-quality service, low work efficiency, and weak finances. The IPO had raised $13 billion, financing the development of telecom industry infrastructure, particularly in the former East Germany, the once Communist state. The deal had strengthened Deutsche Telekom domestically, made it competitive in the vast international market, and allowed it to take care of pension and medical insurance costs for retired and redundant workers.

The last point was a big concern for Zhu Rongji: reforming China's state-owned enterprises would mean breaking the so-called iron rice bowl, the cradle-to-grave care and support guaranteed by the government through the big companies people worked for. The risk was that these changes would result in soaring unemployment that might lead to social unrest, and Chinese leaders feared instability more than anything. The Party had made a simple bargain with the people: economic growth in return for political stability. That in turn meant Party control. Prosperity was the source of Party legitimacy.

National pride was also at stake. "It was not just Deutsche Telekom listing, but also Germany itself listing on the market, and the image of Germany improved as well," I said. "Nineteen ninety-seven is a crucial year, and in keeping with the Handover, telecom reform should start in Hong Kong and become a catalyst for pushing the development of the entire Chinese telecom industry."

I am sure that little I said came as a surprise to Zhu Rongji. He would have been well briefed by Wang Qishan, with whom I had been discussing these issues at length, and I stuck largely to the points Wang Qishan had advised me to make. But it was important that I make a strong case directly to Zhu Rongji to demonstrate Goldman's bona fides and my personal commitment to the success of China's efforts. Moreover, Wang Qishan wanted to work with Goldman, and I had to deliver for him, as well as for Goldman.

When I was done, Zhu nodded and began to speak, addressing two key points on the collective leadership's mind: the importance of reform and

Hong Kong. But first, he spoke with some feeling about the passing of his mentor, declaring that "the Chinese people...will unswervingly carry out Reform and Opening Up. They will turn grief into strength and achieve Comrade Deng Xiaoping's wishes."

I was glad he addressed the subject of Deng, because I had gone against my advisers' counsel in mentioning him (they had believed it would be inappropriate for a foreigner to speak of the passing of the paramount leader). But I simply couldn't imagine meeting Zhu and not expressing my condolences under the circumstances. While I always listened carefully to my China team, and usually took their advice, there were times, like this, when I went with my gut instinct. I had learned that the Chinese valued authenticity and had come to expect me to speak my mind.

"China's favorable economic situation," Zhu said, assured that "there will not be any problems with the return of Hong Kong. I think the majority of people have confidence in the continued prosperity of Hong Kong." He reiterated that after the Handover, Hong Kong would be administered under the "one country, two systems" model and that the "Chinese central government will not interfere with Hong Kong Special Administrative Region political or economic issues." China's leaders took every opportunity they got to make this point. They wanted to reassure the residents of Hong Kong, Macau, and just as important, Taiwan, for which this model was also intended.

As Zhu spoke in Chinese, he mostly engaged me directly, once in a while looking off to where my colleagues sat. No one else from the Chinese side spoke. I happened to look down to where Zhu rested his black shoes in the thick rug, and I noticed the edge of his long johns peeking out under his trouser cuff. He was, as I've said, a very practical man, and the old offices in Beijing in those days could get awfully cold and drafty.

Then he spoke the first of the words we wanted to hear: "Of course, we will consider your opinions, and we hope to cooperate with you. If you are interested in cooperating with the Chinese government in the area of telecommunications, I think you can communicate further with the Ministry of Posts and Telecommunications."

That was it, but it was everything. The meeting had been set up without any representatives from the Ministry of Posts and Telecommunications present. We were scheduled the next day to see Minister Wu Jichuan, a powerful longtime telecommunications official. We had been working for some time with representatives of CICC, the investment bank, and the ministry, but we were concerned (and I think CICC was, too) that MPT might have other ideas about whom to use in the transaction. Zhu's words, of course, would get back to MPT and Minister Wu posthaste.

When Zhu had finished, I jumped in. Keenly aware that the competition for the deal would be intense, I cited Goldman's prowess in doing deals of this sort around the world and noted that we had done more privatizations of state-owned enterprises than the next three investment banks combined. "This will be a complicated program," I said. "But we will spare no effort to provide our skills and specialized knowledge."

Zhu nodded and wrapped up our meeting, saying: "I welcome you to further cooperate with China Construction Bank. By cooperating with your company, CCB will benefit in its commercialization process and speed up its modernization process."

With that he thanked us, and except for some parting pleasantries, the meeting was over.

The Chinese leaders are charming hosts and interlocutors, skilled at making you feel good, leading you to think you've heard what you wanted to hear. It's easy to become giddy and overly optimistic. I had listened very carefully to Zhu Rongji and felt great about the meeting. But once we were outside, I turned to my colleagues for a quick reality check.

"How did we do?" I asked my team.

"I can't imagine that could have gone any better," John replied. Mike and Hsueh-ming agreed.

So, in short, we had just concluded a meeting about doing an initial public offering in which we hadn't said a word about a specific deal, much less its timing, size, or pricing; the powerful senior minister of the business we would work with had not been present; and the company itself did not exist in any real sense: we would have to create it. It was not the kind of deal we could have done, or would have thought about doing, almost anywhere else in the world.

But this was China in 1997, and we felt pretty good about where we stood.

Messages in China are sent in ways that aren't always direct; you have to read the signs. Perhaps the most important aspect of the meeting was not so much what Zhu Rongji had said. It was that we had had the meeting at all. There were plenty of other ways he might have communicated with us. On a day when much of the government's business had been shut down, he made a point of seeing us—about a controversial deal that would be the linchpin and showpiece of his future reform program. The man running China's economy, who would be crucial in all future decisions, had appraised us in person, and we appeared to have passed muster.

He had encouraged us to work with China Construction Bank and the ministry that oversaw telecommunications, and he had lent to us, publicly, his weight and prestige. This was a powerful signal to give to us and to send out to the Chinese state and Party bureaucracies. The meeting would not seal the deal for us. I knew that. Zhu's blessing was a comfort but no guarantee. We would still have to continue to compete, to go through the formalities and navigate layers of decision making below Zhu. We had a leg up, but we could easily lose our advantage if we weren't relentless. I'd been down that road many times. It was the nature of dealing with China: nothing was done until it was done. We'd seen any number of seemingly surefire business opportunities simply fail to materialize. But this deal seemed certain to get done, and every bank would be fighting for it, pulling strings, working the system. Months of hard work and careful maneuvering lay ahead before we could be given the formal mandate for what seemed sure to be the biggest IPO by far of any Chinese state-owned enterprise.

We drove past Tiananmen Square on the way back to my hotel. I caught a glimpse of the giant two-story portrait of Mao on the wall of the Forbidden City and wondered, for a moment, what he would have thought of capitalist bankers selling shares in one of his country's state-owned companies to foreigners. In front of the National Museum of China, which faced the Great Hall of the People across Tiananmen Square, I could see the huge digital clock counting down the number of days until Hong Kong was returned to China: 124.

The sight gave me a start. We weren't on the same timetable as the Handover, but I couldn't help thinking: we had just a few months to complete a deal that in a well-oiled Western economy would take at least a year.

I turned to Mike Evans beside me in the back seat of the car: "How exactly are we going to get this done?"

CHAPTER TWO

Chinese Bodies, Foreign Technology

The key to breaking into new markets is to brand yourself by building strong relationships with the most important clients. Goldman Sachs' initial route into China went through Hong Kong, and one of the most important businessmen I met early on was C. H. Tung, who would eventually become the first chief executive of the Hong Kong Special Administrative Region, the successor to the British colonial administration. He would serve from the Handover in 1997 until 2005.

C.H. ran Orient Overseas Container Line, founded by his father, C. Y. Tung, a visionary shipping magnate who built one of the world's biggest fleets and famously bought the ocean liner RMS *Queen Elizabeth* to convert into a floating university (it caught fire during refurbishing and capsized in Hong Kong Harbor). Orient Overseas had run into trouble in the mid-1980s during a global shipping slump, and had been helped in part by mainland Chinese sources.

Orient Overseas did not have much business for us, but C.H. was a font of wisdom, an astute observer of China, and a big fan of America. C.H.'s closeness to China's leaders had convinced him not only of the seriousness of their long-term vision but also of the nation's likely success. He was a strong supporter of Deng Xiaoping's economic policies and advised me that Goldman Sachs should focus on China if we truly intended to be a force in the region.

On one of my early trips to Hong Kong, Henry Cornell, a young real estate banker who would eventually run our private equity business in the region, described a prime piece of real estate that C.H. was looking to develop in Beijing. Plans for Oriental Plaza called for an enormous multipurpose development, the largest in Asia, with offices, residences, shopping venues, hotels, and restaurants. It couldn't have been better located: the corner of Chang'an Avenue and Wangfujing Street, a stone's throw from Tiananmen Square, and arguably the best real estate in China. As a way to get to know the market, I asked C.H. if Goldman could invest alongside him, and he agreed.

In 1992 I joined C.H. and some other investors when they flew up to see Chinese leader Jiang Zemin about the project. I had worked in the White House in my twenties and had met with President Nixon on numerous occasions, but I still found myself awed to be meeting with the general secretary of China's Communist Party. Jiang Zemin was a force of nature, with a big, outgoing personality. He had been picked by Deng to run the country in 1989 after the Tiananmen crackdown because of his adroit handling of student protests in Shanghai, where he had been Party secretary. Jiang could be easy for foreigners to underestimate because he had a disarming manner, with his thick black-rimmed glasses and unimposing appearance.

We met with Jiang at the Great Hall of the People, the cavernous Soviet-style building that stretches a fifth of a mile along the western edge of Tiananmen Square in the heart of Beijing. Perhaps because I was the only Westerner among the group of eight or ten, I played an outsize role in the discussion. Jiang began speaking in English to me, rattling off the names of U.S. companies like General Electric, Boeing, and IBM, and stressing how important it was that China adopt U.S. accounting methods. He was right, of course: Chinese companies' books were generally a mess, and until the country embraced transparency and adopted stricter accounting standards, it would be impossible to sell the shares of its big companies overseas. He looked me right in the eye and said, "Assets equal liabilities plus equity," and I almost burst out laughing. As I have said since, I'm not sure that our country's leaders could have summed up a balance sheet as succinctly as this born-and-bred Communist.

The trip took place right after the 1992 Olympics in Barcelona, where

Michael Jordan and the U.S. men's basketball "Dream Team" had put on such a show. The world had also been treated to the spectacle of the Chinese women swimmers unexpectedly winning four gold medals. Jiang asked me if I had been following the Olympics.

"Yes, of course," I said.

"What did you think of our swimmers?" he asked. He watched me closely. The Chinese team had come from nowhere to win at record-setting paces, and there were widespread rumors of illegal doping.

"Very interesting," I said, searching for a neutral tone. Jiang nodded, then said with a smile, "Chinese bodies, foreign technology."

I've often thought since of that phrase: *Chinese bodies, foreign technology.* I learned later that it echoed the words of Zhang Zhidong, a 19th-century Qing Dynasty official who championed opening his country to the outside world, advocating, "Chinese learning as a base, Western learning for practical applications." This approach explained much about China's rise over the past few decades: it is the essence of Reform and Opening Up. The Chinese took their enormous store of human power, their brawn and their brains, and coupled it with knowledge and innovation and best practices that they've begged, borrowed, bought, and, frankly, stolen from the West. The combination has allowed the Chinese to turn themselves into an extraordinary colossus that boasts the fastest-growing military among major powers and a rapidly expanding GDP that is expected to pass that of the U.S. in the not-too-distant future.

The idea of China challenging the U.S. for economic superiority any time soon would have been unimaginable back when I met Jiang. China was only just waking up from the political and economic nightmares of its recent past.

When Mao Zedong proclaimed the founding of the People's Republic of China in Tiananmen Square in October 1949, he was charting a new course for a country hobbled by more than a century of colonial oppression and internal rebellion that had culminated in two decades of widespread, constant conflict—against warlords and the Japanese and between the Communists and the Nationalist armies of Chiang Kai-shek in a long-running civil war. In short order, Mao imposed Soviet-style command and control economic planning on the country, collectivizing agriculture and shifting resources to a massive industrialization program that focused on heavy machinery manufacturing, with scant attention to consumer goods and services. The economy grew as it recovered from wartime disruptions, and China made strides in meeting the basic needs of its people. But the imposition of misguided policies and disastrous planning in the midst of a political reign of terror wreaked havoc. Mao's attempt to accelerate industrialization by mobilizing ordinary citizens in the Great Leap Forward (1958–1961) led to widespread famine thought to have killed 30 million or more.

Maneuvering to hold on to power, Mao subsequently initiated the Cultural Revolution, purging the senior ranks of the Communist Party and unleashing the Red Guards to persecute millions throughout the country in the name of class struggle. Universities were shut and educated youth sent to the countryside to do manual labor. Many of today's rising generation of leaders lost years toiling in rural areas before the country's nightmare ended with Mao's death in 1976.

By then the country was in shambles, isolated internationally and adrift economically. Mao's radical egalitarianism had triumphed in a perversely dystopian way: the masses—farmers or factory workers—were all more or less poor. More than half of China's nearly 1 billion people lived in dire poverty, on less than $1 per day, and the country suffered from chronic shortages. Staples like grain and cloth were still rationed into the 1980s and beyond. By contrast, during the years of Mao's reign, the U.S. enjoyed a postwar surge in prosperity: from 1949 to 1976, GDP grew almost sevenfold, to $1.8 trillion, while per capita income nearly quintupled.

In 1978 Deng Xiaoping, who had survived repeated political banishment to emerge as the paramount leader, set the country on a course of profound change. He began by rejecting Mao's corrosive politics and focusing the Party on economic development, encouraging the adoption of market principles to shape "socialism with Chinese characteristics." A pragmatist at heart, he famously said, "It doesn't matter whether a cat is black or white, as long as it catches mice."

The first significant reforms occurred in agriculture. Farmers, forced into collectives, had been required to concentrate on growing grains to meet constantly raised targets and to sell their produce for low prices, effectively subsidizing urban industry. Productivity stagnated and China routinely had to import food. Spurred by Deng, the leadership decided to give the collectives more leeway. Many imitated experiments under way in places like Anhui and Sichuan Provinces that allowed farmers to cultivate small, private plots. Before long, collectives across the country had adopted the so-called household responsibility system in which farms were divided into smaller family-run plots. The households contracted to meet certain quotas and were free to sell any surplus on the open market. With these new incentives, productivity soared. The grain yield rose by 34 percent between 1978 and 1984. By then collectives had all but disappeared. Farmers had expanded into more lucrative cash crops and livestock, giving the Chinese people richer and more varied diets and putting money in the farmers' pockets to spend.

The increased productivity meant fewer workers were needed in the countryside. Many of the excess laborers were absorbed by newly created or energized rural factories; these township and village enterprises were frequently owned by local governments but were not included in the overall national economic plan. They were free to act more like private sector companies, churning out goods in high demand in the market or competing with big centrally controlled state-owned monoliths. Rural Chinese began to look farther afield for work. Millions headed for the coastal cities, drawn to the factories mushrooming there, beginning a wave of urbanization unprecedented in human history: over the next three decades some 300 million people would move from farms to urban areas, massively boosting the nation's productivity but contributing to bouts of unrest and ever-worsening environmental degradation.

Reform came to the urban industrial sector as well. Beijing undertook industry-wide restructuring efforts, hiving off new companies from enormous government ministries. It began to shift its emphasis from heavy industry to consumer goods and took steps to give state-owned enterprises greater autonomy, decentralizing decision making and introducing a dual-track pricing system. Managers were required to meet modified plan quotas but were permitted, beyond that, to produce and sell goods on the open market at flexible prices. This lucrative gray market was meant to help push state-owned enterprises to focus more on profit than on fulfilling plan quotas, and executives were given more latitude to operate and to experiment with incentives.

Keeping his pledge to rejoin the international economy, Deng gave the go-ahead to politicians in Fujian and Guangdong, in southeastern China, to create special economic zones, or SEZs, to take advantage of links with overseas Chinese communities. Shenzhen was next to Hong Kong, Zhuhai bordered the then-Portuguese colony of Macau, and Xiamen and Shantou lay across the strait from Taiwan. Chinese and foreign companies operating in the special economic zones enjoyed lower tax rates, did not have to pay import duties on components and supplies for processing, faced fewer import and export restrictions, and had easier access to investment from foreign sources. Powerful symbols of China's commitment to Reform and Opening Up, the SEZs served as laboratories that, among other things, embraced incentive pay for workers and competitive bidding for construction contracts. In 1984 Deng Xiaoping visited Shenzhen to mark a new round of reforms that accepted the inevitability that some individuals would become wealthier than others. "To get rich is no sin," Deng explained to Mike Wallace of the TV show *60 Minutes* in 1986. "We permit some people and some regions to become prosperous first, for the purpose of achieving common prosperity faster."

That message went out to all, unleashing the pent-up energy and ingenuity of the Chinese people, who were eager to improve their lot after years of privation. The economy boomed. GDP jumped by an average of 10 percent annually in the early 1980s, and incomes soared in urban (up 60 percent) and rural (up 150 percent) areas. Washing machines, color TVs, and motorcycles replaced the bicycles, wristwatches, and sewing machines that had been status symbols under Mao. Millions upon of millions of these must-have items were bought.

Entrepreneurs began to make their presence felt. Eager to use their long-suppressed talents, some jumped from stable jobs in government, state companies, or academia to *xia hai*, or plunge into the sea of business, as a popular phrase from that era put it. Other intrepid souls came from farms to try working for themselves—as street vendors, food stall operators, bicycle repairmen, small-scale manufacturers, insurance salesmen. In the process, they authored improbable success stories to rival any from America's fabled Gilded Age. Though state-owned companies continued to enjoy enormous government-sanctioned advantages, these pioneers would become the engines of China's job creation and innovation and the foundation of many of the country's biggest companies and greatest fortunes.

"People in the U.S. have no way of understanding that before Reform and Opening Up, even if you had the ability, you couldn't do anything with it," my friend computing pioneer Liu Chuanzhi once told me. "But reform gave people a choice."

Liu certainly made the most of his choices. In 1984, at age 40, he and several colleagues decided to leave a computer research institute at the prestigious Chinese Academy of Sciences with the equivalent of a little less than $80,000 in backing from the institute and the use of a former bicycle shed on its grounds. The fledgling entrepreneurs tried selling TVs and digital watches before hitting it big with a circuit card that enabled personal computers to process Chinese characters. Before long, the company was making and selling its own PCs, in addition to distributing those of foreign manufacturers. It soon dominated the country's computer market, on its way to becoming today's mammoth Lenovo, and turned chairman Liu into a national icon.

There were many stories like Liu's in the 1980s. Cao Dewang was born in 1946 in Fujian, the province just north of Guangdong on China's southeastern coast, across from Taiwan. Cao peddled cut tobacco and became a fruit seller and chef after a stint in the countryside during the Cultural Revolution. By 1983 he was running a municipal glass factory. Four years later he set off on his own, launching Fuyao Glass Corporation. He first made panels for water meters, then, specializing in safety glass, he built a global company that is the second-largest, and most profitable, supplier of windows for auto companies like General Motors, Volkswagen, and Toyota Motor Corporation.

Or consider Zong Qinghou: after a decade on a communal farm during the Cultural Revolution, he was peddling popsicles, soda, and notebooks by tricycle in his native Hangzhou. In 1987, along with two retired teachers, Zong, who didn't go to high school, secured a $22,000 loan and began selling tonics for children and later adults. The drinks caught on and turned his company, Hangzhou Wahaha Group (*wahaha* is Mandarin for "laughing children"), into China's dominant beverage company and Zong into the richest person in the country in 2013.

Still, the path of reform was uneven: these early forays into capitalism did not come smoothly or without cost. Political changes lagged economic ones, resources were wasted, pollution worsened, and the unequal distribution of new wealth gave rise to widespread complaints about nepotism and corruption. Reformers had to contend with more conservative elements in the Party that wanted to slow or halt the pace and extent of change. Unintended consequences abounded. The country's leadership had wanted to prohibit a return to family farming even as it loosened the reins on the collectives, but once unleashed there was no holding back the farmers. Six years later collectives were gone and family farms predominated.

Deng understood that change would be unpredictable and fraught with danger. The country, he said, would have to approach reform like crossing a stream by feeling for stones, one at a time. For much of the 1980s, it was two stones forward, one stone back.

Growth accelerated and stalled in abrupt turns as Deng and fellow Party elders like Chen Yun, who had sponsored Deng's rehabilitation in the 1970s, wrestled with how much and how quickly to proceed. Early initiatives led to spurts of overheating that were reined in by Chen, a conservative who advocated careful economic planning and slower growth. A member of the all-powerful Standing Committee of the Chinese Communist Party, Chen was known for his "birdcage" theory, which proposed that the free market in China should have just enough freedom to fly like a bird inside the bars of a planned economy.

A particularly difficult time came in 1988, when the economy turned down after a botched effort to lift price controls. Party General Secretary Zhao Ziyang, a committed reformer, had pressed leaders to adopt market pricing for all but a few staple items to avoid the messiness and potential corruption inherent in the two-track system, where goods could be bought by state entities through official channels and sold for more on the open market. Deng allowed controls to be removed on an increasing number of goods, and prices started rising. Rapid credit expansion sparked economic growth, but inflation soared, spooking a public used to the fixed prices and chronic shortages of consumer goods of the central planning era. When Zhao let it be known that the government had decided to completely liberalize prices, people panicked. They hoarded food, yanked deposits from banks, and took to the streets in protest, causing the State Council to reverse course and reinstitute some price controls.

Conservatives wrested control of economic policy from Zhao, and China headed toward a hard landing. Investment dropped, wage increases stopped, bank lending was curtailed, construction projects were canceled. Growth plunged in 1989, even as inflation remained very high. This tail-spin, coupled with continued anger over corruption, formed the backdrop to the 1989 student protests that were sparked by the April death of Hu Yaobang, the reformist general secretary who had been ousted in 1987. The military crackdown in Tiananmen Square put further market reform and price liberalization on hold. Foreign governments and corporations cut back on trade and curtailed investment to object to the violent suppression of the protests.

By 1991, when I made my first trip to China, the mighty engine of the Chinese people was about to be jump-started again. In January 1992 Deng Xiaoping, though technically in retirement, traveled through the south calling for the pace of reform to be sped up. In Shenzhen, he said the SEZ experiment had exceeded his expectations, and he proclaimed himself reassured. He rebuked hard-liners who feared these changes would lead to capitalism and said the Party had more to fear from ideologues of the ultra-left than liberalizers on the right. Such was the nature of the politics of the day that it took weeks before Deng's Southern Tour, reported by newspapers in Hong Kong and Guangdong, made national news. By then Deng had out-maneuvered the hard-liners, and Party General Secretary Jiang Zemin, who had been contending with conservatives in Beijing, grasped Deng's banner firmly. That fall reformers Zhu Rongji, a vice premier, and Hu Jintao,

Party secretary of the Tibet Autonomous Region, joined the Standing Committee. GDP shot ahead by more than 14 percent as credit spigots opened and provinces tried to outdo one another in promoting pell-mell growth. In 1993 the Politburo endorsed the "socialist market economy."

For the first two-thirds of my life, China was as far from my mind as it was from my hometown of Barrington, Illinois (population 5,012). My grasp of the country was shallow and ill informed. I'd grown up like most Americans of my generation in the shadow of the Cold War, ducking under my desk with my classmates in preparation for a nuclear first strike. My father even built a concrete-lined bomb shelter in the basement and stocked it with canned goods. (My mother still uses it to store Christmas decorations and other odds and ends.) We worried that the Russians would bomb us, and, if they didn't, that the Chinese would develop the ability to do so. And unlike our experience with the Russians, we'd actually fought the Chinese. Stories of the Chinese pouring across the Yalu River or brainwashing captured GIs were riveting and deeply disturbing to me as a boy. Similar impressions stayed with many.

I was as astonished as anyone when President Nixon landed in China in February 1972. I was working in the Pentagon then and moved to the White House domestic policy staff two months later, just before Nixon's trip to Moscow kicked off détente. I grasped the brilliance of his moves, triangulating our strategic interests to throw the Soviet Union off balance even as we prepared for the Vietnam War to end. But I was narrowly focused on my job, shaping ideas for tax reform—like a value-added tax to fund education—that had no chance of getting passed. I wouldn't have predicted that Nixon's trip would form the basis of the U.S. relationship with China for the next 40 years or that it would ultimately have such a deep—and enriching—impact on my own life.

My first trip to Hong Kong came just after I had been named one of three co-heads of Goldman's investment banking division at the end of 1990. I was asked to take on responsibility for Asia because, living in Chicago, I was deemed "closer" than my New York colleagues. That will tell you how important Asia was to the firm's plans back then. Indeed, until the late '80s, we had had no business in China and not much more in Hong Kong. Then the firm moved Moses Tsang, a stellar bond salesman, back to his native Hong Kong. Moses had graduated from Bemidji State University in Minnesota, after which he had earned a master's in social work at the University of Iowa, before joining Goldman, where he sold bonds in New York, Tokyo, and London. In Hong Kong Moses quickly built a business selling U.S. bonds to local institutions and wealthy individuals. By the early 1990s the firm had perhaps a hundred people in Hong Kong, nearly all in bond sales or trading. The banking side had only a handful of folks, and almost no business.

When I saw Hong Kong for myself, I was quickly captivated by its beauty, its sleek modernity and pulsating energy, and the straightforward nature of local businessmen. Not long after, I flew to Beijing for the first time with Henry James, the partner who oversaw Asia from his office in Tokyo. What a contrast to sophisticated Hong Kong! The mainlanders, many of whom still wore Mao jackets buttoned to the neck, seemed like country bumpkins compared with the worldly city dwellers of Hong Kong, who sported bespoke European-cut suits fashioned by their famed tailors. Beijing's streets were filled with bicycles, and riding in the quickly growing fleet of automobiles was harrowing. I remember landing at the old airport and driving to our hotel on a single-lane road jammed with horses and carts, wobbly bicycles, and speeding cars. The driving was so aggressive—ill-advised passing, horns honking—I was relieved that we didn't get killed, or kill someone.

In those days, standing at the corner of Chang'an Avenue and the Second Ring Road, which circles central Beijing at a distance of just 3 miles from Tiananmen Square, you could see mule-drawn carts bringing in the winter cabbage. Looking out to the Third Ring Road, under construction another mile and a half distant, there were still swaths of *hutongs*, the characteristic Beijing neighborhoods centered on narrow lanes and residential houses built around courtyards that had stood for hundreds of years.

All of this was quickly disappearing. On subsequent visits I watched the old neighborhoods being torn down as fast as you could blink, replaced by massive buildings housing government ministries and office, residential, and hotel complexes. The pace of change was stunning. Landmarks seemingly disappeared between trips. As bewildering as it was to a visitor like me, it must have been deeply disconcerting to the Chinese.

Yet the energy and work ethic—and desire—that this change reflected was infectious. China's potential struck me when I visited the special economic zone in Shenzhen, in southern Guangdong Province, where I saw the amazing entrepreneurial spirit in action in factories and ranks of buildings under construction. The skyline was a forest of cranes; fields of bulldozers waited to break ground for new buildings.

Shenzhen was a gold mine for Hong Kong entrepreneurs, who were pouring in money to start businesses they could run at almost no cost. The Chinese government took care of benefits and what little health care there was for the workers, who toiled round the clock. The Hong Kong manufacturers paid bare minimum wages. They transferred their product at cost into Hong Kong, where they paid no corporate taxes. They marked it up and shipped it to the world's consumers. How could you have a better deal than that?

The arrangement worked for the Chinese, too. I'm not minimizing the dreadful working conditions in some factories—long hours, few if any bathroom breaks, poorly ventilated factory floors—but millions of jobs were being created, and the economy was booming. For the first time, people had money to spend and plenty of appealing and desirable goods to spend it on. People from all over Guangdong were flocking to the SEZs, and people all over the country were pouring into Guangdong and the other coastal provinces where the experimentation was most advanced.

To be sure, I was uneasy in the aftermath of the Tiananmen Square crackdown. I found it hard to shake the haunting image of that lone, fragile-looking man with the string shopping bag standing in front of the tank, and I was deeply disturbed by the imposition of martial law. The protesters had sought greater freedom, only to be denied, harshly, by their government.

But I believed then, and still do today, that U.S. engagement with China makes sense—indeed, that more engagement, not less, is the better course, politically and economically. I was convinced that China was making hard, market-oriented choices to improve the welfare of its people, and that an increase in their standard of living would bring them closer to the world community and to achieving the freedoms we embrace in America.

These ideals and rights may or may not come, but they are more likely to be achieved with prosperity than with grinding poverty.

I'm a sucker for action, and the Chinese were nothing if not active. And frankly, I have to say it was quite a refreshing contrast to the gloomy nay-saying that we had gotten used to back home in the States in the depths of the recession that followed the savings and loan debacle. Maybe it was my naïveté and lack of sophistication, but I saw no reason the Chinese on the mainland should not aspire to, or achieve, the success of their brethren in Hong Kong and Taiwan. They would have to make big changes, but it was clear they were trying. I felt we could help them and help ourselves in the process.

I was not without my doubts, though. I remember one trip to Shanghai, when I had a Sunday afternoon to myself and took a long stroll along the Bund. A prerevolution time capsule, the famous waterfront could have passed for Wall Street or the City of London of a bygone era with its historic buildings running along the western bank of Huangpu River. This thoroughfare had been the home of Western and Chinese banks, trading houses, and markets, and they had all but disappeared in an instant after the revolution. The thought gave me pause. Many at Goldman, including such discerning executives as co-chairman Bob Rubin, asked tough, probing questions about China's prospects, in no small part because it was never certain that the reforms would last. I had to ask myself: What makes me think it won't happen again, and how can I be sure Goldman Sachs won't lose its shirt investing here?

CHAPTER THREE

Dealmaking with Chinese Characteristics

Doubts about China inside Goldman Sachs reflected a vigorous debate during the mid-1990s concerning the best long-term prospects in Asia. Some in the firm thought we should focus on the region's other developing economies, the so-called Asian Tigers of Hong Kong, Singapore, South Korea, and Taiwan (not to mention other rising economies like Thailand, Indonesia, and Malaysia). These countries boasted growth stories that were every bit as spectacular as China's but less volatile, with more immediate business opportunities in some cases. Struck by the energy, enthusiasm, and determination of the people, I was an ardent proponent of China's potential. I simply did the math in my head: as successful as all those countries were, together they had about one-third the population of China.

Initially, however, China was something of a sideshow. We focused our earliest efforts on building relationships in Hong Kong. We could see several benefits in doing so. China was courting the colony's business leaders prior to the Handover. These merchant princes could read the writing on the wall and had been cultivating ties to the mainland and investing in all sorts of projects. They had thriving businesses we could work with, and we could use them to piggyback into China.

The most important businessman in Hong Kong was Li Ka-shing. K.S., as friends call him, had come to Hong Kong as a refugee, and in his early 20s he started a business he named Cheung Kong, or Long River, after the Yangtze River. He made and sold plastic combs and soap boxes, progressing to toys and plastic flowers. He thrived and soon began investing in real estate and eventually emerged as the biggest developer in the colony. In

1979 he acquired the venerable conglomerate Hutchison Whampoa, with interests in ports, retailing, and property, and subsequently expanded into new areas like telecommunications while building a portfolio in China. By 1990 he was a billionaire and considered the richest man in Hong Kong.

One day in 1991 I went with Moses Tsang, Goldman's man on the ground in Hong Kong, to meet K.S. for the first time. We were whisked in a private elevator to his offices in the Central District, high over the city. K.S. greeted us warmly, and we chatted amiably in a side area of couches and chairs before moving to a large round table set for lunch with elegant menu cards.

K.S. had two sons, Victor and Richard. Victor worked at Cheung Kong, while Richard, the youngest and still in his early 20s, was in the process of launching Star TV, a pioneering satellite programming venture focused on China and other Asian countries. I don't remember now whether either of them was present, but we were joined by K.S.'s key deputy, Canning Fok, a former Hong Kong high school classmate of Moses's, who had arranged our meeting. Before we went in, Moses had mentioned that K.S. was raising funds for Richard's TV business.

I was impressed by K.S.'s direct manner and incisiveness as we engaged in a wide-ranging conversation about markets and economic conditions in Hong Kong, China, and the U.S. He was shrewd, sophisticated, and global in outlook. He was staunchly anti-Communist but a realist and immensely pragmatic. As I would learn in time, he was also a wise businessman who appreciated the value of a conservative balance sheet with plenty of cash and liquidity in a world he knew from personal experience to be uncertain and frequently volatile.

Sure enough, the subject of Star TV, which was being developed out of Hutchison Whampoa, popped up. Straight out, K.S. asked Goldman Sachs to spend $2 million to buy advertising on it. He certainly did not need the money, and the amount in absolute terms was trivial for him. I saw it even then as a symbolic gesture, but one that was very important to him because he wanted his son's first business venture to succeed.

By nature I'm pretty straightforward, but I hedged, saying that we would have to get back to him. This was for a very good reason: I had absolutely no authority to make such a commitment on behalf of the firm. We were a conservative partnership, and I knew this would lead to a difficult discussion within the management committee, of which I was a member. But I didn't want to offend the most powerful businessman in Hong Kong.

After lunch K.S. walked me to the elevator and rode down with me, a gesture of such politeness and familiarity that I soon found myself adopting it with Asian visitors back home. I thanked him for the lunch and told him I was grateful for the opportunity and that we would weigh and examine it.

"Thank you, Mr. Paulson," I remember K.S. saying as I slid into the car. "I am pleased Goldman Sachs will be taking the advertising package from Star TV."

Back home my colleagues wasted no time in telling me that K.S. had put one over on me. But we were late to Hong Kong, and I had concluded that if we were to catch up and accomplish what we wanted to, we needed to make a commitment. I expected that it would lead to the opportunity to invest in future deals with K. S. Li and his family and to compete for investment banking business. In the U.S. some clients were nervous if you wanted to invest with them. In Hong Kong it was the opposite. Putting your money on the line alongside your clients' earned you their trust and admitted you to the club. I viewed this as a first step in that direction. That was what I tried to explain to the Goldman management committee. It wasn't an easy sell. As a firm that focused primarily on institutional and corporate clients, we had no interest in advertising to the general public. But eventually they went along, and we donated our Star TV advertising to the Children's Cancer Foundation in Hong Kong.

As it turned out, one of the first significant deals we did in Hong Kong took place shortly afterward when we helped Richard Li sell Star TV to Rupert Murdoch. That came about after a chance meeting between John Thornton, then head of banking in Europe out of London, and Richard Li at a World Economic Forum–related event at Davos in 1992. A little later Star began talking to our people about raising funds through a private placement—an opportunity that would not have arisen without our decision to buy advertising. Jumping on this opening, John flew to Hong Kong to persuade Richard that he would be better served by finding a strategic investor. He had in mind Rupert Murdoch, with whom Richard and K.S. had previously failed at least twice to reach an agreement. John turned for help to Brian Griffiths, who was vice chairman of Goldman Sachs International. Lord Griffiths sat on the board of Times Newspaper Holdings, the parent company of Murdoch's *Times* in London. The three had dinner, and John managed over the next few weeks to bring Richard and Rupert to a meeting of the minds, while keeping Pearson PLC, a rival U.K. media conglomerate, in play as a competing bidder. The deal, announced in July 1993, had Murdoch buying 63.6 percent of Hutch-Vision Limited, the parent of Star TV, for about $525 million. (He would buy the remainder two years later.)

The deal was a stunner. It brought Murdoch to Asia and instantly elevated Richard Li in the public eye, confirming that he had the makings of a shrewd businessman. He'd made several times over the initial investment and was launched on a high-flying career.

We subsequently did quite a lot of work for K.S. and his companies, helping him to finance, buy, and sell a number of businesses. Making a simple $2 million commitment didn't win us these other assignments. K.S. was too good a businessman for that: we had to earn every bit of work we did for him. But it did get us a seat at the table so we could compete for the business, and it helped to make our name in Hong Kong, and later in China.

This isn't to say we got the deals we wanted or that the ones we got all worked out so well. Oriental Plaza, the Beijing mega-development on the prime piece of real estate right next to Tiananmen Square, would go through numerous iterations as it became increasingly complicated and controversial. The billion-dollar-plus project broke ground in September 1993 but came to a halt the next year amid protests from preservationists and resistance from McDonald's, which had earlier signed a 20-year lease and opened its first franchise in Beijing on that very site. Eventually, matters were sorted out. McDonald's agreed to move. K. S. Li, who had replaced C. H. Tung as the lead investor, pressed ahead, and the development opened for business in 2000. Along the way, our near–20 percent stake was whittled away to almost nothing, and we made very little.

The circuitous path of Oriental Plaza was not atypical for the deals we encountered when we first started. We discovered quickly the need to be very selective about the business we pursued and never to take anything for granted. That's a wise approach the world over but nowhere more so than it was in China during that early period of rapid economic change. As the country opened to foreign investment, almost every transaction was debated at the highest levels of government; the decision making was complex, diffuse in that it involved the approval of many officials, and opaque to outsiders like us. Many memoranda of understanding were signed that went nowhere; informal negotiations took place with officials who lacked proper authority or couldn't "sell" projects to their superiors. Moreover, China lacked a strong adherence to the rule of law. Instead, the rule of men was the norm, which meant that building strong personal relationships was essential for doing business. For this reason, I traveled frequently to China, especially in the early years. Over time we learned to identify the most viable transactions, involving the right clients and the support of the right Chinese advocates. But on any number of occasions as we were learning to work in China in the early days, we were disappointed by abrupt and bewildering changes in direction. The rug could be pulled out from under you at any point.

We learned this lesson firsthand in our efforts to help build the Chinese power industry. From the start this opportunity had looked like a no-brainer. The fast-growing economy made increasing energy demands that China was struggling to meet, especially in areas like Shandong and Guangdong, two densely populated coastal provinces that were rapidly industrializing and relatively open to foreign investment. Guangdong, across the border from Hong Kong, suffered frequent brownouts—an untenable situation for factories working round the clock to manufacture goods being shipped all over the world.

We devised a solution, borrowed from the U.S. In simple terms, the idea was to sell a stake in one power plant to a group of foreign investors who would become owners of the plant in tandem with the government. This new ownership group would use the proceeds to finance the construction of additional power plants. The financing was straightforward, but we knew arranging the deals would be tricky. Provincial governments were generally more willing to experiment than were central government agencies, but it would still require political courage and savvy maneuvering to push ahead, as the country had never sold part of a state-owned power station to foreigners before.

Tom Gibian, a Goldman Sachs project finance specialist, identified suitable power plants, and by early 1993 we had committed with a well-connected state-owned investment entity, China Venturetech Investment Corporation (CVIC), to invest in electric generating projects. Our efforts in Shandong moved ahead quickly. In November, after winning approval from the China Securities Regulatory Commission (CSRC), China's version of the U.S.'s Securities and Exchange Commission, we and CVIC announced that, along with other investors, including K. S. Li and U.S. engineering and construction concern Bechtel, we would pay $180 million for a 30 percent share of a 1.2 million kilowatt power plant, Shandong's biggest. It would be run through a new company jointly owned by the investors, the power corporation of Shandong Province, and Shandong International Trust and Investment Corporation.

Then the lights on the deal went out. At a conference in Beijing, Gibian gave a presentation that laid out the structure of the deal in detail, including the expected returns for investors—just under 13 percent annually over the first 12 years—necessary to get the deal done.

In the audience was a woman named Li Xiaolin, a young power industry bureaucrat, who happened to be the daughter of Li Peng, the country's premier, and a leading conservative opponent of rapid reform. The next thing we knew, we had been instructed to pull the deal. As we were told, Li Peng was unhappy about the high rate of return to the foreign investors. The Shandong power deal was canceled in December 1993.

We came away with a crucial lesson: many officials could approve a deal, but it took only one well-placed official in a consensus-ruled system to kill it. We subsequently learned to spread our efforts wide to every conceivable person or agency that might have an interest in whatever we were focused on and to work relentlessly to bring them to our side. For a complex, groundbreaking transaction like the Shangdong deal, in a politically sensitive area where the premier had a keen interest, we should have sought the approval of the State Council, which is composed of China's senior government ministers. Even today the Chinese are not great at coordinating among themselves; and in the early 1990s the government approval process for novel policies was very much a work in progress.

Li Peng's intervention also served as a graphic reminder of the intersection of power and family ties in China as the economy was being remade. Apart from being premier, Li had had a long association with the power industry, and his daughter and one of his sons would become heavyweights in that sector as well. This was the first inkling I had of the growing influence of the children of Party leaders. Capitalizing on family connections was common. Many sons and daughters of Party leaders, the so-called princelings, were bright, able, and held productive and legitimate jobs. But many did not, and rampant nepotism had become an open sore, enraging the Chinese public; its patent unfairness stood in stark contrast to the Chinese tradition of strict meritocracy that governs ordinary citizens, whose futures are determined by their performance in a brutally competitive exam system.

As frustrating as it was at the time, our Shandong power setback did reveal a rewarding aspect of doing business in China: the Chinese have a great sense of honor and stick to their word when a commitment is made. A CEO has every right to kill an unfinished deal that he decides isn't in the best interests of his company. Just so, a head of state can back out of an agreement that doesn't serve his country well. When such a reversal occurs, few countries would see a need to do anything more than offer a quick apology, if that. But China is different. Even as Li Peng flabbergasted us by killing the deal, others assured us that we would get Shandong's future business when that became possible. Liu Hongru, a forward-looking and committed reformer who was the head of the CSRC and in charge of handing out the first mandates to take Chinese state-owned enterprises public, promised that we would handle the power company's IPO. And, in fact, we were awarded the mandate in 1994—although it was no walk in the park. Shandong International Power Development Company finally listed in Hong Kong in June 1999 after a very long, difficult process that involved no fewer than three failed road shows, in which bankers and company management traveled to many distant cities to interest investors in the offerings.

As Li Peng's involvement in the Shandong deal taught my partners and me, Chinese leaders were intimately involved in the minutiae of the economy and the changes the reform program was producing. It was the inevitable legacy of a command economy—the top people were involved by design—and reflected the importance of the direction-setting decisions they were making for the country.

As a result, it was easier in the 1990s for foreign businessmen to meet senior leaders and develop relationships. That was not so later on. It was next to impossible, for example, for a businessperson to gain an audience with Hu Jintao after he became general secretary in 2002. It was a bit easier to see Premier Wen Jiabao, although I don't believe he discussed specific transactions. This shift was not just a matter of personal style but the result of a great sea change: as the economy boomed, it was no longer necessary for the country's leaders to court the foreign CEOs, who were beating down doors to build a business in China. The top leadership also had more help. The government was becoming professionalized as more capable and experienced officials populated the ministries and senior ranks of the state.

One of the senior leaders I saw frequently in the 1990s was Zhu Rongji, then vice premier running the economy day-to-day. Our meetings generally concerned financial or economic policy matters. He was smart, well briefed, and focused on finding solutions.

Zhu Rongji had come by his stature the hard way. After a tough childhood in Hunan Province, he had graduated from the prestigious Tsinghua University as an engineer in 1951 and landed a job with a central government planning agency. Always outspoken, he'd been purged twice during Mao's political upheavals. But he was a man of fortitude and persistence. After the Cultural Revolution he returned to Beijing and worked for an economic reform commission before moving to Shanghai as mayor in 1987. There he set up China's first official stock exchange since the Communists had come to power. He also led the effort to turn Pudong, the Singapore-size expanse of vegetable farms and marshes east of the Bund, into China's spanking new financial center, complete with the country's tallest skyscrapers.

Zhu was direct and no-nonsense and, at least with me, a good listener who took blunt advice well when he thought it was in China's best interest. We were advising the country on its sovereign credit rating in 1993, and I sat in on the meeting with the U.S. rating agency Standard & Poor's. I felt that Zhu had not addressed one of the agency's concerns about China as directly as he might have. To the dismay of one colleague, I explained this to Zhu in a matter-of-fact but respectful way after the meeting. He was silent, which my colleagues took as a bad sign. But Zhu was pragmatic to his core, and at a subsequent meeting with Moody's Investors Service he handled the same question frankly and adroitly.

Zhu and other Chinese leaders were keen to list state-owned enterprises on the world's stock markets. Privatization was still a somewhat new concept then, but the Chinese were quick to see its potential for raising capital and restructuring industries. Zhu had already met with our Brian Griffiths, who had led Margaret Thatcher's privatization and deregulation efforts from 1985 to 1990, as well as with other Goldman executives. In my first meeting with Zhu, he asked us to do a feasibility study of which industries would be the best candidates. And he asked me how long it would take to list a company on the New York Stock Exchange.

"Between six months and two years," I replied.

But getting Chinese companies ready for public listings was a daunting task—one far more difficult than I would have imagined. China's state-owned enterprises had grown out of the ministries that, under Communist Party rule, had owned all the property and assets of the nation and had overseen all of its commercial operations and activities, from oil and gas exploration and drilling to farming, manufacturing, and mining. The state determined what businesses to be in and set quotas for production. Product quality, managerial controls, and accounting were neglected.

As the economy had opened up, SOEs had grown like mad. But they remained under government control and were weighed down by all the baggage of the state, including expensive cradle-to-grave care for workers and their families. Companies maintained hospitals, schools, restaurants, stores, and even, in some cases, cemeteries for their employees, and they were proud of the services they provided. I remember Brian Griffiths remarking after a visit to one of these companies that it resembled nothing so much as a medieval village, and, as he put it, "You can't float that on the New York Stock Exchange."

By the 1990s, while the fledgling private sector of the economy—foreign-invested ventures, SEZ exporters, and the township and village enterprises—thrived, most of the SOEs had become bloated and inefficient, debt ridden and money losing. They had almost no knowledge of modern business practices and offered such primitive disclosure that it was almost impossible to measure the extent of their economic losses. Managers had been given greater responsibility to make business decisions, but they often had neither the training nor the temperament for the task. Companies lacked focus and squandered resources. In the first flush of freedom, executives frequently made misguided or corrupt decisions, creating inchoate conglomerates, speculating in real estate, and acting as quasi-banks to extend credit ill-advisedly to other companies.

To make matters worse, the state-owned banks that loaned to these lumbering SOEs were for all practical purposes defunct. They had little knowledge of modern lending, investing, or risk-management practices and had no idea of the extent of their bad loans, or even how to value their assets or measure their losses. Moreover, the banks were regulated at the local level by the same officials who directed them to lend to the SOEs. You can imagine how ineffective it was to have provincial politicians overseeing the banks and inspecting the adequacy of their capital while they were simultaneously seeking loans for their pet projects.

Zhu wanted to overhaul the way the SOEs were managed, eliminate their special privileges and subsidies, and encourage the development of professional managers to invigorate the state sector. Selling shares to the public and "strategic" stakes to leading international companies, he felt, would not only raise capital but also force the SOEs to adopt global accounting standards and become better run. He also recognized that to reform the SOEs, he would have to reform the banking system that, essentially, provided the companies with the corporate version of an iron rice bowl: unending credit and absolute loan forgiveness.

At the time, governments around the world were undertaking privatizations for a variety of reasons—from restructuring assets to make their domestic industries more competitive to raising money, paying down debts, or broadening share ownership. Germany, for one, was eager to create an equity culture. Some governments took the view that their companies would perform better with market discipline than under state ownership and control.

The Chinese embraced a model of their own design. To begin with, they were uncomfortable with the term "privatization," which didn't completely square with "socialism with Chinese characteristics." They preferred to use the terms "corporatization" and "capital restructuring." Government leaders chose to maintain control of companies whose shares they sold in a wide range of industries, keeping them under the Party, which handpicked company leaders. I didn't know then if this was a temporary or long-term plan. But over time, their reluctance to surrender state control has become clearer, and that desire, firmly rooted in politics and ideology, carries negative consequences to this day. Too many of the country's biggest businesses, descended from massive government ministries, stalk the Chinese landscape, creating problems for the government as it attempts to develop best-of-class global companies and to shift to a different economic model that is not so dependent on government investment and exports. And these companies are not being run according to Zhu's plan to make them modern, efficient, market-driven enterprises subject to real competition.

China's interest in privatizations drew the attention of investment banks the world over. For quite a while, Goldman had to play catch-up. British firms like Jardine Fleming, Schroders, and Barings, with their colonial histories in Hong Kong, initially had the upper hand, along with Wardley, the merchant banking arm of HSBC, and Peregrine Investments, a well-connected local start-up. But we sensed the vulnerability of the old-line firms. They were already in decline before the Handover, which would end their historical edge. Among our U.S. competitors, Merrill Lynch and Morgan Stanley had also established themselves ahead of us.

Much of what we did in China in those early days was educational. We might as well have been running a school—indeed, at times it felt as though we were. Even as our bankers sought to build relationships and sniff out business opportunities, they conducted seminars and conferences, gave tutorials in which they explained the benefits of privatization, analyzed Chinese industries, singled out the companies that could be floated on overseas exchanges, and explained such technical details in the IPO process as due diligence, book building, and managing a road show.

All of this was absolutely essential. As smart and capable as the Chinese were, few officials in government ministries, or frankly in the country's fledgling financial system, had any grounding in classical economics, much less hands-on experience in modern banking or capital markets. But they were absolute sponges, taking notes, soaking in information, constantly pressing for more details, more analyses.

We rapidly built up our Hong Kong office to serve as the hub of our Asian activities outside of Japan. The region was booming, and by 1994 we had several hundred bankers and support staff managing our operations throughout Southeast Asia. We began to build our China team. Just as we did elsewhere, we looked for talented young professionals we could train to become outstanding investment bankers.

Some competitors hired employees for their language skills rather than their banking aptitude, or picked up natives of Taiwan and Hong Kong because they were "Chinese." We looked for ones who could thrive in our competitive but collegial Goldman culture.

We sought out bright mainland Chinese like Liu Erh Fei, who had earned degrees from Brandeis University and Harvard Business School as one of the first Chinese students to study abroad. Erh Fei was the first of our serious hires of Chinese bankers and very helpful in building our early mainland relationships. When he left in 1993, we hired Cherry Li, who had taught English at the Beijing Foreign Language Institute—Erh Fei had been one of her students—before switching to economics. Smart and dedicated, she had worked for the State Council's Economic Reform Commission under reformist premier Zhao Ziyang and had been an early recruit at the CSRC. After a short stint in our New York headquarters to learn about our culture and our business, she opened our Beijing office in February 1994. We added a Shanghai office that November, but the bulk of our work in China continued to be run out of Hong Kong.

The business climate in China was frustrating. We were able to underwrite bonds for a number of government issuers, and we found some advisory work, but the equity offerings were slow in coming. In January 1994 the CSRC announced a second batch of 22 candidates for overseas listings that included several power companies, but by the time the last company from the first batch had listed in Hong Kong in June 1994, IPOs of Chinese companies were having a much harder time attracting investors. One reason was the poor quality of the assets being offered in some of the later companies.

Another reason for our frustration was the volatility of the Chinese economy, which had begun overheating after Deng's Southern Tour. After credit controls were eased, bank lending for investment jumped 50 percent in 1992, and inflation hit 15 percent the following year. Speculative real estate projects mushroomed in Guangdong and Hainan, the island south of Guangdong and China's southernmost province. Zhu Rongji, who had become vice premier in 1991, gained greater control over the economy after Li Peng suffered a heart attack in April 1993. Zhu's challenge was to find a way to calm the economy without losing ground on reform. His approach was to tackle both the immediate crisis and fundamental problems in the economy.

Zhu took direct charge of the central bank and instituted a 16-point austerity plan to curb bank lending and restrain price rises. He pushed through the first phase of a revamping of the financial system by setting up three new policy banks and pressing the other banks to be more commercial and less policy oriented in their loan choices. He overhauled the tax and fiscal system and made foreign exchange reforms. Zhu was tough-minded, threatening, it was said, to "chop off the head" of any bank official who did not obey the new rules coming out of Beijing. Zhu and his reformist colleagues had a battle on their hands. Excessive expansion of the money supply and a credit bubble helped push inflation above 24 percent in 1994, before Zhu's stringent measures took effect and led the economy to a soft landing, with inflation falling to 8.3 percent in 1996 and 2.8 percent in 1997.

Meantime, the bottom fell out for Goldman Sachs in 1994—but it wasn't China's fault. A global bond market meltdown, triggered by rapid interest rate hikes by the U.S. Federal Reserve in February 1994, caused our poorly managed trading business in London to blow up. We were soon losing $100 million a month. This firm-wide financial crisis was compounded by our partnership structure, which allowed retiring partners to take half their capital with them. Many did. The firm was on the edge of going under.

Then, in September, in the midst of this crisis, Jon Corzine and I were appointed to lead the firm as chairman and vice chairman, respectively. Jon and I disagreed about a lot but not about the need to act fast. We had to make tough decisions and cut staff by 13 percent worldwide. I tried to protect our business in Asia, especially China, but we had to slash hard to ensure our survival, and in the end I'm not sure we were worse off by cutting back, because we had grown rapidly around the world and hired a lot of the wrong people.

CHAPTER FOUR

Real Gold and Silver

The 15th National Congress of the Communist Party, held in September 1997, cemented the path of economic reform in China. To counter uneasiness in some quarters about the rapidly growing role of private enterprise, Chinese leader Jiang Zemin asserted that the Party did not have to control all aspects of the economy to stay true to its identity.

"Even if the state-owned sector accounts for a smaller proportion of the economy," he declared, "this will not affect the socialist nature of our country." Jiang's argument encouraged the private sector to flourish, while setting the stage for the next crucial phase of economic reform—restructuring the creaky, money-losing state-owned enterprises that employed 110 million workers and accounted for nearly 30 percent of industrial GDP. In his speech titled, in part, "Hold High the Great Banner of Deng Xiaoping Theory," Jiang vowed to reduce these lumbering dinosaurs in number and restructure them through mergers, layoffs, technological upgradings, and sales of stock.

At the time, all eyes were on one state-owned enterprise: China Telecom, which was scheduled to make an unprecedented initial public offering of its shares in Hong Kong and New York in just weeks. The $4.22 billion deal was constructed around the mobile telecommunications assets of two thriving Chinese coastal provinces, but because of the complex, scattered nature of the country's telecom system, a marketable company had had to be built from scratch.

The IPO showed the firm hand of Zhu Rongji, who meant for China

Telecom to become the template for revamping other SOEs. The battle-hardened vice premier knew the devil of reform was in the details, and he understood that the IPO process could press change on companies whose managers were not otherwise up to the task, while reorganizing entire industries and their regulators. Doing so would help clear the roadblocks to China's long-delayed entry into the World Trade Organization (WTO) and better prepare the country for the eventual opening to foreign competition that would follow.

But China was by no means united behind Zhu's efforts; he faced factional and ideological opposition—and inertia. If China Telecom's IPO failed, it could cripple the country's move to a more open, market-oriented system. Unfortunately, the markets had turned ugly, and China Telecom was set to go public in the midst of the worst economic crisis to hit Asia in a generation. Goldman Sachs was leading the deal, and on the hook.

The stakes could hardly have been higher. The future of China's reforms—and our reputation—hung in the balance.

Ironically, Goldman Sachs had won the China Telecom business in part because of another deal that we'd turned down. In the early 1990s Goldman had been asked to help create a Chinese investment bank by entering into a joint venture with a major Chinese commercial bank. We badly wanted to break into the market and to operate with wider latitude than we could as an adviser or investor, but there was a hitch to the proposal: Goldman would only be allowed to own roughly one-third of the firm. Some of my colleagues liked the idea. They saw our being asked as a great coup that would lead to more business. I argued strongly against it. I didn't want any part of running a business we did not control.

I didn't see how we could be successful, guarantee Goldman Sachs quality and execution, maintain our integrity, and obey the law in a country like China with only a minority position. It's hard enough to run an institution—hiring, training, and putting together performance evaluation and compensation systems that reinforce a culture of teamwork, client service, and high ethical standards—when you're all under one roof in New

York. But halfway around the world with our employees answering to non-Goldman executives? No way.

So we turned down the proposal.

Morgan Stanley took our place, forming China International Capital Corporation with China Construction Bank to great fanfare in 1995. And in short order, our archrivals walked straight into the bear trap we'd foreseen. I got a glimpse of how serious those problems had become in September 1996, when Wang Qishan, then head of CCB, visited me at Goldman's offices in New York.

I'd met Wang a couple of times by then and had shared a memorable dinner with him. A committed reformer, Wang Qishan was a savvy up-and-comer with impeccable connections. My wife, Wendy, had joined me on this trip, and along with a Goldman colleague, we'd met Wang at a restaurant in Beijing. Even speaking through a translator, Wendy and Wang Qishan hit it off. Wang was extraordinarily well read; he and Wendy traded theories of education and dissected Chinese, European, and American history and culture while Chinese pop videos played nonstop on a corner TV. Finally, Wang said to Wendy, "Excuse me, Mrs. Paulson. May I borrow your husband for a while?" and we turned the discussion to the state of the economy and prospects for reform in China. Because of his bank's connection with Morgan Stanley, I viewed him as a competitor, although an unusually charming one.

So I was unprepared for what happened when Wang walked into my office in New York a couple of years later. First, he outlined China's plans to reform its telecom sector and sell shares through an IPO, confirming reports we'd heard earlier that summer that the government was looking for the privatization to happen soon—perhaps around the time of the July 1, 1997, Handover of Hong Kong to China.

It was a deal every investment bank wanted to win. The China Telecom offering promised to be a transformational event. Apart from raising capital, it would "brand" China in global markets and pave the way for the sale of shares in other state-owned enterprises. It would also mark the beginning of a wider restructuring of the nation's communications infrastructure. It was easy to foresee additional activity—equity and debt financings, mergers and acquisitions—as the Chinese telecom market grew and took a more modern shape.

As the leading Chinese investment bank, CICC was going to be very involved in the transaction, Wang pointed out. Then he dropped a bombshell on me.

"We need a leading global bank on the deal," he said, "and I would like that to be Goldman Sachs."

"We'd like nothing more than to work with you," I quickly responded. But I couldn't refrain from adding, "I don't see how you're going to be able to do this with us while Morgan Stanley is your partner."

"I understand your point," Wang said simply. "But I've decided to work with Goldman Sachs."

Wang's pronouncement surprised me. Whatever problems the Chinese might be having with Morgan Stanley—and we had picked up rumors of infighting at CICC—they remained partners, and I assumed Morgan Stanley still had the inside track for a deal.

Wang Qishan was the head of China Construction Bank, not the head of the Ministry of Posts and Telecommunications, the actual client. But as another of my Goldman colleagues would later say of Wang, "He was never just a banker." When it came to China Telecom, what mattered was not that he was the head of CCB. What mattered was that he had gotten the assignment to take China Telecom public from Vice Premier Zhu Rongji, who wanted this deal to lead the way for the reform and restructuring of the country's massive state-owned enterprises. Wang was working for Zhu and China, and he would make his decisions accordingly. Zhu depended on a network of allies and protégés, men and women committed to reform, who had the drive and executive ability to cut through bureaucratic lethargy and overcome political opposition to push forward changes while time and momentum were on their side. And Wang Qishan was emerging as one of Zhu's key lieutenants.

Why were the Chinese upset with Morgan Stanley? My sense is it came down to culture and communication: the two sides approached their joint venture with different expectations, and neither completely understood what the other wanted. Perhaps Morgan Stanley wanted to run a successful local operation, pursuing domestic business that purely foreign banks couldn't touch. That's the leg up the joint venture gave them. Wang Qishan had bigger game in mind: he wanted to modernize a country. As one of China's top dealmakers later explained to me, Wang Qishan didn't much care whether CICC made money at first. Success would be measured by how much CICC helped China's reform process.

Where Morgan Stanley saw CICC as a domestic Chinese operation, the Chinese saw it as their flagship global merchant bank. Wang Qishan was thinking about how a Chinese financial institution could grow globally and become a peer of Western investment banks. When Wang and Fang Fenglei, CICC's deputy CEO, approached Morgan Stanley about doing the China Telecom deal, they were told that the New York bank had its own channels in China and did not need its partner to do an international listing. Morgan Stanley's bankers were skeptical that a China Telecom IPO would get done, and even if it did, they expected the deal size to be small. That was not what the Chinese had in mind.

The lesson I drew was that you need to listen hard to what your counterpart is really saying they want—and, if it's not unreasonable or unethical, do your best to meet their objectives or convince them they can't be met. That's true anywhere, but especially in China, where it's so easy to use the same words and phrases and yet mean very different things. You may think you have the same purpose in doing a joint venture, but it turns out your partner's interested in something entirely different.

Even the word *partner* may have been a source of misunderstanding. The Chinese, as I learned later, viewed the joint venture as a minority investment by Morgan Stanley, which would train their Chinese counterparts and receive a few privileges in return. But the Chinese side had total control and wanted to be deferred to and treated almost as if it were a client. Morgan Stanley understandably thought of CICC as a partner that would rely largely on it to manage the JV despite its having only a minority position.

Not having entered into a JV with the Chinese, we found it easier to treat them as a client. We understood that all roads would pass through CICC and that it would benefit us to get close to its people. At first nobody would deal with us because of the firm's relationship with Morgan Stanley. Nobody, that is, except Fang Fenglei, who happened to be the most important person there.

Fang was simply one of the most extraordinary people I'd met in China. Persistent and inventive, a preternatural networker in a country of networkers, he was born in 1952 near Mao Zedong's hometown in Hunan Province and grew up in Beijing. His parents were Communist Party members and midlevel government officials. Like so many of his generation, Fang and his family suffered during the Cultural Revolution. His father and older brother were imprisoned, and he was jailed for three months at the age of 16 for protesting their treatment. After his release he was shipped to Inner Mongolia, where he worked as a farmer and shepherd for two years; he then spent five years in the army, followed by two years in an electrical equipment factory.

After the Cultural Revolution ended, Fang secured a spot at the prestigious Sun Yat-sen University, also known as Zhongshan University, in Guangzhou. After graduation he joined the Ministry of Foreign Trade and Economic Cooperation, now the Ministry of Commerce. He was seconded to a working group affiliated with the Party's Central Commission for Discipline Inspection, which sent him to Henan Province in central China to help implement a 1983 campaign against corruption. He stayed there for two years, transferring to economic work. Fang became head of the provincial agriculture trading company, which among other things shipped half a million pigs each year to Hong Kong, then he helped run the provincial committee in charge of international trade and investment. One of Fang's bosses in his last years in Henan was none other than Wu Jichuan, soon to become minister of Posts and Telecommunications.

When China Construction Bank emerged as the Chinese partner in CICC, Wang tapped Fang, whom he'd previously hired to run an investment subsidiary, to be the joint venture's senior Chinese official. Fang came to feel that he was being treated dismissively by Morgan Stanley. That was particularly galling, since Fang had helped put CICC together. In the early 1990s he had conceived of starting a Chinese investment bank to speed the SOE reform process. He discussed the idea with Liu Guoguang, a noted economist whose daughter had married Fang's younger brother. Liu introduced him to Edwin Lim, who had established the World Bank's office in China and served as its first chief of mission. Fang and Lim set up CICC, with Lim acting as its first CEO until 1996, while he was on leave from the World Bank.

Fang could be headstrong and insist on doing things his own way. He spoke English imperfectly and was green by our standards. But it was a big mistake to underestimate his talent—or drive. Fang was a man of action, a genius at navigating the Chinese system. I've known very few bankers with his ability to get things done—and no one else quite like him in China. A natural storyteller, he could take complex subjects and recast them in a simple manner that Chinese bureaucrats could understand and act on.

We made sure we treated the endlessly animated Fang like a client, with the respect he deserved. John Thornton took the lead. John was a superb strategist, adept at corporate intrigue and client service, which made him a valued adviser in the merger work where he'd cut his teeth—and in wooing Fang. John at times ruffled feathers inside and outside of Goldman, but he was peerless at winning the confidence—and business—of clients. He was brimming with farsighted ideas and suggestions, as befits someone who had been the leader in expanding Goldman's U.K. and European activities.

John approached Fang in a typically blunt way, saying in effect: "You call yourself a banker, but you don't know the first thing about banking. I'm in charge of Asia, but I don't know the first thing about China. I'll teach you banking, you teach me China." Fang took his straightforwardness as a sign of respect.

When Deutsche Telekom made its long-awaited IPO on November 18, 1996, we made sure to invite to Frankfurt a Chinese delegation that included Fang and Ministry of Posts and Telecommunications officials, whom we treated like VIPs. Goldman chairman Jon Corzine met with them as they witnessed our launch of Germany's first mega-privatization. The IPO went off without a hitch, with Deutsche Telekom raising more than $13 billion. We hoped the Chinese would return home with fresh confidence about the potential of their own valuable, if tangled, telecom assets. And convinced that Goldman was the best firm for their deal.

The Deutsche Telekom deal made a big impression on the Chinese. Even today Wang Qishan likes to joke that it took eight years for Germany to spin off Deutsche Telekom, but China completed its deal within six months of awarding the banking mandate. Of course, the Germans had some big issues to deal with during those years, such as the fall of the Berlin Wall and unification. But there were similarities between the two countries. As in China, Germany's postal and telecommunication services were deeply entwined. Until 1989 Deutsche Telekom had been part of the Bundespost, the German post office, which traced its beginnings to the Holy Roman Empire.

In China state ties also ran deep. For a long time, only high-ranking state officials had residential telephone lines. During the Cultural Revolution, the MPT was briefly abolished and the phone system was run by the military. By 1973 the system was in civilian hands but complex and snaggled: a myriad of local and provincial bureaus reported to a reconstituted MPT as well as to their local governments. After the onset of reform, Beijing worked with mixed results to separate commercial activities from regulatory functions and to decentralize administrative power. In the early 1990s, the government created the Directorate General of Telecommunications, better known as China Telecom, to manage the business functions.

Along the way, the government increased investment in the previously neglected sector, adopting preferential tax policies and giving managers more responsibility for profits. Nonetheless, by the end of the 1980s, there was still just one telephone line per 200 citizens (up from one per 500 in 1978). China embarked on a build-out unrivaled anywhere in the world, spending more than $35 billion on infrastructure between 1992 and 1996. The payoff was striking. Fixed-line subscribers leaped from 11.5 million to nearly 55 million; mobile subscribers soared from 177,000 to 7 million. From the end of 1996 to mid-1997 alone, 2.4 million more mobile subscribers would be added. But China still had a long way to go. In 1996 just 4.5 percent of the population had fixed-line access versus 64 percent in the U.S., while 0.6 percent had cellular access versus 16.3 percent in the States. The country's potential was immense, however, and because China had started so late, it had fewer sunk costs in legacy operations and would be able to leapfrog antiquated technologies.

Still, in the 1990s, newly savvy consumers complained increasingly about poor service, long waits for lines, and the high fees the MPT charged for installation and other services to finance its build-out. The government gradually reduced MPT's preferences, and the State Council sanctioned the creation of a competitor, China United Telecommunications Corporation, whose shareholders included the country's rail and power ministries (adding prestige, Henry Kissinger would become an honorary adviser). Though it ran a distant second in size, China Unicom offered mobile services and broke the MPT's monopoly. Fees charged to consumers declined. By the second half of the 1990s, China's ambitious telecom build-out required more capital than the system could generate on its own.

We might have had Wang Qishan and Fang Fenglei as advocates for the China Telecom deal, but we made sure to touch all bases. The team arranged a meeting for me in December 1996 with Wu Jichuan, the powerful head of the MPT. The meeting got off to an inauspicious start when Cherry Li and I got snarled in traffic not far from the ministry. We kept nervously glancing at our watches, knowing that we simply could not be late. That would be taken as a near-unforgivable insult. Five minutes to go, and we were still stuck.

"What do you suggest we do?" I asked Cherry.

"I suggest we run."

So we did, jumping from the taxi and, overcoats flapping, sprinting down Chang'an Avenue to the amusement of pedestrians. We managed to get to the ministry, a drab hulk of a building, on time. The bespectacled, 60-year-old Wu was already waiting for us. He had spent nearly all his career in the industry, graduating from the Beijing Institute of Posts and Telecommunications, then working his way up from technician to division chief to vice minister and, in 1993, to minister. He'd even married into the business: his wife of nearly four decades was an expert in telecom transmissions. A tough and wily bureaucrat, Wu had over the years outmaneuvered and crushed competitors who threatened his control of the telecom sector.

Our aim was to get Wu's support for Goldman Sachs to host a much-needed symposium on privatization for ministry executives. I also wanted to establish a personal rapport with Wu and to demonstrate how high a priority we placed on China Telecom. As chief operating officer of a global investment bank, I could not oversee the deal day to day, but I could take direct responsibility for it. This was essential to the Chinese, who may be among the most status- and rank-conscious people on earth. I promised to attend the symposium, which we agreed to hold in January in Sanya on the island province of Hainan, in the South China Sea. Sanya was a tropical resort with beaches and big hotels popular with honeymooners and Minister Wu. The MPT, surprisingly, owned a hotel there that we could use.

The conference and our team were organized by Hsueh-ming Wang, who had joined Goldman after several years as a founding partner in an aircraft-leasing firm in Hong Kong. She played a vital role, developing relationships with Chinese clients and officials, particularly Minister Wu and Wang Qishan. She understood the importance of "face" and worried that we would send the wrong people to Hainan. If we sent junior bankers to talk about finance before a senior minister like Wu, we might lose any chance of a mandate right then and there. John Thornton made sure that senior Goldman partners attended, and our team worked through Christmas preparing presentations on all aspects of finance.

In mid-January 1997, two weeks before the scheduled date of the conference, I had to withdraw, creating a minicrisis. We needed someone with comparable status to Minister Wu to attend or he might pull out, too, damaging our prospects. We had just appointed John Thornton chairman of Asia, but he was in his early 40s, and it was felt he lacked Wu's stature. Fortunately, 53-year-old Bob Hormats, vice chairman of Goldman Sachs International, agreed to make the trip. John, who was on our six-member executive committee, far outranked Hormats internally, but Bob had been on the U.S. National Security Council staff when Henry Kissinger had made the opening to China in 1971, and he had been involved in the discussions that led to normalization of relations in 1979. The Chinese, with their abiding respect for such long-term connections, were pleased for him to substitute for me.

Several dozen people gathered for the conference—Goldman bankers, their CICC counterparts, and a raft of MPT bureaucrats from Beijing and the provinces. Minister Wu kicked off the proceedings, while John led the sessions. The presentations were meant to give officials of the MPT and CICC a primer in taking a telecom company public. As Fang Fenglei had told us, "I don't know much about finance or the rules and regulations of IPOs, and if I don't, you can be sure the MPT doesn't either."

Our team used the Deutsche Telekom offering as a template to walk everyone through the IPO process, instructing the Chinese in everything from how to structure a company and arrange its accounts to writing the prospectus and conducting a road show. They lapped up the information, despite the language challenges, taking copious notes in Chinese fashion. In one particularly unusual moment, the Deutsche Telekom CFO's remarks had to be translated from German to English to Chinese.

The Chinese had ambitious goals. They were keen to complete the deal by September, a date that coincided with two high-profile events that would draw lots of attention: the World Bank/International Monetary Fund annual meeting, which would be held for the first time on Chinese soil, in Hong Kong, and the Chinese Communist Party's National Congress, which meets every five years and ratifies key Party decisions, including leadership changes. We'd learned, moreover, that the Chinese wanted to raise upward of $2 billion—an eye-popping number for a country that had yet to do a deal bigger than $625 million. It was not a number based on any economic analysis; it was just a goal. A firm goal.

The most obvious challenge we faced was that, in conventional terms, there was as yet no actual company to underwrite. The China Telecom (Hong Kong) holding company was officially unveiled in late March, but it was, in the beginning, a shell with no assets: the entity whose shares would be sold to the public had yet to be created. We would have to help the MPT fashion a company that would meet listing requirements and appeal to investors. This was the opposite of a normal underwriting, where you start with an operating company with known assets, measurable revenues or cash flows, and audited books, and work with management to prepare it for public markets. We simply had to create new models as we went along.

John and Mike Evans explained to Minister Wu that for a $2 billion deal to succeed the ministry would have to meet a number of conditions. Although the government wanted to keep tight control, it would need to float a substantial enough chunk of China Telecom (Hong Kong)—between 20 and 25 percent—to satisfy listing requirements in Hong Kong and to generate the capital it wanted to raise. The company would have to include its highest-quality assets to demonstrate future growth—after all, investors would be buying the huge potential of China's telecom market. It would need a strong management team willing to go on a two-week road show to sell the deal, and it would need to be listed on the New York Stock Exchange, as well as in Hong Kong, to assure investors that it met the exacting accounting and financial standards of the United States. The government would also need to set up a transparent regulatory framework that made telecom tariffs clear, allowing investors to assess growth prospects. Minister Wu agreed, and the five conditions were written down. Mike signed the document. It wasn't a contract, but we were on the hook and would have to deliver.

From a practical point of view, the government couldn't just sell a small piece of China Telecom itself. It was too big, too complex, and its business was too concentrated in landlines, which did not much interest investors. The solution was to focus China Telecom (Hong Kong) on the mobile business and seed it with the cellular assets of various Chinese provinces. The ministry would have to help us identify which provinces met the requirements for revenues, growth potential, and a compelling story: millions, not thousands, of customers; commercial, not rural, subscribers (for higher revenue per customer); and high profit margins. Then the deal team had to sort through the administrative and political tangle and tease out the mobile from the fixed-line assets, which in most provinces were intermingled.

Figuring all of this out wasn't easy. Ministry accounts at all levels were, at best, opaque, and it wasn't long before there were upward of 350 full-time accountants from accounting firm KPMG digging through the books as they did due diligence. All day and into the night, they grilled the MPT officials, trying to reconcile the numbers, until finally some of those officials begged our people for just one day off.

Meantime, a number of provinces, which exercised control over their local telecom businesses, resisted participating. Why would they want to surrender their most promising operations—and the money these made—to a public company that would be controlled by the MPT in Beijing? Indeed, as they figured out the value that could be unleashed from the mobile assets, they wanted to do their own deals and not be included in the China Telecom (Hong Kong) structure. The ministry used its clout to quash that resistance. In this case, reform efforts led initially to more central control, not less.

The ministry came up with three provinces as candidates for inclusion in the deal: Guangdong, Zhejiang, and Jiangsu. All were booming coastal areas with rapid growth potential. It was decided to start with Zhejiang and Guangdong, which had the largest number of mobile subscribers. Together they accounted for just under 30 percent of all the mobile subscriptions in the country; their revenues and growth prospects would justify a market valuation that could get the company a market capitalization of $8 billion. Floating 25 percent of the shares would raise the $2 billion the government was looking for.

It was crucial to the deal that China Telecom (Hong Kong) wasn't just promising investors the markets of Guangdong and Zhejiang; it was promising investors China's mobile telephone future. The mobile assets of Jiangsu—and other provinces—could be acquired later. Thus, from the beginning, it was assumed that the company would essentially roll up the provincial mobile networks to create a massive national operating system. This would remove a roadblock to economic development and give China Telecom (Hong Kong) two attractive sources of growth: the organic growth from rising demand in the provinces that it would control at the outset, plus growth from the cellular assets of other provinces that it would systematically acquire. We could tell investors: "Think of this almost like an open-ended fund. Every year or so, we're going to add more provinces."

Initially, I had my reservations about this audacious plan, which was a bet on China's future. What if China didn't continue with asset injections from the other provinces? Investors would have bought into a hollow promise. But I realized that the Chinese had no choice but to follow through. They wanted foreign know-how, they wanted capital, and they wanted other state-owned enterprises to be able to come to market as well. China Telecom (Hong Kong) would be the lens through which the world would view China and decide whether its big companies could become competitive, well managed, profitable, and thus worth investing in. The Chinese would do what it took to make this deal a success.

On May 20, 1997, the MPT awarded Goldman and CICC the official mandate for the role we wanted as the deal's joint global coordinators, which meant we would take primary responsibility for helping China Telecom (Hong Kong) prepare to be a public company and for coordinating the marketing and pricing of its shares. MPT finance director Shi Cuiming, who would become chairman and CEO of China Telecom, drew up the document by hand in Minister Wu's office and signed it, along with China Telecom president Chen Zhaobin. John Thornton signed for Goldman while Fang did the honors for CICC. Not long afterward, the ministry named J.P. Morgan and Bear Stearns as its financial advisers, a limited role that essentially involved providing independent advice to the company, particularly when the IPO was priced.

At the time, our Beijing offices consisted of a couple of rooms in a building next door to the Great Wall Sheraton Hotel, and once we had the mandate, they began to get crowded. We soon employed 16 full-time people on our team, which worked around the clock to prepare the offering. We put people on the ground in Beijing, Hangzhou, Guangzhou, and Hong Kong, and every Tuesday they reported to Shi at the MPT. The world would be watching this deal, and we were determined that there would be no screwups.

In June, China Telecom (Hong Kong) announced that it would buy 5.5 percent of Hong Kong Telecom, the territory's primary provider of service, for $1.2 billion from its controlling shareholder, Cable & Wireless, the British concern that had been among the first of the U.K. state-owned companies privatized by the Margaret Thatcher government in the 1980s. Wang Qishan and Minister Wu had been pushing for China Telecom to purchase a stake for two years after hearing that British Telecommunications might bid for Cable & Wireless. That offer never materialized, but Wu had kept raising the idea of a Chinese bid for control: he did not want Hong Kong's phone services to stay in British hands after the Handover. It was decided, however, to keep Hong Kong Telecom separate from the China Telecom (Hong Kong) listing. The market was interested in "red chips"—mainland companies listed in Hong Kong; we didn't want to muddy China Telecom's story with Hong Kong assets.

Fang Fenglei had an iron constitution and an insatiable desire to learn. During the intense months leading up to the IPO, Fang would show up at all hours at the Great Wall Sheraton, Hsueh-ming Wang in tow, to pick Mike Evans's brain. He would park himself in the lobby, order a scotch, and talk with Mike and Hsueh-ming for hours about every aspect of the deal. One night it might be investment banking fees, another the details of book building. Fang was determined to learn the business. And he was learning from the preeminent capital markets banker in the world.

If anyone had the stamina to outlast Fang it was Mike. Confident and competitive, Mike and his twin brother, Mark, had won gold medals rowing on the Canadian men's eights team in the 1984 Los Angeles Summer Olympic Games. Mark had overseen Asian operations from Hong Kong for us beginning in 1994 and moved in 1997 to New York to run global equity capital markets. Mike had come to Goldman from Salomon Brothers in 1993; by 1996 he was head of European equity capital markets. Having brought Deutsche Telekom to market, Mike was the logical choice to oversee China Telecom's IPO. Tall, lean, and aggressive, he had the oarsman's disregard for limitations. He combined superb financial engineering with incisive strategic thinking; he rolled up his sleeves and immersed himself in every detail of a transaction, connecting as easily with a CEO or head of state as with the most junior analyst.

In late June I went to Hong Kong for the Handover. The British were formally giving the colony back to the Chinese after 156 years, ushering in a new era for both China and Hong Kong, and there were festivities for days. Goldman hosted a big dinner to mark the occasion.

During the celebrations I bumped into an old friend, Phil Purcell, who had just become CEO of Morgan Stanley following its merger with Dean Witter, Discover & Company. I knew Phil from Chicago, where he had led corporate strategy for Sears Roebuck and was a client of mine. Now there he was in Hong Kong with Morgan Stanley Asia head Jack Wadsworth. I had a high regard for Phil, but I couldn't resist bragging a little bit about our China Telecom mandate.

Finally, Phil turned to Jack Wadsworth, right in front of me, and said, "Explain to me again how our joint venture partner brings this business to Goldman Sachs."

Jack, a first-rate banker and professional, was speechless.

I had always cautioned our folks not to take victory laps or to rub people's noses in our successes. But I couldn't resist ribbing Phil. He was a friend, and this was one of the most extraordinary turn of events I had seen in my investment banking career.

My gloating was short-lived. On July 1 Hong Kong was returned to China. On July 2 all hell broke loose in the markets. After months of battling speculators, Thailand gave up defending its currency. The baht plunged nearly 20 percent against the dollar that day, triggering the onset of the Asian financial crisis that would batter many of the high-flying economies of the region for months.

Thailand was the first country affected, but the pain would soon spread, reversing the successes of the previous decade. In general, these economies had overheated, fueled by hot money, too-easy credit, property speculation, and the inevitable sins of crony capitalism: corruption and insider dealings. When the bubble burst, capital took flight and bank lending dried up. The countries were also mainly export-driven, which left them vulnerable to currency fluctuations. A strengthening dollar, to which some had pegged their currencies, led to a dramatic reduction in demand for their exports, which were now more expensive. A weak Japanese economy further softened the market for Southeast Asian exports.

Signs of trouble had emerged in 1996 but at first appeared localized. Speculation against the baht peaked in May 1997 with a massive attack on the currency. Thailand spent billions in defense, but by July the government could no longer afford the fight and let the baht float. Within days the Philippines devalued its peso and the currencies of Malaysia and Indonesia came under attack. Money fled the region and the contagion spread. Regional stock markets were hit hard, currencies swooned, liquidity dried up, banks failed, and sovereign debts were downgraded. The IMF would eventually put together a $40 billion fund to prop up the currencies of Thailand, Indonesia, and South Korea.

It wasn't the best time to be planning the biggest-ever Chinese IPO.

To be sure, this would all take place over several months, and in the earliest days of the crisis, Hong Kong markets held up. The Hang Seng stock index had risen more than 30 percent in 1996 and continued its climb into January 1997 before retreating. It recovered in April and climbed steadily, perhaps inspired by the impending Handover. Though the index dropped more than 3.2 percent in that fateful week after the baht collapsed, it regained its momentum to reach a new record of 16,673 on August 7.

The volatility was unsettling, and I couldn't help remembering our early days in Asia, when some at Goldman had favored Southeast Asia over China, figuring it was a safer bet. In the midst of this crisis, we took a hard look at our Asian efforts. Led by John Thornton, we scrutinized operations, business by business, and decided to focus on pursuing a smaller number of the highest-profile deals and relationships while fielding fewer, higher-quality bankers. The idea was to pursue clients like China Telecom and avoid getting scattered chasing lots of less consequential deals. Once you branded yourself with marquee deals, other transactions would follow. That was the Goldman strategy worldwide, but in Asia we'd gotten a bit unfocused.

The IPO had originally been planned for mid-September, but even before the onset of the crisis that target had been a tall order. As the Goldman and CICC team examined China Telecom, we pressed the MPT to provide what investors would demand from a company trying to raise so much money in this closely followed sector. The very process of preparing the IPO—challenging assumptions, forcing questions to be answered, reconciling accounts, nailing down business plans, examining the quality of management, and focusing on the bottom line of profit and loss—helped steer the ministry to make critical changes in how it operated the company and how it organized the industry. Our focus extended to the administrative and regulatory arena as well. How would fixed-line assets be handled in the future? What would the national government's role be, and how would the provinces fit in? How would mobile be regulated?

Zhu Rongji's approach to these issues embodied his genius as a reformer. He was using the market to instigate changes that ministry and management could not or would not do on their own. As I've said, he was not an ideologue but a fierce pragmatist, a socialist willing to use market mechanisms to speed reforms needed to enhance the efficiency of the country's enterprises and improve the nation's well-being.

"Management," he told me with typical bluntness in a meeting later that year, "is backward and needs to become more modern and progressive."

But he felt he could go only so far. State-owned enterprises needed foreign capital, but the Chinese could not surrender control—for a simple reason. SOEs lost money in part because they had too many workers; if foreigners took control, they would lay off many employees—he estimated up to 80 percent. Doing that without an adequate social security system would threaten stability. China would have to build a safety net and in the meantime use the equity markets for its version of partial privatization.

Meantime, our team raced against the odds to prepare the IPO, which had been pushed back to October 23, 1997.

Mike Evans and his counterparts at CICC devised a plan to sell the shares in three main tranches: U.S., Asia, and international (primarily Europe). The Asian leg would include a Hong Kong retail offering, an institutional offering, and an allocation to key corporate investors, whose presence in the deal we judged would help anchor the offering and inspire confidence in the market. A dozen Hong Kong business magnates and the Hong Kong arms of mainland entities like China International Trust and Investment Corporation (CITIC) agreed to buy at the offering price and retain their stakes for at least a year. Collectively, they would account for nearly half of the initial offering of shares, and 10 percent of the company. This concept of cornerstone investors hadn't been tried before; we created it for China Telecom, and we would use it on many successful future IPOs.

But some of these investors got nervous as the expected size of the deal increased and the market got precarious. At our suggestion, Minister Wu called them to an emergency meeting in Shenzhen. Mike Evans updated the group, letting them know there was strong demand for China Telecom shares, both on the retail front—where the deal would be oversubscribed 30 times—and among global institutions. But some of the corporate investors were in a sour mood. They worried the deal might tank while they were locked into holding shares at the IPO price.

It was up to Minister Wu to reassure them, and he did just that, with a short, stirring speech in which he argued that whatever the state of the markets was right then, the long-term benefits of investing in China Telecom (Hong Kong) would more than reward them. The corporate investors hung in after Minister Wu assured them, "This is just the appetizer. The main course is to come."

On September 29 we gave investors a first look at China Telecom's price range: 2.6 billion shares from HK$7.75 to HK$10.00. Then Mike and the CICC team led a caravan on a whirlwind two-week road show to about a dozen cities in the U.S., Europe, and Asia. The first U.S. stop was New York on October 8. I hosted a luncheon presentation at the Plaza Hotel. Prospective investors in the audience relied on earpieces that simultaneously translated the Mandarin presentation. With demand clearly building, we did a rare thing—we repriced the offering in the middle of the road show, raising the range to between HK$9.39 and HK$12.48.

Heading into the meeting to price the deal, Mike felt the offering price should be in the middle of the range, but China Construction Bank chief Wang Qishan wanted to issue the shares at a higher level, one that would drive speculators away. He and other officials also favored a price that included the number 88, which many Chinese consider doubly lucky. They were set on HK$11.88 per share. Mike worried that the weak markets were going to give way. Wang Qishan was supremely confident but compromised a little.

"We're just going to go with HK$11.80," he calmly told Mike.

"I'm not being asked," Mike remembers thinking. "I'm being told."

In Hong Kong shares are priced one week before they are listed and begin trading. That's in contrast to the U.S., where IPOs are priced at the day's close and trade the next day. We announced the price on October 16, one week before the IPO trading date of October 23.

Mike had his finger on the pulse of the market, and his apprehensions turned out to be justified. The financial crisis, which had begun in earnest in July, turned its fury for the first time on Hong Kong. On October 17, the day after we priced the IPO, Taiwan stopped defending its currency. Speculators attacked Hong Kong, the last regional currency pegged to the U.S. dollar. The new Hong Kong SAR government vowed to defend the currency and ratcheted up short-term interest rates, which alarmed Hong Kong's all-important property markets. By October 22, the day before the China Telecom shares would open for trading, Hong Kong stocks had fallen 14 percent. We were setting sail into a raging headwind.

Thursday, October 23, turned out to be a very wet day in Hong Kong, with dark skies pouring rain. To Canadian Mike Evans, the weather boded ill. Walking over to the Hong Kong Stock Exchange with Shi Cuiming that morning, he said, "Can you believe how hard it's raining?"

"This is a good sign," Shi corrected Mike. "It's a good omen."

With Hong Kong's currency under attack, the Hang Seng index dropped like a rock; it would fall more than 10 percent that day, which was quickly dubbed Black Thursday. China Telecom opened down sharply at HK$10.50 and stumbled through the day, before ending the first day of trading at HK$10.55.

China Telecom had raised $4.22 billion, but we were all nervous about what would happen next, as Hong Kong shares continued to be pounded. China Telecom shares climbed above their offering price on Friday (HK$12.15) and held on to some gains Monday (HK$11.95), even as markets cracked wide open. The Hang Seng dropped 6 percent on Monday, triggering a mini-crash in New York, with the Dow Jones Industrial Average falling 7.2 percent; trading had to be halted twice before the market was closed early. Tuesday was worse: the Hang Seng plunged 14 percent, and China Telecom was back to its first-day close of HK$10.55.

The Chinese were worried, too. Wang Qishan later told me that in the midst of the frenzy, his boss, Vice Premier Zhu Rongji, called him back to Beijing from Hong Kong. Before he went in to see Zhu, he phoned to check on China Telecom and heard that the stock had bounced back.

"Did you get the $4.2 billion?" Zhu asked him.

"Yes," Wang said. "*Zhen jin bai yin*—real gold and silver."

That, I learned, was a Chinese expression that means, in effect, "real money."

"I'll only be reassured when it's in your pocket," Zhu said. "Only then can you be really sure that it's there."

It may be hard to believe today, but back then China was worried about money.

Fortunately, the demand for China Telecom was strong and persisted through the fall. By year-end, its shares were trading up 26 percent from its first-day close and 13 percent above its offer price. The Hang Seng index was up 3 percent.

Afterward, Mike told me that during pricing, when Wang Qishan kept reassuring him that demand would be there, he had thought, "These guys know nothing about pricing deals."

Later he said he had changed his mind, concluding: "Maybe I don't know anything about pricing Chinese deals."

Fang Fenglei had another take on things, turning to Chinese superstition. China Telecom's listing code number on the Hong Kong Stock Exchange was 941. These numbers, as pronounced in Chinese, mean "survival in the midst of dangers."

Not quite a month later, my wife, Wendy, and I flew to Beijing for the China Environment Forum, where I would be giving a speech on behalf of the Nature Conservancy on the economics of conservation, a passion of mine.

On November 21 I met with Zhu Rongji at the Purple Light Pavilion at Zhongnanhai. Our group included John Thornton, Mike Evans, and Wendy. She has a sharp eye for detail, and I could see her making mental notes of the rich blue carpet and splendid floral arrangements, and of the elegantly dressed young women who, with military precision, strode into the room to serve us tea. As we had in February, Zhu and I sat facing each other across a side table, accompanied by interpreters. It was almost nine months to the day Zhu had given us his implicit backing for the China Telecom assignment. As ever, the Chinese had been slow to decide, astonishingly quick to act.

Zhu asked me, "Are you confident about the performance of China Telecom?"

"It's been the best-performing stock in Asia, despite the crisis," I pointed out. "And those people who didn't subscribe to the IPO will regret that for the rest of their lives."

Zhu quoted a Chinese proverb about "the one beautiful flower in the garden." He was referring to China Telecom, the symbol of Chinese stability in the middle of the Asian financial crisis.

"Goldman Sachs did a great job," he told me. Then he pointed to Mike Evans, sitting along the rim of the horseshoe.

"How many people like Mike Evans do you have in Goldman Sachs?"

"Only one," I said. "He's the best in the world at what he does."

"Mr. Evans," Zhu said, "if I had ten people like you, I'd turn around all of the state-owned enterprises. If I had 100 people like you, I'd turn around our whole country."

The China Telecom deal had given Zhu Rongji a start on that goal. The first high-profile example of state-owned enterprise reform, it was a true landmark. Its success signaled the international markets' approval of the country's economic direction and confirmed Zhu's supposition that Western capital markets could begin to do for China's industrial base what bureaucrats who lacked the resolve or skill or fresh perspective could not.

The deal also marked the beginning of a widespread corporate restructuring of the telecom system that would create a nationwide mobile system and lead to a more competitive domestic marketplace through a series of complex corporate reshufflings. Not long after the offering, the government would restructure MPT, combining it with elements of other ministries to create the Ministry of Information Industry under the redoubtable Minister Wu. China Telecom (Hong Kong) eventually became China Mobile;

what it left behind would retain the China Telecom brand, consolidate the country's landline businesses, and eventually expand into mobile. Another start-up challenger, China Netcom, would appear in 1999, take over China Telecom's northern China landline business, and in 2008 merge into China Unicom. All this would leave China with three massive and competitive national carriers.

CHAPTER FIVE

Your Chairman Has Gone to Sleep

Zhou Yongkang, the head of the China National Petroleum Corporation (CNPC), was eager to meet former U.S. president George H. W. Bush. It was early 1998, and we had learned that Zhou was planning to attend an energy industry conference in Houston, Texas, the president's hometown. CNPC, the biggest and most important energy concern in China, was expected to be the next big state-owned enterprise to go public, and I was eager to get to know Zhou and his colleagues better. I'd met him for the first time the previous November in Beijing over lunch near CNPC's headquarters. Zhou was a career oilman, educated at the Beijing Petroleum Institute, who had gone to the frozen fields of Northeast China after completing his studies. Unlike many government bureaucrats of that era, who still sported white socks with their dark business suits, Zhou was nattily dressed and meticulously groomed. A sharp, serious man, he had taken charge of CNPC the year before, knew his business cold, and had clear ambitions for how to transform his company.

We invited Zhou and his colleagues to visit us in the States and arranged a meeting with the former president through his cousin George Herbert Walker IV, who worked in Goldman's asset management division. On February 12 John Thornton, Mike Evans, and I flew down to Houston. We met Zhou at the former president's office. President Bush's son Neil greeted us and then took us to see the president. Zhou beamed, calling Bush an old friend of China. The president had founded Zapata, an oil driller, in the 1950s, and served as the head of the U.S. Liaison Office in Beijing in 1974–1975 before normalization of relations.

"I've been an oilman all my life," Zhou told President Bush, "and you can always trust an oilman."

Bush was in fine form, expansive and familiar. He explained the memorabilia on the walls and proudly described his presidential library, which had opened in November in nearby College Station. The president invited us into his inner office, and we chatted for a while about world affairs, the outlook for oil prices, and the character of oilmen generally. He reminisced fondly about his days in Beijing and how much China had changed for the better. He took out a sheet of paper from his desk and wrote a note that he asked Zhou to deliver to Chinese Premier Li Peng.

I can only surmise why Zhou wanted to meet with President Bush. I've found that many Chinese like to meet prominent Americans when they visit the States, out of a combination of curiosity and an inherent preoccupation with rank—such visits confer status on them back home. In any case, the point wasn't to have a substantive discussion. As I had learned in dealing with China, the meeting itself was the substance. It would help us forge a relationship with Zhou, who would perhaps gain a little more cachet at home. I don't know what President Bush wrote to Li Peng, but it didn't escape my attention how he had used Zhou to deliver the note. Years later I, too, would turn to Zhou to deliver an important message to a different Chinese leader. By then, in one of those twists and turns that careers can take, he had become minister of Public Security and I was U.S. Treasury secretary.

We flew back to New York at noon, and the next morning, bright and early, we took Zhou and his colleagues through a series of presentations that we had designed to demonstrate the depth of our industry expertise as well as our capital markets skills. We showed Zhou our equity trading floor; experts from banking and research presented our views on the oil and gas business and explained the nuts and bolts of raising capital. After lunch, the group headed up the street to the New York Stock Exchange, where Zhou was delighted to see his name and that of CNPC whiz by in a welcoming message on the ticker.

We had more on the agenda, but the group was running late and Zhou Yongkang was scheduled to visit Morgan Stanley. This was a delicate matter and not something we were eager to help out with. After the success of the China Telecom offering, Fang Fenglei was eager to work with us again, a guaranteed way to enrage our archrivals. Having lost out on China Telecom, Morgan Stanley was working hard to repair its relationship with China Construction Bank and win the CNPC mandate. CCB chief Wang Qishan, who had brought his boss "real gold and silver" on the China Telecom IPO, had been tapped to become vice governor of Guangdong, the biggest and most economically important province. The new head of the bank would be Zhou Xiaochuan, another protégé of Zhu Rongji's.

With Zhou Xiaochuan's appointment, I truly appreciated Zhu's deft touch. A brilliant economist, he would use China Construction Bank as the model to begin the crucial restructuring of the ailing banking sector. State-owned enterprise reforms were driven by share offerings, and CICC would be involved in every one. If the public markets were to be the fulcrum of change, Zhou Xiaochuan would help Zhu Rongji lean on the lever.

We heard later that Morgan Stanley was unhappy about the limited time their executives had secured with the CNPC team. Zhou Yongkang had a packed schedule when he was in New York—although he did take a break to enjoy a night on the town. His party ate dinner at famed steakhouse Smith & Wollensky then went en masse to see the new movie *Titanic*. Goldman would secure the CNPC deal, while Morgan Stanley would be awarded the mandate for the IPO of the oil giant's main rival, Sinopec.

Oil occupied a special place in China's psyche. More than just a crucial source of energy, it had become over the years a symbol of independence and self-reliance, a literal wellspring of national pride. Not long after Mao Zedong took power in 1949, he had turned to the Soviet Union to help break China's dependence on imports. Until then oil exploration in China had largely been a disappointment. Mao's Cold War ally dispatched thousands of experts, along with equipment, technology, and financial support. Drilling began in 1958, and oil was discovered the following year at a field in Northeast China known as Daqing, or Great Celebration. But amid ideological differences and growing acrimony, Russia withdrew nearly all of its technical advisers in 1960. Two years later the countries severed relations.

China was determined to develop its energy resources on its own, substituting sheer resolve for a lack of technical expertise. The government approached the challenge like a military campaign, sending waves of workers to the oil fields. One team, led by Wang Jinxi, labored famously through temperatures as low as –30°C before finally striking oil. Mao lauded the achievements of "Iron Man" Wang and his Number 1205 drilling team, exhorting the country to embrace "the Daqing spirit." Wang was celebrated as a model worker and national hero and was even elected to the Central Committee of the Communist Party of China in 1968. He died two years later at age 47.

Daqing, where Zhou Yongkang went to work in 1967, would become one of the most productive fields ever discovered. In the 1960s and 1970s, it accounted on average for some three-quarters of China's oil output and at its peak produced more than 1 million barrels per day. As China drove toward its goal of energy independence, other fields were developed, and by the late 1970s, the country had become the world's ninth-largest producer and a net exporter of oil, particularly to neighboring Japan. The timing was fortuitous, as crude prices soared during the decade's oil shocks. Deng Xiaoping and China's other leaders came to believe that they might be able to pay for modernization initiatives with surging oil revenues.

Instead, the explosive growth sparked by Deng's reforms placed ever-greater demands on the country's energy resources—from newly sprung factories to consumers switching on their first refrigerators—and by the late 1980s it was becoming apparent that China would need to import oil again. Even as demand boomed, reserves had plateaued, in part because of the below-market prices for domestic oil sales mandated by the government. While a boon to energy-guzzling state-owned enterprises, this pricing scheme left little in the till to fund exploration and production. By 1994 China was once again a net importer of oil.

This time China's leaders could not rely on a revival of the Daqing spirit to provide energy to a country that was much more closely integrated into the world economy. Instead they would need to diversify their sources of supply, developing other types of energy and venturing overseas for additional oil and gas production. Doing so required capital and carried wide-ranging economic, political, and national security implications. If China were to turn again to imported oil, it would need its supplies to be safe from interdiction. Moreover, the state-controlled energy industry would have to become better run and more globally competitive to find, secure, and manage needed resources.

From the onset of reform in 1978, China's leaders had sought to retool the sector into more efficient and logically structured entities. In 1982 the government created the China National Offshore Oil Corporation (CNOOC) to develop offshore gas and oil fields in waters deeper than five meters through joint ventures with foreign companies. A year later the refining and petrochemical sections of the Ministry of Petroleum Industry were carved out and combined with chemical and fiber manufacturing enterprises that had previously come under the Chemical Industry and Textile Industry Ministries to form the China Petrochemical Corporation, or Sinopec. This company would be responsible for petroleum refining and the production and marketing of petrochemical products. CNPC was formed in 1988 to undertake onshore oil and gas exploration and production as well as some refining and chemical production. CNPC controlled major pipelines and all onshore oil fields plus offshore oil fields in waters up to five meters deep. It owned Daqing, which remained China's largest oil field.

Still, as the 1990s drew to a close, Chinese oil and gas companies badly lagged their Western competitors, weighed down by high operational costs, low productivity, overstaffing, and out-of-date equipment. Among other measures, CNPC suffered from higher-than-average production costs.

We could see that the restructuring and IPO of CNPC would be even more politically difficult and organizationally complex than that of China Telecom. With China Telecom we had helped the Ministry of Posts and Telecommunications pluck out its most attractive assets—the mobile telephone services of the major provinces—to create a company that would interest the market. CNPC was another matter. The macroeconomic picture was dim. The Asian financial crisis had sapped demand, the Organization of the Petroleum Exporting Countries cartel was in disarray, and oil prices had dropped to levels not seen since before 1973. On top of that, the changes required at the company itself were daunting.

We were nevertheless eager to push forward, and Mike Evans suggested to Zhou Yongkang that we hold a "summit" with a wider group of CNPC executives and Goldman experts modeled on the presentations we had done on Hainan Island for China Telecom. Zhou appeared eager to do so.

After his New York visit, Zhou Yongkang had traveled to Moscow for meetings. The head of our China team, Ziwang Xu, went along. "Z," as we called him, was an energetic and resourceful banker, with master's degrees from Shanghai's Fudan University (economics) and from the Fletcher School of Law and Diplomacy at Tufts University (international business relations), whom we had recruited the year before from Morgan Stanley. In Moscow Z had a conversation with Zhou that gave him a better understanding of some of the barriers to pushing the deal forward.

One obstacle was that Zhu Rongji, who was set to become premier in March 1998, had reservations about an IPO, reflecting internal government debates about the energy industry. Zhu was said to have a low opinion of the competence and prospects of CNPC and its sister companies and frowned on CNPC's acquiring overseas assets. Zhou Yongkang favored the international strategy, as did outgoing premier Li Peng, who exerted a strong influence over the energy and power sectors. It was also thought that Zhu held the view that oil prices, at $13 per barrel, might sink further. He was not alone. The *Economist* would run a piece the following year predicting that oil prices would fall to $5 per barrel. We had also picked up talk that some Chinese decision makers were pushing to merge Sinopec and CNPC before any deal.

When Zhu became premier, the whip hand driving reform cracked sharper than ever. He gave state-owned enterprises three years to become profitable by cutting workers and upgrading technology or be restructured out of existence. Government bloat was also a target. Zhu proposed cutting China's army of 8 million bureaucrats in half and paring the number of ministries from 40 to 29. The responsibilities of most industrial ministries would be reduced, their regulatory functions handed over to the State Economic and Trade Commission, and their commercial assets spun out into separate state-owned enterprises. Three new ministries were created, including one for labor and social welfare to deal with layoffs that would result from downsizing. Zhu's aim was to move government out of business, making state-owned enterprises more commercial by separating regulators from operators.

Zhu Rongji's changes had an immediate impact on the energy sector. The State Council decided to leave CNPC and Sinopec as separate companies that would be restructured through asset swaps to create vertically integrated nationwide oil and gas companies. Previously, CNPC had been focused on "upstream" exploration and production, while Sinopec had concentrated on the "downstream" business of refining and sales. CNPC would transfer several oil fields to Sinopec and receive a number of refineries, petrochemical plants, and retail distribution companies in return. CNPC's exploration and production assets would now be concentrated in the north, northeast, and northwest, while those of Sinopec would mostly be in the south and east. With a few simple pen strokes, the government had created China's own versions of Exxon, Royal Dutch Shell, and BP. The moves came at a crucial moment in the global oil business: low crude prices and increased competition would soon lead to a wave of mergers creating the so-called super major companies. BP would merge with Amoco in 1998, the same year Exxon and Mobil would announce their impending combination.

The Chinese government made another crucial change. Until that spring the price of nearly all oil-related products had been set by the state at a discount to market rates, which effectively subsidized consumers but limited profits for CNPC. Now the prices of domestic crude oil and refined products would be pegged to international markets.

The government shifted oversight and administrative responsibilities from CNPC and Sinopec, which had been regulating themselves, to the State Economic and Trade Commission and the newly minted Ministry of Land and Resources to encourage the companies to focus on management and operations. The big surprise, and seeming setback for us, was that Zhou Yongkang was put in charge of Land and Resources, which was set up to manage China's mineral riches, granting permits for petroleum exploration and estimating and evaluating reserves. He had only taken over CNPC at the end of 1996 and had been focused on restructuring and taking it public from the get-go. But the Party had bigger plans for Zhou Yongkang.

Zhou arranged for us to meet his successor, Ma Fucai, at a lunch in mid-March. Ma shared a similar background to Zhou's. Both were petroleum industry veterans, and Ma had followed in Zhou's career footsteps. But in terms of our working relationship, Ma would prove to be quite different. Zhou was ambitious and eager to restructure CNPC. Ma was a hands-on operator new to the world of strategy and finance. He seemed uncertain and slow to move. This did not make our team's job any easier, and he would delay the deal at numerous stages.

Getting CNPC to market may have been the most difficult assignment that Goldman had in China during my tenure. Even today Goldman veterans groan when they talk about the IPO of PetroChina Company, which became the name of the CNPC subsidiary that was listed in Hong Kong and New York in April 2000. To begin with, economic conditions were inauspicious. The dot-com bubble was rapidly inflating, and investors had little interest in "old economy" companies, much less one in an industry wracked by historically low prices. The PetroChina offering would also inspire the first organized protests against a Chinese company listing in the States.

That was the world outside CNPC. Inside, the effort to reposition the company to attract investors, satisfy listing requirements, and pass muster with international regulators was nothing short of extraordinary. CNPC, like so many other state-owned enterprises, was less a company in the Western sense than a self-contained city-state, with company-provided housing, schools, hospitals, mortuaries, commissaries, and police departments—all catering to the needs of more than a million workers. Disentangling this conglomeration of essential and nonessential functions to fashion a modern public corporation was a challenge of enormous proportions that would test the ingenuity—and stamina—of all involved. More than a thousand professionals worked on the deal at one point or another. Goldman fielded a team of 40, twice the number it had devoted to China Telecom. They were joined by a contingent from CICC, consultants from McKinsey & Company, lawyers from seven firms, and a battalion of auditors from PriceWaterhouseCoopers.

The asset swaps between the oil giants were completed, and CNPC reincorporated as a so-called integrated group, in June 1998. I dropped a note to CNPC's new head, Ma Fucai, congratulating him and reiterating my personal commitment to the company's restructuring. We were working closely with

CICC, but we didn't have a formal mandate, and CNPC couldn't say definitively when—or if—a deal would go to market. This was an all-too-typical frustration in China; things could be in flux for months, with ministries requesting presentations and research papers on this or that aspect of a proposed deal, soliciting the analyses of competitors, going back and forth repeatedly with the State Council as its members scrutinized and refined options. Then, all of a sudden, a decision would be reached behind closed doors, and the Chinese would want everything done in record time. You had to be on your toes, constantly probing to see where you stood, what else you could do. Your team had to be assembled and ready.

In February 1999 Ma set up an internal IPO team. It was headed by Jiang Jiemin, Ma's eventual successor as CEO. A slight, almost gaunt executive, he was gifted with great skill and decisiveness and would be more responsible than anyone on the Chinese side for getting the deal done. CNPC would need to establish a subsidiary that could be listed. Figuring out what should go into this subsidiary would be complicated and politically difficult. After the asset swap the now vertically integrated CNPC was an even more sprawling enterprise, with a massive oil and gas exploration and production business, refining and marketing operations, and a slew of petrochemical plants. It dominated the production and sale of crude oil and natural gas in China but needed to turn around the money-losing natural gas and chemicals businesses.

I empathized with Ma and the heads of other SOEs as they prepared for their IPOs. I was going through the same exercise myself in early 1999. After a gut-wrenching internal debate, Goldman had decided, after 130 years as a private partnership, to become a public company, and I was devoting much of my time and attention to our own IPO, which would come in May 1999.

To create PetroChina, Goldman and CICC guided CNPC executives through a painstaking exercise in identifying and separating core assets from noncore assets. Core assets would be put in PetroChina; noncore would stay with CNPC, which would own 90 percent of the subsidiary and sell 10 percent to the public. Much of this exercise was fairly obvious. CNPC's social service functions made little sense in a globally competitive company. But separating them out wouldn't be easy to accept for employees and executives who had come up through a system with deeply rooted expectations of cradle-to-grave care. Before the onset of reform, a person's employment meant far more than a nine-to-five job and a salary. The work unit, or *danwei*, was the central organizing force in people's lives in urban areas. On leaving school Chinese men and women were assigned a specific workplace for life; they were fed, housed, and given social and medical services there. They needed permission from work to travel, marry, and have children. Over the years competition from private companies had eroded the system, but it remained in place at state-owned enterprises, which were, as a result, weighed down by excess employees, immense financial obligations, and management distractions.

Such inefficiencies were what Zhu Rongji and his fellow reformers sought to eliminate, and they were prepared to endure the short-term pain that would accompany reorganizations and forced layoffs. I can only imagine how disruptive and wrenching this process must have been for workers, their bosses, and the country as a whole. While liberating for those able to take advantage of new opportunities, it had to have been terrifying for laid-off and older workers—especially since China had only a rudimentary, government-sponsored social security system. CNPC alone was responsible for some 1.5 million active workers and their families—perhaps 6 million people in all. By contrast, global oil giant BP employed about 80,000 people in 1999. The clear implication was that CNPC would need to shed hundreds of thousands of workers to begin to be competitive. Yet CNPC officials were understandably reluctant to lay workers off. Petro-China would eventually keep approximately 480,000 workers. It targeted an ambitious goal of cutting $1 billion, or 8 percent of costs, within two years and projected a workforce reduction of 50,000 by 2002.

CNPC's numbers only hint at the dimension of the problem for the country. The statistics on state employment and layoffs are squishy for that period, but the International Monetary Fund, for one, estimated in 2004 that the state-owned sector shed more than 40 million jobs between 1990 and 2001.

These workers received meager severance pay, and the vast majority of them were unable to find new employment. Their hardships were severe and in many ways grossly unfair. That these disruptions produced a market-based system that lifted hundreds of millions out of poverty was cold comfort to those who weren't equipped to deal with this new world. Many would later come back demanding more money, often in noisy protests, and the companies generally paid to keep peace, but Zhu Rongji and his team of reformers, backed by President Jiang Zemin, were determined to press ahead on SOE reforms, despite the pain and political risk involved. They knew that the iron rice bowl crippled the companies' efficiency and China's prospects.

CNPC's social service functions were easy enough to identify, but they accounted for only part of the excess staffing. Another factor was that just about every operation was done in-house—dozens of functions, from surveying and drilling to construction and engineering. This no doubt reflected the legacy of self-sufficiency, as well as the fact that before reform, no private marketplace existed in which companies could be formed to compete to supply these services. Outside of China major oil companies outsourced most similar functions, reducing overhead and other expenses.

The idea was that PetroChina would leave the noncore functions and business operations with CNPC. In time CNPC would turn the social services over to the central government, which had agreed to gradually assume these obligations; senior officials were pushing reluctant, financially strapped local governments to share, and eventually take over, the burden. PetroChina meantime would contract with parent company CNPC to provide the services it needed for a fee.

A number of well-known and well-regarded operations didn't fit with the new PetroChina. Among those were certain international exploration and production assets, as well as the iconic drilling operations made famous by Iron Man Wang. For historical and sentimental reasons, this was a controversial decision, but multinational energy companies like Exxon and BP Amoco were not in the drilling business, either, as our bankers noted and as Ma and company learned in their investigations and meetings.

PetroChina acquired some of the most attractive assets from CNPC, including oil and gas exploration and production, refining and marketing operations, and the petrochemical business. PetroChina would also own the prized Daqing oil fields, as well as pipelines that transported 84 percent of China's natural gas. It would control more than 70 percent of China's proven oil and gas reserves and two-thirds of its 1998 production.

Meeting the stringent U.S. accounting and regulatory standards necessary to do the listing was not easy. The Securities and Exchange Commission required five years of accounts, and its demands sent U.S.-trained analysts off to Manchurian oil fields to pull files, when they could find them, to put together such things as depreciation schedules. We, along with PriceWaterhouseCoopers, had to answer hundreds of SEC questions concerning accounting decisions that had been taken. One issue related to reserves—a key measure for energy companies. We had hired a respected consulting firm to do an international standard reserve estimate—the first ever for China's reserves.

It took weeks to hear from the SEC. We finally did, but it was the eve of the Chinese New Year, when just about everyone in China disappears to return to their hometowns. The SEC was unhappy that PetroChina was required to renew its production permits annually with the Chinese government. The requirement, though a formality, created uncertainty. What if regulators suddenly denied the renewal? PetroChina's reserves would be worthless.

We had to get a government waiver from the Chinese right away. We couldn't wait until after the holiday, and we lacked high-level contacts at the Ministry of Land and Resources—Zhou Yongkang had left to become Party secretary of Sichuan in 1999. In an amazing feat given that all of China was on holiday, one of CICC's top bankers managed to find an official who, with a little coaxing, processed the request on New Year's Day. The banker was Jinyong Cai, a World Bank veteran and graduate of Peking University with a Ph.D. in economics from Boston University, who had joined from Morgan Stanley during the past year. The waiver was subsequently signed by Wen Jiabao, then vice premier (and future premier), whose economics portfolio included the Ministry of Land and Resources. The SEC gave us the green light, so the IPO could move forward.

The PetroChina offering had to contend with a host of obstacles. Asia was still recovering from the 1997 crisis. China's economy had softened, with GDP growth dipping to 7.6 percent in 1999 from 9.3 percent in 1997.

Hong Kong–listed H-shares were underperforming, while the Internet stock market frenzy had reached full cry. Although oil prices were on the rise—from $10 a barrel in 1998, they would reach $27 a barrel in February 2000—energy was viewed as stodgy and unappealing. In October 1999 China National Offshore Oil had been forced to pull a planned $2.5 billion IPO that was being led by one of our competitors in difficult market conditions. The PetroChina offering simply had to succeed. A second failed IPO would be globally embarrassing and demonstrate a lack of confidence in China and its energy sector. For PetroChina's Ma it would also mean the end of his career.

We devised features to appeal to the market. Investors would naturally wonder whether a Communist state-owned relic could actually change its habits and follow through on all of its promises. So we encouraged the company to put in place an innovative incentive compensation structure. In a groundbreaking move for China that would set a precedent for other SOEs, PetroChina granted stock options to 300 senior executives and designed an incentive package for more junior managers. Some 70 to 75 percent of senior managers' pay would be contingent on meeting performance targets linked to net profits, return on capital, and cost reductions. PetroChina also set explicit financial targets for each business segment. Since most of the variable compensation came from stock ownership, the interests of shareholders and executives were aligned.

To help anchor the offering, we followed the China Telecom model and recruited several cornerstone investors, who agreed to purchase $350 million of shares and hold them for a minimum of six months. All of the investors, including K. S. Li, had also been investors in China Telecom.

We added another wrinkle, inviting in a major strategic investor as well. The idea was not just to raise capital, but to help PetroChina forge a relationship with a world-class oil company whose experience, management know-how, and technical skills it could tap. This approach was another first for China. The government would welcome strategic investors in subsequent major offerings, most notably in banking.

The oil company was BP Amoco, whose CEO, John Browne, we knew well. He had joined the board of Goldman as part of our own IPO in May 1999. The British concern was completing its acquisition of Atlantic Richfield (ARCO), which would significantly hike its Asian oil reserves. Browne had been eyeballing China for some time. I flew to London and met up with Mike Evans. We went to see Browne at his offices and ran through our proposal.

It was not an easy sell. BP had recently taken a $200 million write-down on an investment in a venture to develop a huge Siberian gas field in 1999, and Browne was wary of making a commitment.

"Is this deal going to get done?" Browne asked. "And is it going to be successful?"

When we assured him it would be, he responded, "That's good, because I can't afford to have another failure."

Our bankers were eager for CNPC to reach an agreement with BP before the road shows began. But BP wasn't in quite the same hurry and wanted to be sure it got its money's worth. Browne proposed that his company be permitted to get into the retail fuel business in the prosperous southern Chinese provinces in return for a sizable stake in the IPO. There was a problem, however. China was at a critical stage in its application for entry to the World Trade Organization. Although CNPC was willing to cut a deal, BP's ask was far ahead of what would be permitted by the schedule China had agreed to under its WTO agreement.

We completed the London road show without BP's agreement. Investor interest was tepid. BP had still not agreed to invest as we were about to begin marketing in New York. Ma Fucai was getting nervous. He didn't want PetroChina to falter as the IPO for CNOOC had.

CNPC needed to provide a government guarantee that BP would be able to acquire the gas stations it wanted, despite China's pending WTO application. Ma was able to track down Vice Premier Wu Bangguo, who oversaw the state-owned enterprises, and explain the situation. Wu agreed to provide a letter of support and asked CNPC's team to prepare one for him. A draft with language approving a gas station deal was hurriedly faxed to him.

The next morning a reply came from the vice premier, but it was ambiguous: He didn't explicitly say CNPC could sell the gas stations to BP. Instead, he noted that once China got into the WTO it would be more open to such deals. Browne accepted this vague pledge and agreed to buy up to 20 percent of the shares sold in the offering. That would eventually come to just under $600 million. In the end, though it took time, BP would form a joint venture with PetroChina for 500 gas stations in Guangdong by 2007.

That was living on the edge, China style, but that was how you had to operate. In China you frequently had to work in a gray area. Deals often had to be completed before the country, reinventing an entire economy on the fly, had put in place laws and regulations that had not been necessary in the days of centrally controlled planning. You had to take it on faith that the Chinese would live up to their word and deliver, even if they could not, for one reason or another, put something in writing as precisely as you had hoped. It was then and remains to a great extent today a nation ruled by men, not laws. Trust and face were uppermost: you had to trust that if the Chinese committed to doing something, they would deliver, even if they danced around the point. In dealing with China's most senior government and business leaders for two decades now, it has been my experience that they have come through, without fail, when it was in their best interest to do so. Making sure PetroChina's IPO succeeded clearly was. For its part BP understood correctly that China needed Western know-how and capital, and that it wasn't in its interest to mislead its foreign partners.

The agreement from BP was crucial, because the underwriting had sparked an outcry. Protests had started in the fall of 1999, when word of the CNPC offering began to appear in the press. The first came from religious groups denouncing CNPC's activities in Sudan. In addition to wells and drilling rights, CNPC owned 40 percent of Sudan's Greater Nile Oil Project, the country's main exploration and production arm. The U.S. had imposed sanctions on Sudan in 1997 for its support of international terrorism and its poor human rights record. Activists argued that the Sudanese government would use oil revenues to fund its civil war against Christians and animists in the southern part of the country. They protested that the IPO proceeds would help to finance the government's actions.

We impressed upon the Chinese the seriousness of this criticism and worked to separate the new company from the taint of Sudan. It was named PetroChina to distinguish it from its parent, and Sudanese operations were left, along with noncore assets, at CNPC. Additionally, we set up accounting firewalls and tracking mechanisms to ensure that the IPO proceeds would not be used in Sudan.

I wasn't entirely satisfied with the structure of a listed company that was overwhelmingly owned by a state-owned enterprise under the control of the Chinese Communist Party. That's one reason we insisted on setting up such tight financial controls between the parent company and PetroChina. But I saw this solution as a pragmatic first step that would subject much of the company's operations to public scrutiny and tough international capital market standards. Because so many Chinese economic experiments were widely imitated, I believed the deal would lay down a blueprint that would simplify and speed up the process of badly needed reform for many other industrial SOEs. I expected that the PetroChina IPO would be followed by public listings of the other viable businesses left behind at CNPC, once management had gained experience running a public company and the Chinese were able to see how the discipline of the market and the pressure to meet the expectations of new shareholders led to a more successful company. I believed, as I'm sure Zhu Rongji did, that over time the Party's controlling ownership in publicly listed SOEs would become more passive in nature, with the government no longer interfering as much in business decisions or conferring special advantages that would impede the evolution of competitive market-driven companies.

Meanwhile, the protests against the deal grew. Environmentalists concerned about Tibet, and union members, led by the AFL-CIO, joined in. The protests were a dress rehearsal for a last-ditch fight by labor leaders and other opponents to prevent China's admission to the World Trade Organization. China had first applied to join the General Agreement on Tariffs and Trade, the WTO's predecessor, in 1986; the United States and China had achieved a critical breakthrough in November 1999, agreeing on terms of a WTO pact. Now President Bill Clinton had to persuade Congress to give China permanent access to U.S. markets rather than continuing to subject the country to an annual review that generally featured activists agitating against Beijing. WTO opponents, who had violently disrupted the organization's meetings in Seattle in December, meant to use PetroChina as part of their campaign to persuade Congress to reject the president's overtures.

Union leaders railed against working conditions in China and tried a new tactic, expanding from labor and human rights issues to pan the deal on its investment merits. An AFL-CIO report contended that the Sudan concerns, expected worker layoffs, and the company's governance structure posed financial risks to investors. Meantime, U.S. sanctions against Sudan caused a number of pension funds, including TIAA-CREF and the California Public Employees' Retirement System, to announce that they would not buy shares.

The campaign put us in a tough spot. I understood these concerns and why some investors would not buy shares. To begin with, I didn't much like the structure of separating the listed company from a holding company that continued to do business in an opaque manner. And I certainly didn't approve of the repugnant actions of the Sudanese government. But I have never been an all-or-nothing person. I will take half a loaf if it leads to more progress. And I believed that a public offering for a large part of the business did just that. I felt that the deal would jump-start needed reform in a vital sector of the Chinese economy and would lead in time to the rest of CNPC's assets being privatized and subjected to the scrutiny and discipline of public shareholders. I believed it was important to continue to encourage China to integrate its economy with the world's, to open its markets and endorse free trade.

Because the IPO was in an SEC-designated "quiet period," we could not comment on the accusations in the press. Behind the scenes we did our best to counter the criticism. Goldman chief of staff John Rogers took an active role, explaining the safeguards in the deal to key figures in the Clinton administration. Before joining Goldman he had been undersecretary of State and knew his way around Washington. He was a convincing advocate for the view that reform was causing a sea change in China that would better life there and improve relations with America and the world. Despite efforts by members of Congress to lobby the Clinton administration to intervene, the Treasury and State Departments did not get involved.

From a human rights standpoint, I believed strongly that China's embrace of markets over central planning would inevitably lead to more economic and political freedom there. As I wrote after the IPO in an op-ed article published in the *New York Times*, "The case for permanent normal trade relations with China is the story of PetroChina repeated a hundred-fold or a thousandfold.... The individual freedom, initiative, and responsibility inherent in free markets are, by their very nature, at odds with authoritarian rule."

Progress has been slow in China, but I still believe this today.

We needed to raise at least $2 billion from investors to satisfy the requirements in Hong Kong for how much of a company's shares had to be available to the investing public. In the early days of discussing a Petro-China IPO, there was talk of raising upward of $5 billion. But even after BP finally signed on, we were getting only a lukewarm response from investors. By March 14, 2000, we had cut back the target of PetroChina's IPO to between $2.8 billion and $3.4 billion. It was not clear we could raise even that much.

Ma Fucai did not appear to be happy, and I could understand why. He was under a great deal of pressure. He'd been a bit hesitant about the deal to begin with, and now he had to worry about letting down the Chinese leadership. At one point he delayed for hours a team of bankers about to fly to Hong Kong to start the road show, to argue again about the price range for the offering, which we had recommended be lowered to reflect the soft demand. Ma seemed reluctant to authorize this change.

"I cannot sell state assets like that," one banker recalls him saying at the time. "I just cannot do this."

The process of putting the deal together was so intense and difficult, and Ma came under so much pressure, that communication issues led to a breakdown in trust during the negotiations. Ma would prove an obstacle at the very last minute, when it came time to determine the final price at which we would sell PetroChina's shares to the public on March 30. The pricing meeting took place in our offices in New York, with senior management from CNPC and PetroChina, senior bankers from CICC, and our team. The discussions started at 7:30 p.m. We figured it would be a short meeting. It was clear to us, because of the light demand, that we would have to set the price near the low end of the price range of HK$1.24 to HK$1.51. The indications we were getting from big institutions were closer to HK$1.28—and we weren't even sure that price would stick.

Ma Fucai thought it would be a black mark against him for the deal to be priced so low, and he resisted signing off. I wound up going home a couple of hours in, asking Mike Evans to call me when the decision was finalized. I never got the call: the meeting did not end until 5:30 the next morning. There was a lot of arguing among the CNPC and CICC officials in Chinese; I am told the Chinese word for "traitor" was tossed around liberally. Around 2:00 a.m. Ma fell asleep on the conference room table, and it was up to Jiang Jiemin, the executive whom the government had appointed to oversee the IPO, to carry on.

"Your chairman's gone to sleep," Mike told Jiang. "You and I have worked for two years on this transaction. This is the only price the deal works at. You have to trust me that this is what we've got to do."

At last Jiang Jiemin agreed. When Ma awoke, he reluctantly accepted the decision, but Goldman Sachs would remain in his doghouse for years to come.

The PetroChina restructuring was a difficult, even ugly, but absolutely necessary event for China. Fifteen years after its IPO, which raised $2.9 billion, PetroChina ranks as the biggest oil producer among listed companies in the world, having passed ExxonMobil in 2011. Its market capitalization briefly topped $1 trillion, when its yuan-denominated shares debuted in Shanghai in 2007, ranking it as the biggest company in the world by market cap. PetroChina earned more than $21 billion in 2013, compared with $3.3 billion in 1999.

In reorganizing and revitalizing state-owned enterprises like Petro-China to make them more competitive, the Chinese were willing to endure the loss of tens of millions of jobs. The immediate result was pain, dislocation, and instability. Longer term, many SOEs that went public became bigger, stronger, and more efficient, contributing to the country's rapidly growing economy. But reform efforts stalled in the early 2000s, and the performance and business practices of China's best-run SOEs still badly lag those of their global competitors.

Many still feel the pain of their restructurings. Laid-off workers at PetroChina and CNPC were given severance payments, but by 2002, when their money had run out, they came back to the companies demanding more. Widespread protests and riots followed in Daqing and other locations. A similar story played out at Sinopec, which also did an IPO in 2000, and dozens of other restructured state-owned enterprises in the country, presenting a difficult challenge for them and the political leadership. Many SOEs responded by making additional payments and agreeing to rehire former workers to keep the peace while continuing to find ways to grow their businesses. As recently as 2012, when disaffected workers laid off during the run-up to the 2000 Sinopec IPO threatened to protest in Beijing, company chairman Fu Chengyu agreed to increase the pensions of 200,000 workers or put them back on his "inactive" payroll. Fu concluded that these workers had been treated unfairly and were living in great hardship. In the end, no matter how well designed or generous company packages might have been, China lacked, and continues to lack, a well-funded, nationwide pension and social safety net. This remains an urgent task for the country to address.

CHAPTER SIX

Cleaning the Stables in Guangdong

In the West the arrival of China as a major player in capital markets is often seen as the culmination of a smooth and steady march, but the road from the special economic zones in places like Guangdong to a Chinese company's first listing on the New York Stock Exchange was not without its disasters. Deng Xiaoping's great reforms sparked an extraordinary burst of productivity and prosperity, but they also led to waste, mismanagement, fraud, and corruption on an epic scale, as the forces of capitalism were released without sufficient transparency and oversight. I became acquainted firsthand with this dark side of the Chinese miracle when we agreed to steer a wayward investment group, Guangdong Enterprises (Holdings), or GDE, through the tortured restructuring of nearly $6 billion in total debt and liabilities owed to international lenders, bondholders, and other creditors.

Goldman Sachs got involved with GDE through a familiar source, Wang Qishan, who had been appointed executive vice governor of Guangdong Province in late 1997 to clean up a burgeoning financial mess in a crucial test for reform. Born in Shandong and educated in history at Northwest University in Xi'an, the widely read Wang Qishan was clearly a force in the making: steeped in traditional Chinese ways, he also possessed a keen understanding and appreciation of Western thinking and practices that was crucial to Reform and Opening Up.

China had withstood the onslaught of the Asian financial crisis but remained vulnerable, particularly in Guangdong, with its dependence on exports and close ties to Hong Kong, which had come under siege by currency speculators. Wang asked Goldman Sachs to help resolve the problems at Guangdong Enterprises, a big investment company owned by the province. GDE and a similar entity, Guangdong International Trust and Investment Corporation, or GITIC, were among the country's biggest, most visible companies, and both were in dire shape—unable to roll over short-term loans and on the brink of insolvency.

The thought of getting involved with this kind of work was unappetizing to me. Bankruptcy workouts or similar corporate restructurings are notoriously difficult for advisers like Goldman. Technically complex, labor intensive, and inevitably contentious, these transactions require you to persuade companies to take painful actions they want to avoid even as you try to negotiate tough terms with their disgruntled creditors, who may well be your own customers. All too often you burn out your best people and risk damaging your reputation and alienating clients. We had very few at Goldman who were temperamentally suited for such adversarial work. Our best bankers were trained to build bridges, not to burn them, which is what too often happens when creditors squabble about how to share the losses in a bankrupt company.

When Wang Qishan asked for help, I took a deep breath and said, "Are you sure you can't find someone better to do the job, Qishan?"

"This is for me, Hank, and it's important," he replied. "I want *you* to handle this."

The reason soon became clear. China's senior leaders had decided to make a radical break from the past. These two companies, unlike other faltering behemoths before them, would not be propped up or bailed out, and their debts would not be treated as sovereign obligations. The companies would either be restructured or liquidated. This would shock the foreign business community, but the leadership felt it was necessary to send a clear message that they were serious about imposing market discipline on investors and creditors. The training wheels were off, and the government was done safeguarding its reckless children.

The stakes were high for the country's ongoing reforms and for Wang Qishan's credibility. I initially pushed back because I wanted to be sure he knew how difficult a challenge it would be. But there wasn't a chance I would say no in the end. How could I? Goldman had gotten the opportunity to manage landmark Chinese transactions, and we had worked closely, and well, with Wang Qishan. So we agreed to take on what I thought surely would be a thankless task. Relationships are a two-way street. When an important client asks you to do something that is difficult and not very profitable, you say yes. That's especially the case when that client has already given you the very lucrative, franchise-building assignment that led to the IPO of China Telecom (Hong Kong).

The restructuring of GDE turned out to be even more difficult than I had expected. But it also proved to be among the most important pieces of work we would ever do in China.

The mess that Wang Qishan had inherited in Guangdong was two decades in the making. Beginning with Deng's reforms in 1978, China had cautiously opened its economy to foreign trade and investment. Along with setting up special economic zones in Guangdong and neighboring Fujian to attract investment from the Chinese diaspora, the government okayed the creation of investment trusts to borrow money overseas—from banks and eventually in the bond markets—and to use the proceeds to spur development at home. The borrowers were encouraged to enter into joint ventures with foreign companies to bring in capital, technology, and expertise. CITIC, founded in 1979 under the direct supervision of China's State Council, was the first and most famous of these. Copycat trust companies, including ones that raised funds domestically, were launched by provinces, municipalities, and state-owned banks throughout the country.

These vehicles, known as ITICs, provided a crucial funding source for an economy that lacked effective modern capital markets or commercial banking options. At the time, foreign banks could lend only to foreign companies doing business in China, while state-owned banks financed big state-owned enterprises. The trusts gave foreign banks entrée to a promising new market and local governments access to a new source of funds they could direct to much-needed infrastructure projects like bridges and power plants. ITICs weren't the only route to obtaining money from abroad. The same legislation that authorized special economic zones permitted provincial and municipal governments to establish in Hong Kong so-called window companies that would turn out to be little more than fronts to finance mainland activities. These companies flourished—especially after the 1984 agreement for Hong Kong's return to China in 1997—because of lax oversight by Beijing and the pressure to raise funds locally. By the end of the 1980s there were hundreds of trust and investment companies in China, and many more companies backed by local Chinese governments in Hong Kong and Macau.

Along the way, local politicians moved beyond the original mission of supporting infrastructure and began to direct investments into real estate developments, construction companies, and, eventually, businesses of all kinds, often outside their home provinces. In addition, some mainland companies incorporated subsidiaries in Hong Kong, where they listed their shares and raised debt capital. These so-called red-chip companies joined the ITICs and other window companies in pouring money into increasingly risky activities, from sizzling property markets to big bets on volatile stocks.

As much as the casual observer might think of the central government as an all-knowing, all-powerful monolith, Beijing doesn't always find it easy to control, much less dictate, activities in the provinces, especially ones as big and energetic as Guangdong. The tension between central administration and regional autonomy is an enduring concern in a country that has been beset by warlords for long stretches of its history, including the decades leading up to the Communist takeover in 1949. Even today China rotates its senior political leaders and military brass through provincial posts and regional commands to prevent anyone from building up too strong a local power base.

Speculation financed by excessive leverage is never a good thing. To make matters worse, the central government had no idea how much debt local governments were racking up. Estimates put the total of bonds, bank credits, guarantees, and other liabilities in the tens of billions of dollars. Foreign creditors accommodated this borrowing binge in the belief that the central government would back the debts as it always had.

Beijing tried to rein in the excesses to little avail. The investment vehicles had become the honey pots of provincial and local leaders, who borrowed to produce the growth they needed to advance professionally and, occasionally, to line their own pockets. Many so-called *guanxi* loans were made solely on the basis of relationships, not on any solid financial or legal analyses, in an unsavory confederacy of incompetent or corrupt borrowers and their foreign enablers, who earned higher returns than they would have on loans to the central government but got to tell their bosses in Paris, Frankfurt, Tokyo, or New York not to worry because these instruments were still backed by the state. Despite Beijing's directives that they reduce their activities, local leaders kept doing deals. As the old Chinese adage went, "The mountains are high and the emperor is far away."

Dodgy financial activities were part of the ugly underbelly of China's historic rise. Partly they were the inevitable result of rapidly shifting a vast nation of more than 1 billion citizens from a command and control economy that dictated every action to one meant to have a more free-flowing, market-oriented approach. Entire areas of law needed to be written or rewritten, and where rules already existed, the country lacked the public institutions—from a truly independent judiciary to fully empowered regulatory agencies—to ensure effective governance. Moreover, China was short on properly trained officials to run existing institutions.

Meeting these challenges would take time, but the Communist Party leadership had staked its legitimacy in the reform era on providing growth and prosperity. It could not put the economy on hold while it designed the ideal, comprehensive blueprint for all aspects of the country's evolving vision of capitalism with Chinese characteristics. Thus, even as China's leading intellectuals studied which international standards and practices to adopt, the country threw itself into a vast economic improvisation that was by turns creative, chaotic, and at times criminal, as elements of the government all too often turned a blind eye to lawlessness.

Chinese authorities encouraged widespread experimentation as they cast about for ways to boost the economy. Ambitious regional leaders were allowed to run broadscale test cases—such as encouraging private farm plots in Anhui Province or establishing special economic zones in places like Shenzhen. Their experiments often morphed into national policy that would, in time, transform the country. Just about every organization of the state, from scientific think tanks to the military, plunged into business. If the advocates of change succeeded, they could become heroic figures and, eventually, incredibly rich. Entrepreneurs, government officials, vendors in the streets: all had to make it up as they went along. Even the most upright businessmen found themselves operating in gray areas, skating along a thin edge of legitimacy, in the absence of a consistently applied rule of law.

"There were rules prohibiting bribes. They were enforced selectively, so it incited fear, but everyone broke them," one of China's most respected business leaders once told me as we reminisced about that period. Reflecting on his distinguished career, he said, matter-of-factly, that his greatest success had been "surviving in the system for so long."

All of this gave China's fledgling capitalism a Wild West feel. Millions embraced stock ownership in the 1980s through nascent over-the-counter markets that were nominally supervised by the People's Bank of China, but trading was far more widespread—and risky—on unregulated black markets. Officially sanctioned exchanges opened in Shanghai in 1990 and Shenzhen in 1991, but "share fever," as local newspapers called it, raged unabated. In August 1992 nearly a million people lined up over three days in Shenzhen to enter a lottery for the right to buy shares in future IPOs. When the government ran out of forms, 50,000 people rioted overnight, accusing officials— accurately, as it so happened—of keeping the forms for themselves. This debacle helped lead to the establishment of the China Securities Regulatory Commission. State-backed securities firms proliferated in the 1990s, when market manipulation was rife. Dozens would go belly-up.

Meantime, the People's Liberation Army had turned itself into a commercial juggernaut. By the 1990s it owned thousands of enterprises. Many were run as the private fiefdoms of princelings, the sons and daughters of prominent Party leaders. From airlines and mines to karaoke bars and a telecommunications company, these concerns earned billions of dollars annually. And that was just the legitimate activity. PLA officers also ran or abetted widespread smuggling operations that brought in cars, mobile phones, oil, cigarettes, and more. In 1998 President Jiang Zemin ordered the military to sell its commercial assets, increasing the PLA's budget in return. The government cracked down on smuggling, and customs revenues jumped 81 percent in one year.

Few places were as wild as steamy Guangdong, with its long tradition of commercial hustle and entrepreneurial flair. It was in Guangdong that the first special economic zones had been opened, and it was to Guangdong that Deng Xiaoping had gone in 1992 on his famous Southern Tour to reignite reform when he feared it was flagging. Manufacturers from Hong Kong and elsewhere in Asia shifted production lines to Guangdong's Pearl River Delta to take advantage of the cheap labor of the millions of migrants flooding in from all over the country. By the early 1990s, growing at 14 percent or more a year, Guangdong had become the world's factory floor.

The province was also a hothouse of speculation, improvident management, and financial irregularity. Wang Qishan confronted on his arrival scores of dicey nonbank financial companies—Guangdong had an estimated 40 ITICs of its own—that he would eventually have to prop up, restructure, or close. By far the most pressing challenges were Guangdong Enterprises and GITIC.

The pair were fearless highfliers. As the first provincial government allowed to establish operations in Hong Kong, Guangdong had launched GDE in 1980 to promote exports and to import key materials. GDE diversified wildly and paved the way in 1987 for red-chip companies when it acquired control of a Hong Kong–listed property and investment concern, Union Global Development Limited, which it renamed Guangdong Investment Limited. By 1998 GDE had become an unfocused and unwieldy conglomerate controlling a mind-bending range of businesses in China, Southeast Asia, and Europe that included five red-chip subsidiary companies. GITIC had embarked on a similar pell-mell expansion, growing into the second-biggest trust company in China and the biggest property developer in Guangdong. It owned stakes in manufacturing concerns, pursued joint ventures with foreign companies like McDonald's, and controlled two red chips of its own.

Both companies were on the verge of collapse thanks to inept managers, among them local politicians who had glommed onto Guangdong Enterprises and GITIC as plush sinecures in retirement. They were both built on shaky capital structures and borrowed to excess. Like all financial pyramids, they hid their troubles with "irregular" accounting and remained solvent only so long as they could attract new funds to cover their mounting losses. When the Asian financial crisis hit and creditors began to pull their money from the region, the companies were caught in a credit squeeze and couldn't refinance their loans.

As Wang Qishan related it, he had hardly taken up his duties in Guangdong when the two companies were in his office looking for help in meeting their creditors' demands. At first, he advanced them the funds they needed, but in no time they were back for more. Wang Qishan knew better than to keep extending aid.

"The hole was too big to fill," he told me. "You could not see the bottom."

In December 1998 I flew to Hong Kong to announce that Goldman Sachs would advise Guangdong Province on the restructuring of GDE. I joined Wang Qishan at the Island Shangri-La, a five-star luxury high-rise hotel, and after we signed our agreement, we laid out our plans to a local press corps eager to get the story. GDE was a major player in Hong Kong, and cleaning it up would mark the first time that the reform-minded Chinese government had undertaken a restructuring of such magnitude. Wearing matching red boutonnieres, Wang Qishan and I sat on a low stage, behind a baize-draped table bristling with microphones, to take questions. The room was mobbed by the most raucous, importuning group of reporters I'd ever seen. One after another, repeating or rephrasing each other's questions, the reporters grilled us about GDE's future and the province's commitment to the company.

The media reflected the jitters in the markets. Two months earlier Wang Qishan and the Chinese leadership had decided that GITIC was too far gone to be salvaged as an operating entity. Rather than throw good money after bad, they chose to shut it down. The move stunned investors. The central bank had assured foreign creditors that registered lenders would get repaid, but many of GITIC's debts were not registered; banks had been busy lending funds outside of official channels. Rating agencies downgraded China's major trust companies, and nervous lenders pulled back even more, tightening the noose around GDE's neck, prompting statements of support from some members of the provincial government. And when Zhu Rongji visited Guangdong in late October as part of the crackdown on smuggling, word had leaked that the government would lead a reorganization of GDE, and that, with Zhu's approval, the province would inject assets into the company to prop it up. But no details had been forthcoming, and the press was eager to find them out.

I was taken aback by the aggressiveness of the Hong Kong press, but Wang Qishan appeared unfazed, even though I couldn't imagine that he had ever encountered anything like this on the mainland, where the media was far more docile—subservient to the government and not infrequently paid under the table by the companies it covered. He had a simple, direct message to impart, namely that the provincial and central governments fully supported a reorganization of GDE designed to make the company financially independent and commercially viable. China was committed to reform, he said, and GDE's restructuring would serve as a model for other Chinese state enterprises. The revamping would focus on corporate, financial, and management issues, and he assured everyone that success meant making certain that GDE had quality assets and top-notch management and that it understood and followed best international practices and standards. Meantime, he made clear that Guangdong, with its booming economy, had ample resources to provide capital and would inject assets into GDE as needed, pending Goldman's advice.

"Major shareholders are like parents," he said. "Although the children have grown up, if they have encountered very big problems, and we are still capable, we have to take care of them and give them a helping hand."

I'd known Wang Qishan as a banker, but I saw him now for the first time as a political leader, a supremely able and self-confident one at that. It wasn't so much what he said but how he said it. He was substantive and direct, blunt and charming by turns, unflappable and utterly in his element. It was, altogether, a virtuoso performance. Years later, when I was besieged by reporters during the 2008 financial crisis, I had occasion more than once to recall Wang Qishan's coolness and clarity under fire and wish that I had been born with some of his grace and eloquence.

My part in the proceedings that day was much more modest. I was there to provide technical and, ultimately, moral support. Hiring Goldman Sachs was proof to the press and creditors that China was not going to resolve this crisis arbitrarily but in a way consistent with international best practices. I emphasized how hard we were going to work and underscored our commitment by announcing that we would put our own capital on the line. Once the restructuring was completed, I said, Goldman would invest up to $20 million in the company that emerged.

"We're not doing this to get a specific, targeted return," I said. "We're investing to signal our confidence in Guangdong."

The son of a senior engineer at the Ministry of Construction, Wang Qishan was a born leader who became student body president at his Beijing high school. When the Cultural Revolution came, his family suffered like so many other intellectuals: his father, a standout student who had been admitted to Tsinghua University in 1929, was forced to clean toilets.

Wang was sent down to the countryside to Yan'an, in Shaanxi Province, where Mao and his fellow guerrillas had famously holed up in caves following the Long March. Wang arranged for a group of classmates to be assigned there as well, including a friend of his older sister's named Yao Mingshan, who would later become his wife. Michelle, as she is also known, was the daughter of Yao Yilin, a former minister of Commerce, who would rise to first vice premier and member of the Standing Committee of the Communist Party at the end of the 1980s. One day, while digging for coal for her work team, Michelle fell 20 feet into a mine, injuring her back. It was feared that her feet would have to be amputated, but doctors painstakingly pieced together the shattered bones. She and Wang Qishan would marry in 1976, and she went on to become a doctor herself.

In 1971 Wang went to work in the Shaanxi Provincial Museum, then studied history at Northwest University in the provincial capital of Xi'an, which would become world famous for the 2,000-year-old life-size Terracotta Warriors discovered there three years later. After a second stint at the museum, he returned in 1979 to Beijing and a research post at the Modern History Institute of the Chinese Academy of Social Sciences. Like so many of his contemporaries, Wang Qishan was driven by an almost kinetic sense of mission, pushing himself relentlessly to improve the lives of the hundreds of millions of Chinese whose destitution and hopelessness he had come to know firsthand on the hardscrabble plains of Yan'an. He made a name for himself when he and three other young intellectuals jointly published a paper proposing a new framework for reform in an influential

Party journal in 1980. The "four gentlemen," as they were known, were soon recruited to the influential think tanks that sprouted under reformist premier Zhao Ziyang. Wang Qishan subsequently spent much of the 1980s helping to shape crucial rural reforms. He joined the Party in 1983 and the following year spearheaded a famous conference of young economists that led to China's officially adopting a dual-track pricing system, a key component of the gradualist reforms that enabled a freer market for goods to develop outside the formal state sector. He got his first exposure to banking in 1989 when he became vice governor of the People's Construction Bank of China, the forerunner of China Construction Bank. Though the bank was taking on more commercial banking functions, it remained at the time a government policy arm that doled out funds for construction and infrastructure-related projects in keeping with the state economic plan.

Wang Qishan began a close association with then vice premier Zhu Rongji in the early 1990s, when Zhu called Wang to his office and grilled him for two hours. Though the two had met before, this was their first substantive conversation. Shortly after, Zhu took direct charge of the People's Bank of China. Impressed by Wang Qishan's abilities, Zhu brought him to the central bank as a vice governor to tamp down rampant foreign exchange speculation, which he did. It was the first of many jobs that established Wang as a Mr. Fix-it for cleaning up the messes that festered in pockets of China's booming economy.

I met Wang Qishan shortly after he left the central bank in February 1994 to head China Construction Bank as it shed its role as an agent of the government to become a full-service commercial bank. I could see right away that he was a quick study, with a nimble intelligence and a rare combination of commercial savvy and political skills. He had a gift for knowing how to separate the possible from the desirable in order to get things done. And as I saw at the GDE press conference that day in December 1998, he was also a master communicator. Still, for all his bravado with the press, he was deeply concerned about the situation—and for good reason, as he explained over a lunch we shared afterward. To begin with, GDE was in sorrier financial shape than anyone had expected. More than half of its debt was short-term, which gave it little breathing room, and its assets were likely worth less than previously thought. Among other things, a team of accountants had uncovered fraudulent activity in various subsidiaries.

GDE's troubles reverberated beyond the company. Chinese leaders were concerned about the stability of Hong Kong and its markets. GDE and GITIC had made investors squeamish about other mainland trust companies and highlighted concerns about the country's big state-owned banks, which were plagued with bad debts. China's overall economic strength was not in question. More resilient than its regional neighbors, the country had dodged the Asian financial crisis because its financial system and capital accounts were closed, it had a healthy trade balance, and its currency wasn't market determined. Even when exports dipped, it had refused to devalue the renminbi because it didn't want to set off a round of competitive devaluations that would have made matters worse. Its foreign exchange reserves, at about $145 billion, were substantial and growing. Beijing had tested the market earlier with a bond offering that proved so popular that Goldman Sachs, acting as co–lead manager, had been able to double the amount sold to $1 billion.

Zhu Rongji and Wang Qishan saw an opportunity to flex some new-found muscle and create a model for reforming China's shaky financial system by cleaning up the ITICs, red chips, and window companies. The first step was to make clear to creditors that the central government was not responsible for the companies' debts. This was not, in fact, a new policy. Rating agencies had periodically warned investors that ITIC obligations were not guaranteed by China. But experience suggested otherwise: since the Chinese government was wary of driving away foreign capital, it had repeatedly paid off creditors of failed enterprises in full. So, while in theory provincial borrowings were not sovereign credits backed by the central government, in practice they appeared to be just that. This allowed companies like the provincial ITICs to borrow at lower rates, encouraged risky behavior, and sheltered incompetent and corrupt officials. Foreign lenders kept the spigots open, substituting a perceived government guarantee for due diligence and proper market pricing of loans and bonds.

Zhu Rongji wanted to modernize banking practices and eliminate the presence of this moral hazard. Making sure that bad decisions led to bad consequences was crucial for developing a market economy. Doing this would also rein in out-of-control borrowers by reducing their access to funds and bring local and provincial governments under the thumb of the central government. Clarifying what was and wasn't a sovereign obligation was an important step as the country moved to restructure and privatize its state-owned enterprises.

Zhu Rongji was resolute in his belief that, as Wang Qishan told me, "whoever makes the mistake must be responsible for it."

Creditors were not eager to hear this. They had grown comfortable having their bets covered by the house. And in fairness, Chinese officials had sent out mixed signals. Shutting GITIC and telling banks to get in line to register their claims by early January 1999 was a warning shot. But in December, the municipal government of Tianjin—China's fourth most populated city, located 75 miles southeast of Beijing on Bohai Bay—was allowed to cover a shortfall on yen-denominated debt coming due for its local ITIC, giving GITIC creditors hope that China would in the end bail them out.

Wang Qishan faced a delicate task. The wounds of the Asian financial crisis were still raw, and he had to find a way to get tough with GDE's creditors—but in a manner that didn't so alienate them that they turned their backs on Chinese securities just as the country sought to raise even more capital through the initial public offerings of state-owned enterprises. Fortunately, we had the perfect person to lead the Goldman team and advise Wang Qishan. Steven Shafran, the Singapore-based co-head of our Asian principal investing business, was experienced in managing corporate workouts and was a true financial engineer—a whiz at analyzing and dissecting complex financial structures. He was tireless, loved to look under the hood of everything, and most important, he was personable but hard-nosed, evenhanded, and decisive—absolutely crucial qualities for managing difficult negotiations.

Steve took the train up to Guangzhou from Hong Kong to meet with Wang Qishan, whom he told straight out that the provincial government was being too accommodating. Creditors, Steve told Wang Qishan, "must have thought that Christmas had come early." He boarded the train back, and before he'd returned to Hong Kong I'd gotten a call from Wang Qishan with a simple message: "I want that guy."

Steve moved to Hong Kong to oversee the GDE workout. He assembled a team of 20, drawn from a mix of Goldman divisions. Among its members were Hsueh-ming Wang, who had played such a key role in China Telecom; Martin Lau, an up-and-comer with a degree from Northwestern University's Kellogg Graduate School of Management who had worked as a consultant before joining us (he would later become president of Tencent Holdings, the enormously successful Chinese social media pioneer); and Brian Li, a mainland-born lawyer who had come on board that year from Davis Polk & Wardwell and would serve as our Beijing representative.

Steve's main counterpart on the Chinese side was Dr. Wu Jiesi, Wang Qishan's right-hand man. A trained economist, Dr. Wu had worked for Industrial and Commercial Bank of China and served as deputy mayor of bustling Shenzhen before joining Wang in 1998 as assistant to the governor of Guangdong. One of a very rare group of Chinese officials with both technical and leadership ability, Dr. Wu was a relentless worker who managed both the GDE restructuring and the GITIC liquidation on a day-to-day basis.

The Goldman team's first task was to identify GDE's assets, assess their value, and decide what should be kept, sold, or shuttered to salvage a profitable, self-sustaining enterprise and offer creditors a chance to recoup their capital. Deconstructing Guangdong Enterprises was much easier said than done. In its brief corporate life, it had evolved into a phantasmagorical assemblage of hundreds of subsidiaries spread over a dozen lines of business with no clear focus, strategy, or logic. In conjunction with a battalion of accountants, Steve's team had to reconstruct the history and makeup of each of these companies. Records, when they existed at all, were inadequately maintained, and frequently Steve's team had to become corporate folklorists, piecing together the shaky recollections of employees. Quite a few of GDE's subsidiaries were valuable and running reasonably well—including much of Guangdong Investment—but far too many were worthless, and few had anything to do with infrastructure development in the province.

What Steve uncovered was alternatively hilarious and horrifying. Apart from mainstream companies like a brewery, a tannery, and a washing machine maker, there was an eel farm whose eels allegedly had been washed away by a flood—if there had been any in the first place—a hotel on the outskirts of Paris, and beachfront property in Thailand that was periodically submerged.

Then there was the criminal activity. GDE owned nearly 60 percent of Guangnan Holdings, a high-flying red chip that was one of the biggest suppliers of Hong Kong's freshwater fish, poultry, vegetables, and livestock. It was also a sump of fraud; some executives had conspired to falsely inflate profits, others had embezzled, while still more had schemed to swindle banks into issuing letters of credit for phony transactions. Three of Guangnan's directors would eventually stand trial, several others fled to the mainland and went into hiding, and 16 people were convicted in a series of fraud cases related to the company and its subsidiaries.

Company financials were a mess. Accounting firm KPMG, working with GDE, estimated that for the first nine months of 1998 the company had lost about $2.3 billion. The loss included one-time charges taken to clean GDE's books, among them sums that had to be set aside for unrecoverable loans that had been extended to municipalities in Guangdong and other government entities.

As one of Goldman's team members later recounted: "GDE was an encyclopedia of what not to do in business."

The company's liabilities were as complicated as its organization. Altogether, GDE and its affiliates owed almost $6 billion to some 170 foreign and Chinese banks, more than 300 bondholders, and over 1,000 trade creditors. Slightly more than $2.2 billion was in bank loans, most extended by foreign banks.

Much would have to be written off. The government was willing to inject income-generating assets to rebuild the company, but it wanted to make clear it would not cover all of the losses. At the first meeting with creditors, in Hong Kong in January 1999, the government proposed delaying principal payments for GDE Group and Nam Yue, a Macau-based window company also owned by Guangdong Province, which would be part of any restructuring. Both companies would continue to pay interest.

The banks balked. Initially, they resisted GDE's request that they form a creditors' committee, which is an organization composed of the representatives of those with secured and unsecured claims who work together to salvage some value from an ailing company. Instead, the banks clung to the idea that the Chinese would come around and cover losses as they had in the past. But Zhu Rongji and Wang Qishan were determined not to: they intended to follow Western practice. They wanted state-owned companies to act, and be treated, like truly commercial enterprises, not wards of the state.

The creditors had plenty to worry about. Most of GDE's bank loans were unsecured, meaning lenders had relied on the promise of the now-insolvent company, not a pledge of specific assets, to guarantee repayment. Barring a government bailout, the alternative to a negotiated restructuring was liquidation, which would mean even greater losses. The Chinese made it clear they were prepared to go that route when it was announced in January that GITIC, whose debts were twice as big as previously thought, would be placed in bankruptcy and liquidated. Creditors would get what they could as they picked over the carcass. The decision alarmed investors, who were looking at recovering less than 10 cents on the dollar. China had had bankruptcy laws in place since 1986, but GITIC would be the first major company to go through the process. It was a crucial step in the evolution toward a more market-oriented economy, and an effective warning to GDE's creditors. The Chinese had, as the expression goes, killed the chicken to scare the monkey. Banks and bondholders sent delegations to see Wang Qishan and complained in meetings with Zhu Rongji. But the leadership held firm.

GDE's creditors finally got religion and formed a creditors' committee for the banks—led by London-based Standard Chartered Bank and Europe's ABN-AMRO Bank and BNP Paribas—and for bondholders, advised by U.S. private equity powerhouse Blackstone (Asia). Negotiations would take nearly two years to complete. First, everyone had to learn the awful truth about GDE's finances. In March, after weeks of digging, KPMG informed shocked creditors that GDE's debts exceeded assets by about $1.6 billion. The province was willing to inject the Dongshen Water Supply Project, which had supplied most of Hong Kong's fresh water since 1965, to bolster GDE's assets and cash flow. Even so, Wang Qishan warned creditors they would have to take steep losses, or "haircuts" in the banking vernacular. Wang Qishan was quoted in *BusinessWeek* as saying, "Even after I said 'thank you,' there was no applause. That is very rare, in my experience."

The team prepared the first formal restructuring proposal, to be unveiled by Wang Qishan to 500 grim-faced bankers at the Grand Hyatt Hong Kong in late May. I won't go into too many of the details here—it was fiendishly complex—but in essence the proposal envisioned GDE's being restructured so that its red-chip subsidiary, Guangdong Investment, or GDI, would be the surviving company and the valuable Dongshen Water Supply Project would be injected into it. A host of subsidiaries would be shut, and the remainder, including GDE's Hong Kong real estate, would be collected into two other entities, which would be managed to achieve better-than-liquidation recoveries. Creditors would receive a mix of stock, including preferred shares, and debt, in GDI and the other two units, as well as a small amount of cash.

There was an elegance to this proposal. The lenders and the Chinese government would share losses equally, because the value of the water company being injected was roughly that of the proposed haircut. Creditors nonetheless rejected the proposal, some because of the terms—which also featured low interest rates and long maturities—and others because they still did not want to take a haircut. We had expected this reaction; we wanted to get creditors to the table but had set stiff terms for negotiations to convince them that they were going to have to take a loss. Wang Qishan insisted that GDE would be liquidated if they didn't agree to the restructuring. The team presented an analysis that showed unsecured creditors could expect to recover just 11 cents on the dollar in that event.

Steve's team and GDE's officials made clear that the specifics could be adjusted, but certain principles had to be observed. These were laid out at a July 1999 meeting. Among them: Guangdong would inject the Dongshen Water Supply Project into GDI only after creditors agreed to share the losses with the government. Dongshen was the only asset the province would use, and it could only be injected into GDI. Guangdong would negotiate only with the representatives on the creditors' committee. If the creditors would not negotiate, the government would liquidate GDE.

In addition, GDE announced that it would stop paying interest on its debt. This tough stand upset creditors but helped bring them around. By December a preliminary agreement was reached that saw a number of terms sweetened from May. It took another year, or until December 22, 2000, for the final agreement to be signed. The recovery rate for bondholders and lenders was estimated at signing to be approximately 63 percent of the value of creditors' claims, but those who held on to their securities ultimately would have recovered all their money, thanks to the strong performance of the water company and a revival in the Chinese and Hong Kong economies.

"Capitalism without bankruptcy is like Christianity without hell," Frank Borman, the former astronaut turned CEO of Eastern Air Lines, once quipped. Wang Qishan gave the same idea a different spin when he told reporters after the first restructuring proposal for GDE was announced in May 1999, that "the fundamental principle of a market economy is that the winners win and the losers lose."

Wang Qishan's deft handling of the mess he inherited in Guangdong was a major milestone for reform and a key advance along the path to an increasingly market-oriented economy. It established precedents for dealing with inevitable corporate failures through bankruptcy proceedings and restructurings, and it made plainer the crucial distinction between commercial and government obligations that was an important precursor to the corporatization and privatization of state-owned enterprises. The actions he took reset relationships with foreign investors and creditors, began the cleanup of the banking system, and laid out a blueprint for future SOE reforms. They also marked an important step toward eliminating the moral hazard that had led to a host of unsavory financial practices, signaling China's seriousness in embracing commercial market principles as Zhu Rongji worked toward WTO accession.

The GDE workout established Wang Qishan as a force to be reckoned with in China, propelling him upward in power and influence. From Guangdong he was called back to Beijing to be director of the State Commission for Restructuring the Economy, putting him in the engine room of the reform process throughout the country.

Goldman's involvement in the GDE restructuring cemented our reputation for getting even the most difficult things done in a way that supported and advanced the important changes that China was undertaking. It also brought the firm, and me personally, much closer to a rare, gifted leader who would be in the vanguard of reform for years to come.

CHAPTER SEVEN

School for Success

The incompetence and venality that led to the Guangdong Enterprises debacle underscored dramatically China's shortage of well-trained executives. No one understood the problem better than Zhu Rongji, who had become premier in 1998 and did not want to see his ambitious plans to reform state-owned enterprises derailed by poor business practices. When I had met with him shortly after the China Telecom IPO in the fall of 1997, he pressed me to find ways to train good managers for the companies that we were helping to restructure and take public. "Management is backward," he'd told me with typical bluntness.

Zhu Rongji raised the subject of management development again in March 1999, when several of my colleagues and I met with him at Zhongnanhai. We were knee-deep in the GDE quagmire at the time and working, as well, through the early stages of the immensely complicated IPO of China National Petroleum. Though crucially important, these and other restructurings weren't going to succeed, I told Zhu, unless China could find first-rate talent to run its companies. Wu Jiesi, Wang Qishan's deputy on GDE, was an excellent executive, as were Jiang Jiemin, who was overseeing the oil company IPO, and Wang Xiaochu, chairman and president of China Telecom (Hong Kong), but the ranks of top-notch leaders at SOEs were thin.

This weakness was partly a legacy of Mao's later years. The shutdown of universities during the Cultural Revolution had held back a generation of men and women who ought to have been coming into the prime of their careers. To put this in perspective, when Chinese universities were closed in 1966, I had just finished my sophomore year at Dartmouth College; when

China held nationwide university entrance exams in December 1977 for the first time in more than a decade, I had finished college, graduated from Harvard Business School (HBS), worked at the Pentagon and in the Nixon White House, and had been a banker at Goldman for four years. During that time my contemporaries in China had been harvesting crops, tending pigs, digging coal, and performing a host of other backbreaking chores. These wrenching experiences fueled their ambition and helped cement their desire for reform but cost them years of training that the country needed.

Moreover, the transition from a centrally administered economy was only two decades old in the late 1990s. That wasn't much time for aspiring executives to gain hands-on experience or for the country's educational system to adapt to the newfound needs of a market economy. China's universities were plenty good at churning out engineers to build roads, dams, and factories but much less adept at producing capable managers. We encountered this firsthand at Goldman, while recruiting in China. We concluded it made more sense to hire recent graduates of local universities or Chinese students who had studied abroad and train them ourselves than to bring in veterans of China's companies, particularly those from SOEs. Most had the wrong skill sets or had picked up bad habits; many were too cautious, reluctant to suggest new ideas, and overly deferential to their bosses.

China needed topflight business schools to lead the way, but Premier Zhu had concerns about the program at Tsinghua University, known as the MIT of China, and asked if I would evaluate the school and come back to him with ideas for improvement. John Thornton, by then president and co–chief operating officer of Goldman, encouraged me to take on the challenge. We both knew how crucial improving management was—and how devoted Zhu was to Tsinghua, his alma mater. Not only had he graduated in 1951 with a degree in electrical engineering, but he also had courted his wife there, spending long hours with her in the library, one of the few heated buildings on campus during Beijing's bitterly cold winters. He had founded Tsinghua's School of Economics and Management (SEM) in 1984 and continued as dean even after becoming premier.

During the spring of 1999, I was preoccupied with Goldman's impending IPO, but after it took place in May, I was able to focus more on Tsinghua.

I was scheduled to meet with the premier again in October, and I wanted to present him with a concrete plan of action for the school, which had trained China's elite for nearly 90 years and enjoyed the kind of reputation and influence that even top schools in the United States like Harvard or the Massachusetts Institute of Technology might envy. In the late 1990s two of the seven members of the Politburo Standing Committee, Zhu and Hu Jintao, were Tsinghua grads; by 2002 the number was up to four of the nine members. China's leader today, Xi Jinping, is a Tsinghua graduate.

The quality of students wasn't an issue; Tsinghua and nearby Peking University attracted the highest-scoring students from each year's national examinations. But the SEM's curriculum and teaching methods were dated, and new faculty members were needed. To be a world-class school required world-class professors, but many instructors, holdovers from a bygone era, knew little about markets or modern business practices. The school's teaching was largely confined to economic theory, which wasn't very practical. China needed corporate leaders, not Marxist theoreticians, and Tsinghua's curriculum placed too little emphasis on such critical areas as finance, marketing, strategy, and organization.

The way I see it, a business education should be as much vocational as academic. Teaching business is like teaching medicine: theory is important, but hands-on practice is essential. Medical students learn from cadavers and hospital rounds; business students learn from case studies—a method pioneered more than a century ago by Harvard Business School that engages students in analyzing complex real-life dilemmas faced by actual companies and executives. Tsinghua's method of instruction, like too much of China's educational system, relied on rote learning—lectures, memorization, and written tests—and did not foster innovative, interactive approaches to problem solving. Students needed to know how to work as part of a team—a critical lesson in China, where getting people to work collaboratively can be difficult. At Harvard Business School we weren't told the "right" or "wrong" answers but were encouraged to think for ourselves and defend our ideas before our peers and our at-times-intimidating professors. This helped hone my analytical skills and confidence, and I believed a similar approach would help Chinese students.

By October I had worked out a series of proposals after numerous discussions with educators I knew at Harvard Business School and Goldman colleagues like Thornton, Brian Griffiths, Hsueh-ming Wang, and Fred Hu, a razor-sharp Tsinghua grad who oversaw greater China economics for Goldman Sachs from our Hong Kong office while serving as co-director of Tsinghua's National Center for Economic Research. Among other things, I planned to recommend that the school form an international advisory board. It would be composed of globally renowned business figures—who could give the SEM practical guidance and prestige—as well as academic deans and Chinese business and government leaders.

The school needed a new long-range plan that would involve not only shifting to the case study method but also creating China-specific cases. Meantime, I would suggest that SEM launch a reinvigorated executive education program grounded in the practical realities of doing business in China. This would get help to the group that needed it most immediately. And because of the higher tuitions such programs can charge, Tsinghua's executive training courses would be self-sustaining almost from the start. Some of the money they generated could be used to build research centers that would attract and retain the best faculty and improve the reputation of the school.

A few of my acquaintances in New York wondered how we could possibly set up a program to teach Western methods without running into ideological roadblocks or issues of academic freedom. Had we been designing coursework in history, journalism, political science, or similar subjects, I don't doubt there would have been difficulties. China's concern for political stability allowed its people little latitude to discuss human rights issues or civil liberties, much less argue the merits of the Chinese system of government or one-party Communist rule. But the pragmatic Chinese leadership tended to take a different view of economics, and public discussion or criticism of government economic policies was more tolerated. Within the government itself there was a healthy debate on economic issues, and the Chinese looked everywhere in the world for best practices that they could adopt. Effective business management was an area where they knew they had much to learn. This made designing an improved business education, particularly an MBA program, an easy area in which to collaborate. The Chinese wanted to learn and to give their students and up-and-coming leaders the best practical business education they could.

The day before I was to meet with Zhu Rongji in October 1999, I stopped by Tsinghua to visit with students and to give a speech. As we drove through the entrance, I was struck by the quiet, almost bucolic, beauty of the campus. It had been laid out in 1911 on the grounds of a Qing dynasty imperial garden in the northwest corner of the capital, far from the bustling government ministries and SOE headquarters where I usually had meetings. The mix of Chinese, Greco-Roman, and German architectural styles reflected the rich history of a school founded to prepare students for study in America. Tsinghua had been financed in part with donations that U.S. president Teddy Roosevelt had ordered be taken out of the indemnity Western powers had forced China to pay after the nationalist Boxers rose up against foreign interests in 1900. The U.S.'s influence could be seen in the Jeffersonian echoes of the domed rotunda of the auditorium designed in 1917 by American architect Henry Murphy.

SEM had just moved into a new, five-story white stone building whose entryway bore an inscription in Chinese by Zhu Rongji that I was told read in part, "Let's work together toward the goal of building a world-class school of economics and management." I walked with my colleagues Fred Hu and Hsueh-ming Wang past a wall lined with portraits of Nobel laureates in economics into an auditorium so jammed with students that some had been sent to overflow rooms to listen to me over loudspeakers. I spoke for a half hour or so on various aspects of corporate management and closed with some thoughts on the importance of finding a work-life balance. Then I asked for questions, and over the course of an hour of wide-ranging give-and-take, the students simply floored me with their energy, earnestness, and attentiveness. After the session they literally mobbed me, imploring me to autograph notebooks or newspaper articles about me or Goldman Sachs. It was the closest I've ever come to feeling like a rock star.

Now, I didn't delude myself into thinking I'd just delivered a second Gettysburg Address. I don't read prepared speeches too well, and I'm sure I went on too long. But investment banking had become a hot profession in a country trying to reform its economy and escape centuries of poverty. Still, some of my words struck a chord, especially with the women in the audience. I knew many Chinese were looking for more to believe in than work and making money. So I talked about the importance to me of my family, prayer, and conservation work. I described how, when I was climbing the ladder at Goldman, I came home early to read to my kids at bedtime, then resumed making client calls after they had fallen asleep. Afterward, I was surprised by how many students—all women—came up to me to ask me more questions about prayer and my religion.

There was one drawback to my day at Tsinghua. I had a hard time with the students' heavily accented English. I had to rely on the translator to restate their questions in a way I could understand. Since there are few secrets in China, word got back to Zhu Rongji. The next morning my colleagues and I met with him at the Diaoyutai State Guesthouse complex in western Beijing, not far from Tsinghua. Zhu invited me to speak first, and I carefully laid out my plans. Before he addressed them, however, he offered me an apology.

"I'm so embarrassed," he said. "Our students' foreign language skills aren't good enough. It's the same with the teachers. They are the cream of the crop, but their English proficiency isn't strong enough."

Zhu was determined to enhance the education provided by Tsinghua. Improving students' English-language skills was a concrete step that could lead to their advancement. Looking back now, I wonder if he didn't have another, more subtle motive, as well. He knew that the school needed to upgrade its teaching staff. Many were not qualified to teach their courses, and lacked, as he put it, "practical experience and knowledge of enterprise management." But they were entrenched and could not easily be removed. Requiring professors to teach in English, which many couldn't do, might just make it easier to bring in new blood.

"For many years I have wanted to establish a world-class management school to complement China's reform," he told us. Then he turned to me and said, "We need to rely on you for this."

With the premier's blessing—and no small sense of responsibility—I grabbed hold of the Tsinghua project with both hands. I approached my friend Kim Clark, then dean of the Harvard Business School, who agreed to have his institution partner with Tsinghua SEM. Harvard brought an unparalleled mastery of the case study method and a sterling reputation for its executive education programs. In a stroke of good fortune, Warren McFarlan, an acclaimed HBS professor and prolific author who had taught for years in HBS's renowned Advanced Management Program for senior executives, was doing research and teaching in Shanghai. He was eager to pitch in and began developing China-specific case studies while reshaping Tsinghua's executive education program. Consultants at McKinsey & Company, which actively worked with HBS, agreed to develop a five-year strategic plan for Tsinghua.

I worked the phone, inviting prominent business leaders to join the board, CEOs like Eastman Kodak Company's George Fisher, BP Amoco's John Browne, and Nokia's Jorma Ollila. I reached out to Irwin Jacobs of Qualcomm, Masayoshi Son of Japan's SoftBank Corporation, and Victor Fung of the Hong Kong manufacturing and sourcing giant Li & Fung. Hank Greenberg of American International Group, Nobuyuki Idei of Sony Corporation, Marjorie Yang of Esquel Group, Chris Galvin of Motorola, Claude Bébéar of AXA, Lee Scott of Wal-Mart Stores, and Richard Li, CEO of Pacific Century CyberWorks, would also join.

In my zeal to create a strong board, I went ahead and filled in the Chinese side, too, reaching out to leaders I knew like Lenovo founder Liu Chuanzhi; Liu Mingkang, the new head of Bank of China; and Zhou Xiaochuan, who had just moved from China Construction Bank to head the China Securities Regulatory Commission. I also recruited Harvard's Kim Clark.

To my surprise, almost all of the executives I approached agreed to join. In fact, so many people accepted so quickly that I faced the problem of potentially having too many talented CEOs—the board would lose its effectiveness if it got too big.

Really, though, that was the least of my problems.

In China they say the high nail gets hit by the hammer. While I prepared for the first advisory board meeting, I learned that the school and Zhu had been fed criticisms and rumors about me and my motives. As best I could tell, this "information" was coming from competing bankers, who evidently resented the prominent role I was taking. "Paulson's putting all of his clients on the board," the whispering went. "He's doing it for his own aggrandizement."

The intrigue came to a head as I was preparing to fly from New York to attend the opening of Goldman's new Singapore office, with plans to travel to Beijing afterward for the Tsinghua advisory board's inaugural meeting on October 6, 2000. Just before boarding my flight, I learned from Hsueh-ming Wang, who was in daily communication with SEM's then deputy dean Zhao Chunjun, that it was no longer clear whether I would chair the board or what role I would play at the meeting. Normally, I tried to rest on the long night flights to Asia, but I couldn't sleep; the uncertainty and misunderstanding ate at me. I took out a pen and paper and spent hours drafting a long memo to the premier, explaining exactly why I'd done what I'd done. I made clear that I had been acting solely for Tsinghua and for China, not for myself or for Goldman. I hoped that the straight-shooting Chinese leader would appreciate an equally straight-shooting, no-BS note. When I landed in Frankfurt to change planes, I called Hsueh-ming and dictated the letter for her to deliver to Zhu Rongji. After I got on the plane to Singapore, she got my letter to Zhou Xiaochuan, who delivered it personally to Zhu Rongji. A prominent graduate of Tsinghua, Zhou had been consulting with me as we developed our proposals for the school.

Once there, I checked in with my team, only to hear that our people in China were unhappy with me for having the temerity to write such a letter to Zhu and with Hsueh-ming for getting it delivered. I'd been way too direct, they said, and was only making things worse. The vehemence of their admonitions made me plenty nervous. After the Goldman office opening, I flew to Beijing. When I arrived at Tsinghua the next morning, I had no idea what to expect.

Swallowing hard, I walked into the SEM building, past the premier's calligraphy, all too aware that my hard-driving personality was considered pushy even by my countrymen. A school representative led John Thornton, Hsueh-ming, Fred Hu, and me to a ceremonial holding room where we joined the dozen or so newly appointed international members of the advisory board who had been able to attend. Then we walked down a marble hallway and into the school's old library. Zhu Rongji strode toward me. I was prepared for the worst. But the premier smiled with his usual friendliness and clasped my right hand in both of his.

"I read your whole letter," he said in English. "I agree with everything you said."

As we took our seats Zhu turned to me and said, "Mr. Chairman, please start the meeting."

That first meeting of the board was a great success. It was clear that Zhu Rongji meant business and that Tsinghua—unlike many institutions I've known—would be very receptive to advice from board members. With Zhu's backing I confidently pushed forward our plan to start the executive education program, to begin upgrading the faculty, and to attract visiting professors. For months Hsueh-ming Wang practically lived at Tsinghua to oversee the project and work hand in glove with deputy dean Zhao. Her judgment, people skills, discretion, and ability to get things done were extraordinary.

HBS's Warren McFarlan was able to get the executive education program off the ground almost immediately, inaugurating the use of the case study method at Tsinghua and in China. Initially, some of the Chinese companies were reluctant to share the information needed, but Victor Fung, who was much respected on the mainland, helped convince them they weren't giving away state secrets in doing so.

The first program, Managing in the Internet Age, was held in January 2001, barely three months after the inaugural board meeting; it featured seven new China-centered case studies written by Warren's team. CEOs from five of the companies in the case studies attended and provided their insights to the 85 executives from across China who participated. Warren and two other HBS professors conducted the program with Tsinghua professors, and as they taught the classes, they trained the faculty. By June 2002 the program would be entirely taught by SEM faculty. Today the Tsinghua SEM China Business Case Center develops and compiles scores of new cases each year on Chinese companies, from China Merchants Bank to the wildly successful hot pot restaurant chain Hai Di Lao Huo Guo. Many of the cases are developed by Tsinghua faculty; the collection currently stands at more than 400. (HBS has produced more than 7,500 cases.)

Since that first training program, more than 50,000 mid- and senior-level executives have gone through Tsinghua's non-degree-granting executive training programs, of which there are now more than 60. Degree-granting executive MBA programs began in June 2002, and Tsinghua's flagship 18-month executive MBA program has trained more than 4,000 Chinese senior managers and high-level government officials. Tsinghua offers another 18-month EMBA program with the international business school Institut Européen d'Administration des Affaires (INSEAD).

The executive education programs, with higher tuition rates than undergrad and traditional MBA programs, helped strengthen the school's bottom line, allowing it to hire internationally trained faculty. Tsinghua recruited 30 new lecturers and distinguished professors from HBS, the Massachusetts Institute of Technology's Sloan School of Management, Columbia Business School, the Yale School of Management, and the Haas School of Business at the University of California, Berkeley, to come for three-year rotations starting in 2002, significantly boosting the strength of SEM's faculty. The school now has 18 affiliated research centers, including the National Center for Economic Research, the China Business Case Center, and the National Institute for Fiscal Studies.

After the June 2002 board meeting, I stepped down from my chairmanship to focus more attention on another nonprofit I was co-chairing, the Nature Conservancy's Asia-Pacific Council. BP's John Browne proved a more than capable successor, and I stayed on the SEM advisory board, attending every meeting until I became Treasury secretary in 2006. My favorite part of the board work was the student presentations—not least because they became increasingly easy for me to understand. Zhu's determination to improve English at the SEM bore fruit; today two-thirds of the school's classes are taught in English.

I tend to approach all challenges the same way: start with a big vision, choose a concrete first step that can be accomplished quickly to build momentum, then push forward relentlessly, holding people to tight schedules. Otherwise it is too easy to lose your focus and drive. This approach worked for me in business, and it worked for me with Tsinghua, in good measure because the results-oriented Zhu Rongji liked to work that way, too. He wanted to create a business school grounded in the practical realities of doing business in China while adopting best international practices, as he sought to do in his economic reforms generally. We were not educators at Goldman, but we cared about education and understood how important improved management training was to China's ability to press ahead on needed reforms. Moreover, we had demonstrated that we got difficult things done.

All of this appealed to Zhu Rongji, who was in a hurry to reform and modernize his country.

CHAPTER EIGHT

Saving Shangri-La

About the time we were working with Guangdong Enterprises, I found myself increasingly drawn into efforts to preserve one of the most singularly beautiful areas in the world: Yunnan Province in the southwest part of the country. China, frankly, was the last place I had expected to find a wilderness of such spectacular biodiversity. Everywhere I went in the late 1990s, I could see—and smell and taste, for that matter—the horrific cost of China's economic miracle. Not only was rapid industrial development fouling the air and water and threatening the health of citizens, but the country's natural wonders were ill cared for and poorly protected, overrun by rapacious developers and hordes of littering tourists.

It pained me to see this ecological disaster unfolding. I've had a deep and abiding interest in nature and wildlife, an affinity for unspoiled places, since my childhood on a farm in Barrington, Illinois. As a boy I raised pet crows and raccoons and dreamed of becoming a forest ranger. I devoured books on animals and plants. The highlight of my year came every July when my family canoed for two weeks in the pristine Boundary Waters on the U.S.-Canadian border. Catching bass and lake trout, picking blueberries, watching bears, beaver, and otters—that was heaven to me. After business school, when I worked in Washington, D.C., at the Pentagon and in the Nixon White House, I traveled with Wendy on October weekends to Assateague Island, which straddles Maryland and Virginia, to band peregrine falcons during their annual migration. Perched at the top of the food chain, raptors captivated me for their fierce beauty and for what they told us about our world: if they were healthy, the environment was healthy.

Wendy and I moved back to Barrington in 1974 and built a house on five acres that we bought from my parents. My wife, who loves wild, beautiful places as much as I do, began the hard work of restoring the native prairie grasses and forbs in the nature preserve bordering our home. I had just started at Goldman, and money was tight, so I was dumbstruck when she spent $500 to join the Nature Conservancy (TNC), the U.S.-based nonprofit dedicated to preserving biodiversity. But as Wendy got more involved—first as a volunteer, then as chairman of TNC's Illinois and New York chapters, and eventually as vice chairman of the national board—I began to appreciate the reach and effectiveness of its work.

As it happened, the Conservancy wanted to become more active in the Far East and China. But when I was asked to help jump-start the work of its Asia-Pacific Council, I was initially reluctant. Given the breakneck pace of development, I half joked that I doubted much would be left to preserve in the region before long. But I also questioned how effective TNC could be, considering the weak regulatory environment and the indifference that I had observed firsthand. Though Chinese friends, ever the polite hosts, frequently offered to arrange expeditions to remote areas when they heard of my interest in birding and the wilderness, I had yet to hear one express a personal interest in conservation. This was true of most officials I knew as well. Like the leaders of other developing nations I had known, their chief goals were to create jobs and reduce poverty. Dealing with pollution was a distant priority. One exception was Wang Qishan. During his stint in Guangdong, he spoke fervently of the need to clean up the province's rivers, which festered with toxic waste and industrial pollutants.

Moreover, I like to be involved in projects where I can see tangible results. I join where I feel I can make a difference. In the late 1980s I got involved with the Peregrine Fund, which had a clearly defined mission, and demonstrated success, in saving birds of prey from extinction. I'd become chairman in 1996, and I wasn't sure if TNC could hope to have such an immediate impact.

My skepticism faded as I listened to a remarkable woman named Carol Fox, the Hawaii-based director of program development for TNC's Asia-Pacific programs, whose ambitious initiatives included protecting forests and reefs in Indonesia and Palau. Carol had learned Mandarin while living some years before in Taiwan and in Hong Kong and was keen to bring TNC's expertise to the mainland. Carol described a project the Conservancy had been working on in northwestern Yunnan, in a remote area in the Himalayan foothills that many thought had inspired the mystical paradise of Shangri-La in James Hilton's 1933 novel *Lost Horizon*.

The project had begun in cooperation with a Thai businessman who had sought TNC's help in developing for ecotourism the picturesque 800-year-old town of Lijiang and, towering above it, the Jade Dragon Snow Mountain range, whose tallest peak reaches 18,360 feet. That plan had fallen through, but Carol was determined to involve TNC in protecting the area's extraordinary cultural and ecological diversity.

One of the most spectacular and biologically rich ecosystems in the world, the mountainous area of northwest Yunnan is home to the higher-elevation watersheds of four of Asia's largest rivers—the Irrawaddy, the Salween, the Mekong, and the Yangtze. The last three of these run parallel from north to south, through spectacular gorges, some plunging nearly 2 miles from peak to valley. At their closest point the rivers are separated by fewer than 55 miles. Warming monsoon winds from neighboring Myanmar allow rhododendrons to bloom at 14,000 feet, while deep, fertile valleys help the region to shelter more than 20 percent of the country's plant species and about one-third of its mammal and bird species, nearly a hundred of which, like the black-tufted, 2-foot-tall Yunnan snub-nosed monkey, are endangered. Many of the region's plants and animals were left over from the last ice age, when species now unique to Yunnan survived in the temperate gorges.

The area's diversity extends to its inhabitants. Some 90 percent of Chinese people belong to the Han ethnic group. They speak Mandarin or some variant of it and live in densely populated coastal or central regions. But the country claims 55 other ethnic groups, who live mainly in its vast and inhospitable border regions. Though the restive areas of Tibet and Xinjiang attract more international attention, Yunnan, with its mountainous terrain and porous borders, contains many minority groups that make up more than a third of its population. In the northwestern part of the province where TNC was working, nearly 20 of these groups live in close proximity. Among them, Buddhist Tibetans herd yaks and build monasteries high on exposed mountainsides; animist Naxi, centered in Lijiang, boast a rich musical tradition and communicate with one of the world's last pictographic written languages; the Lisu, who live in the upper reaches of the Salween River valley, are more closely related to people across the border in Myanmar than they are to the Han.

Some of these areas had been set aside as nature reserves in the 1980s but suffered from weak protection and poor enforcement. There were few incentives to stop impoverished natives from eroding steep hillsides by chopping down trees for firewood and grazing their goats and yaks or to discourage local governments from allowing overdevelopment that would destroy what was meant to be saved. TNC's long-term goal was to identify the highest-priority sites for conservation. These would be turned into national parks that would adhere to international standards, generate revenue for local governments, and help to alleviate poverty by putting some tourism profits into the hands of the region's ethnic minorities so they could make a living from preserving nature, not exploiting it.

I agreed to co-chair TNC's Asia-Pacific Council, and in November 1997 Wendy and I represented the Conservancy at one of the country's first environmental conferences, in Beijing. Several hundred people attended, including representatives of large multinational corporations and international organizations like the United Nations. Yunnan vice governor Niu Shaoyao introduced what we called the Yunnan Great Rivers Project to the many Chinese government and business leaders present. I described how the Conservancy worked closely with the government and the private sector to solve problems through compromise and cooperation. TNC's nonconfrontational, science-based approach was ideal for China, which bridled reflexively at the reproaches of outsiders. The last thing the Chinese wanted to hear was a lecture from foreign industrial powers that, it could be argued, had polluted their way to power and were now proffering advice that might put obstacles in the path of China's own progress.

I acknowledged that China's headlong growth demanded that tough choices be made, but that a healthy economy did not have to be at odds with a healthy environment. Protecting the environment was good business. It was cheaper to prevent damage than to clean it up afterward. I noted, too, that according to one study I had seen, U.S. states that took environmental protection seriously outperformed other states in every economic category, from overall growth to nonfarm employment to construction.

I witnessed firsthand how difficult these choices could sometimes be when, along with a small group from the conference, I met with Premier Li Peng in the Great Hall of the People. Going back to the days of our stumble on the Shandong power plant venture, I had not seen eye to eye with him on much, including his reluctance to embrace reform. Li began by saying that rich Western nations should help pay for China's environmental cleanup as the price for having polluted during our own industrial development. He assured us that his country was doing its part, citing the work that had begun three years earlier on the massive Three Gorges Dam on the Yangtze River. Li was an engineer, and the controversial dam was his baby; he was proud of all the clean energy it would soon produce. I was concerned that the dam would also displace hundreds of thousands of people, submerge hundreds of historic sites, and disrupt the great river's flow, destroying natural wetlands that filtered out pollutants, reduced the impact of storm flooding, and provided habitat for rare species.

Li Peng's approach didn't jibe with mine at the time. I saw the benefit of clean, renewable hydropower compared with coal-fired electrical power plants, but I questioned a project that was so big and complex and involved so much environmental risk and social disruption. Nonetheless, I came away from the Beijing conference encouraged by China's growing commitment to conservation, having met any number of officials determined to tackle the country's considerable challenges.

Fundraising posed a challenge. I knew that it would be difficult to solicit money in the U.S. if I couldn't show that wealthy Chinese were also prepared to give. But philanthropy in China at the time generally took the form of patronage to a hometown as a way of honoring ancestors, or "donations" made to local officials to curry favor. Bringing together like-minded people to raise money for a cause like biodiversity? That was a tough job, made harder by the Asian financial crisis then raging.

I decided to start in Hong Kong, whose business leaders rose to the occasion. In June 1998, we arranged a dinner for the Nature Conservancy's

Asia-Pacific Council, a group of leading government and business figures committed to working to preserve biodiversity in the region. Hosted by shipping tycoon C. C. Tung, the brother of Hong Kong chief executive C. H. Tung, the event was held at Hong Kong's private Island Club and raised $1 million. Just as important, we made progress in increasing awareness among potential donors. Mainland Chinese would also prove generous with their money and time once they understood the cause. Indeed, I was to discover over time that there were plenty of Chinese people who cared deeply about clean air and clean water and who were unhappy with the environmental damage that was accompanying the country's growth. There were others, including political leaders, who took great pride in the wild and beautiful places that still existed in China and wanted to preserve their natural heritage.

After the dinner I had to cancel plans to fly to Yunnan and returned home because of pressing business at Goldman Sachs. I had been named co-CEO in the run-up to our scheduled September IPO, which ended up being postponed because of poor market conditions. Wendy and our daughter, Amanda, along with some TNC members and staff spent several days hiking, camping, and meeting with government officials in the areas TNC sought to protect. But it would be more than four years before I would make it to Yunnan myself.

There were encouraging developments. The Yunnan provincial government signed an agreement with TNC to start the Great Rivers Project, and more broadly, Beijing began to pay greater attention to environmental issues. In 1998 it created the State Environmental Protection Administration (SEPA) from the existing environmental agency, upgraded it to a ministry, and strengthened regulation and enforcement. Meantime, massive floods along parts of the Yangtze that summer left more than 4,000 dead and 15 million homeless and brought home the dangers of rampant deforestation in the upper reaches of the river caused by overdevelopment and large-scale commercial logging.

The Yunnan project leadership team began to take shape. Carol had earlier recruited Rose Niu, a Lijiang-born Naxi, to lead efforts on the ground. After working for the government's Quarantine Service in Yunnan for nearly a decade, Rose had earned a master's degree at the Asian Institute of Technology in Thailand. Her thesis, "Nature Tourism and Environmental Protection: A Strategic Analysis for an Ethnic Minority Region, Southwest China," could not have been more perfectly suited to TNC's mission. Rose had moved to New Zealand with her husband, but Carol persuaded her to return home. In early 1999 Edward Norton, a co-founder of the Grand Canyon Trust and an expert on America's national parks (and father of the American actor), joined the team, moving with his wife, Ann McBride, to the provincial capital of Kunming. McBride, a former head of Common Cause, the U.S. citizens' advocacy group, would establish an innovative program in which local villagers were given cameras and encouraged to photograph special places and describe what these places meant to them.

All conservation, like politics, is local. If local people don't buy into a project, it won't be successful. In the field TNC staff used a comprehensive approach called Conservation by Design that brought together all stakeholders—state agency administrators, provincial and municipal officials, community members, and conservation interest groups like TNC—to hash out the issues and develop a plan. The approach fit with the Chinese tradition of consensus decision making. Conservation by Design was used to identify sites for preservation and to develop strategies to reduce the threats to their biodiversity. Working with Chinese scientists and officials, and gathering input from skilled American biologists and conservation experts, TNC staffers spent a year and a half collecting data on the region's animals, plants, and geographic features, as well as on social and economic conditions, in order to target specific areas for action. Along the way, they trained their Chinese counterparts in environmental management and data collection.

With the help of Hong Kong–based Tim Dattels, who headed Goldman Sachs' department for managing investment banking relationships in Asia, I sought out business and government leaders from the region to build a strong board of trustees to support these efforts. Most crucially, I was able to recruit as my co-chair of the Asia-Pacific Council Lee Kuan Yew, the Republic of Singapore's founding father and its prime minister for more than three decades until 1990. Lee's involvement instantly raised the

Conservancy's profile and gave it much higher status in China, where he was widely admired for having overseen the pint-size city-state's extraordinary economic success as a leading center of trade, finance, and innovation.

At the start few of the board members were ardent environmentalists; an exception was Edward Tian, a native of Liaoning Province, who had co-founded AsiaInfo, a provider of software and infrastructure solutions for the Internet that would become the first Chinese company to list on Nasdaq. Edward, a born entrepreneur who would become the number two man at China Netcom Group Corporation (Hong Kong), was a trained biologist like both of his parents and had studied North American rangeland while working for his Ph.D. at Texas Tech University in Lubbock. Over time, however, thanks to their work with the Council, a number of other businessmen, like Victor Fung, chairman of Li & Fung in Hong Kong, and Douglas Tong Hsu, chairman of Taiwan's Far Eastern Group, also became committed conservationists. And Wang Qishan still thanks me for the environmental training he received in the early days as a member of TNC's advisory council.

We gathered for the first time in August 2000, in Singapore, at a meeting chaired by Lee Kuan Yew. TNC soon brought in millions of dollars to support our projects. But all the money in the world wouldn't help if the Conservancy couldn't operate effectively on the ground in China, and there were challenges to overcome.

Though the Yunnan provincial and local government leaders had backed our project from the beginning, TNC had to contend with rivalries and weak coordination among central government agencies. In the 1980s China had created two kinds of protected spaces with national significance. "Scenic areas," ranging from sections of the Great Wall to Tibetan villages in Sichuan, were developed for tourism and run, oddly enough, by the Ministry of Construction, whose idea of a park was, all too often, a patch of open land on which impressive buildings could be built. "Nature reserves," by contrast, were administered by the State Forestry Administration, which kept a tighter rein on commercial activity. These restrictions were often brushed aside: local officials pushed for development, while poor, indigenous people who lived in or near designated reserves routinely ignored regulations as they struggled to make ends meet—cutting down trees for firewood or wildcatting small mines.

TNC's approach—protecting natural and cultural treasures while generating income for locals through sustainable ecotourism—split the difference between the two models but stoked bureaucratic friction. Some officials in the Ministry of Construction and the State Forestry Administration, otherwise an ally, worried that the Great Rivers approach would undermine the system administered by their agencies. The State Environmental Protection Agency was more accommodating, seeing a chance to expand its own authority.

One conflict concerned the very terminology we used. At one point a Ministry of Construction official rather imperiously told Carol and her colleagues that they had no right to call the areas we were trying to protect national parks. Why? National parks, this official said, fell under the Ministry of Construction, and since the ministry was not involved, TNC could not use the term.

As Carol replied, it didn't matter to us what the Chinese called the areas we identified for conservation as long as they were protected. But beyond setting up Yunnan's pilot parks, we wanted to create an appropriate model for the rest of China. Great Rivers was a classic Chinese test case for conservation, much like the Shenzhen special economic zone had been for economic reform.

Fortunately, the Conservancy was able to gain the support of the powerful State Development and Planning Commission. How that came about illustrates the importance of touching base with all possible constituencies. As part of its effort to educate officials, the Conservancy sponsored study trips for local and national officials to visit the national parks of other countries. These trips made a big impression on the delegations, one of which included Madame Hao Jianxiu, an SDPC vice minister. The final report from her delegation's visit to the U.S., which included stops at the Grand Canyon and Yellowstone and Yosemite National Parks, strongly recommended that China move forward with our proposed Yunnan Great Rivers Project.

SDPC had no mandate for action in this area, but it played a crucial role in putting together China's five-year plans for economic growth and wielded plenty of clout. Madame Hao was a force in her own right. A textile mill worker by trade, she was just 16 in 1951 when she devised a method to reduce waste while spinning thread and catapulted to national fame as a "star model worker." She rose to become one of China's highest-ranking women, serving on the Party's elite Central Committee.

In the spring of 1999, she helped convene a workshop in Lijiang co-hosted by the Conservancy and Yunnan's provincial government that brought together officials from numerous agencies, including the State Environmental Protection Administration and the Ministry of Construction, to discuss the future of northwest Yunnan. TNC and Yunnan provincial officials subsequently drew up a blueprint that, among other things, called for setting aside a large swath of land for new nature reserves and national parks. It gave targets for alternative energy use by local communities; proposed replacing small mines with bigger, more cost-efficient ones employing better technology and pollution controls; and recommended a halt to tilling fields steeper than 25 degrees and the introduction of terracing for other sloped fields. The provincial government adopted the proposals, which were incorporated into Yunnan's part of China's tenth five-year plan (2001–2005). In the end the government would set aside nearly 26,000 square miles—an area just larger than West Virginia, or twice the size of Taiwan—for the Yunnan Great Rivers Project.

This success still left TNC operating in a gray area—since we had yet to get official approval from Beijing. As always in China that could be good or bad. On the one hand, TNC had freedom to experiment. On the other hand, the project could be shut down at any point. Beijing distrusted nongovernmental organizations (NGOs). Few were sanctioned in China at the time, and TNC was active in a highly sensitive area on the border of Tibet that was home to many ethnic Tibetans. Anything concerning Tibet had the potential to be a problem for China's leaders.

It made sense to get a sign-off from the highest levels of the state. That meant arranging a meeting with President Jiang Zemin. The question was how to do that. The days when any group of foreigners working on a project or deal could meet with China's president were long over. An added complication was that I hoped to discuss another issue with the president—the continued reform of the country's capital markets. Goldman had long wanted to set up a fully owned and operated securities business in the country but was restricted to joint ventures. Keeping out the world's best banks was self-defeating and limited China's own development potential, I believed. A number of Chinese reformers agreed with me, but there was resistance in top state bodies to opening the markets further. Some of this came from ideological intransigence, some from the domestic securities industry, which had a vested interest in limiting competition, and some, I think, came from an understandable case of the jitters. Global markets were rocky—the Nasdaq Composite Index had collapsed in March 2000 after the dot-com bubble blew up, then U.S. energy highflier Enron Corporation imploded in late fall 2001. And Chinese markets were notoriously volatile.

Although meetings with senior officials had to be sponsored by a state host, no government agency in the financial sector would have helped us. If Goldman were seen to have secured a meeting with Jiang, every major financial services company in the world would have demanded their own one-on-one, and there was no way the Chinese could or would accommodate that. But there weren't a lot of environmentally focused NGOs operating in China asking for meetings with Jiang Zemin. So we decided to go through the State Environmental Protection Administration.

To be clear: we were not trying to pull a bait and switch by asking to talk about the environment only to start discussing finance. Far from it. The Chinese were eager to discuss both topics—securities regulator Zhou Xiaochuan was planning to attend and helped facilitate the meeting. But it was important that our approach conform to the established process, so that we could discuss environmental *and* financial matters without opening the floodgates to every importuning bank in the world.

The wrinkle was that the environmental agency was not very powerful and lacked easy access to Jiang Zemin. Officials at the agency felt they would be putting an awful lot on the line to request a meeting with the president on our behalf and did not want to appear to overreach. So, working through Ziwang Xu, Goldman's head of China, we approached Jiang's eldest son, Dr. Jiang Mianheng, who had a strong interest in the environment, to secure the president's informal acceptance of a meeting. Once we had done that, we had to convince SEPA officials that we had learned through our own back channels that they could get the meeting if they asked. It's a measure of just how cautiously Chinese officials operated that it would take three months and multiple trips by TNC staffers to Beijing before SEPA finally felt confident enough to ask to see the president.

We met with Jiang Zemin at Zhongnanhai in the first week of February 2002. All around us the capital was busily preparing for Chinese New Year festivities, with its noisy fireworks and train stations jammed with travelers heading home. But inside the leadership compound's thick walls all was as serene and orderly as ever. At 4:00 p.m. we were ushered into an ornate meeting room and seated in a horseshoe of plush armchairs beneath an enormous ink landscape painting. I had brought along Carol Fox, Ed Norton, and Rose Niu, as well as Goldman chief of staff John Rogers, Ziwang Xu, and Hsueh-ming Wang.

Among the Chinese attendees was State Environmental Protection Administration chief Xie Zhenhua, a Tsinghua-trained engineer who'd spent much of his career in the thankless work of fighting for China's environment while serving in the haphazard bureaucracy that predated SEPA. (In 2006 Xie was appointed to serve as China's chief climate change negotiator.) Also attending were Yunnan governor Xu Rongkai and Zhou Xiaochuan.

President Jiang looked as relaxed and friendly as ever, sporting a well-cut dark suit and his trademark square black-rimmed glasses. He got right to the point. "China needs to learn more about stock markets and global economic policies," he told us. "I'd like to start off talking about those issues."

Jiang quizzed me about financial topics, particularly the importance of equity markets to economic development. In his typically wry way, he quoted Sir Isaac Newton's famous remark that he could grasp the movements of objects and celestial bodies but not those of stocks. Jiang said he had been puzzled to see the collapse of the Nasdaq index, down more than 60 percent from its peak. I understood his concern might be closer to heart: the Shanghai Stock Exchange Composite Index had fallen by one-third since mid-2001. Jiang acknowledged the advantages of having a stock market in China, but expressed concern about his countrymen's proclivity to speculate.

I explained that stock markets provided a means to invest China's rapidly growing capital in the nation's economic activity rather than leaving it in banks. I emphasized, too, how important it was to have excellent managers running the companies that people were investing their money in. During our colloquy I tried to shift the topic toward Yunnan and conservation, pointing out how a healthy economy and a healthy environment depended on each other, but Jiang kept his attention focused on capital markets for longer than I expected.

When I was done, Jiang asked me if I could expand my thoughts in a report and send it to him.

"Don't charge any fee," he said, adding wryly, "of course, I could always ask J.P. Morgan instead."

The president then gestured to the Chinese side of the horseshoe and told me we had better start talking about the environment, or SEPA administrator Xie and Governor Xu would become angry with him.

So I spoke very briefly about the Nature Conservancy, which I called "the best conservation organization in the world," and then I introduced Rose Niu, suggesting that she explain the Yunnan Great Rivers Project.

"I'm a simple Naxi girl from Lijiang," Rose began, addressing Jiang directly, "and I was very nervous about my assignment of reporting our work in Yunnan to you. Then I heard you speak. Your hometown is right across the river from my husband's, and I thought, gosh, you talk just like my father-in-law."

It was a masterful opening, completely disarming, and from that moment, the diminutive Naxi woman, sitting on the edge of a big red chair, her feet barely touching the ground, was in absolute command of the room. Speaking without notes for perhaps 20 minutes, she gave an incisive, nuanced presentation, explaining what TNC was doing in Yunnan and the importance of the Great Rivers Project, not just for the province but for China as a whole.

The president was riveted, listening intently, and leaning in close, the better to see and hear Rose, who was seated to my right. I almost felt I should offer him my chair.

He interrupted her at one point to ask how to pronounce a particular term of art in English, and then repeated aloud after her: "Conservation by Design, a very systematic and science-based approach."

Jiang, being an engineer, liked systematic things.

When Rose was done, Jiang praised her effusively, commending the clarity and precision of her report. He asked her where she had learned her English and said he knew the Asian Institute of Technology, where she had studied. Then he turned again to his side of the room and declared: "All Chinese government officials concerned should work together with TNC to make this project a success and take this model to all China."

It was exactly what we were hoping to hear.

Afterward, flashbulbs popped and TV cameramen jostled for an angle as they squeezed together to document the first meeting between representatives of a foreign environmental NGO and the president of China. After the meeting, Jiang wrote me a letter endorsing TNC's Yunnan program as a model for environmental protection efforts in other areas of China. The same day the Conservancy also signed an agreement to cooperate with SEPA. TNC had been active in Yunnan for years; now Jiang Zemin had provided the official blessing, opening doors to Chinese government agencies at all levels. No one could question whether a foreign NGO like TNC should be so active in China—even on the borders of Tibet.

Rose framed Jiang's letter and took it to meetings with any officials who were giving her a hard time. TNC established a Beijing office that October and not long after was invited by SEPA to develop a scientific ecoregional plan to identify China's conservation priorities, which led to the creation of the country's first centralized biodiversity database. The resulting blueprint was incorporated into the government's National Biodiversity Conservation Strategy and Action Plan, which was approved by Premier Wen Jiabao and released in 2012. The plan called for strengthening nature reserves to protect 90 percent of China's endangered species and important ecosystems; conducting complete biodiversity surveys by 2015 in priority areas; and stopping the loss of biodiversity in China by 2020.

In 2003 a significant part of the Yunnan project area was designated a World Natural Heritage Site. Known as the Three Parallel Rivers of Yunnan Protected Areas, the site is one of the largest recognized by the United Nations Educational, Scientific, and Cultural Organization (Unesco). In June 2007 China's first pilot national park opened in northwest Yunnan under provincial supervision. The 500-square-mile Pudacuo was designed to encompass Tibetan villages, soaring peaks and alpine lakes, forests, and meadows and to adhere to strict international standards for environmental protection, biodiversity conservation, and ecotourism. In total, the Yunnan provincial government has approved plans for a dozen pilot national parks to be established by 2020.

After the meeting with President Jiang, Yunnan governor Xu invited the Asia-Pacific Council to hold its next board meeting in his province, so the members could see the place they were working to protect. We accepted, and in late October 2002 Wendy, Amanda, and I flew out early to explore the area before attending the meeting in Lijiang.

This being China, we couldn't just sneak in. We were met at Kunming airport by Governor Xu, who had stayed there overnight so as not to miss our early morning arrival. After a ceremonial breakfast Wendy, Amanda, and I set out with TNC science director Bob Moseley, Ed Norton, and a few local Chinese staff for Meili Snow Mountain. We took a short flight up to the newly christened town of Shangri-La. In a marketing coup to attract tourists, the Zhongdian town and the surrounding county had beaten out other local jurisdictions to win approval from the State Council the year before to officially change their names to Shangri-La.

That night we stayed in the small city of Deqin, and in the morning we visited a school the Nature Conservancy had provided with rooftop solar water heaters, clean-burning biogas stoves fueled by methane from pig waste, and greenhouses that provided fresh vegetables for the students and staff. Though these improvements were not conservation work per se, they helped to engage local families happy to see their children enjoy better conditions in the mostly residential schools. Many villagers nearby were motivated to install ultra-efficient, wood-burning stoves in their homes, as well.

Over the next four days, we explored a part of Yunnan that was even lusher and more jaw-droppingly beautiful than we had been led to expect. Leaving Deqin we traveled by four-wheel drive to a trailhead that led to the tiny village of Yubeng, which we reached on foot. From there we made arduous climbs and descents through old-growth hardwoods, cautiously navigated narrow traverses that overlooked dizzying, thousand-foot drop-offs, crossed alpine meadows where a few late gentians were still in flower, and followed the Yubeng River down to the Mekong, through villages with clusters of whitewashed houses whose roofs were covered with corn spread out to dry.

Because it was October, few of the area's spectacular wildflowers were in bloom, but the monsoon season had long gone, leaving behind high crystalline skies against which the soaring peaks of the Meili range stood out in stark, almost surreal relief. Looking at the vistas—the peaks, waterfalls, and valleys—it was easy to understand why the area was considered sacred by locals, most of whom are Tibetan Buddhists. I remember in particular one hike up a steep grade to a waterfall above the timberline. We stopped for a lunch of instant noodles and *baba*, a traditional Naxi bread. Wendy and I wedged ourselves between some boulders and, with the waterfall behind us, watched in wonder as the mountain sun glinted off the ethereally white wings of a flock of Himalayan snow pigeons.

As Bob Moseley explained, Yubeng, where we stayed two nights, lay within a complex, religion-based zoning system that was maintained by villagers and supported by religious leaders from nearby monasteries. I wasn't surprised to learn this, having seen throughout the day prayer flags flapping in the stiff upland breezes. In Yubeng there were zones open to all extractive uses, including timber harvest and hunting. There were other zones where hunting was prohibited but yak grazing and the collection of medicinal plants and mushrooms were allowed. Some areas, where certain deities were believed to reside, were off-limits to humans. Punishments for breaching the rules were enforced. This sacred zoning system was not something Western-trained conservation planners (or even most Chinese natural scientists) would have thought to include in the design of a protected area at Meili. Luckily, Bob Moseley helped us recognize and catalog this otherwise unseen world. Working with this centuries-old system gave our team a much better chance of protecting biodiversity in the area. It was a clear reminder to me that as much as successful conservation requires building relationships at the top, it demands that we work hard and take the time to understand the needs of local people as well.

Sometimes China can move very fast; other times the pace of change can be maddeningly slow. It pays to have patience—never my strong suit—persistence, and a little ingenuity. Conservation in China was never going to offer a simple, quick fix. Given the country's huge population and limited remaining natural areas, it is simply impossible to set aside very large portions of its territory for strict protection. With roughly the same landmass as the U.S. (and nearly one-third less arable land), China must support a population more than four times that of America's. And as with any country, numerous stakeholders make competing claims on the land and its resources, from indigenous populations trying to maintain a traditional way of life, to local officials eager to boost revenues through land sales, to the country's power producers looking to build dams in pristine gorges to meet the country's surging electricity needs, to mining interests eager to exploit the abundant mineral resources, and on and on.

The tension between development and conservation is particularly high in this resource-rich region. Many dams and mines have been built and many more proposed. TNC has worked to help minimize ecological damage, bringing in experts, for example, to advise on the location and construction of dams. But in some cases, such as a recent proposal to build a series of 13 big dams on the upper reaches of the Salween River, TNC has joined other Chinese and international conservation organizations in opposition.

To its credit, as our efforts at the Nature Conservancy showed, the Chinese government was open to new ideas and willing to experiment as it sought solutions to address the unprecedented challenges of protecting its environment while balancing the needs of nature and people. If the pilot national parks in Yunnan prove successful, the concept will be embraced by other provinces. When that happens, China will have gone some ways toward securing part of its threatened natural and cultural heritage.

CHAPTER NINE

One Bank, Two Systems

I was in the air over the Pacific, bound for China in the dead of the night, when the pilot came out of the cockpit of our leased private jet to tell me I had an urgent call from the office. We had taken off only half an hour before after a brief refueling stop on the Kamchatka Peninsula, where I'd checked in with Julie Becht, my assistant, so I was surprised to be hearing from her again so soon.

Mike Evans and I were on our way to two days of meetings, beginning that morning in Hong Kong with the president of China's massive state power company. It was planning to spin off its grid, which was responsible for transmission and distribution throughout the country, and we were hoping to win a piece of the business. Then it would be on to Beijing and meetings with members of the executive committee of Tsinghua University's business school, as well as a breakfast with Zhou Xiaochuan, now heading the China Securities Regulatory Commission. Goldman Sachs was in the thick of preparations for the multi-billion-dollar restructuring of Bank of China's Hong Kong assets, which involved the first international IPO of a Chinese bank. It was scheduled for February 2002, just under five months away, and it was meant to serve as the model for Premier Zhu Rongji's plans to restructure the shaky banking sector. Zhou was the brains behind the financial reforms, and I was eager to discuss them with him.

I called Julie, who connected me to John Rogers, Goldman's chief of staff, and I wasn't on the line long before any thought of those meetings and deals went right out of my head.

"Hank," he said. "A plane's flown into the World Trade Center."

Calm and precise as ever, John said he didn't know whether it was an accident or something worse. But while I was on the line with him, I heard a loud shout in the background that I later learned had come from Goldman employees on the 22nd floor of our 85 Broad Street headquarters—a few blocks south of the World Trade Center—who were watching from our windows as a second plane crashed into the other tower. John had spent more than a decade in government service before joining Goldman in 1994. He said, "There's no way it's an accident now."

I signaled to Mike. "Tell the pilots to turn the plane around. We've got to go back. Right away."

The plane swung into a long curve and started flying east, but after a while it reversed course again. I asked immediately what was going on, only to be told that U.S. air space had been closed except to military aircraft. We understood just how serious matters had become. We had no choice but to proceed to Hong Kong.

The next few hours were interminable. We checked on our families— all safe—and every few minutes I called for updates, and, of course, the news kept getting worse. We learned about the collapse of the Towers, the attack on the Pentagon, the plane going down north of Shanksville, Pennsylvania, the mounting toll of death and destruction. Fortunately, we knew of no one at Goldman who had been hurt, although sadly, we would learn, a number of our staffers had lost family members. It was surreal: floating aloft in the filtered, humming quiet of a small private jet, just the pilots, Mike Evans, and I, full of questions, unable to get answers, unable seemingly to do anything useful, calling the office repeatedly with just one more thing we'd forgotten to ask about, all the while racing away from the very place I wanted to get back to as soon as I could.

We landed in Hong Kong at 7:00 a.m., having decided to go straight to our meetings. I wanted to show resolve and determination. And I wanted to lead by example. I didn't want anyone to think we could be stopped by these attacks. In the car on the way in, I started drafting a voice mail to send throughout the firm to reassure our 23,000 employees worldwide. I knew they would be worried about family, friends, and colleagues from Goldman and other firms in New York.

My first meeting was a breakfast, at the upscale restaurant Felix on the top of Hong Kong's Peninsula Hotel, with Gao Yan, the CEO of the State Power Corporation and a protégé of former premier Li Peng's. I could not believe how indifferent he seemed to the news of the tragedy in the United States. When I mentioned the attack, trembling with shock and sorrow, he didn't say a word. I mean not one word. He seemed far more interested in having the restaurant play a favorite song repeatedly on its sound system as he ate a huge breakfast. I excused myself a couple of times to get updates from John Rogers, who was still in the office, where he would spend every night until my return. I couldn't wait for the meeting to end and free me from the presence of that self-absorbed, arrogant man. As it happened, barely a year later, Gao fled China in the wake of a $1 billion corruption scandal. He's been a fugitive ever since.

Fortunately, Gao's attitude was markedly different from that of the other leaders and executives I met or who called me expressing their condolences, their concerns for the U.S., our people, the markets. His rudeness was unlike anything I had ever encountered, before or since, from a senior official in China.

Mike and I rushed back to our Hong Kong office. Though I was relieved that no one at Goldman had died, I was concerned that our people were frightened and emotionally devastated by the horrific events of the day. Many were worried sick over friends and relatives who worked in New York. I made it clear that Goldman placed the highest priority on their personal safety, and I did my best to encourage everyone to look ahead and focus their energy in positive ways, contacting family and comforting friends. Mike and I had lunch with Antony Leung, the financial secretary of Hong Kong, then met with K. S. Li and C. H. Tung, who was chief executive of the Hong Kong Special Administrative Region. All had been watching the events on television, and they were shocked and saddened— and perhaps a little frightened, just as we were. The world was changing before our eyes, and no one could quite imagine what might come next.

I shelved my plans for Beijing and worked with John Rogers and my office to get us home fast. Meantime, I sent out a very personal voice mail to all of Goldman's employees assuring them that I was returning in a few hours and that "we are going to go forward as a team and a firm that is strong... [and] a force for stability in a time of crisis."

We were among the first overseas travelers allowed to fly back, because I ran a major investment bank and it was considered a matter of vital national importance to restart the markets, closed since the attacks. Mike Evans and I jumped on a NetJets plane in Hong Kong on Friday, September 14. When we stopped in Osaka to refuel, I recorded another voice mail in which I urged everyone to come back to lower Manhattan for work, saying simply, "We are returning to normal business operations."

I remember vividly, as we flew over Alaska, and then across America, being accompanied by an F-16 fighter jet on each wing. We landed in White Plains, New York, and were met by Alex Noreddin, my driver, who asked if I wanted to go home to my apartment on the Upper West Side of Manhattan.

"No," I said. "Straight to the office."

It was a dripping, overcast day, and we sped through empty roads to the city and down the FDR Drive. When we cleared the barricades at Canal Street and entered the frozen zone near Ground Zero, I was shocked by what I saw, even though I had been trying to prepare myself: debris was everywhere, a storm of ash, the streets empty except for emergency and police vehicles, National Guardsmen, and the awful stench of burning.

The next few days were extraordinary. The U.S. bond market had reopened Thursday, and the bulk of our employees had returned to our offices, joining operations and technology teams that had been working day and night. But we had to go to great lengths to get people in. A Goldman Sachs crisis management team had organized ferries from New Jersey, buses with police escorts to pass through security cordons, and fuel trucks to supply our backup generators. We had another team working around the clock with the New York Stock Exchange to be ready for Monday, when the NYSE would open again for business. I was on the floor of the exchange with the heads of other Wall Street firms for the bell ringing, then literally ran back to be on our trading floor when we executed a big trade of Walt Disney Company shares.

It was, as I had anticipated, an ugly day for the markets, as investors' pent-up fears exploded into a selling rout that saw the Dow Jones Industrial Average plunge by more than 7 percent, or 684.81 points—still the third-largest point drop in history. As rattling as it was, I was not overly concerned.

I was confident in America and the resilience of our economy and financial system. I knew we would bounce back. I was relieved to see that the markets were functioning smoothly and that our people were coping with the shock and sorrow of those awful days. I was so proud of our team at Goldman, and frankly of all our colleagues at other Wall Street firms who were working so hard under unbelievably difficult conditions. I saw that no matter how hard we competed with one another, we were united by things even more fundamental and important: love of country, surely, but also a powerful, pervasive sense of shared humanity that made us all determined to prove that terrorists would not defeat us or weaken our resolve.

That day I worked the phones hard, calling Goldman partners and clients around the world. I ended with calls the next morning to Zhou Xiaochuan and to Wang Qishan, who had moved up from Guangdong to be director of the State Council General Office of Economic Reform, the nerve center of the government's far-reaching economic changes. I wanted them to hear straight from me that we in the U.S. and at Goldman were undaunted. They and Premier Zhu Rongji and all of China could rest assured: we weren't going to miss a beat. Their plans for reform would stay on track—at least as far as Goldman Sachs was concerned.

In Mao's China there hadn't been much need for commercial banks. The Ministry of Finance funneled money to state-owned enterprises, which handed profits back to the ministry in a stultifying, closed loop. Urban workers belonged to SOEs, which provided their basic needs directly. In the countryside farmers eked out a subsistence living and had little or no money. Household savings, at just 6 percent of GDP, were low for a developing country. Today they are half of GDP. (U.S. household savings, by contrast, account for 5 percent of GDP.)

One institution dominated the financial arena: the enormous, all-purpose People's Bank of China (PBOC). It acted both as central bank—managing the money supply, setting interest rates, and overseeing the country's foreign exchange holdings—and as a commercial bank, making nearly all the loans in China and holding four-fifths of all deposits. A few other financial institutions existed, vestiges of the pre-Communist economy that had been folded into the Ministry of Finance and the PBOC after 1949. Bank of China, founded in 1912—and until 1928 the central bank of the Nanjing Provisional Government and the Northern Warlords' Government—had become a bureau of the PBOC concerned with foreign exchange transactions. The Agricultural Bank of China (ABC), formed in 1951 to finance rural projects, spent most of the next three decades as part of the PBOC. The Ministry of Finance created the People's Construction Bank of China in 1954 to disburse funds for infrastructure and construction projects.

To switch from a command and control economy to one that is more market oriented requires commercial banks and, eventually, capital markets. Banks come first. They play a crucial role in allocating capital efficiently. They make loans to businesses and individuals, help depositors safeguard and grow their savings, and provide a host of day-to-day transactions—from letters of credit and trade finance to lockbox services and funds transfer—that most people don't think much about but that grease the wheels of commerce.

With the start of Reform and Opening Up in 1978, China's leaders set out to build a set of banks that would compete to provide a wider range of needed services. Bank of China and Agricultural Bank were separated from the PBOC and became stand-alone commercial banks operating directly under the State Council. In October 1979, the People's Construction Bank was spun out of the Ministry of Finance (it would later be renamed China Construction Bank). In 1984 the State Council put through a series of reforms to make the PBOC act more like a traditional central bank. Its commercial activities were shifted to the newly created Industrial and Commercial Bank of China (ICBC), which immediately became China's biggest bank, with more than 20,000 branches and offices and nearly half of all bank lending.

The idea was that the newly minted Big Four commercial banks—ABC, Bank of China, ICBC, and People's Construction Bank—would provide financing for the SOEs as they grew out of the state economic plan. The banks would gradually exert greater discipline on the loans they made and the companies that borrowed from them. The approach proved to be flawed. The banks were created but the discipline was not. The 1984 financial reforms decentralized decision making, giving considerable discretion to local branch managers with scant training and no experience in operating profit-making enterprises. These executives were, moreover, under the thumb of local government and Party leaders, who were hell-bent on financing growth at all costs: their political futures—and personal well-being—depended on it.

The Big Four banks grew quickly, scooping up deposits from households made increasingly prosperous by burgeoning entrepreneurial activity and lending these funds to SOEs. This propelled breakneck growth and helped fuel the inflationary spiral that contributed to the unrest underlying the Tiananmen Square protests of 1989. Eventually, the feverish expansion would lead to mountains of bad loans.

Along the way, to gradually increase competition, a dozen joint-stock banks of modest size were created or reconstituted from prerevolutionary institutions like the Shanghai-based Bank of Communications, and in 1995 the State Council authorized another new class of banks, so-called city commercial banks that were owned by municipal governments. But the power of the banking system remained concentrated in China's Big Four.

As he tackled inflation and introduced fiscal and tax initiatives, Zhu Rongji moved to reshape the banking system, aiming, among other things, to halt local government intervention in bank-lending decisions and to reform the central bank, whose departments had overlapping and conflicting responsibilities. Too frequently, provincial branches of the decentralized PBOC came under pressure to cover the losses at local branches of the Big Four banks. (The government would go on to introduce measures that shifted authority from local bank branches back to headquarters in Beijing, while a new central bank law revamped and strengthened the PBOC. Beijing would replace the 31 provincial PBOC offices with nine regional ones, whose presidents would be appointed by the central bank instead of local authorities.)

The government also created three new banks—the State Development Bank of China, the Export and Import Bank of China, and the Agricultural Development Bank of China. They were meant to finance government projects: roads, bridges, power plants, and the like. Such "policy" lending typically had higher default rates and had previously accounted for a third or more of the loans made by ICBC, the People's Construction Bank of China, Bank of China, and ABC, which were now directed to focus strictly on making commercial loans.

Some of these well-intentioned moves fell flat. The new policy banks soon wanted to make commercial loans of their own, while the big commercial banks continued to have to contend with political pressure to prop up faltering industries, which led inevitably to poor credit decisions. The vast majority of their loans went to struggling state-owned enterprises, which increasingly used the money to pay operating expenses, while China's dynamic but fledgling private enterprises went begging for credit.

Moreover, while the reforms were meant to improve future credit decisions, they did not address the problems already festering on the banks' books, and the bill for these was rapidly coming due. Borrowing freely while hemorrhaging money, the SOEs had run up enormous debts, crippling the banks and threatening to derail economic growth and undermine China's standing in world markets. By 1997 the government calculated that a staggering 25 percent of the Big Four's bank loans were nonperforming. Later it would turn out that even this figure was a gross understatement: when the government began using stricter methods of loan classification, the proportion of bad debts rose to closer to 50 percent of loans.

The Asian financial crisis laid bare the problem. Countries in the region fell victim to a nasty mix of weakening exports and plunging currencies that accompanied the collapse of speculative property lending, widespread bank failures, and the specter of panicky global investors withdrawing their money. The shakiness of China's banks led many to question whether the country would stumble, too. China was hit by the recessionary fallout of the crisis, and GDP and export growth slipped sharply, but China's leaders vowed to stand strong. Zhu Rongji refused to devalue the renminbi, which would have made China's exports more competitive but would have led to beggar-thy-neighbor devaluations throughout the region. Instead, he embarked on a vast program of infrastructure spending to stimulate the economy and moved to revamp the banking system.

In 1998 the government injected 270 billion yuan (roughly $32.5 billion), or more than 3 percent of GDP, into the Big Four banks to bring their capital levels up to the international minimum standard of 8 percent of assets. But bad loans still threatened the system, and the problem was too big for a simple fiscal solution. The total value of nonperforming loans (NPLs) far exceeded the government's annual revenues as well as the country's foreign reserves of $145 billion.

Goldman bankers, including Jerry Corrigan—a former president of the Federal Reserve Bank of New York, who served as co-chair of both our risk committee and our global compliance and controls committee—had begun conferring with the government on various solutions. They flew regularly to Beijing to share their experience and advice with government and banking leaders like Zhou Xiaochuan, who had been tasked by Zhu Rongji with taking the lead in devising a pilot for bank restructuring. The premier wanted a systematic plan that would address nonperforming loans, capital issues, and corporate governance across the industry. With Goldman's help, the government studied various international models—including bad-loan workouts in Sweden, bank restructurings in Central and Eastern Europe, and the efforts of the Resolution Trust Corporation to deal with the U.S.'s savings and loan crisis in the 1980s.

Zhou designed a plan to move bad loans off China Construction Bank's balance sheet and into a specially created asset management company that would try to recover what it could by selling assets, using debt-equity swaps, reorganizing the operations of defaulted borrowers, and employing other loan workout practices. In October 1999 the three other big banks set up their own asset management companies. By the end of 2000 the four AMCs had acquired more than a fifth of the loan portfolios of the big banks, or $170 billion, a whopping 15.5 percent of China's 1999 GDP. This move shrank the nonperforming loans on the banks' balance sheets, though it didn't eliminate the problem.

Dealing with these staggering sums required some fancy financial engineering. To pay for the $32.5 billion recapitalization in 1998, the government resorted to the expedient of having the central bank lower the reserve requirements of the big banks, freeing up funds the banks could use to buy bonds issued by the Ministry of Finance. The Ministry of Finance then injected the funds back into the banks as capital. A similar circularity was used to deal with the nonperforming-loan problem. The asset management companies were capitalized with equity from the Ministry of Finance. They paid for their purchase of the bad loans by borrowing from the central bank and issuing low-coupon bonds that the banks themselves purchased.

The plan, which ultimately succeeded, was inspired if flawed. The asset management companies acquired the bad loans at face value but hadn't a prayer of recovering anything on that order. Most of the loans were dreadful, and loan recovery rates would run closer to 20 percent, foretelling massive losses for the AMCs. The AMCs were empowered to swap debt for equity and take stakes in debtors, but they lacked the clout to force operating changes at the politically connected SOEs. Crucially, however, the asset management companies were not meant to wind down for ten years, and that allowed the Chinese to buy time, putting off any financial reckoning until they were better able to afford it.

The architect of the banking sector restructuring, Zhou Xiaochuan, had been on the front lines of reform for two decades and would go on to become, in 2002, the head of China's central bank, where he still serves today. I first got to know Zhou in early 1998, soon after he had taken the reins at China Construction Bank. We had a lively discussion inspired by the IPO of PetroChina, which we were vying to lead-manage alongside China International Capital, CCB's investment banking joint venture with Morgan Stanley. Tall and graceful, Zhou is a man of many talents: fluent in English, he learned to play a crack game of tennis in the 1980s, and he nurtures an abiding love of Western classical music, opera, and Broadway musicals (at one point, he compiled a guide to Western musicals with the help of graduate students).

A penetrating thinker, Zhou was also exceptionally well connected, always a huge plus in China. His father, a powerful official in the postrevolution First Ministry of Machine Building, had been an early mentor of Jiang Zemin's, when the future Communist Party leader was a young official at the same ministry. Both of Zhou's parents studied in the Soviet Union in the 1950s. They were central planners—his mother worked as an official in the Ministry of Chemicals—who developed a deep skepticism of the ability of central planners to effectively manage such a sprawling economy. Zhou's graduate research would dissect, with mathematical models, the practical challenges of the command and control economy, analyzing what kind of information could be collected and correctly reported to the State Planning Commission, comparing resource allocation in planned and market economies, and examining incentive structures—or lack thereof—in top-down planned economies.

Zhou, his parents, and three siblings were scattered across China during the Cultural Revolution—all in different remote locations. He spent four years as a farm laborer in Heilongjiang Province in Manchuria, where the brutal winters last from October to May. Zhou found time to read and cultivate his love of music, listening to a 5-foot-tall stack of records that he managed to collect. As he told me once: "During the Cultural Revolution they tried to stop people from listening to classical music, but in the countryside, no one cared!" Most important, Zhou used those frigid sent-down years for introspection, to examine what was right and wrong in his country, and how people's lives could be improved.

Beijing in the early 1980s was a fervid laboratory of experimentation, and Zhou, working toward his Ph.D. in automation and system engineering at Tsinghua University, emerged as one of a group of energetic young reformers, alongside his contemporary Wang Qishan. While Wang focused on rural reform, Zhou delved into pricing, trade, and foreign exchange issues, working with Zhu Rongji, then vice minister of the State Economic Commission, on plans for comprehensive reforms in these areas. After earning his Ph.D. Zhou began working in 1986 as deputy director of the Institute of Chinese Economic Reform Research and became a commissioner of the State Commission for Restructuring the Economy later that year. Along with Wang Qishan, Zhou was involved with the group of scholars and returnees from overseas who tried to set up a stock exchange in Beijing in 1988.

In 1991 Zhou Xiaochuan became vice president at the Bank of China, and his hand became increasingly evident in banking sector reforms after Zhu Rongji took direct control of the central bank in 1993. He co-authored a paper recommending the separation of commercial and policy-based lending before taking charge of China's foreign exchange regulator, the State Administration of Foreign Exchange (SAFE), in 1995 and joining the

People's Bank of China as deputy governor the following year. The PBOC was in the process of being revamped into a more tightly managed operation modeled after the U.S. Federal Reserve System.

In 1998, after Zhu Rongji had dispatched Wang Qishan to clean up the financial mess in Guangdong, Zhou Xiaochuan took over China Construction Bank. The move positioned Zhou to implement the reforms he had helped design, since Construction Bank's investment banking arm China International Capital Corporation would act as the lead or co–lead manager on China's major restructurings and IPOs in the late 1990s. Relations with Morgan Stanley were tidied up, and the premier's son, Levin Zhu, was appointed to the management committee of CICC.

Zhou continued to work on broader reform themes. In 1999, at Zhu Rongji's behest, Zhou wrote a paper outlining a long-term plan for comprehensive bank reform detailing how the banks should restructure—improving their management and lending practices by upgrading their accounting, technology, and transparency—and then incorporate as stockholding companies and prepare for IPOs. To sell their shares successfully, the banks would need to assure prospective investors that legacy loan problems had been resolved and mechanisms had been put in place to prevent any reoccurrence.

Zhou originally suggested reducing government ownership to 30 percent, enough to maintain control while raising plenty of capital, but the premier told him that proposal would never get past other senior leaders. Instead, the paper called for government to maintain a majority share of the banks. At Zhu Rongji's insistence, Zhou published the paper in the *People's Daily* in 2000, the same year he would move to head up the China Securities Regulatory Commission (CSRC).

Bank of China (Hong Kong) was chosen to be the guinea pig for Zhu Rongji's plan. The bank, it was thought, would be in better shape and better run than those on the mainland. After all, it had competed for decades with major international institutions like HSBC Holdings and Standard Chartered in the sophisticated Hong Kong market, where it operated under the supervision of the Hong Kong Monetary Authority, a stricter and more highly regarded regulator than the PBOC at the time. These factors would make Bank of China (Hong Kong) the bank with the greatest attractiveness to international investors and the least baggage as a Communist institution.

Concluding that BOC(HK) was in better shape than its mainland brethren wasn't saying much. To begin with, it was not a single institution, but rather a motley collection of a dozen or so banks that included the 84-year-old Hong Kong branch of Bank of China itself, as well as the Hong Kong branches of seven mainland banks that the People's Republic of China government had nationalized after coming to power, plus two additional banks the PRC government had established in Hong Kong. In the 1980s BOC had tried to rope them together as part of a newly formed Bank of China Hong Kong Group, but apart from a common ATM network and some shared software, the effort was largely window dressing. Though jointly headquartered in the bank's stunning I. M. Pei–designed tower by the Hong Kong waterfront, the banks were run independently, with their own brands, back offices, and information technology systems. Their books were not consolidated. There was no chief financial officer or chief risk officer for the group. All in all, this was an unusual set of deficiencies in a modern bank.

Not surprisingly, group results were underwhelming. In 2001 it had earned $355 million pro forma, a meager return on assets of $98 billion. Problem loans were modest compared with mainland banks but still substantial by Hong Kong standards. At the end of 2000, nonperforming loans stood at 10.19 percent, compared with 3.3 percent for a local competitor, the Hang Seng Bank.

For most of the 1990s Bank of China had been run by Wang Xuebing, whom everyone called HP after the Cantonese pronunciation of his given name. A graduate of the Beijing Institute of Foreign Trade, he had worked for Bank of China in London and New York, where he took over U.S. operations in 1988 after a stint as a trader. He returned to Beijing in 1993 to head the bank. I'd first met with him in the winter of 1996. He was a man of medium height who wore prominent dark glasses, and with his very big smile, boisterous personality, and command of English, he was popular with foreign bankers. He had recently sought advice from our old friend Fang Fenglei at CICC, who in turn enlisted our help.

In October 1999 Fang arranged to meet one Saturday at the Kunlun Hotel in Beijing with Ziwang Xu, our lead China banker, and Tracy Wolstencroft, who ran our Asia financial institutions practice and was co-head of Japanese banking. On arriving, they were surprised to be directed to the hotel's steam room, where Fang awaited them, draped in a white towel with a cold orange washrag on his head. They were the only guests in the room; two associates of Fang's guarded the entrance. He'd chosen the rendezvous so that he could describe, with utmost confidentiality, a specific plan for bank reform. Focusing on Bank of China, Fang sketched a "one bank, two systems" strategy that drew on Deng Xiaoping's "one country, two systems" formula for reincorporating Hong Kong. He outlined a plan to create two separate legal entities (one for mainland China and one for the international assets) that would be incorporated under a parent holding company that would straddle both.

Tracy worked through that Christmas with Fang hammering out a plan for restructuring Bank of China (Hong Kong), and in January, over lunch, Wang Xuebing reviewed the details with me and the Goldman team. The approach—to clean up bad loans and broaden ownership from the state to multiple shareholders, then raise capital through a public offering—would morph over time, but it became the basis for the Bank of China (Hong Kong) offering and the blueprint for future IPOs as each of the four major state-owned banks was restructured.

HP wouldn't be around to see the plan through, however. Not long after our lunch, in one of the frequent, mystifying leadership round-robins in the Chinese hierarchy, he was transferred to China Construction Bank, replacing Zhou Xiaochuan, who moved to the CSRC. HP was succeeded by Liu Mingkang, the chairman of China Everbright (Group) Company, a Hong Kong red-chip conglomerate, who had previously served as deputy governor of the People's Bank of China.

Zhu Rongji knew the key to success was getting the right person in the right job. We concluded that the Chinese had foreseen that Liu Mingkang would be the right person to drive the Bank of China IPO forward and wanted him to work with Goldman Sachs, following our success on other big deals.

By May we had signed a cooperation memorandum, and Liu Mingkang, whom I had taken to calling by his Western nickname, LMK, pronounced himself impressed with our teamwork and "knowledge, skills, and experiences." It had helped that our work in the Guangdong Enterprises restructuring in 1998 and 1999 had built credibility with members of Liu's management team; their bank had been significantly exposed to Guangdong Enterprises, and they had appreciated our transparent workout process. We also received high grades for taking heat in the market—and politically—during the PetroChina IPO.

In October 2000 I met with LMK, who confirmed that the State Council had settled on the two-stage strategy to take Bank of China (Hong Kong) public first, followed in time by the mainland bank. John Thornton signed a technology transfer agreement with LMK under which Goldman would help train BOC personnel in best practices. By the time John and our bank team made our formal pitch for the IPO on January 2, 2001, the deal was ours to lose. We would be lead underwriters with Switzerland's UBS and Bank of China's investment banking arm.

The bank faced a huge task in restructuring Bank of China (Hong Kong), especially on the timetable Zhu Rongji had initially set: to list by the fourth quarter of 2001. For all the preliminary work we had done, we were in some ways starting from scratch—at least when it came to the bank leadership. Tracy Wolstencroft attended the first board meeting after the mandate was awarded to walk the directors through what they should expect during the restructuring process. One asked what multiple of book value we thought the bank should be priced at. A banker from one of the other underwriters said, flatly, "2.8 times book." That was a high, even mischievous, valuation, given that the best banks in the world were then trading between two and three times book value—which measures the value of a company's assets minus liabilities and intangible assets. Liu Mingkang asked Tracy his opinion.

"We have no idea," Tracy answered forthrightly. "For the next six months, the exercise is precisely to find out what the book value is. Only then can we tell you what's the right multiple."

To find out what the book value was meant we would have to dig through the nonperforming loans and see how much they impaired capital and whether the government was willing to take over the bad loans. The reorganization of the bank, already under way, would take another year and a half to wrap up. During that time we would play a combination role of policy adviser, management consultant, and investment banker, pushing hard to accelerate changes. I made it clear at an April 2001 meeting with LMK that a successful IPO depended on a thorough restructuring.

This was not just about selling shares. It was about building a good bank. A successful IPO would signal to the world that China's banks had arrived on the global financial stage. But the IPO would fly only if the new shareholders owned a piece of a successful bank, and that would be possible only if BOC was restructured. LMK assured me that he understood, and wanted and needed, the same outcome I did—a good bank. The 2001 restructuring involved a total of 15 subsidiaries with assets of $105 billion that made Bank of China (Hong Kong) the second-biggest bank in Hong Kong after HSBC. It cut several hundred workers, put most of the banks under one brand name, consolidated their books, management, and IT, and established uniform lending criteria. BOC became the first Chinese bank to implement a more stringent loan classification system. The banks were officially merged in October 2001. By then, however, the world had been shaken to its core by the events of September 11, 2001.

The attacks disrupted markets worldwide, and the Chinese government continued to dawdle in finalizing the size of its nonperforming-loan position and in determining how much of the losses from those loans it was prepared to absorb. This caused the IPO date to be pushed back. When we'd won the mandate, the offering had been scheduled for year-end 2001. That had become February 2002, and then even later. Keenly aware of the time pressure, I had stressed to LMK at a December meeting in Beijing that his team had to speed up its decision making if it wanted to have a successful offering in the first half of 2002.

A new set of problems emerged that threatened to delay the offering even further—and turned our relations with the bank testy. The immediate issue was an eruption of bad publicity related to allegations of fraud and corruption at the bank. Liu Mingkang's predecessor, Wang Xuebing, had been deposed in January as chairman of the rival China Construction

Bank, after barely a year in charge. The reason: alleged illicit activity that had taken place at Bank of China's New York and Los Angeles branches when he had been in charge of those activities at the bank. Separately, press outlets had revealed that a group of Bank of China executives had pilfered almost half a billion dollars through just one branch in Guangdong Province over a nine-year period ending in 2001. (Wang would subsequently be expelled from the Communist Party, tried, and sentenced to 12 years imprisonment for taking bribes.)

Under any circumstances, this was bad news. On the eve of an IPO, it spelled a potential disaster. Bad timing compounded matters. In December 2001 Enron had imploded in the then biggest-ever U.S. bankruptcy amid revelations of accounting fraud. The stunning collapse of the U.S. energy conglomerate dominated headlines for weeks, triggering intensified scrutiny of company accounting practices and heightened concern over the adequacy of market oversight. (These would lead to the July 2002 passage of the Sarbanes-Oxley Act, which put in place much stricter standards for financial governance in U.S. markets.) Enron captured the interest of investors, corporate executives, and government leaders the world over. Not long after the Enron news broke, I'd met with Vice Premier Wen Jiabao, who was expected to take over the reins of the economy from Zhu Rongji. He quizzed me extensively about the company, how such a collapse could have happened, and what it meant for the U.S. and global economies.

The fallout in the U.S. capital markets had reached LMK and his colleagues. We had been planning for listings in New York and in Hong Kong. Now the Chinese wanted to skip the New York Stock Exchange and issue shares only in Hong Kong. They were concerned that increased market vigilance and demands for wider disclosure in the States would delay their offering, especially now that the bank's dirty laundry had been aired. Our equity markets team disagreed. Its members believed that an NYSE listing would help generate demand and that the Big Board seal of approval would lay the groundwork for the parent company, and other Chinese banks, to come to market.

The Chinese were adamant and became increasingly frustrated with our position. They wanted their first bank deal to succeed, and they were eager to press ahead as quickly as possible. Zhu Rongji wanted bank reform well under way before he left office the following year, and he wanted to ensure that China's banks were ready when the financial sector was scheduled to be opened fully to foreign competition in 2006 in keeping with the newly struck WTO accession agreement.

I was hoping to iron out our differences with LMK. Although I had known him for only a couple of years, I considered him a friend and enjoyed working with him on the Tsinghua SEM international advisory board. He maintained close relations with a number of Goldman bankers and had been very supportive of our efforts. He seemed to appreciate the way our team pushed his to produce results. He saw the process as a way to train his people.

LMK himself fascinated me. I could see in him the grit and ingenuity so many of the Chinese leaders of his generation had used to survive the Cultural Revolution and then thrive in its aftermath. He was a smart, determined man of high character who knew banking well but was always eager to learn more. He had grown up in Shanghai, and after graduating from high school in 1965, had been sent down to do manual labor on a farm in Jiangsu Province, where he taught himself flawless English in secret, studying tattered BBC textbooks and on long winter evenings listening clandestinely to Voice of America's Special English program. In 1979, at 29, he was one of just two people in Jiangsu Province, population nearly 57 million, to pass a civil service exam aimed at identifying sent-down youths who could go straight to work without a college degree. By 1984 he was working at Bank of China's branch in London, where he got an eyeful of Margaret Thatcher's privatization efforts. Returning to China, he was tapped in 1993 as vice governor of Fujian Province. He subsequently took increasingly powerful jobs at the China Development Bank, the People's Bank of China, and China Everbright Group, which he ran for a year before joining Bank of China.

I was scheduled to meet with LMK in February 2002 for breakfast at Beijing's Grand Hotel, which was close to where I was staying. Though I appreciated the pressure that LMK must have been under, I wasn't looking forward to seeing him. LMK was always courteous and considerate, but it was clear we were stretching him to the limit by insisting on our position.

In the end, he was a loyal Party member, and a very efficient bureaucrat, who needed to get this deal done without delay for the very demanding head of his government.

I got into the car with Tracy Wolstencroft for the short ride. Tracy, a tall Massachusetts native who had superb people skills, summed it up for me: come hell or high water, Liu Mingkang was going to complete this IPO. We'd have to be flexible or risk getting fired.

I had time to think things over, because what should have been a 15-minute drive took twice as long in the heavy Beijing traffic. And the more I thought, the more I saw things very clearly, and simply. Essentially, we were saying, "This is how we have done things before; it worked then, so we should do it the same way again." I wondered if we were just being obstinate or, as Mike Evans would say later, "bloody-minded." After all, we were turning blue in the face with our arguments, but LMK wasn't buying any of them. The imperative for him was timing. Yes, he wanted to get the deal done right, but he couldn't wait, and it was going to be easier to issue out of Hong Kong. Delay would affect not just Bank of China, but also the entire banking sector reform effort.

It dawned on me then that this was a classic case of not listening to what our client really needed. I turned to Tracy and said, "Tracy, you and I are just going to have to forget about the equity capital markets people. We're just going to say 'fine' to LMK, 'we can do the time schedule, and you don't have to list in the U.S.'"

I made the snap decision out of instinct—and good judgment. I had a ton of faith in Mike Evans and his people in capital markets. I knew somehow they'd get the deal done.

Now, I'm not naïve. We could have stood our ground and insisted on the New York listing, and I'm sure LMK would have been perfectly gentlemanly and understanding and then gone out and found another bank to replace us.

"I agree," Tracy said. "But won't New York think we've caved on a matter of principle?"

I told Tracy I'd stand on a principle all day if that meant opposing something that was immoral, illegal, bad for investors, or not right for the client. But that wasn't the case here. The judgment we had to make was this: Are the Chinese going to make this a successful deal? Is it basically a clean company? Are they honorable people?

My conclusion was yes to all.

Moreover, I reasoned, they couldn't afford to try to sell a problem bank to international investors.

When we got to the hotel and caught up with LMK, he told me he had been pleased to see me the previous night on TV. I had met with President Jiang Zemin the day before about creating national parks in Yunnan Province, and the nightly news shows had covered the meeting at some length. LMK had many interests aside from banking—he was a talented artist whose work decorated the cover one year of the China Banking Regulatory Commission (CBRC) annual report after he took that agency over—and he was deeply interested in the environment and clean energy. He said he had been touched by our conservation efforts.

"I am confident that with you in charge," he said, "Goldman Sachs is focused on China's best interests with both your minds and your hearts."

I told him we were also focused on the best interests of the Bank of China (Hong Kong).

Tracy may have been the only one in the room not surprised when I told LMK that we had changed our mind and decided to go with his plan. I explained that skipping the NYSE meant we would have to press for greater transparency and disclosure, particularly about the nonperforming loans, and LMK agreed. He was so delighted and relieved that he might have agreed to anything at that point. LMK had been working hand in glove with our bankers for two years and wanted to proceed with us. Switching bankers also might have delayed the deal.

In the end, the choice I made was practical and considered. I had to decide whether the bank was serious about dealing with its problems and had the management capability to do so. I concluded that the Chinese had more to lose than anyone if they failed to get these problems under control. Another blowup or scandal at Bank of China would set back all the other bank IPOs and bank reform, and the government wouldn't want to risk that. A New York Stock Exchange listing would have given them more time to make sure everything was in order, but I decided that if LMK and the government wanted to go ahead, then they must have had things under control. If I did not trust them on that score, an NYSE listing and another three to six months were not going to make a difference in any case.

I staked the firm's future in China on LMK's abilities and the government's sincerity. Neither one let me down.

The offering itself came to market five months later, in July 2002. Bank of China (Hong Kong) raised about $2.8 billion, slightly below some expectations, but Liu Mingkang and the Chinese leadership were thrilled with the results. It was the biggest Chinese IPO since Sinopec had raised $3.3 billion in October 2000, and the largest Hong Kong–only IPO ever. Most important, Bank of China was the first Chinese state-owned bank to sell shares outside of the mainland, and it helped turn around the negative views many international investors had held about the country's banks.

The offering would generate some $18 billion in global demand. Most of that was Hong Kong retail, whose strong buying made BOC(HK) the second most widely held company in Hong Kong behind the local Mass Transit Railway Corporation. It was not an easy sell, for a number of reasons. The markets, shaky since 9/11, continued to be soft and erratic. The bank had gotten the government to take an additional $1.5 billion in bad loans in June and place them in an off-balance-sheet workout vehicle. This brought the NPL ratio down to a still worrisomely high level of about 9 percent, which caused some institutional investors to shy from the deal. They have no doubt kicked themselves several times over since then: BOC(HK) shares have more than tripled in value.

The key to our success, as bankers in this new market, was a willingness to look beyond short-term problems and make a bet on China and its leadership. A number of corporate investors, such as K. S. Li's Cheung Kong and the Kwok family's Sung Hung Kai Properties, took that same bet and invested in the IPO. As with PetroChina and China Telecom, we also brought in a strategic investor, Standard Chartered, which purchased a 1 percent stake for about $50 million, with a 12-month lockup. It was important to Liu Mingkang that Bank of China (Hong Kong)'s share valuation be competitive with other Hong Kong banks, and the final pricing reflected a price-to-book ratio of more than 1.6, compared with Standard Chartered's price-to-book ratio at the time of 1.8. LMK was delighted, as were his colleagues.

More important, the process of bank restructuring and reform in China had begun.

CHAPTER TEN

The World's Biggest Mattress

The outbreak of severe acute respiratory syndrome (SARS), a virulent form of pneumonia, paralyzed travel to and from Asia for months in early 2003. China and Hong Kong were at the epicenter of the outbreak, and the initial efforts of China's Health minister to ignore or conceal the dangers—the government didn't report its first cases to the World Health Organization until February 2003—helped sow panic around the world. People were not only afraid to visit China, but some also were afraid to meet with anyone Chinese, almost anywhere.

I saw this fear firsthand. My wife, Wendy, had arranged for Rose Niu, who headed the Nature Conservancy program that was working to create national parks in Yunnan Province, to make a presentation in New York City to some of her Chinese friends, a number of whom hailed from prominent families and split their time between New York and Hong Kong or China. Wendy assured everyone that Rose was well and that Yunnan had not reported a single SARS case, but she was forced to make the presentation without her because none of the Chinese was prepared to get in the same room with Rose.

"How can we be sure Yunnan doesn't have a SARS problem?" one demanded.

Like every organization I knew, Goldman wisely restricted travel and took many other precautions, and I was forced to cancel several planned trips. But I was scheduled to be in Japan for business in early June, and one of my colleagues, Deborah Lehr, suggested that I continue on to China. The crisis appeared to be abating, though very few people were traveling there because of lingering fears. Deborah had worked for the U.S. Trade

Representative's office during the WTO negotiations with China, as well as for the National Security Council, and was advising me on what proved to be a successful effort to get a domestic securities license. She understood China exceptionally well and had great instincts, so whenever she made a suggestion, I paid heed.

We checked with Wang Qishan, who had been installed as acting mayor of Beijing to fix the SARS problem in April. He sent word back that it was safe to travel. Although many at Goldman Sachs advised me not to visit, others, like Fred Hu in our Hong Kong office, urged me to come. Besides, if Wang Qishan said it was okay, that was good enough for me. I flew in from Tokyo on a nearly empty United Airlines flight on the night of June 3. I've been told I was the first Western CEO to come to China post-SARS. I was certainly treated like I was. I was put up in sumptuous accommodations in the Diaoyutai State Guesthouse complex, in a suite with a bathtub that might have been a small swimming pool. My visit led the evening TV shows and was splashed across the front pages of the newspapers the next morning. The publicity was a great boost for China, which was seen as open for business again, and for Wang Qishan, who had addressed the crisis head-on.

Glad as I was to help China get back on the right foot, I hadn't gone just to show the world the country was safe. Goldman had postponed lots of business for months, and I packed in a set of meetings on what could only be a one-day stopover. The morning of June 4, 2003, began over breakfast at the Guesthouse with Jiang Jianqing, then president of ICBC, China's biggest bank. Although John Thornton and Fred Hu had been working with him for some time, it was the first time I'd met Jiang, who was confident and energetic and determined to transform his gigantic institution. We were interested in doing more with ICBC and the other banks. Indeed, after meeting with Jiang I rushed off to see the new head of Bank of China, Xiao Gang, a charming 44-year-old rising star of Chinese finance. Over lunch we discussed the restructuring strategy and outlook for the bank.

Then it was off to visit Wang Qishan at the mayor's office in a grand compound that had housed the Japanese mission in the old Legation Quarter just east of Tiananmen Square. Following his stint in Guangdong,

Wang Qishan had spent two years in Beijing at an economic reform office before being dispatched to Hainan as Party secretary. He hadn't been there long before he was called back to Beijing to deal with the SARS debacle. After the virus had emerged in Guangdong Province in November 2002, the Chinese government had hidden its problems and even patients while hundreds died and thousands more were infected in China, as well as in Southeast Asia and Canada. China had finally stopped the cover-up in April, firing the Health minister and Beijing mayor and bringing in Wang Qishan. His straightforward, candid response saved the day: he shut schools, quarantined thousands of people, released accurate case numbers, and designated new SARS-only hospitals—one of which was built in just eight days. By June the crisis was finally under control; it had infected more than 8,000 people worldwide, killing nearly 11 percent of them.

The Chinese government and Wang Qishan had put strict measures in place to control SARS. Body temperature sensors were everywhere—at airports, rail stations, and hotels. Everyone had to have their temperature taken before entering any government offices. The day got hotter, and I worried as we raced from office to office that I'd trigger the sensors and be banned from a meeting. I turned out to be just fine, but not my colleague Richard Gnodde. A tall, broad-shouldered South African who ran our Asia business out of Hong Kong, Richard worked up such a sweat hurrying across the baking grounds at Zhongnanhai that he three times triggered the alarm set up outside the room where we were to meet Executive Vice Premier Huang Ju. Wang Qishan had just detailed the strict quarantine regimen he had put in place for suspected SARS patients, and we had great fun teasing Richard that he'd be locked up for days. Finally, the Chinese brought out an oral thermometer to determine that Richard didn't have a fever and allowed him through.

I didn't know it at the time, but this would in some ways become my most important trip to China while at Goldman. For years afterward, Chinese friends referred fondly to my visit, while others I met for the first time often said I was well known to them thanks to the publicity it had generated. To my delight, as they saw Goldman awarded plum assignments, jealous competitors often commented on my lucky timing in going there when I did. In truth, I had long before learned the importance of a gesture to the

Chinese, and I was rewarded with a deep and enduring sense of personal satisfaction and pride.

I was happy to have had the chance to finally get back into China and to be received so well. But the flight home was bittersweet. I caught a charter out of Beijing and was joined in Seoul by John Thornton for the return trip. It was John's last month at the firm. He had decided to leave Goldman after more than 20 years. This did not come as a surprise to me, because John and I had been discussing his career goals for some time.

Typical of John, he had chosen to do something completely out of the box: he was joining Tsinghua University, the first non-Chinese to be named a full professor there since 1949. He would commute between Beijing and the United States, where he would serve as chairman of the board of trustees of the Brookings Institution, the famed Washington, D.C., think tank, as well as, later, chairman of Barrick Gold Corporation. John and I had worked closely for years, and I would miss his advice and my daily exchanges with him. John was an extraordinary strategic thinker, an idea generator of the first order, and a terrific adviser to our clients—a rare combination of visionary and rainmaker. He possessed a loathing of bureaucracy that had made him a natural ally of many of China's reformers as he helped design and build our China business in the late 1990s, before becoming co-president and co–chief operating officer of Goldman prior to our own IPO in 1999. No one deserves more credit than John for establishing Goldman's franchise in China.

In the fall of 2004, I had another meeting with ICBC's Jiang Jianqing that would set the stage for Goldman's most extraordinary, and contentious, deal in China. It was a crucial time for China's big banks, which were restructuring in preparation for IPOs. Our involvement with ICBC would underscore a shift in the way Chinese and Western banks worked together. Early on, investment banks like Goldman had advised our Chinese counterparts; now we were looking to become financial partners as well. All of the Western banks sought a leading role in the big bank IPOs, but I can think of no banker who was more eager to win a mandate than Fred Hu. He was the Goldman banker closest to ICBC, and he arranged a lunch for us in early November that year with Jiang Jianqing at a restaurant that overlooked the beautiful Imperial Archives building just off Chang'an Avenue.

A brilliant economist turned exceptional investment banker, Fred understood the economy, the priorities of China's leaders, and the policy changes needed to achieve them better than just about anyone I knew. He was very well connected and quietly influential to boot. Gifted and driven, Fred typified the rising generation of ambitious, hyperfocused young leaders unleashed by Deng's reforms. Born in 1963 in a small village in Hunan Province in south central China, Fred was just three years old when the Cultural Revolution began. He endured hardships in the countryside, but his education was largely uninterrupted, despite the decade-long political turmoil. He joined millions in taking a competitive nationwide test for university admission in 1978, and at 15 he went off to the most prestigious, Tsinghua, where he would earn a master's in engineering science. Most of his classmates were much older and driven to make up for years lost laboring on farms and in factories. Inspired by Deng's program of change, Fred and his generation of university graduates—like fellow 1978 Tsinghua matriculant Lou Jiwei, who became a key adviser to Zhu Rongji in the 1990s and was named Finance minister in 2013—took up the banner of reform, determined to make a difference in China.

Fred subsequently earned an M.A. and a Ph.D. in economics from Harvard University then worked as a staff economist at the International Monetary Fund. Training central bank governors and finance ministers, he was on the front lines as the Fund pushed for market reforms in countries of the Eastern Bloc and the former Soviet Union. Fred returned to China on several IMF missions and helped to train Chinese officials who visited Washington. He turned down invitations to work for the Chinese government and instead joined Goldman Sachs as the firm's chief China economist in 1997. We soon saw the potential in Fred's unique blend of pragmatic knowledge of the economy and proven ability to win the trust of clients, so I made him co-head of China investment banking in 2003. His ability to get things done—he is a prodigious worker and a great networker, whose insightful thinking built strong relationships—was something to behold. Over the years I would increasingly rely on him for strategic advice.

Chinese officials also turned to him regularly for advice. As meetings with senior leaders from Zhu Rongji to Xi Jinping wound down and we were saying our good-byes, Fred could often be seen handing over a memorandum with economic reform proposals or fielding requests for his views on one topic or another. Among our corporate clients, I don't think anyone appreciated his talents more than the CEOs of China's state-owned banks.

Jiang brought to lunch several colleagues, including Dr. Pan Gongsheng, his right-hand man. Fred and I were joined by John Rogers, Mike Evans, and Chris Cole, our most senior financial institutions specialist and a superb banker who had become co-head of investment banking at Goldman in 2002. Before Jiang's party arrived, we had a few moments to strategize. ICBC was China's biggest bank and had the strongest domestic franchise, but Bank of China and China Construction Bank were slated to go to market first. We had the inside track at Bank of China after doing the IPO of its Hong Kong assets. Since it was highly unlikely that we could win all of these assignments, and getting one might complicate getting another, we debated how hard we should pitch for ICBC. I figured the best course was to trumpet our qualifications and make a strong play to lead the IPO. If Jiang decided he wanted us, we would have a high-class problem that we could sort out later.

We had a lively discussion at lunch, ranging from the health of the economy to whether Bank of China would go public before CCB, how much capital they would raise, what investors they might attract, and how bad each bank's nonperforming loans were. Jiang candidly acknowledged ICBC's mixed story: the bank was not making much money, capital levels remained low, and it continued to wrestle with its bad loans. But he also highlighted the strengths of ICBC's domestic franchise and put a positive spin on the changes he was introducing. ICBC had adopted more stringent loan classification standards, strengthened credit policies and procedures, installed a new credit management system, and invested heavily in IT infrastructure. It had separated what it called the Old Book, loans made before January 1, 1999, from the New Book, loans made afterward. The ratio of nonperforming loans among the old corporate loans had reached nearly 57 percent by the end of 2003; the NPLs in the new corporate loans came in under 2 percent. That was progress, but ICBC had a long way to go by any stretch.

I described Goldman Sachs' experience in advising banks and our capital markets prowess, emphasizing what we had learned guiding the biggest Chinese companies, like PetroChina, through major restructurings that led ultimately into the public market. I reminded him that Mike Evans had personally led these marquee underwritings and would oversee future Chinese deals. I added that Mike had just been named chairman of our Asian business and would be moving to Hong Kong to take an even more hands-on role. Chris Cole, I said, had advised many of the world's best-known banks and insurance companies, and both Chris and Mike had worked closely with me on Goldman's IPO. I noted that after the IPO of Bank of China (Hong Kong), Fred Hu and his team had successfully advised Bank of Communications on implementing a comprehensive restructuring program that gave it a stronger balance sheet and secured HSBC Holdings as a strategic investor—the first-ever foreign strategic partner for a Chinese bank. Bank of Communications was almost ready for an IPO in Hong Kong.

Jiang and I were sitting side by side at the big round banquet table, and when the interpreter had translated my remarks, Jiang shifted in his seat to face me more directly.

"Hank," he said. "Would Goldman Sachs be interested in becoming one of our strategic investors before we do our IPO?"

His proposition caught me off guard. I'd expected to pitch for the underwriting and had not focused on this option. The idea itself wasn't new: we'd been discussing and debating investing, pre-IPO, in Chinese banks, including ICBC, for more than a year. Fred had been an early advocate and in his persistent way converted Chris, Mike, and others to his thinking.

I was the biggest skeptic. The financial rationale was tempting: investing in banks, especially in emerging markets, is essentially a leveraged play on their home countries' economies, and the booming Chinese economy was set to grow faster. But I was preoccupied with the potential pitfalls. While Chinese banks were cleaning up their bad loans with government assistance, even the best teetered on the edge of capital impairment and insolvency. Committing a big chunk of Goldman's capital carried financial and reputational risks that made me nervous.

Jiang's direct approach made me a bit uncomfortable, as well. I'm sure Fred had discussed investing with him, but I would have expected our staffs to have hashed out the details before he floated the idea publicly. But that, I would learn, was Jiang's style. He was bold and brash, cut from a different cloth from most of the CEOs of Chinese state-owned enterprises I'd met. They tended to be careful and scripted; they avoided making a request like this unless they knew the answer beforehand, for fear of being turned down and losing face. Jiang was forceful, direct, and spontaneous.

I would come to admire these characteristics, but I didn't know him well then. A tall man with jet-black hair, strong features, and an athlete's gait, Jiang moved quickly, with power and purpose, no wasted motions. He smiled easily and openly. He struck me as perhaps a bit too self-confident. He'd been at the bank for years, and I wondered if he wasn't underestimating the problems he faced and overestimating his ability to deal with them. I feared, as Donald Rumsfeld might have put it, that he didn't know what he didn't know, and I sure as heck didn't know what he didn't know, either. That made me uneasy.

"We'd like to work with you on the IPO," I responded. "But as for investing—"

I hesitated for a moment, searching for a diplomatic way to say no—that Goldman, while grateful to be asked, wouldn't want to invest. I didn't want to offend him and lose the chance at underwriting the IPO. I was about to finish my thought when I heard someone clearing his throat. It was Mike Evans.

"Hank, perhaps we should consider doing both?" he said in a low voice. Knowing my opposition to the investing idea and my propensity for saying what's on my mind, he didn't hesitate to interrupt me before I closed the door on that opportunity.

I quickly surveyed my colleagues' faces: John, Mike, Fred, and Chris were all nodding in agreement. Despite my concerns, I made a snap decision to give my team the benefit of the doubt and keep the investing option open. We could always find a graceful way out later if we had to.

I turned back to Jiang and said, "We'd also like to work with you in exploring a possible investment in ICBC. Thank you."

I made sure to add that this would obviously be a major undertaking and that we had a lot to learn, as well as our own internal processes to go through. I reiterated that we were eager to help by lead-managing the IPO, and that we could also help him find other strategic investors.

"Fred and the entire Goldman Sachs team will be here to help you every step of the way," I assured him.

When I finished, Jiang nodded and thanked me. I could see he was pleased. I know how to read clients, and I knew that Jiang—Mr. Self-Confidence himself—would want a direct answer, and I gave him as direct a one as possible. He was sophisticated enough to know that I couldn't be more definitive until I knew more than I did then.

I followed up shortly after with a letter saying that we would begin careful internal evaluations and that we took the opportunity to invest "seriously." Fred has since told me that he did his best, in the Chinese version we sent to chairman Jiang, to emphasize our seriousness.

If I was skeptical of investing in ICBC, it was for good reason. Chinese banks continued to suffer from the corrosive legacy of so-called policy lending directed by the government, particularly to prop up loss-making, unviable state-owned enterprises. In the late 1990s Premier Zhu Rongji had tried to redirect policy lending into new, specialized institutions while strengthening the internal controls and risk management skills of state-owned banks to transform them into more commercially oriented banking institutions. He injected $32.5 billion to recapitalize the four biggest state-owned banks, but as bold as that effort was at the time, the amount soon proved to be far from adequate. The magnitude of bad loans turned out to be a gross underestimate because of the antiquated accounting and loan classification system the banks used. Four years after that recapitalization, the government estimated that another 1 trillion yuan ($121 billion) was needed to bring the banks up to the 8 percent international standard minimum capital ratio. That was half of China's annual fiscal revenues, or nearly 10 percent of GDP.

ICBC was a perfect example of the problem. Beginning in 1999 it had transferred roughly $50 billion in bad loans to Huarong Asset Management Company, the entity created to work out and recover bad debts. But five years later ICBC still had $85 billion to $95 billion in bad loans on its books, or about one-fifth of its total loans.

Zhou Xiaochuan had taken the lead in finding a way to avert a looming banking crisis and accelerate reform down the path he had drafted for Zhu Rongji. His influence had only grown with his appointment to head the central bank, after a stint as the nation's securities overseer. Zhou was also a member of a newly minted policymaking group that cut across government agencies to lead financial sector reform. Set up in 2003 by new premier Wen Jiabao, the group was headed by Executive Vice Premier Huang Ju, with day-to-day operations run by Zhou. At the same time, the government established the China Banking Regulatory Commission, with Liu Mingkang as its first chair, to take over the regulatory and supervisory role of the banking industry from the PBOC, which would focus on monetary issues. The new agency would function like the present-day Office of the Comptroller of the Currency in the United States.

Zhou Xiaochuan's original bank reform plan envisioned that banks would list after restructuring and attracting foreign strategic investors that would shore up the banks, share advanced technology and business practices, and strengthen corporate governance. Zhou had concluded that selling stakes to foreign investors was the best way to attract stable capital to bolster the banks' fragile balance sheets. Later he would be criticized in some quarters for having given away Chinese assets too cheaply, but looking back, I believe that this was an absolutely crucial and wise decision his country made. Had China not taken this approach, it's entirely possible that its banks might have failed to strengthen their capital bases and suffered the fate of Europe's overleveraged, undercapitalized institutions, many of which foundered when the financial crisis hit in 2008.

But before the banks could begin the IPO process, they were going to have to clean up their balance sheets once again. Zhou Xiaochuan decided to use some of the country's foreign exchange reserves, which were growing rapidly thanks to booming exports and soaring capital inflows, to boost the banks' capital bases and dispose of tens of billions in additional bad loans. In contrast to the restructurings of industrial companies like China

National Petroleum, the Chinese wisely decided to include all of the banks' operations in their IPOs. Rather than listing a subsidiary, like PetroChina, that would remain under the control of an opaque Party-led parent company board, the entire bank would be publicly listed.

The central bank created a new vehicle, Central Huijin Investment Company Limited, to hold the government's shares of the systemically important banks so that they could be recapitalized to ensure stability of the financial system. At the end of 2003, the central bank injected $22.5 billion apiece into Bank of China and China Construction Bank. This increased their capital levels to 8 percent and wiped out the Ministry of Finance's stake in each of the banks, which found themselves under the control of a new stakeholder, the stricter but more reform-oriented central bank.

Despite this mop-up work, many sophisticated investors questioned the quality of the bank loans and, ultimately, the solvency of the industry. We were as acquainted with this skepticism as anyone. Bank of Communications had by far the cleanest books of the big banks, but working on its planned IPO, expected in mid-2005, we found that most foreign banks were reluctant to invest in the Shanghai bank because of concerns over nonperforming loans and an expected capital shortage. After our team came up with capital replenishment solutions, HSBC agreed to buy up to 19.99 percent.

Jiang Jianqing later told me he had approached more than 40 potential strategic investors, a global who's who of leading financial institutions, but the only ones that were interested were Allianz and Fortis in Europe and, later—after our negotiations leaked—JPMorgan Chase & Company and Citigroup in the U.S. Even these were reluctant to commit to anything on the order of the multi-billion-dollar sum he was looking for.

I had given my word to Jiang—and my colleagues—that Goldman would take a very serious look at the investment, and I directed Fred, Chris, and Mike to organize a thorough examination of the bank. Convince me, I challenged them. I soon began to see the results of their work, and the numbers just about blew my mind. I had been focused on asset quality, and all those sour loans. But the other side of the balance sheet was a revelation. ICBC had more than $600 billion in deposits, and new deposits were flooding in at a rate that worked out to nearly $225 million every business day. In one year that would bring in enough money to rank among the top 15 of all U.S. banks.

The economics were incredible. The Chinese government set the rates for what banks could charge companies on loans as well as what they could offer customers in interest on deposits, and it kept the spread between the two rates artificially wide, ensuring a hefty return to lenders. With all that cash pouring in, ICBC was minting money. A profit-making machine like that would easily erase the losses on a lot of bad loans.

"This has got to be the world's biggest mattress," I said one day to Chris Cole.

The arguments of Chris, Fred, and Mike in favor of investing were beginning to persuade me. China's vitality and growth potential were inextricably linked to its banking sector, and few institutions stood as a better proxy for the booming economy than ICBC, with its 150 million retail customers, 2.5 million corporate customers, and 17 percent share of the country's banking assets. It was hard to imagine any company that would benefit more from China's growth on such a massive scale. Moreover, we knew the government was committed to the bank's success. It wanted healthier, better managed, and profitable banks. After all, following the IPO, the government would remain the controlling shareholder. It was a perfect alignment of interests.

I grew to like and trust Jiang Jianqing. I realized that his confidence came from hard work and application. Jiang had been born in Shanghai; his father had been a chemist in a hospital and his mother a teacher. After graduating from junior high school, he was sent down to the countryside in remote, poverty-stricken Jiangxi Province, where he grew rice and taught at a rural elementary school before he went off to work in a coal mine in Henan Province. When the Cultural Revolution ended, he returned to Shanghai, attended Shanghai University of Finance and Economics, and joined the Shanghai branch of the People's Bank of China as a clerk. The years of hardship had made him, like so many of his peers, stronger and more determined.

Jiang had an uncanny facility and familiarity with accounting. "Numbers in banking books are like tones in music. They always have a logic," he once told me. "When I read a financial report, I read it like I'm reading a sheet of music. I enjoy that feeling."

Jiang worked his way up the ranks, earning a master's in engineering and a Ph.D. in management from Shanghai Jiaotong University in his few spare hours. He became ICBC president in 2000 (he would become chairman in October 2005) and proved himself to be a dynamic leader willing to spearhead needed reforms by unleashing a wave of changes on the culture, people, and processes of the organization where he'd spent nearly all of his career.

Ultimately, apart from ICBC's amazing domestic franchise, what persuaded me to invest was Jiang—his skill and enthusiasm for banking, for digging in and doing the work, for motivating his employees and transforming his institution. We had to make sure the numbers made sense, but it was absolutely crucial to be sure the institution had a strong leader. Boy, did it. He was a true believer. Sometimes, I thought he was too optimistic. As it would turn out, he wasn't nearly optimistic enough!

I ran the idea of investing in ICBC past every wise head I could find in the firm. We subjected it to a formal vetting process that involved a series of rigorous checks and cross-checks from one internal committee to another all the way up to the board of directors. Yet in the end, I understood that making this investment would be about more than number crunching and due diligence. As I explained to senior executives and board members, it wasn't just a financial investment in the conventional sense. We would ultimately be making a bet on China itself, knowing that the Chinese government needed ICBC and its sister banks to succeed. Their IPOs would be as much about the validation and global legitimacy of China's banking system as they were about raising money. The importance of the banks was difficult to overstate. With no real capital markets to speak of, the big banks were the four financial pillars that held up the entire Chinese economy. The government could not let them fail; our money would be safe as could be. And, of course, this was a two-way street: the Chinese were looking for the Goldman Sachs investment to validate ICBC.

We began to negotiate specific terms with ICBC, aiming to shrink any margin of error. Our agreement gave us the right to scour ICBC's portfolio and sign off on decisions about loan valuations. These "marks" ultimately determined the valuation of the bank, because any losses would come out of capital. The scrutiny gave Chinese regulators confidence that there was a process in place to ensure the bank would be adequately recapitalized. We also began coordinating with American Express Company and Germany's Allianz, which would join us as investors in ICBC.

We thought a lot about both sides of the potential partnership: What would ICBC get from having Goldman Sachs as a partner, and what would we gain from partnering with them? Being a strategic investor would mean sharing technology and know-how. Drawing on a key strength of the Goldman franchise, we established a strategic cooperation team and helped install much better risk management systems, information technology, and management controls, helping ICBC improve in such areas as reporting, transparency, and governance. Senior Goldman executives like former New York Fed chief Jerry Corrigan flew to Beijing to lead seminars and training sessions on the culture and practice of good credit risk management for ICBC's board of directors and executives.

Meantime, the Chinese leadership and Jiang Jianqing pushed ahead on a sweeping restructuring. ICBC would ultimately slash its branches and other outlets from about 42,000 in 1997 to 18,000, while trimming employees from some 390,000 at the end of 2003 to 355,000. (It had had nearly 570,000 in the mid-1990s.) During the spring of 2005, ICBC began to overhaul its balance sheet. In April it received a capital injection of $15 billion from the country's foreign exchange reserves, while the Ministry of Finance retained a $15 billion ownership stake.

ICBC also dumped two huge batches of bad loans. In May the bank shifted about $30 billion in NPLs directly to the Ministry of Finance in return for an interest-bearing bond. One month later it sold $55 billion to the four asset management companies at auction. Including the NPLs hived off in 1999 and 2000, China's biggest bank had disposed of $135 billion in bad loans in less than six years, an extraordinary number that underscored just how shaky ICBC and the banking industry had been and how determined the government was to clean up the mess. By June we had reached a handshake agreement with ICBC, and we were eager to organize formal due diligence and engage outside auditors to comb through the bank's books.

A number of events were combining to change the way the market looked at Chinese banks. For one, a feeding frenzy among Western banks to own a piece of the Chinese financial sector had begun. In June China Construction Bank announced that Bank of America Corporation had agreed to invest $3 billion in return for a stake of approximately 9 percent, with an option to purchase up to 19.9 percent. If that didn't catch the eye of skeptical investors, the following week's IPO of Bank of Communications certainly did. Its shares, which we underwrote with HSBC, jumped 13 percent the first day, driven by massive demand for the $1.9 billion offering. HSBC, which had gone out on a limb to buy its 19.9 percent stake the previous summer, now looked brilliant, and the dynamic for investing in Chinese banks suddenly changed. In short order, Temasek Holdings, the investment arm of the Singapore government, agreed to invest $1 billion in CCB. A group led by Royal Bank of Scotland announced the purchase of a $3.1 billion, 10 percent stake in Bank of China, which was advised by Goldman. Temasek agreed to take an additional 10 percent stake, while UBS bought a 1.6 percent stake. Pariahs barely a year before, the Chinese banks had become the belles of the global investment ball.

By July, along with Allianz and Amex, we had reached a handshake agreement on the key details of an investment in ICBC. Because of the success of the BoCom IPO, our group would pay a slightly higher valuation and purchase 8.45 percent of what was perceived to be the shakiest of the banks that were being readied at that point for public listings but that we believed was the strongest thanks to its domestic franchise and deposit base. (Agricultural Bank of China was in much worse shape than the others and would not debut on the market until 2010.) At $3.8 billion, the deal represented the single biggest foreign direct investment since Deng Xiaoping opened China to foreign capital.

Despite the agreement and Jiang's strong backing, we knew we had a way to go before getting final approval, since we needed sign-offs from the central bank, financial regulators, government ministries, and, ultimately, the State Council. We were optimistic but knew approval was by no means assured.

By an unlucky coincidence, word of our agreement with ICBC came out on August 30, 2005, the same day that Bank of China publicly announced that we had been selected as a lead manager, or bookrunner, for its IPO. It was a classic embarrassment of riches: we had already managed the high-profile IPOs of Bank of China (Hong Kong) and Bank of Communications. Now we had won two more huge plums. Moreover, it was widely assumed we had the inside track to lead the ICBC underwriting as well. And, indeed, we did: the memorandum of understanding for the investment stipulated that we would be the bookrunner on the IPO.

This was exactly what Jiang wanted—for us to manage the IPO as well as do the investment. But he was concerned that Goldman would be stretched too thin to manage both his IPO and that of Bank of China at more or less the same time, and he wanted to rush ahead and beat Bank of China to market. Jiang came to the States in September 2005 for the World Bank/IMF meetings in Washington, D.C. First, he stopped off in New York, where he gave a terrific presentation on the bank's prospects to the management committee, after which we hosted a lunch introducing him to New York financial luminaries. To his delight we had invited David Rockefeller, knowing that his fascination with the Rockefeller family's history had led him to visit the clan's estate in Pocantico Hills outside of New York City.

I saw Jiang several times at the World Bank/IMF meetings, and he emphasized how much he wanted Goldman to lead the underwriting, while pressing me to abandon our work with Bank of China. He was relentless. We spoke at Goldman's D.C. office and on the sidelines of a dinner we hosted where Goldman Sachs International chairman Peter Sutherland, who had been the first director-general of the WTO, interviewed former president Bill Clinton on world events. At the dinner Jiang insisted we meet again the next morning before he flew home. Each time the message was the same: give up the Bank of China mandate. I did my best to convince him that Goldman would have no problems handling both transactions.

I was being optimistic, as it turned out. The ICBC and Bank of China announcements had stunned the investment banking world, and the blowback was sharp and intense. Our rivals were up in arms, sniping in the press and behind closed doors that Goldman was getting too much business and that our assignments were riddled with conflicts of interest. We argued that our unmatched reach and experience in the Chinese financial sector should be seen as a unique strength that could be leveraged to serve our clients. And since they were state-owned sister banks, it was in the Chinese government's best interest to coordinate the offerings so as not to have them come to the market at the same time in a direct head-to-head competition for investors. That's what I told Jiang and Bank of China chairman Xiao Gang.

But the drumbeat of criticism grew louder. A number of our competitors employed princelings, and they were only too happy to use their influence against us. How much this affected officials' thinking I can only guess, and there were clear differences among the financial sector's leaders about our activities. Zhou Xiaochuan supported our roles in ICBC, because as part of the effort to improve governance he supported Jiang's right to make decisions for himself, just as a CEO and his board would do in Western markets. But clear pockets of resistance had emerged. The Ministry of Finance did not believe that it made sense for investment banks to be strategic investors in China's commercial banks. The China Banking Regulatory Commission's new chief, Liu Mingkang, wanted to see China's financial sector opened up, but, like the Ministry of Finance, he preferred that a commercial bank invest in ICBC.

Complicating matters, some terms of the deal leaked, unleashing a wave of popular criticism that China was selling state assets on the cheap. The invective wasn't directed at Goldman alone: the ICBC investment had been priced at 1.18 times book value, while the China Construction Bank and Bank of China deals had been, respectively, 1.15 and 1.14 times book. We knew the pricing reflected how hard it had been to persuade foreign strategic investors to risk so much of their capital, but these deals were now being compared to the incredible success of BoCom: its shares were up 32 percent since listing and were trading at the equivalent of twice book.

Matters soon came to a head. On November 3, 2005, a year after Jiang Jianqing had asked us to invest in ICBC, I had lunch with Zhou Xiaochuan in the dining room on the ninth floor of the central bank headquarters on Chang'an Avenue. Normally, lunch with Zhou was a pleasant, intellectually stimulating affair that touched on topics ranging from economic conditions in both of our countries to reform in China and the development of the nation's fledgling capital markets or to progress being made at the Tsinghua School of Economics and Management. Not that day.

Zhou was as poised and urbane as ever, but apart from running the central bank, he also served as director of the State Council's leading group for state bank reform, an interagency coordinating body with decision-making power. He reported directly to Executive Vice Premier Huang Ju and played a key role in designing and implementing the restructuring plan for each of the four biggest state-owned banks. In that capacity he had a sobering message for us, straight from the top. The leadership had decided that one investment bank managing two big deals like these at the same time wouldn't create a fair competitive environment. Goldman would have to choose which assignment to drop. It was clear Zhou hadn't invited us in to debate the issue or to hear our side so much as to impart the news, as pleasantly but as firmly as he might.

Perhaps to emphasize the urgency, Zhou left the dining room so that Mike Evans, Chris Cole, Fred Hu, and I could decide right then and there. After a brief but intense conversation among us, I told Zhou Xiaochuan that we would underwrite Bank of China, invest in ICBC, and waive the condition that we serve as a joint bookrunner on the IPO for ICBC. We felt we could do more for ICBC as a strategic investor than as a lead underwriter, and a landmark investment in the bank would be far more significant in the medium and long term for both ICBC and Goldman Sachs' role in China than our doing just the IPO. We were also concerned that it could hurt Bank of China if we had to decline the IPO we had already been entrusted with. I confirmed our decision in a note a few days later.

In the end, we did win the right to invest in ICBC. In January I flew to Beijing for the ICBC strategic investment signing ceremony. Our investment of $2.6 billion was the biggest investment we had ever made.

ICBC held its formal beauty pageant for the lucky bank that would take Goldman Sachs' place as lead underwriter. It awarded Merrill Lynch, Credit Suisse, Deutsche Bank, ICEA Capital, and CICC the mandate for the deal, which was expected to come to market later in the year. The press, which loved to chronicle battles among rival investment banks, went to town with what they chose to portray as a stunning humiliation for

Goldman. And it's true we didn't receive the mandate for what would, in October 2006, become the world's biggest IPO. Instead, Goldman made an investment that would yield billions in profits over the years. Moreover, we had found a real partner in Jiang and ICBC, and we were able to make a significant contribution to restructuring ICBC and to bank reform in China.

The Goldman team, under Fred Hu's lead, brought Bank of China public in Hong Kong in June 2006. The bank raised $11.2 billion—making it the biggest such offering since 2000. The bank raised a further $2.5 billion through a Shanghai offering a month later. It was the first mainland company to list in both places and became the most valuable company in China's A-share market. ICBC went public in October 2006, the first bank to list simultaneously in Hong Kong and Shanghai, raising $21.9 billion.

These transactions were the high-water mark of financial reform in China. After years of restructuring, many of the biggest SOEs had stabilized. They dominated domestic markets and had become influential vested interests blocking further advances. Turf fighting had increased among the ministries, and more conservative factions resisted changes, which required their relinquishing power. Antireform, protectionist rhetoric became more pronounced.

Success can lead to complacency, and the push for reform stalled with its most senior advocates now on the sidelines. Zhu Rongji had stepped down from the premiership in 2003, and Jiang Zemin, the former leader, gave up his last official post as head of the Central Military Commission in late 2004. Their successors, Hu Jintao, as general secretary of the Party, and Wen Jiabao, as premier, shifted their attention from reform to social stability and harmony. Executive Vice Premier Huang Ju, a Jiang Zemin ally and the member of the Communist Party Standing Committee who oversaw finance and the economy, had the backed the reformers, but he developed a terminal illness in 2005 and died in 2007. Notably, control of Central Huijin, the institution that held the government's stakes in the Big Four banks, was moved from under the central bank to the Ministry of Finance, which was less favorable to reform then.

Meanwhile, the state-owned banks continued to capitalize on their domestic franchises on their way to becoming enormous, lushly profitable machines. By 2012 ICBC ranked as the biggest bank in the world by market capitalization, followed in second place by China Construction Bank. Agricultural Bank of China ranked fifth, with Bank of China seventh. When the global financial crisis erupted in 2008, China's banks, five years removed from the brink of collapse, would emerge as a force to stabilize the Chinese economy and to help prevent the world's markets from going into free fall. But this came at a further price to reform efforts, which had aimed to get the banks to act in a more commercial manner. In 2009 the Chinese government would push the banks to extend an enormous 9.6 trillion yuan ($1.4 trillion) in stimulus lending. This was a sharp U-turn back to the policy lending approach of the past and one that has undoubtedly led to an increase in bad loans as the banks financed many projects that were uneconomical or inefficient.

Government-bestowed subsidies, regulatory protections, or other advantages all too frequently become sacrosanct entitlements, and changing that mind-set is difficult to sustain without a strong push from the top. But China's leaders seemed to have become more interested in preserving stability than in continuing to press for change, as if the rapid economic growth they had inherited from the groundbreaking reform efforts of their predecessors would continue on its own momentum. In my view, China needed to approach its economy very much as a work in progress. It was still near the beginning of a difficult evolution that had to be completed for the country to realize its full potential. China risked stumbling—and undermining stability—more by going slow on reform than by going too fast.

PART TWO

Breaking New Ground

September 2006: Visiting with future president Xi Jinping at Hangzhou's famed West Lake State Guest House on my first trip to China as Treasury secretary *(REUTERS/Nir Elias)*

December 2006: Jawing with President Hu Jintao at the Great Hall of the People after the first meeting of the Strategic Economic Dialogue in Beijing *(REUTERS/Elizabeth Dalziel/Pool)*

February 1997: We get our marching orders on China Telecom at the Zhongnanhai leadership compound. With Goldman's Cherry Li (behind me with interpreters) and Executive Vice Premier Zhu Rongji

November 1997: Celebrating the success of the China Telecom IPO at Zhongnanhai.
Front row (from left): Wang Qishan, me, Zhu Rongji, Wendy, John Thornton.
Back row (from left): Fang Fenglei, Ziwang Xu, Mike Evans, Bi Mingjian, Kong Yongxin, Hsueh-ming Wang

October 1998: Minister of Posts and Telecommunications Wu Jichuan (left) visits Goldman Sachs' New York headquarters with Mike Evans and Hsueh-ming Wang

December 1998: How one Hong Kong paper covered a meeting Wang Qishan and I held with Guangdong Enterprises creditors. In this account, I'm quoted as saying, "Relax, I will take care of it!" while Wang Qishan is thinking, "I will rely on you for this one!"

October 2000: First Meeting of the Advisory Board of the School of Economics and Management at Tsinghua University. Front row (from left): Rajat Gupta, Wang Xuebing, Jorma Ollila, Wang Dazhong, me, Zhu Rongji, George Fisher, Chen Zhili, Kim Clark, Liu Mingkang. Back row (from left): Zhao Chunjun, Warren McFarlan, Liu Chuanzhi, Masayoshi Son, Zhou Xiaochuan, Li Wei, Irwin Jacobs, Victor Fung, John Thornton, Levin Zhu

July 2002: Celebrating the closing of the Bank of China (Hong Kong) IPO at the Great Wall. Goldman's Tracy Wolstencroft and Ziwang Xu flank Bank of China's Liu Mingkang

February 2002: Discussing the establishment of parks in Yunnan with President Jiang Zemin. Goldman's Ziwang Xu is behind me

April 2013: Before lunch with chairman Jiang Jianqing at ICBC's Beijing headquarters

December 2007: Vice Premier Wu Yi shows off the elaborate "veggie art" table decorations at SED III in Grand Epoch City; Commerce Secretary Carlos Gutierrez is to her right

May 24, 2007: A meeting in the Oval Office of the White House during the second Strategic Economic Dialogue. With China's Ambassador to the U.S. Zhou Wenzhong (at left),Vice Premier Wu Yi, President George W. Bush, and interpreters
(David Bohrer, courtesy George W. Bush Presidential Library and Museum)

December 2006: Getting the real work done behind the scenes before SED I at the Great Hall of the People in Beijing. Taiya Smith (center), her counterpart, Zhu Guangyao (standing to her left), Deputy Secretary General of the State Council Xu Shaoshi (standing, far right), and their colleagues

June 2008: Trading insights on the grounds of the U.S. Naval Academy in Annapolis, Maryland, during SED IV with Vice Premier Wang Qishan and Secretary of Health and Human Services Mike Leavitt *(Courtesy of the U.S. Department of Treasury)*

November 2014: It's always a pleasure chatting and discussing world affairs with central bank chief Zhou Xiaochuan, here at the People's Bank of China headquarters in Beijing

December 2014: Exploring cross-investment with Vice Premier Wang Yang and Secretary of Commerce Penny Pritzker at a Paulson Institute–sponsored event in Chicago on the margins of the U.S.-China Joint Commission on Commerce and Trade *(Mark Tolbert III, Office of Public Affairs, Department of Commerce)*

December 2011: "Uniting knowledge and action": Li Keqiang, now premier, inscribes the Paulson Institute's motto at the Great Hall of the People in Beijing

July 2014: Discussing the government's priorities with Liu He, Xi Jinping's right-hand man in driving economic reform

April 4, 2012: Zhou Qiang, then Hunan Party secretary and now president of the Supreme People's Court, shows me a new app on his smart phone in Changsha

April 11, 2014: Wendy and I tour an auto glass manufacturing facility with Fuyao Glass founder Cao Dewang (second from left) and his son Cao Hui (far right) *(REUTERS/Nir Elias)*

January 2011: With Wanxiang founder Lu Guanqiu and his son-in-law Wanxiang America president Pin Ni at a private dinner in Chicago

July 2000: Carol Fox (left) and Rose Niu, both then with the Nature Conservancy, flanking NDRC vice minister Hao Jianxiu at Yellowstone National Park

November 2013: Wendy consults a bird book with 12-year-old prodigy Tina Lin, a local guide, and Tina's mother, also named Wendy, at the Beidagang wetlands in Tianjin *(Courtesy RARE)*

August 2008: In China for the 2008 Olympics, the Paulson family gathers at the Great Wall. From left with me: Wendy, Amanda and her husband, Josh Rollins, Heather and Merritt Paulson *(Tod Hamachek)*

August 2008:
Mastering the fine
points of tai chi in
a Beijing park
(Tod Hamachek)

August 2008: Wendy
with granddaughter
Willa Rollins in
Beijing *(Tod
Hamachek)*

July 2012: I am revealed as a panda hugger at the Chengdu Research Base of Giant Panda Breeding in Sichuan. From left, Fang Fenglei, Paulson Institute vice chairman Deborah Lehr, and PI chief of staff Rebecca Neale; in my lap, Jun Jun, one happy panda

June 1998: Wendy and Amanda on a hike in Bita Lake Nature Reserve, now part of Pudacuo National Park in Shangri-La, Yunnan

October 2002: Wendy and I take a welcome rest on a climb in the mountains of Yunnan

November 2014: The Paulson Institute team at the Fourth Annual Cities of the Future Conference in Beijing. Front row (from left): Damien Ma, Jenny Xu, Rose Niu, Ellen Carberry, Amy Wan, Chelsea Eakin, Hortense Hallé-Yang, Dorinda Elliott, Evan Feigenbaum, Bo Sun, Emily Hemmings, Lily Zhao. Back row (from left): Liwei Chen, Jerry Yu, Richard Xie, Lini Fu, Cindy Jiang, me, Merisha Enoe, Anders Hove, Julian Schwabe, Cynthia Zeltwanger, Gracie Sun

Fall 2006: My former colleague and partner Fred Hu stops to visit at my Washington, D.C., home *(Wendy Paulson)*

July 2007: Surveying the ecological damage at Qinghai Lake with William Chang, then the China representative for the U.S. National Science Foundation *(REUTERS/David Lawder)*

CHAPTER ELEVEN

A Call to Serve

I'd been to China at least 70 times, but my first visit as U.S. Treasury secretary, in September 2006, was very different from anything I'd experienced before. The sirens, the long motorcade, the six-lane highway emptied of cars as we raced to West Lake in the booming city of Hangzhou: all of this was thrilling, of course. Yet it was more than that—I didn't kid myself into thinking any of that pomp was for me. No doubt I had made many friends as a businessman in China, but now, for the first time, I was representing the United States of America, and I felt an enormous sense of pride and purpose—and not a little pressure, because I had come to nail down the details of a plan for a new way to develop and manage U.S.-China relations—and I wasn't 100 percent sure the Chinese would go along with it.

I had debated long and hard about taking the job at Treasury, and as we whipped along I remembered the words that Zhou Xiaochuan, the respected head of China's central bank, had spoken to me privately just a few months before: *Hank, you can make a difference.*

Now, beginning with America's relationship with *his* country, I believed I might be able to do just that.

Because symbols matter so much in China, we had put a great deal of thought into the details of this visit. First, we decided I should make a point of breaking with tradition and stopping some place other than Beijing, some place with a lot of private sector economic activity, to highlight the importance of reform. Located just southwest of Shanghai, Hangzhou was the capital of coastal Zhejiang Province and renowned for its entrepreneurship and vibrant, homegrown private sector. Low-cost goods poured out of its factories and onto container ships to be carried across the globe. I wanted to send a powerful signal that the new U.S. Treasury secretary understood economics and reform, had relationships that went well beyond the leaders of the state, and knew there was more to China than Beijing. I had also put a lot of thought into the person I would meet with first, and the province's Communist Party secretary, Xi Jinping, was the perfect choice. A rising political star, Xi had been an extraordinarily effective leader in promoting Zhejiang's private sector, and I thought that a meeting with him would send another strong signal to Beijing.

I had come to China on a very specific mission. U.S. president George W. Bush and Chinese president Hu Jintao had agreed to launch what we were calling the Strategic Economic Dialogue between our two countries. President Bush had placed me in a kind of "super-Cabinet" position to lead and coordinate the other Cabinet members in this effort, which I considered the best possible way to manage our economic relationship with China—in my view the most important bilateral relationship that our country had. Our dealings with China had become mired in perhaps a hundred diffuse low-level exchanges and needed to be coordinated and prioritized better. (I had learned, for example, that efforts to halt illegal logging practices had been stymied by inadequate communications made worse by poor translation of documents.) I intended to establish a top-down process that would address long-term concerns while delivering short-term results.

So here I was, two months into my new job at Treasury, speeding through Hangzhou to meet with Xi Jinping, who, as it turned out, would become China's next leader. Joining me were National Economic Council director Al Hubbard, a tall Midwesterner with a boisterously infectious laugh; Treasury undersecretary Tim Adams, a Kentuckian who had also served in George H. W. Bush's administration; and my soon-to-be SED coordinator from Treasury, Taiya Smith, a New Jersey native from a Quaker family, with a radiant smile and an iron will.

Born in 1953, Xi was the son of Xi Zhongxun, a veteran of the Red Army and onetime vice premier, who had played a crucial role in helping to launch China's first special economic zones as Party secretary of Guang-dong. Known for his personal integrity and unblemished reform creden-tials, the elder Xi was a close ally of reformist Party chief Hu Yaobang, whose death helped to trigger the student unrest in 1989. Xi Senior was sidelined soon thereafter.

Years earlier, when Xi Zhongxun was jailed during the Cultural Revo-lution, the 15-year-old Xi Jinping went from being the privileged son of a respected Party leader to seven years of hard physical labor in the country-side. Xi found his way back to China's version of our Ivy League, earning degrees in chemical engineering and law at Tsinghua, then rose steadily through the Communist Party. He gained military experience serving as personal secretary to Geng Biao, a respected revolutionary general who was secretary general of the Central Military Commission and Defense min-ister in the early 1980s. Xi then worked in a series of local, county, and provincial government positions. Before coming to Zhejiang in 2002, he had been governor of the affluent coastal province of Fujian, just across the strait from vibrant Taiwan and home to one of China's first designated special economic zones. In a glamorous contrast to the usual life story of faceless Party bureaucrats, Xi married the beautiful and much loved folk singer Peng Liyuan.

I had visited with Xi a few months before when he had come to New York at the head of a Zhejiang delegation looking to visit their sister state, New Jersey, and build relationships with select U.S. business and finance leaders. Tall and self-confident, Xi was a big presence who lit up a room and I could see why he had moved up the leadership ranks quickly. He was inci-sive and forward-looking. He stressed that China should replicate elsewhere the entrepreneurialism of Zhejiang's thriving private sector before it lost its low-cost advantage in manufacturing as the price of labor rose because of growing prosperity. He was focused on the need to help industry in Zheji-ang and other coastal regions move up the product value chain the way, say, Singapore had done in past decades.

"We need to foster a better climate for innovation," Xi told me. "Small and middle-size companies in the private sector can lead the way."

Crucially, too, he wanted China to make these changes while treating environmental protection as an "urgent priority," as he put it. He commended my work in Yunnan with the Nature Conservancy and expressed his delight with a book on the birds of Central Park that my wife, Wendy, had suggested I give him.

This time I met with Xi at Hangzhou's famous West Lake State Guest House. Richard Nixon and Zhou Enlai had come together at this beautiful lakeside spot during the American president's groundbreaking 1972 trip to China, two days before the historic Shanghai Communiqué had proclaimed our two countries' commitment to normalizing relations. Clearly, Xi had put as much thought into the symbolism of my visit as I had. He told me that he wanted to take the same walk with me that Zhou Enlai had taken with Nixon. It would underscore, he said, the importance of what I was trying to do for U.S.-China relations. As we traced the route Nixon and Zhou Enlai had taken, Xi's words drove home the important responsibility that President Bush had given me. I saw myself as a custodian for this profoundly important relationship, and I dearly wanted to improve the way it was managed.

Talking through our interpreters, trailed by our security details and entourages, we strolled through an old pavilion, down a winding path planted with gorgeous red salvia, and under an ornate carved wooden gate to the shore of West Lake, rimmed with weeping willows and dotted with islands connected by graceful white bridges. The landscape was a marvel of botanical engineering, with perfectly cultivated gardens stretching to the water. I explained my view of the U.S.-China relationship and why the Strategic Economic Dialogue was important to it. As news photographers jostled one another trying to get a shot of us, we halted briefly to pose side by side under the gate, just as Nixon and Zhou Enlai had done. Xi was in great spirits and very friendly. As friends later told me, he was very appreciative that I had chosen to see him first on my maiden trip to China as U.S. Treasury secretary.

Meeting with Xi had another benefit as well. I had not yet been able to schedule a private meeting with President Hu, but I was determined to secure one and thought Xi might be able to help out. We'd heard that Hu was nervous about seeing me, that he didn't want any surprises and was concerned that I might use the occasion to lecture him publicly about China's undervalued currency—the single biggest issue that members of Congress cited when they complained that China was costing Americans jobs. But that was not my intention. I simply wanted to discuss the SED agenda with the president, and I made that clear to Xi. Even though I would be in Hangzhou just one night, I was betting that the message would get to Hu.

After meeting with Xi, I had dinner with a group of Chinese entrepreneurs at the 158-year-old Louwailou, a sprawling, noisy seafood place that an official from Zhejiang's Foreign Affairs Office cheerfully noted had been Chiang Kai-shek's favorite restaurant. I wanted to signal U.S. backing of private enterprise in China and lend support to Xi, who was pushing entrepreneurial efforts in his prosperous province. Among my dozen or so dinner companions were Lu Guanqiu, the son of peasants, who became an ironsmith at 15 and went on to found Wanxiang Group Corporation, China's biggest auto parts manufacturer; Guo Guangchang, the son of a stonemason who, with three university classmates, had turned sales of a hepatitis testing kit into the Shanghai-based Fosun Group, a diversified holding company with interests in pharmaceuticals, real estate, steel, and retail; and Zong Qinghou, who had co-founded Wahaha, China's biggest beverage company, with the help of two retired teachers. My dinner companions took the opportunity to argue for policies that supported their businesses—including the continuation of a cheap renminbi.

After dinner my Treasury team and I took a walk around town, officially for sightseeing but also to get some privacy. Indoors we were subject to the Chinese government's pervasive eavesdropping; outdoors we could speak under cover of traffic and crowds. We headed down the hotel drive toward the lake only to become the focus of a minor power struggle as Chinese security forces joined our walk, positioning themselves in front and in back of our Secret Service detail and forcefully clearing pedestrians from our path. We wrapped up our discussion quickly to avoid causing a scene.

Still, I went to bed that night feeling good about my first day in China as Treasury secretary. I felt even better the next morning when I arrived in Beijing and learned that I had gotten the meeting with Hu Jintao.

When President Hu came to Washington in April 2006, I was invited to attend a lunch given in his honor by President Bush at the White House. I had been approached to become Treasury secretary and was asked to meet the president the night before, but I had decided not to accept the offer and would see President Bush only in passing at the luncheon.

A big Chinese delegation was in the capital for the event, including central bank chief Zhou Xiaochuan, who was visiting at the International Monetary Fund before the lunch. I went there to catch up with him outside the official whirl. Zhou asked me if I was going to take the job of Treasury secretary. There had been speculation linking me with the post, including an article in the *New York Times*, but Zhou sure seemed to know a lot more than what was in the papers. I told him I had declined an offer, as I did not see how I could be effective in the last two years of an unpopular administration. That was too bad, he said, adding that he spoke as a friend.

"It is a great honor to serve your country," Zhou said. "More important, you never know what opportunity you may have to make a difference."

Zhou's words stuck with me, and I returned to them again and again over the next month or so as I began to second-guess my decision after some soul-searching and conversations with close friends. As it turned out, the White House was still interested in me, and I flew back to Washington in May to meet with the president to discuss the scope of the job.

President Bush and I talked about the need for entitlement reform, which I considered the most pressing economic issue facing the U.S. We discussed the important role the banking system could play in cutting off funds to terrorism and pressuring rogue countries to change their behavior. And I made sure to let the president know how interested I was in China. I told him how I thought the U.S. could improve its approach to the relationship.

"The Chinese think long term and strategically," I said. "We should do the same."

Since the 1972 rapprochement our relations with China had been determined by security concerns. That emphasis was a natural by-product of Cold War superpower politics that aligned China with us against our mutual enemy, the U.S.S.R. The world had changed dramatically—most obviously, the Soviet Union had long since collapsed—and we needed to refine our approach. Economic concerns were now paramount to the Chinese, as the president well knew. We needed to engage with them on that basis.

I recalled what President Hu had replied when President Bush had asked what gave him nightmares: having to create 25 million new jobs each year. The Chinese leadership sought stability above all else, and that meant having a strong economy. That in turn required additional market-oriented reforms and a mutually beneficial relationship with the U.S., its most important trading partner. The Communist Party had essentially made a deal with the people to provide prosperity in return for continued political power. The Chinese leaders' credibility with their citizens was rooted in economic opportunity, job creation, and an ever-improving standard of living. It was the glue that held the system together. But China's continued success had given its citizens higher expectations, and these were growing more difficult to meet as many more social stresses accumulated—from dirty air and water to gnawing disparities in income distribution.

If we got the economic relationship right, the rest of our issues with China would follow, I reasoned; the Chinese would respond positively to initiatives that contributed to a stable, growing economy. Alternatively, if economic relations spun out of control—through protectionist legislation that sparked a trade war, for example—it would fray the overall relationship. We would find it easier to solve almost any major global problem with the Chinese on board; without them, it would be much more difficult. To deal with China, we would need to be strong and clear, and we would need to get the right people from both sides involved. This would require a high-level, cross-agency approach with top decision makers from both countries sitting across from one another. We needed commitments from senior leaders, beginning with both presidents, to ensure the direct, top-down engagement necessary.

I was completely frank as we sat together that Saturday morning in the Treaty Room, which served as the president's study in the residence on the second floor of the White House. Nothing could substitute for long-standing personal relationships with top Chinese decision makers, and I told the president I wanted to put mine to good use.

"Of course," President Bush said. "I would like to take advantage of your experience." He said he hoped that among other things I would help us make progress with the Chinese on the hard issues of Iran and North Korea.

Even before my talk with President Bush, I had decided to accept the Treasury job. You certainly don't agree to meet with the president and then turn him down, but I wanted to be clear on the scope of the job. I didn't immediately tell anybody at Goldman Sachs of my decision. On May 25 I took a two-day trip to China—my last as head of the investment bank. One highlight was a dinner Fred Hu and I had with Xiao Gang, chairman of Bank of China, who was basking in the glow of his company's just-launched $11.4 billion IPO, which my colleagues at Goldman Sachs had managed.

The next day Fred, Mike Evans, and I also met with Finance Minister Jin Renqing, and to my astonishment Jin said, "I understand from my friend John Snow that you're going to be the next Treasury secretary."

Now, John Snow—the former chairman of CSX Corporation who was then Treasury secretary—certainly didn't know I was going to succeed him. I had only known for a few days myself. I made a joke and changed the subject, and Jin let the matter drop. Afterward, Mike said, "How could the Chinese think you'd leave your job as CEO of Goldman Sachs to join the sinking Bush administration?"

That summer, after I'd accepted the Treasury job, I sat down to figure out how a new engagement with China might work in practice. I turned for help to Deborah Lehr, who had frequently advised me on China when I was at Goldman Sachs. A trained economist, she had served in the Clinton administration as a top China trade negotiator, dealing, among other things, with China's accession to the WTO. She had worked with Chinese companies as well as with U.S. companies doing business in China, and I trusted her advice. She is married to Goldman chief of staff John Rogers, and that summer I often met with her in the living room of their D.C. home to hash out the basics of the Strategic Economic Dialogue.

With Deborah typing, the two of us would sit side by side on the Lehr-Rogers family sofa, batting ideas back and forth. The SED, we eventually decided, should have three overarching goals: to advance the economic relationship between the U.S. and China by improving cooperation between our two countries; to speed up China's economic reforms; and to encourage China to be a responsible member of the global economic system by opening up more markets to competition, doing more to protect intellectual property, and accelerating its move to a market-based currency. We focused less on particular policies than on the process itself: what was the most efficient way to build trust and get things done, how to concentrate on shared strategic interests and avoid getting bogged down by ad hoc disputes.

We wanted to design a structure that would deal effectively with China's complex mix of top-down yet consensus-driven decision making. Because of China's concentrated power structure and legacy of state planning, we knew we had to involve officials at the pinnacle of the hierarchy to win approvals for policy changes. But China's strong tradition of consensus meant we would also need to find a way to win the approvals of as many ministers and influential officials as possible, including those who did not have direct responsibility for a given issue. As I had long since learned: no one person could say yes, but many could say no. And you always wanted to get a blessing from the very top.

The way the U.S. managed relations when I started at Treasury was simply too diffuse to be effective. We maintained well-intentioned dialogues across many departments and agencies; there were joint commissions, forums, and partnerships on subjects ranging from commerce and trade to economic development and science and technology. But discussions got mired in detail, and people lost sight of the big-picture issues. Though our China policy was coordinated at the highest levels of government, each Cabinet secretary inevitably thought his or her issues should have top priority. The Chinese needed a clearer message about what we wanted and what we would give in return.

We concluded that while the SED would focus on long-term strategic goals, it would have to deliver short-term results to show we were making progress and win political support. Accomplishing this would require not just periodic official meetings but a continuous process of negotiation and discussion at ministry and agency levels to build trust and help defuse any crises that would inevitably arise. This trust building would make it easier to discuss sensitive subjects, such as China's aggressive quest for resources in developing countries. All decisions would be carefully tracked and followed up on to make sure they were implemented.

The SED would not replace but rather supplement and help coordinate ongoing discussions and existing entities. Each Cabinet member would continue to direct his or her own interchanges, while gaining a more prominent platform through the SED. The Joint Commission on Commerce and Trade, for example, would continue to be led by the Commerce secretary, Carlos Gutierrez, and U.S. Trade Representative Susan Schwab, and their forum would follow up with Chinese officials to resolve day-to-day trade and investment problems ranging from intellectual property protection concerns to antidumping trade disputes in the steel and textile industries.

Traditionally, high-level conversations with China could be frustrating gabfests, with each side talking past the other as they read prepared statements—an unsatisfying process with little substance. We envisioned a more dynamic approach with the SED. The U.S. would make, say, environmental arguments not just to China's environmental officials, who likely had limited power, but to other ministers, vice premiers, and members of the Party's Standing Committee—that is, officials with broad portfolios and wide-ranging powers. When we had a big breakthrough in negotiations, top government officials, from the U.S. Cabinet and China's State Council, would be there to ratify it on the spot.

The president had assured me I would be in charge of all economic issues for his administration, and we decided to define "economic" broadly, as the Chinese did. Why shouldn't it include such vital matters as energy and the environment—or food and product safety? The way I saw it, the SED should embrace everything except national security and foreign policy. This would require me to take on a leadership role with my fellow Cabinet members on U.S.-China relations. I understood the inherent problems with that. Some would surely see it as a power grab. That wasn't the intention: if the SED was going to be successful, someone on the U.S. side had to prioritize our objectives and then negotiate at China's highest levels across a range of subjects and controversies. President Bush couldn't do this twice a year, but I could.

The super-Cabinet position would make clear to the leaders in Zhongnanhai that we took the enterprise seriously and would give me the "face" I needed in China, which regarded the positions of our Cabinet members as ranking below that of their vice premiers. At the same time, it would give me the standing necessary inside the U.S. government to make things happen. I wouldn't just lead the delegation. I would coordinate everything we did. Treasury staff began feeling out Chinese contacts to see whether they would be receptive to a broad dialogue with the U.S. I broached the subject within the administration, starting right after my July 10 swearing-in.

President Bush was, of course, the most important person who had to sign off on the SED. Despite his earlier encouragement of my ideas on improving the U.S.-China relationship, and despite positive feedback from White House officials, I knew that I was tiptoeing through a bureaucratic minefield and that selling the SED to my fellow Cabinet members might prove tricky. Fortunately, I had a great source of immediate support in National Security Adviser Stephen Hadley. He had worked after me in the office at the Pentagon where I had my first job following business school in the early 1970s. We had many mutual friends, and he welcomed me to the Bush White House and helped me to explain the idea to the president and others in the administration—and ultimately to make the interagency process work.

Among those with the most at stake was Secretary of State Condoleezza Rice, with whom I had lunch the day after my swearing-in. I'd met Condi only once before, when she had been interviewing for a job at Goldman Sachs before deciding to join the Bush campaign. Although we got along great, she had some understandable initial reservations—she did not want two secretaries of State when it came to China. I assured her that I had no intention of usurping her role, and she ended up being a great backer of the program. I also won the support of Defense Secretary Donald Rumsfeld, whom I had known as an active director of Sears when I was advising the board on restructuring the company. I expected him to oppose the SED and was surprised when he didn't. He left office, in any case, just a few months later, in December 2006. Officials who might have been justifiably suspicious of a power play on my part, like Commerce's Gutierrez and U.S. Trade Representative Schwab, became big supporters once they saw how the SED could work, particularly in the way that it gave them access to a wide range of Chinese ministers and allowed them to make their case directly to President Hu Jintao and Premier Wen Jiabao.

Not everyone was as accepting. Some of my colleagues were none too keen initially about being subordinate to the Treasury secretary in the SED. Some didn't think we needed another U.S.-China forum and weren't eager to add annual trips to Beijing to their busy schedules. Others cautioned me that the timing could not be worse: U.S. midterm elections were a few months away, the 2008 presidential campaign was beginning to take shape, and China was always a touchy subject for our politicians.

In addition, China was on the verge of announcing a leadership change in 2007, and we still had to sell the idea to the Chinese. We knew that we could not rely on the usual bureaucratic channels to get our message across. These could prove slow and counterproductive—everyone on the State Council would want to weigh in, there would be endless debate, and our elegant idea for a joint dialogue would get turned into so much Chinese sausage. We needed to find someone who had the connections in Beijing to take our message directly to the top levels of the government.

The messenger would turn out to be an old acquaintance, Zhou Yong-kang, whom I had first gotten to know nearly a decade earlier when he was in charge of China National Petroleum and Goldman was preparing for the landmark PetroChina IPO. In the middle of that process, he had been shifted over to run the Ministry of Land and Resources, a post he didn't much care for. I'll never forget visiting him once in early 1999 in his Beijing office, when he said to me, "Hank, you know important people in our government. Use your influence and get me out of here." I laughed. The Party later that year appointed him secretary of Sichuan Province. By December 2002 he was back in Beijing as minister of Public Security. As head of China's internal police system—with 1.6 million to 1.7 million police officers and commissioners—Zhou had become one of the most powerful officials in the government.

He had come to Washington on an official visit, with a substantial delegation, to confer on matters of mutual security. He was scheduled to see, among others, Steve Hadley, Attorney General Alberto Gonzales, and Michael Chertoff, secretary of Homeland Security. We decided to take advantage of my prior relationship with him to request a meeting at Treasury to raise concerns about illicit activity in the Chinese financial system. I knew that Zhou Yongkang, as a member of the Politburo, could help us leapfrog the bureaucracy and bring our idea for the SED directly to Hu Jintao.

I met with Zhou Yongkang and his delegation on July 27 in my large conference room, which, in keeping with the Treasury Building itself, was decorated in the 19th-century style, complete with antique wall sconces, gas chandeliers, and mahogany chairs with U.S. dollar signs on their backs. Zhou and I faced each other across the long table, as we moved through an agenda that included everything from the proliferation of weapons of mass destruction to financial system abuse by North Korea. After a while, I laid out my thoughts for the strategic dialogue, which didn't come as a complete surprise to Zhou. The evening before, I'd given our ambassador to China, Sandy Randt, a heads-up that I planned to do this, and we had requested the meeting through an old friend, China's ambassador Zhou Wenzhong, telling him we had an important initiative to present. The ambassador, who was at the Treasury meeting, later told me that our request raised eyebrows in the Chinese Ministry of Foreign Affairs; they wondered what important matters the U.S. Treasury secretary could want to discuss with China's head of Public Security.

"Minister Zhou," I said, "we'd like you to take the proposal back to President Hu and present it to him."

Zhou was clearly pleased to be asked and promised to relay the idea to Hu "as soon as I return to Beijing."

After the meeting formalities were over, I gave him a quick tour of my office, showing him some Treasury memorabilia. Zhou Yongkang showed a particular interest in the pistol confiscated from Roaring Twenties gangster Al Capone.

We heard soon enough through back channels that Hu Jintao had responded positively to my overture. In early September we had arranged a call for President Bush with Hu, and the two leaders agreed to launch the Strategic Economic Dialogue by year-end in Beijing.

The SED was scheduled to be announced officially in Beijing on September 20, the day after my meeting at West Lake with Xi Jinping. I was to meet with China's top officials on September 21 to hammer out the details, but I had more on my mind than just the SED. Back home, protectionist pressures were rising in advance of the midterm elections. Senators Charles Schumer (D-NY) and Lindsey Graham (R-SC) had drawn up bipartisan legislation to punish China for manipulating the value of the renminbi. It was heading toward an up-or-down vote by the end of September, and I hoped to emphasize the need for currency flexibility to the Chinese.

China's exchange rate policy had increasingly become a hot-button issue. Dating back to the days of the command economy, Beijing had pegged the value of the currency to the dollar. As the economy opened up, the renminbi had been continually devalued, from 1.50 to the dollar in 1980 to a low of 8.62 in 1994. As China's current account balance improved, the government stabilized the exchange rate at 8.27 to the dollar from the late 1990s to 2005, when it decided to take the renminbi off a strict dollar peg. The renminbi was still tightly managed by the central bank, but it was now valued against a basket of currencies, whose composition was kept secret, though it was widely assumed the dollar was the main component.

Many Americans believed China was still holding down the value of the renminbi to give its exports an unfair advantage. Its manufacturers were booming, and its coffers were overflowing, while our companies, the argument went, were unable to compete on price and were closing or shipping work overseas. And the U.S. trade deficit with China was gaping. I empathized deeply with the concerns of the public and their representatives on Capitol Hill about job losses and the pressure on American workers. Global trade had brought benefits like cheaper imported goods and lower inflation, but companies had been forced to downsize, and families, businesses, and in some cases entire communities had been devastated. A good deal of this pain had hit close to my home in the Midwest.

This suffering resulted in part from the artificially low value of the renminbi: economic analyses indicated that it should have been stronger but for Chinese market interventions. But the problem, and its solution, were much more complex. China's currency, while important, had become an oversimplified and misunderstood issue. It wasn't the main cause of our trade balance woes. After all, we ran negative balances with just about every major economy. Rather, the deficit with China stemmed from a range of structural issues that caused the U.S. to save too little and borrow too much, even as the Chinese saved too much and consumed too little. Fixing this was the key, and getting the currency policy right was one part of that.

And there were clearly other reasons for U.S. job losses. These included the advent of new technologies that were squeezing out jobs in manufacturing and in many professions, as well as an education system that was no longer producing enough workers with advanced skills to meet the needs of our fast-evolving economy.

A currency should reflect the strength and dynamism of a country's economy. I've always been an advocate for a strong dollar. It should be the result not of exchange market maneuvers but of a strong economy whose sound macroeconomic policies and commitment to property rights and market principles inspire investor confidence. An artificially weak renminbi was not the way to maintain a strong dollar.

Because China had become such a major factor in the world, its constant interventions to keep the renminbi artificially low created harmful distortions that were not good for it, the U.S., or the global economy. One of these distortions was an overreliance on export-led growth at the expense of developing domestic consumption. This would become painfully apparent when the financial crisis hit in 2008 and dried up much of the demand for China's goods in Europe and the United States.

If China truly wanted a market-based economy, it needed its currency to reflect economic realities. A freely exchangeable, market-determined renminbi was very much in China's interest—and ours. It would yield more accurate, more realistic prices, which are necessary for efficient markets. It would lead to better capital allocation and help China rebalance its economy, spreading the benefits of prosperity more broadly.

Before China could fully float the renminbi, though, it would need to develop a modern banking system, which was why I would eventually lean on the country to open up its capital markets to foreign competition. Structural reforms and greater market access for U.S. companies and products would benefit U.S. workers more thoroughly than adjusting the currency alone. A stronger Chinese economy would become a magnet for U.S. investment and exports.

Ultimately, the currency issue mattered because it was a highly visible indicator of the pace of reform in China. To move forward on necessary changes to its economy, it was essential for China to keep appreciating the renminbi to reflect economic reality. The Chinese knew this very well. Our public disagreement was over the speed and amount of change.

One week before this trip, I raised the debate in a speech at the Treasury Department that some in the press, including the *New York Times*, had interpreted as a "warning" to China. My remarks may have been what had concerned Hu Jintao about being lectured on currency matters, but they were also useful in holding off action by Senators Schumer and Graham, who were waiting on the results of my trip before they pushed forward with their legislation. Chuck and Lindsey were smart and generally well informed about China, but they were locked onto the currency issue because it was an easy one for the public to understand, and they saw it as a way to goad China to reform. Fortunately, they were willing to give me a chance to prove the SED could work. "I hope that Hank returns with tangible results," Schumer said publicly. "But if the disconnect between China's rhetoric and actions is any guide, we'll have no choice but to call for a vote."

It was still not decided who would lead the Chinese side in the SED, and that was proving to be a thorny issue. Just as President Bush had agreed to give me super-Cabinet status, it was essential that my counterpart rank high enough, or be given the authority, to wield power over the ministers in the State Council. The logical choice would have been Executive Vice Premier Huang Ju, a member of the Communist Party Standing Committee, who had oversight of finance and banking, but Huang was terminally ill.

In his place, we pressed for Wen Jiabao, but we got a lot of pushback from Beijing that was understandable, given the unequal pairing of China's premier with the U.S. Treasury secretary. But we were also told that it wasn't clear whether Wen would even be part of the SED or what role he would play. This was perplexing until someone on the Chinese side took one of my key people aside and said, "Would you stop pushing for Wen? Hu Jintao wants to do it."

This was a development we hadn't foreseen, but a very fortunate one indeed. The Chinese were basically saying that Hu Jintao was such a big supporter of the SED concept that he wanted to keep it under his own control. For obvious reasons, he could not be my counterpart, but he would be actively involved. Instead, the Chinese appointed Vice Premier Wu Yi to lead the Chinese side.

Wu Yi was one of four vice premiers, but she was handling much of Huang Ju's job and effectively acting as executive vice premier. She was the most senior woman in the Chinese government. A chemical engineer by training, the 67-year-old Wu had been born in Wuhan, in central China, and began her career at a refinery in western China's desolate Gansu Province, before rising through the ranks of the petroleum industry and then being named vice mayor of Beijing in 1988. In the 1990s she had served as minister of Foreign Trade and Economic Cooperation, where she helped negotiate China's entry into the WTO—indeed, Wu Yi played a critical role in making her country an export powerhouse. With her reputation for getting things done, she had been asked to take over the portfolio of an incompetent minister of Health during the SARS crisis, and she was respected for having helped guide the country through the pandemic. Wu Yi was already involved in discussions with the U.S. as the senior Chinese official on the Joint Commission on Commerce and Trade; her portfolio as vice premier had expanded as she took on more responsibilities after Huang Ju's illness.

I had a few concerns about Wu Yi at the start. To begin with, she was a longtime trade negotiator, and she hadn't earned the sobriquet Iron Lady for nothing. In my experience, professional negotiators don't believe in win-win; they just want to outmaneuver you—to get as much as they can while giving up as little as possible. And she was a relentless negotiator. I was also concerned that Wu Yi didn't have the background for many of the issues we'd be dealing with in the SED. Furthermore, I doubted she had the power to make deals on behalf of China.

The important thing, to me, was that China's president, Hu Jintao, wanted to be actively involved and that I would have direct private access to him when I was in China. In turn, the Chinese delegation as a group would meet with President Bush in the States. As the protocol evolved, our entire senior delegation would be invited to see Hu at the Great Hall of the People after each SED meeting. Then, following a 45-minute meeting that enabled my fellow Cabinet secretaries to make their case on key issues directly to the Chinese president in front of his ministers, our delegation would file out while I stayed behind to visit with Hu. At that time, it was unprecedented for someone who was not a head of state to meet privately and alone with China's president. (The SED would open the door for other ranking U.S. Cabinet members to enjoy similar access on occasion.) I remember discussing the arrangement with President Bush sometime later. When I told him that I saw Hu alone, the president replied, "Alone? What do you mean by 'alone'?"

"Alone," I said. "Just the two of us."

"I've got small-meeting envy," the president said.

To announce the creation of the Strategic Economic Dialogue, the Chinese hosted a big press event at the Great Hall of the People. Every ministry in China involved with economic matters attended. At this gathering I met my official counterpart for the first time. Gray-haired, barely 5 feet tall, Vice Premier Wu Yi grabbed my hand and gave it a hearty squeeze.

"I know you didn't want me," she said bluntly. "I know you don't think I'm strong enough. But I'm going to show I'm as strong or stronger than you are."

That was my introduction to China's Iron Lady, and the beginning of a soft spot in my heart for her. I appreciated her directness, not to mention the strength of her grip. She was a force of nature. I would find her, in time, to be a tough negotiator and an efficient communicator who didn't twist words and was never discourteous or disrespectful. That day, looking around the vast high-ceilinged reception room thronged with dark-suited men, I instantly understood the struggle it must have been for her to make her way to the top ranks of the Party and state. China is in theory an egalitarian society, and I've met many dynamic and powerful women in business throughout the country, but Wu Yi was the only woman in the top government ranks—there was no other woman in the 25-member Politburo and just four among the 205 members of the Central Committee. I felt an admiration for her that would shift over time into professional affection.

It was still unclear how much time I would get with Hu Jintao on that trip. My calendar was stuffed with other meetings. One memorable sit-down came with Commerce Minister Bo Xilai at the ministry's offices on Chang'an Avenue, a short distance from Tiananmen Square. Bo was a rising star, a smooth politician with a strong populist bent, a flair for publicity, and a love of the limelight who was thought by many to have a shot at the Standing Committee of the Politburo, the most powerful body in the country. There was no hint in 2006 that Bo and his wife, Gu Kailai, would end up at the center of the country's biggest political scandal six years later.

Bo Xilai had been born in 1949, the year of Mao's victory, and was a true princeling. His father, Bo Yibo, was a leading economic planner and swimming partner of Mao's, who was purged in the 1960s, then rehabilitated after Deng Xiaoping came to power. He was one of the "eight immortals," influential Party elders of the Chinese Communist Party, under Deng. The younger Bo, like so many others of his generation, suffered during the Cultural Revolution, spending time in jail and at hard labor, but he'd followed those travails with a swift climb up the Party ladder. As mayor of the northeastern economic hub of Dalian in Liaoning Province from 1992 to 2000, he had overseen rapid growth and prosperity. He'd next served as governor of Liaoning, where he'd helped oversee the revitalization of its troubled industrial sector before becoming Commerce minister in 2004.

This meeting proved Bo to be a shrewd, exceedingly well-prepared advocate for China. He told me that he welcomed the launch of the SED and that Hu Jintao placed great importance upon it. For every point I brought up with him, he had a swift and dismissive response. Why were we so worried about the currency? he challenged me. The U.S. deficit with Asia-Pacific countries as a percentage of U.S. GDP had declined over the past six years. That was good, wasn't it? He pointed out that U.S. exports to China were up 20 percent, and that, in any case, most of China's exports to the U.S. came from foreign-invested enterprises operating in his country. I assured Bo that President Bush and I both believed protectionist measures were unhealthy and that I would work to persuade senators not to pass the Schumer-Graham bill. Bo conceded that a flexible rate would be good in the long term, but he contended that China's cheap labor would always give it a competitive edge. I was struck by the difference in his approach to that of Xi Jinping in Zhejiang. Xi was already looking to the day China lost that cost advantage and thinking of how the country could learn to innovate and compete higher up the value chain.

Bo's confidence and communication skills were impressive, as was his memory for facts, but I also found him overbearing and aggressive. I'd seen him correcting his translator on certain interpretations. This made quite an impression on me—not just his understanding of English but the peremptory way he overrode the translator, who was, I should note, a remarkable character in her own right. Our people knew her to be absolutely precise and nuanced in her translations, which meant, of course, that Bo was grandstanding when he interrupted her. She also had a flair for the dramatic. She would passionately deliver Bo's arguments in her dead-on English, then throw her pen down on the table for emphasis.

The following day I met with Hu Jintao, who was accompanied by a large group of Chinese officials at the Great Hall of the People. Hu was warm and welcoming and very supportive of the SED, acknowledging the importance of having a forum to discuss long-term policy issues. I made the point that, while the SED wasn't the venue to hash out short-term differences in areas like trade, nonetheless, we did need to deal with the most serious or politically sensitive issues as they arose, sometimes unexpectedly.

As our session wrapped up, the U.S. delegation left the room, along with most of the Chinese, except for Wu Yi, Finance Minister Jin Renqing, and Dai Bingguo, vice minister of Foreign Affairs. This gave me the chance for a brief, intimate meeting with Hu. I pressed the currency issue some, explaining that apart from long-term concerns, each side needed to point to short-term successes to show that our dialogue was making progress. I noted that outside of China—and to the U.S. Congress—currency flexibility was seen as an indicator of his country's reform efforts. That was about as much as I felt I could say in front of the other Chinese officials. But, as the meeting ended, I was able to get the president and his interpreter alone so I could be more specific on currency.

I began by emphasizing that I was not asking him to do something that wasn't good for China. In fact, I was making this request because I believed moving the currency was very much in his country's best interest. At a minimum, it would help us avoid protectionist actions from the U.S. Congress. Then, in a way that could only be done in a truly "private" meeting, I said something that I never divulged to members of the Congress or even to my fellow Cabinet members. (I did, of course, report this exchange to President Bush.) I gave him a number to work with.

"Mr. President," I said, "if your currency appreciated 3 percent against the dollar before the end of our first SED session this December, the result would be good for China and it would help me convince Congress that the SED is working."

There was no magic to the number I gave. But I knew that with less than three months until the first SED, a 3 percent bump would amount to an almost 15 percent annualized increase. I was looking for a good-faith gesture that was tangible and meaningful but that wouldn't seem insurmountable or impertinent to the Chinese, who rightly viewed the currency as a sovereign matter. So I took care to present my proposal as a constructive suggestion and not as a demand to be negotiated. Moreover, I believed that specifying a reasonable amount and timing for the move would encourage the Chinese to act. It would also preempt a Chinese rejoinder that almost any realistically achievable appreciation in their currency would not make a big difference in the trade deficit, which was largely determined by other factors, and would always be labeled as insufficient by their critics unless and until China had a market-determined currency.

The renminbi had increased by 2.4 percent since July 2005, when China dropped the dollar peg. The Chinese were determined to keep moving the currency—but not too fast, because they believed that doing so would not be good for stability in China.

Hu listened carefully to my proposal and said: "I understand."

Still, he was cautious and noncommittal. But he heard my message very clearly. I subsequently took Wu Yi aside and emphasized that it was important that we see some movement in the renminbi soon, even though there were more important concerns for the U.S. and China.

"If currency isn't the issue," she asked, "why do you keep talking about it?"

"It's a huge symbol in the U.S.," I explained. "If I don't talk about it, I'll lose credibility back home."

I came away confident that the Chinese would move the currency. I briefed President Bush on my return and called Senators Schumer and Graham. They withdrew their bill on September 28.

My confidence in the Chinese was well placed: they had listened and let their currency appreciate more rapidly. It would climb 1.3 percent from September 2006 to the end of our first SED meeting in December, and 2.2 percent through the end of our second SED meeting in May 2007. In what would become a familiar pattern, the pace of appreciation quickened as we approached each new SED and picked up even more during the meeting. By the time I left Treasury, the renminbi was up 13.8 percent from that September 2006 meeting with President Hu in Beijing, but the critics of China's foreign exchange policy were not satisfied, nor, frankly, should they be—until the value of China's currency is completely determined by the marketplace.

The first Strategic Economic Dialogue was held in Beijing on December 14 and 15, 2006. The 28-member delegation—the greatest number of Cabinet members and agency heads to travel in a single group to China from the U.S. until then—included our ambassador, Sandy Randt, and six of my fellow Cabinet members: Carlos Gutierrez of Commerce, Elaine Chao of Labor, Michael Leavitt of Health and Human Services, Samuel Bodman of Energy, U.S. Trade Representative Susan Schwab, and Environmental Protection Agency administrator Stephen Johnson. Federal Reserve chairman Ben Bernanke and Export-Import Bank head James Lambright also came. The Chinese side included 14 ministry-level officials, including central banker Zhou Xiaochuan, Finance Minister Jin Renqing, National Development and Reform Commission chairman Ma Kai, Labor and Security Minister Tian Chengping, and Commerce's Bo Xilai. This unprecedented high-ranking lineup showed the seriousness of both sides.

No one took the SED more seriously than I did, and I meant to leave nothing to chance. I had slow-boiled through too many ceremonial meetings in China and elsewhere at which delegate after delegate would deliver a speech, then sit down and nod off while the next delegate rose to deliver his or her prepared remarks. That was not how I intended the SED to work. I didn't want speakers drily reciting scripted talking points. I wanted real working meetings, where key issues were identified through candid presentations and frank discussions that fostered the kind of understanding and trust that would help us reach agreement on various actions, or so-called deliverables. The formal SED sessions themselves wouldn't be for nitty-gritty negotiations; these took place through my regular phone calls with my counterpart, on the margins of our sessions, or between meetings at the staff level, led by Treasury's Taiya Smith and her Chinese counterpart, Zhu Guangyao, then head of the international department at the Ministry of Finance.

"We're not just going to talk," I promised the Chinese. "We have to get short-term deliverables as well."

To the U.S. delegation I laid down Paulson's Rules of Order: "No using your BlackBerry. No taking calls. Everyone has to participate in every session. This is a real dialogue, and in a real dialogue, you focus on what's being discussed."

The two large delegations met inside the Great Hall of the People, in the cavernous Golden Hall, facing each other across long tables covered in green baize. Video screens were set up between the tables to allow for easier viewing of PowerPoint presentations. Each place was set with a name card that could be turned on its side to signal a participant's desire to speak: all were equipped with state-of-the-art microphones (superior to those in use at Treasury, though I noticed they appeared to be foreign-made, despite China's government procurement rules requiring domestic content). Decorated with fine paintings and hung with chandeliers, the vast yellow-walled room was hardly an intimate setting for discussion. But the Chinese had taken their usual care with details, setting pots of bright poinsettias around the room and, as ever, dispatching elegantly dressed young women to pour tea with near-synchronized precision. I learned later that the exacting Wu Yi had personally reviewed all the preparations, from menus to flower arrangements.

For the first SED we had placed several key topics on the agenda for discussion: China's economic development strategy, making China's growth sustainable, promoting trade and investment, and addressing specific energy and environmental issues. We spent some time discussing the renminbi, but we also talked about sulfur-dioxide controls, high-tech trade, restrictions on the U.S. entertainment industry, pirated DVDs, and China's efforts to increase consumption, as well as health and rural development. We discussed China's view that the U.S. refused too many visas and our belief that China's financial services sector should be opened to outside investment. And we explored China's rural-urban imbalance, encouraging leaders to address the structural causes of recent unrest in the countryside, including official corruption, the lack of property rights, and the need for better access to health care and education.

There were promising moments of frank talk. Fed chairman Ben Bernanke urged Chinese officials to increase public spending on pensions and health care and to improve access to private insurance. With China's high level of precautionary savings hobbling consumption, such measures would do more to address the underlying cause of our negative trade balance with China than appreciating the renminbi. National Development and Reform Commission chairman Ma Kai—who in 2013 would become vice premier responsible for industrial, transportation, and financial services policies— admitted that insufficient health insurance was a problem but pointed out that the government was trying to raise the incomes of farmers and poor city dwellers. When Trade Representative Schwab asserted that China was backtracking on reforms, Wu Yi and Ma Kai gave spirited responses. Ma Kai politely, but doggedly, questioned Schwab's facts, then challenged her analysis, arguing that some macro control by the State was inevitable even in a market economy. What is regulation, after all?

"Our reform has to be market oriented," he declared. "The key criterion to determine whether China's market-oriented economic system is established should be whether the market is playing a basic role in allocating resources instead of equating any macro control with backtracking on reform."

Striking a more defiant tone, Bo Xilai went on the offensive in responding to Secretary of Commerce Carlos Gutierrez, who had said, "We welcome Chinese investment." Bo shot back, "America is not open to Chinese investment. Look what happened when China National Offshore Oil Corporation tried to buy Unocal."

That was an episode I knew only too well, since Goldman Sachs had advised CNOOC on its high-profile, controversial deal. I can only imagine Bo thought he'd put me on the spot by mentioning it. If anything, though, I welcomed his assertiveness. He was saying what his Chinese colleagues were thinking, and I wanted the SED sessions to be lively, open, and thought provoking. To be honest, Bo aside, the initial SED was a bit too formal and static, as each side felt the other out, and speakers relied too frequently on set pieces or talking points. That would change over time as the principals got to know one another and the staffs for both sides worked closely between sessions to reach the milestones we set.

As for CNOOC, it was true the company had been forced to withdraw its $19 billion bid for a U.S. company, Unocal Corporation, which had most of its oil reserves in Asia. I explained that we were as open as any country in the world to foreign investment but that CNOOC had run into a political backlash because it was a contested deal and Unocal had already signed a contract with Chevron. I didn't say what everyone knew to be the case: that CNOOC had offered a higher price but was forced to withdraw its bid for political reasons. Bo, in fact, was right. It was an early example of China's growing global ambitions running up against reflexive U.S. protectionism. I did note that China's energy sector was not open for investment.

The first SED gave the U.S. Cabinet officials an opportunity to meet, and raise issues directly with, Premier Wen Jiabao and President Hu. Without the SED they would have had very little chance of seeing these leaders. Wen clearly had arranged our meeting with him to let us know he expected to participate in the dialogue. He told us he would speak for 35 minutes— and to our amazement he spoke for exactly 35 minutes, during which he said that China had selected a U.S.-based corporation, Westinghouse Electric Company, to provide the technology for four nuclear plants, something I had pushed hard for. China had been reluctant to approve the Pennsylvania-based Westinghouse because of its Japanese parent, Toshiba Corporation. Wen's news came as a bit of a surprise, since the Chinese had not yet received our last changes to an agreement we had been negotiating through the SED.

After our formal meeting with Hu, I met privately with the Chinese president, conveying President Bush's best wishes. I pressed Hu again on continued currency flexibility, warning that the next Congress would be tough on this issue. I emphasized that opening up financial services would be critical for China's development and beneficial for its relationship with the U.S. Hu agreed about the importance of opening financial services. But he cautioned me that in this area, leaders had to proceed slowly and "eat one mouthful at a time."

As I had hoped, the first SED was able to claim some immediate, specific successes. On the touchy subject of trade, we concluded an agreement that facilitated financing to support U.S. exports to China. The Chinese allowed the New York Stock Exchange and the Nasdaq Stock Market to open business offices in China and agreed to restart stalled negotiations to expand flights to and from the country for U.S. carriers. And we agreed that both sides would work to enable China to join the Inter-American Development Bank, which provides development financing in Latin America. These were modest accomplishments, but the important thing was that we had met, wrangled over hot topics, reached agreements, and, most important, set a tone of cooperation and put in place an effective process for the future. As soon as the sessions ended, I called Schumer and Graham, as well as their fellow senators Max Baucus (D-MT) and Chuck Grassley (R-IA), to report that we were off to a good start, noting that the renminbi had popped by more than 1 percent since September.

The most moving moment for me came on the first night of the SED. Our delegation had taken an evening tour of the Forbidden City. It was followed by a splendid banquet, complete with a Chinese band playing Western music, at the Beijing Hotel, which is located at the corner of Wanfujing Street and Chang'an Avenue. Wu Yi proudly announced that she had arranged something special for us. We were led out to a windy hotel balcony, high up over the city, with Wu Yi warning me, "Please stand back when you go outside." Apparently, she was worried that I might topple over the low railing.

Coatless, I shivered in the December night air. Aides cautioned me against staying outside and catching a cold, but there was no way I was going to miss what our hosts had arranged for us, especially given Wu Yi's obvious excitement about the treat.

Then I forgot all about the temperature as I beheld an astonishing sight just a few blocks away: all of the lights in and surrounding the Forbidden City had been turned on. The vast old palace complex, witness to centuries of empire, war, revolution, and protest, was ablaze in a welcome just for us.

CHAPTER TWELVE

The Great Patio Debate

On the day of the midterm elections, November 7, 2006, Democrats routed Republicans to capture control of the U.S. Senate, the House of Representatives, and most governorships and state legislatures. This "thumpin'," as President Bush called it, deepened an already bitter divide in Washington, except for one key area: both parties remained united in bashing China, which they blamed for currency manipulation, widening trade deficits, and stateside job losses. I expected the rancor to only get worse as the 2008 presidential campaign kicked into gear.

In January 2007 I was called to testify before the Senate Banking Committee, chaired by Connecticut Democrat Chris Dodd, who had just declared his candidacy for president. I tried to beg off, assuming that Dodd would want to score points by beating up on the Treasury secretary. I asked to defer testifying until after we'd finished budget negotiations, but Dodd insisted, telling me that I would never have a working relationship with him if I did not appear as scheduled.

Treasury was required by law to review twice a year the foreign exchange practices of the U.S.'s major trading partners to determine if any were manipulating their currencies against the dollar and to report its findings to Congress. In Treasury's December 2006 report I had declined to label China a currency manipulator, because I knew that doing so would only backfire. It would offend the Chinese and make it harder for them to let their currency appreciate; they wouldn't want to appear to be bowing to foreign pressure. Treasury had last cited China in 1994, but I was pushed hard on my decision. I told the senators that the best approach was not through confrontation—which would only lead to retaliation—but through the kind of tough-minded engagement we were getting in the SED, which was already producing results.

"My goal is to make significant progress toward a fully market-determined, floating Chinese currency," I said, adding that it was up to the International Monetary Fund to take China to task for any manipulation.

"We meet our constituents, and they are livid," Dodd replied. "Congress isn't going to wait necessarily for us to get some sort of vague definition of how this is kind of progressing when they watch 3 million manufacturing jobs leave this country."

The hearing reinforced in my mind how much pressure we would soon be facing. In February a bill emerged in the House of Representatives that specifically targeted China in proposing to levy countervailing duties on "nonmarket economies," and a number of other bills were in the works in the House and Senate. Although I knew much of the legislation was for show, and not intended to become law, I worried about one of the bills reaching the floor. If it went to a vote, Congress was sure to pass it, because that was what their aggrieved constituents back home would demand, and no one wanted to appear to be "soft" on China. I believed that congressional leaders were looking for good reasons not to move the legislation, but I was also concerned that some unforeseen economic or political incident, or some Chinese action, might cause the leaders' judgment to change.

I took the position that China needed to move toward a more flexible currency not because *we* said so but because ultimately it would be in its best interests. A more flexible currency would lead to a strengthened renminbi, which would encourage economic activity within China by, among other things, boosting household consumption and domestic-led growth. It would make it easier for policymakers to control inflation, and it would minimize economic dislocations and speculative bubbles.

President Hu and other Chinese leaders said they were committed to moving toward a market-determined currency, but only gradually, because they worried about disrupting economic growth and threatening social stability. By SED II, in the spring of 2007, the nominal value of the renminbi had risen by nearly 6 percent from 2005, when China had taken the currency off its peg to the U.S. dollar.

To my mind, there were more immediate, pressing issues. Among these, the Chinese needed to speed key reforms in financial markets. Freeing banks from government control and noncommercial lending directives while developing efficient, competitive capital markets would help China transition to an economy that was less reliant on low-cost exports and better able to produce higher-value-added products and provide crucial financing to private sector companies. Reformers had strived for such changes against powerful resistance, some of it ideological and some the unanticipated by-product of the very success of China's reforms. Cleaned-up, newly profitable state-owned enterprises had become powerful vested interests that pushed back against the prospect of greater competition from the private sector or foreign companies.

In addition, China's boom had led to gaping disparities between rich and poor, urban and rural residents, and the eastern and western regions of the country. President Hu and Premier Wen had set out to create a "harmonious society" to quell dissatisfaction, proposing to spend political capital not on market-oriented reforms they saw as risky but on populist support for the groups left behind, like migrant workers, poor farmers, and pensioners. China's rapid development mirrored in some respects the kind of wealth creation and income disparities that were seen in the U.S. during the Gilded Age of the late 19th century, when huge fortunes were created and social tensions were exacerbated.

I decided to try to influence the leadership by launching a campaign for capital markets reform, which I viewed as critical to rebalancing China's economic growth model. So in March, after bilateral meetings in Japan and South Korea, I flew to China to give a speech in Shanghai on capital markets liberalization. I stopped over briefly at Beijing's main airport for an unofficial visit with my SED counterpart, Wu Yi, who arrived accompanied by, among others, Commerce Minister Bo Xilai, Finance Minister Jin Renqing, and central bank chief Zhou Xiaochuan. The fact that she was accompanied by six officials who held full ministerial rank, Wu Yi said, indicated the great importance President Hu placed on the SED.

Picking up on that point, I told Wu Yi I had made the case to Congress that the SED was the proper forum for resolving our differences with China. So, I stressed, we absolutely had to get results. I pressed her on currency and pushed for opening the financial markets further to foreign commercial and investment banks. At the time, China had some of the most restrictive equity ownership rules among big emerging-markets countries. No single foreign entity could own more than 20 percent of a Chinese bank; total foreign ownership was limited to 25 percent. Foreign securities companies could own up to 33 percent of a joint venture, while foreign asset management firms were limited to 49 percent of a JV. There was a 20 percent limit on single direct ownership stakes in Chinese securities firms. I thought there should be no caps at all, but at a minimum I wanted to see them raised above 50 percent. At the time, other developing countries, like Brazil, Russia, and India, allowed foreign firms to own 100 percent.

I knew from experience that some Chinese officials believed that the securities sector was a strategic national asset and wanted to keep foreigners out: Goldman had spent the better part of four years trying to set up a securities firm in China. Finally, through a creative structuring and patient negotiation, Goldman Sachs Gao Hua Securities Company had emerged; it was a joint venture in which Goldman owned the permissible 33 percent but had full operating control.

While Wu Yi pushed back on currency reform, she was encouraging on changes in financial services. This squared with information I'd gotten right after the first SED, when Finance Minister Jin told me he was confident the equity caps would be raised. Some of my staff had cautioned me not to get ahead of myself, but I was feeling pretty optimistic.

I spoke on March 8, 2007, at the Shanghai Futures Exchange. It had been established eight years earlier in Pudong, the new financial center of China that lay across the Huangpu River from the historic Bund and was replete with bright lights and shiny skyscrapers. I told the audience of several hundred gathered on the trading floor—government officials, the heads of the biggest securities companies, prominent academics and journalists—that if China wanted to live up to its promise, it should quicken the pace of financial services market reforms. Efficient capital markets, based on transparency, clear property rights, strong institutions, and robust supervision, drive economic growth. They funnel money to the best ideas and allow people to invest in their country's future.

Despite great strides, Chinese markets remained rudimentary and fragmentary. There was little in the way of debt, including government paper; real estate was illiquid and beyond most people's means; the stock market, barely a decade and a half old, was volatile and rife with fraud, from rigged accounting to pump-and-dump schemes. The country urgently needed sound alternatives to invest its newfound wealth and to cope with changes in demographics and social structure that had led to a soaring savings rate that crimped consumption. Disappearing cradle-to-grave government care and the fear of widespread job losses from the restructurings of state-owned enterprises had led workers to save more for retirement and other contingencies. So, too, did the one-child policy, which put a greater burden on individuals to care for aging parents in a society governed by filial piety. But there were few appropriate investment vehicles for these "precautionary" savings beyond bank deposit accounts, whose government-fixed interest rates were so paltry that people had to put aside an even greater share of their earnings to build their nest eggs.

Capital markets liberalization would provide Chinese citizens access to a wider range of investment products and services, promoting the development of a more diversified economy. Greater foreign participation would speed this process, which was why I recommended removing the equity caps. I wasn't asking China to do any favors for foreign banks. I simply believed that limiting the participation of the world's best banks hurt the country.

"I don't know of a single country in the world with a successful and sustainable well-balanced economy that doesn't have a strong capital market in place," I told the group in Shanghai. "And I cannot think of any such country that isn't open to competition—both domestically and from abroad."

Some of the issues raised in my Shanghai speech were on the agenda for SED II, set for May 22–24, 2007, in Washington. Since the first SED in Beijing, teams from the U.S. and China had been working on deliverables, and the agenda included progress reports on financial services, balanced economic development, and cooperation on alternative energy and pollution reduction, among other things. A number of major agreements would be unveiled, including opening China's skies to U.S. airlines.

The SED was constructed so that the deliverables were negotiated and nailed down between our semiannual conclaves. Our various departments and agencies had been dealing with their Chinese counterparts all along and would continue to have direct discussions with them, but the SED process prioritized issues for the Chinese and allowed us to resolve matters that had gotten lost in the bureaucratic tangle of years past. Before we set up the SED, each U.S. department and agency had independently lobbied for its concerns with the Chinese. Now, under the direction of my deputy chief of staff, Taiya Smith, deputies from every department sat down together and hashed out our government's top five to ten priorities. We looked for "big ideas": initiatives that were both transformational and solidly in the mutual interest of both the U.S. and China. The Chinese did the same. Then the U.S. and China worked on something known as the outcomes document, which listed every item being worked on for each SED. The semiannual SED meetings themselves were reserved for dialogue: substantive presentations followed by honest discussion. Both sides meticulously tracked the agreed-upon outcomes—a simplified version of which was released as a fact sheet at the end of each SED—knowing that they were expected to carry them out and that any failures would be reported to me or to my Chinese counterpart.

The Chinese had their own list of priorities, of course. They were eager to modify or postpone new U.S. export control rules to gain greater access to technology in areas like clean energy, civil aviation, electronics, and software. And they also pressed us to consider granting their country so-called market economy status so that their companies would receive preferential treatment.

Ahead of SED II, I called Wu Yi to give her the lay of the land. Again I reported Washington lawmakers' growing impatience with her country and recommended to the vice premier that she personally meet with U.S. lawmakers and tell them China's story.

"This round of the SED will determine the dialogue's viability," I said. "We need a breakthrough package of results."

I believed that a breakthrough might come with China agreeing to increase the caps on foreign investment in its securities firms, but right before the start of SED II, as the Chinese delegation flew to Washington, we learned from Taiya Smith's counterpart, Zhu Guangyao, that lifting the equity caps had not been approved by President Hu and Premier Wen. This surprised me, given how encouraging Finance Minister Jin had been after the first SED; I knew we might not get the 50 percent–plus I wanted, but I thought we'd get at least 35 percent.

When the Chinese delegation landed at Andrews Air Force Base on the morning of May 21, I was there to meet them. The formal meeting of the SED was to begin the next day in downtown Washington, and we had arranged my official greeting as a show of respect for Wu Yi, but I also hoped to raise the issue of equity caps and win the concession we sought.

"We've got a big problem," I told the vice premier after a few polite preliminaries, as we walked along the warm, windy tarmac. "We need to figure out how to resolve this issue before the SED gets started."

"We've given you much more than you have given us," Wu Yi asserted. "But we will talk."

I knew I'd have one more shot later in the day. When my team at Treasury and I heard we weren't getting the equity caps concession, we had decided to invite Wu Yi and colleagues to dinner at my home to work on her some more. I'd asked my assistant, deputy executive secretary Lindsay Valdeon, to alert my wife, Wendy, who happened to be at Treasury that day, working on a project to make the department more "green."

Fortunately, I had married a woman who is unflappable, resourceful, and incredibly understanding. Wendy had accompanied me on many trips to China, helping me build relationships there—and building many of her own. She'd cooked for plenty of Chinese guests, but that May day she didn't have time to plan a dinner, so she simply drove to the local Whole Foods Market and made a beeline for the takeaway hot tables. She loaded up on noodles, Chinese beef with peppers, and other dishes she hoped would please our visitors from Beijing.

A small group gathered that evening at my place, a French country-style house in the Massachusetts Heights area of Washington, D.C. On the Chinese side Wendy and I welcomed Wu Yi, Bo Xilai, NDRC chief Ma Kai, central bank head Zhou Xiaochuan, Finance Minister Jin, Ambassador to the U.S. Zhou Wenzhong, and Zhu Guangyao. From the American side were, among others, Taiya, U.S. Ambassador to China Sandy Randt, and Ambassador Alan Holmer, Treasury's special envoy to the SED.

Tucked into the side of a hill, our three-bedroom home was small and cozy inside. The main floor, down a small flight of stairs, was open plan, with the living room flowing into the dining room, and both facing a flagstone patio that overlooked a wooded ravine and quiet stream. As soon as the guests arrived, I took Wu Yi aside on the patio and shut the glass door. We had neighbors fairly close on either side, including a reporter for the *Washington Post*, but I was frustrated, and I got a little loud.

"Madam Vice Premier, I've been telling Congress that currency isn't the problem, structural issues are, and I believe we're going to have some breakthroughs," I said. "That means I have to show real progress on issues like equity caps. You and I promised each other that there wouldn't be any surprises, but here I am, surprised and embarrassed."

It got so heated that Wendy, who could hear us from inside, worried we wouldn't sit down together to eat, but she succeeded in shepherding everyone into the dining room. We filled our plates buffet-style and found places to eat on the patio and in our living room. Wu Yi and I sat down together. Taiya and Zhu Guangyao joined us, and this time the conversation was softer.

"I've been working so hard on this," Wu Yi confided about the equity caps, "but you're not going to get it now."

As we went back and forth, it dawned on me that perhaps Wu Yi simply didn't understand why the issue was so important. She was a trade negotiator, not a finance official. Her background was in petroleum and chemical engineering, not economics. Furthermore, she had little or no experience with an untethered private sector and the economic growth it could provide. Or maybe she simply couldn't accomplish what we wanted done.

Wendy's Whole Foods takeout was a hit. The beef and peppers disappeared, and, as is their custom, the Chinese prepared to leave as soon as the meal was finished. But I could see that Wu Yi was still upset. Our argument on the patio had clearly distressed her. This SED meeting was very important to the vice premier, who was making her first visit to the U.S. as my counterpart. The Iron Lady would be retiring the following year, when the Chinese made government changes. She clearly wanted to go out on a successful note.

Sorry that I had upset her, I just put my arms around Wu Yi. I'm not much for the touchy-feely side of things, so my spontaneous hug surprised my Treasury colleagues—and me—perhaps as much as it did the Iron Lady of China.

"Don't worry," I assured her. "This is going to be a success."

The formal meetings of SED II were held in the magnificent setting of the neoclassical Andrew W. Mellon Auditorium on Constitution Avenue, at the base of the Federal Triangle. Built in an imposing temple style and named for a previous Treasury secretary, the gilded auditorium was part of a complex that housed, among other entities, the Environmental Protection Agency.

As with the first SED, I reminded the U.S. team that the Chinese tended to give long speeches and that we should mind our manners. The Chinese wanted us to understand them and their needs, and they took the SED very seriously. They worked hard on their presentations to make sure they were detailed and thorough. So we had to be serious, too.

"They'll be performing for their delegation peers in Washington as well as those back in China," I explained. "The opportunity to give their speeches is exceptionally important to them. Your listening to their perspective constitutes a real deliverable to them."

We were able to unveil several key milestones. First, we announced the "open skies" agreement liberalizing air travel to and from China—one of President Bush's top priorities. This was a good example of the value of the SED process. Flight allotments to China from the United States were way too low—only 11 daily nonstop passenger flights, compared with 55 daily nonstop flights to Germany. And while the benefits to China were huge—one estimate said the country gained more than $200 million in economic activity annually for each additional daily flight—their domestic air carriers, fearing a loss of market share, had pressured their officials to resist opening to our carriers. Our Transportation and State Departments had negotiated to expand air service in April 2006 only to have China pull out four months later.

The SED recharged the discussion by allowing us to present the issue

at a higher political level, beyond the narrow considerations of China's aviation industry, and appeal to the country's broader interests. At the first SED
we had agreed to restart talks, and six months of diligent staff work later we
announced an agreement to double the number of passenger flights and to
lift the limits on cargo routes and carriers.

SED II also announced some much-desired liberalization of China's
financial services regulations, including the gradual expansion of the activities that joint venture companies could pursue to include securities broker-
age, proprietary trading, and asset management. The quota for so-called
Qualified Foreign Institutional Investors would triple to $30 billion from
$10 billion—a change I'd pushed for in my Shanghai speech two and a half
months before. The increase benefited dozens of big investors around the
world, from banks like the Swiss giants UBS and Credit Suisse to professional money managers like the U.S.'s Templeton Asset Management and
such institutional investors as the Bill & Melinda Gates Foundation and
Yale University, which could now buy and sell bigger stakes in Chinese
yuan-denominated shares on the Shenzhen and Shanghai Stock Exchanges.

We also took up the grave subject of the safety of Chinese exports to the
U.S. The spring of 2007 had deeply bruised the "made in China" brand.
The Food and Drug Administration had announced one of the largest-ever
recalls of pet food after the industrial chemical melamine had been found
in imports from China. Some of the animal feed had worked its way into
the human food supply in the U.S. Mike Leavitt, secretary of Health and
Human Services, dispatched an investigative team to China, but it became
clear that the SED would need to focus on this thorny issue, which cut
across several economic sectors.

The protocol of our operating agreement with China meant that I
would have a private discussion with Hu after the SED meetings. These
were frank and, I think, quite useful to both sides. To reciprocate, at the
end of SED II, President Bush met with the U.S. and Chinese delegations
at the Eisenhower Executive Office Building. I had explained to the president that a meeting with Wu Yi in the Oval Office would mean a lot to
her. She had never been there and had not gotten her picture taken with
President Bill Clinton after the successful WTO negotiations. I still felt bad

for upsetting her at my house, and the president happily invited her to the White House.

President Bush knew how to turn on the charm. As we walked down the steps of the Executive Office Building and toward the West Wing, he guided her between us, and we each held a hand as photographers snapped our picture. Once in the Oval Office, he talked with Wu Yi about U.S.-China relations and the importance of her role, then made a point of posing for pictures with her. Then, as our private meeting ended, he took her by the hands, bent down, and kissed her good-bye.

Wu Yi didn't say anything that day, but four years later, hosting a lunch for me in Beijing, she recounted with a twinkle in her eye, "I've met with a number of foreign leaders, but that was the first time I've ever been kissed in the Oval Office."

Wu Yi was in a feisty mood for her trip to Capitol Hill to meet some of our legislators. The vice premier was a forceful advocate for China's women, and she eagerly looked forward to meeting with Speaker of the House Nancy Pelosi. She told me she'd been warned that meeting the California Democrat would be like walking into the den of a tiger, but she wasn't intimidated; she'd been born in the Year of the Tiger. Turns out, Nancy had been born in the Year of the Dragon, and the dragon let the tiger know that "members of Congress are following closely the Strategic Economic Dialogue."

We put a lot of thought into how we hosted the Chinese delegation. Entertainment may seem like a trivial subject compared with trade balances or energy development, but the Chinese take it very seriously, lavishing great expense and planning on dinners, fireworks, singers, and acrobats to share their culture and amuse their guests. At Treasury we had nowhere near a comparable budget for entertainment, and our team had to scramble to come up with something good on a shoestring, lest we lose too much face.

The solution turned out to be one of the highlights of the meeting. Our team found an astonishing singer, Tyler Thompson, a 12-year-old African American from Oakland, California. He attended school in a predominantly Chinese American neighborhood and had an extraordinary affinity for traditional Chinese music. We welcomed our guests with a dinner at the

State Department in the elegant Benjamin Franklin State Dining Room, where red faux-marble Corinthian columns soar to the gilt-edge plaster-work of the ceiling, hung with splendid cut-glass chandeliers. Tyler sang a Mongolian folk song so beautifully that at least one minister had tears in his eyes as he listened. A number of members of the delegation approached Tyler afterward to praise his performance, with several telling him, "My mother sang that to me when I was a child."

Over my years of close contact with China, I'd learned that it was impossible to separate the country's environmental challenges from its rapid growth: China's dazzling economic leap forward had taken a horrific toll on its environment. You saw and felt that firsthand everywhere you went: in the choking smog that increasingly blanketed Beijing and other big cities; in the fetid rivers and lakes that made China's water undrinkable for much of the population; in the reports of basic foodstuffs like rice tainted by industrial heavy metals like cadmium. The problem played out in the streets, putting at risk not only the nation's health but also its social and political stability. In 2005 China had seen an estimated 50,000 protests, some of them violent, that had been prompted by environmental issues.

The very structure of the Chinese economy encouraged abuse, with state-owned enterprises run at the regional level by officials who were rewarded for growth at any cost. The toll was startling: in 2007 the World Bank estimated that pollution cost China 5.8 percent of GDP annually and caused 750,000 premature deaths each year. An earlier World Bank report had found China home to 16 of the world's 20 most polluted cities. Suffering from severe water and air pollution, the country faced the prospect of an unprecedented environmental catastrophe.

Nor were China's environmental problems contained by its borders, as particles of air pollution were carried across the Pacific on westerly winds to the U.S. Power plants burning coal to meet an insatiable demand for electricity combined with record numbers of cars and trucks rolling onto a rapidly growing highway system helped cause emissions of the greenhouse gas carbon dioxide to nearly double from 2000 to 2007, on China's way to surpassing the U.S. as the largest emitter of CO_2 in the world. If China couldn't get a better handle on environmental protection, the rest of the planet would suffer along with it.

The country was taking steps to deal with its environmental challenges. In June 2007 it unveiled a plan to address climate change, and it had vowed to make the upcoming 2008 Summer Olympics in Beijing "green." But competing interests, and the leadership's determination to pursue relentless economic growth, put environmentalists at a disadvantage. Moreover, the State Environmental Protection Administration (SEPA) had been cobbled together in 1998 out of a weak predecessor, and the agency was new and inexperienced, vastly understaffed, and lacked clout in Zhongnanhai.

Not that everything was perfect in the U.S., but after decades of public discussion, overdue legislation, and government regulation, we had demonstrated that a healthy environment could coexist with a strong economy. I hoped the SED could help China improve its approach, for everyone's sake. At the first meeting in December 2006, we had agreed to cooperate on efficient and sustainable energy use, and the just-completed SED II had included an agreement on a range of environmental issues, including clean-coal technology and discussions aimed at securing an eventual bilateral pact to end illegal logging, which contributes to erosion, desertification, and the loss of vital natural habitats for wildlife.

The environment was the chief item on my agenda when I returned to China in July 2007. I landed at a time of ecological disaster. Severe flooding in the country's central and coastal regions had affected more than 105 million citizens, killed more than 500 people, destroyed crops, and threatened dikes and levees. Just a week before my arrival, President Hu had traveled to the city of Chongqing to assess the damage. China had been experiencing droughts and serious flooding for years, and there was no question that deforestation, overfarming, and overdevelopment had contributed to the problem.

At the suggestion of Dan Wright, a key member of my Treasury SED team, I had decided to visit the far western province of Qinghai, on the Tibetan Plateau, before my scheduled August 1 meeting with President Hu. It was an unusual place for a U.S. official to venture, but Qinghai's huge, endangered saltwater lake exemplified many of China's—and the world's—challenges. I wanted to highlight the importance of environmental issues for both our countries, while showing that we knew there was far more to China than Beijing and Shanghai and that we understood the reach and complexity of the country's challenges.

President Hu had spent years in western China, running the Tibet Autonomous Region as Party secretary from 1988 to 1992. Qinghai was a poor province, where Hu had been encouraging economic development. I knew that my going there would command his attention and respect, in much the same way that working with Tsinghua University to revitalize its School of Economics and Management had strengthened my connections to its famously loyal alumni body, which included Hu himself.

Traveling to the region took me 1,300 miles west of Beijing and 10,000 feet above sea level. China's largest lake, Qinghai is also one of its most beautiful. The surrounding province is known as "China's water tower" because seven of Asia's biggest rivers, including the Yangtze, Mekong, and Yellow, originate in the mountains there, and the region's glaciers contribute to downstream water flows. Equal in size to Western Europe, the Qinghai-Tibetan Plateau stretches to Central Asia, embracing Tibet, Mount Everest, and part of Kashmir. It plays a key role in the Asian monsoon system, thus touching the lives of more than half of the world's population.

But the lake and the surrounding plateau had been under threat. The province was beset by droughts and desertification—partly because of overgrazing and land reclamation, partly because of climate change. Like Utah's Great Salt Lake, Qinghai Lake is endorheic. It doesn't drain to the sea; rather, it is a basin filled by streams and rivers. The lake itself had been shrinking for a century—maximum depths, which once reached 100 meters, were now closer to 30 meters—and its waters had become increasingly saline as tributaries dried up. Before the 1960s 108 freshwater rivers emptied into the lake; by the time of our visit, close to 85 percent of them, including the lake's largest tributary, the Buha River, had disappeared.

Ironically, in 2004 the shrinking had reversed and the lake had begun to expand. But the new water was coming in part, scientists believed, from the rapid shrinking, caused by climate change, of the great glaciers of the Tibetan Plateau. Local temperatures were rising four times faster than elsewhere in China, with potentially adverse implications not only for weather patterns in the region but for much of the rest of the world as well, because of the plateau's influence on the global jet stream. As I told foreign and local reporters who accompanied me, my purpose in going to Qinghai was to demonstrate that "what's happening with the environment in the middle of China not only affects the local climate and economy but also the global climate and economy."

To reach the lake, our group, which included Taiya Smith, Dan Wright, and Lindsay Valdeon, among others from Treasury, plus a number of Chinese and U.S. scientists, drove 75 miles from the provincial capital, Xining, on a brand-new four-lane highway that eventually wound slowly up a wide gorge. Along the way we began to see more ethnic Tibetans: young children with cherry-red cheeks, their parents with the weathered-dark skin of people who seemed to have completed a lifetime of work by age 20. All wore bright-hued clothing with woven belts and sashes. There were herds of grazing yaks and short native horses in colorful tack, and as we reached the top of the gorge, which opened onto fields of brilliant yellow rapeseed, we could see Qinghai Lake, seemingly as boundless as an ocean.

At those heights, nearly 2 miles above sea level, it was, literally, a breath-taking view. But it wasn't long before I could see the damage as we trudged over mountainous dunes of powdery white sand that spilled down to the water's edge. If not for a tree-planting project aimed at restoring vegetation, we might have been standing in the Gobi desert. The Chinese government had pledged nearly $900 million to help fix the lake's problems. The Nature Conservancy, World Bank, Asian Development Bank, and other institutions were working hand in hand to improve the province's ecosystem.

My hosts led me down a marked path through the dunes to the lake-shore, careful not to disturb the sparse vegetation. Qinghai Lake was a popular destination for tourists from China and throughout the world. Many who came were bird-watchers; the lake was an important wintering and breeding ground for the endangered black-necked crane and the bar-headed goose, a bird that migrates over the Himalayas to feed in India in the winter. Because I was visiting Qinghai strictly to explore environmental issues, I'd vetoed a proposed side trip for birding, though I had brought my binoculars just in case. We strolled along the lake, joined by local government officials, security teams, and our delegation. Our walk led us past the

scattered trash of what must have been a recent beer party. The local officials standing near me saw the cans the same time I did, and for a moment I
worried that the cleaning crew was going to get in trouble for having missed
them. So I reached down and picked a can up and examined it. Then I
dropped it and stepped on the can to flatten it. Then I crushed another.

"Everyone's responsible for keeping the lake clean," I said. "I'll do my part."

The local officials joined in. Soon we were all crushing the cans and
dropping them into garbage bags.

After touring the lake we stopped for lunch with some of the local
leaders. Tibetans are not known for their cuisine, but I was curious to see
what the locals ate. We went into a small restaurant in a village along the
road, where we were served several courses, including what turned out to
be yak knuckles—big, bony, gristly chunks of meat swimming in broth.
Caught up in a discussion about the challenges facing Qinghai Lake, I
absent-mindedly fished a knuckle out of the broth and began to chew on it.
Shortly after, I felt Taiya tapping me on my shoulder and heard her whis-
per: "Hank, no one else is eating that." She was right. Everyone else at the
table, including local officials, was steering clear of that one dish, which on
reexamination appeared to have seen better days. Fortunately, I suffered no
negative consequences.

Seeing up close the threat to the spectacular plateau left a profound
impression on me. I went away from Qinghai Lake convinced that working
to mitigate climate change had to become an essential component of U.S.-
China cooperation and that the place to start was to promote clean energy,
clean transportation, clean air and water, and greater biodiversity. Eventually, this line of thinking would lead to a groundbreaking agreement on
energy and the environment, which the U.S. and China would announce
the following year.

The next day I had a full slate of meetings in Beijing that concluded with a
visit with President Hu at the Great Hall of the People. Hu exuded an enthusiasm I had not witnessed before as he told me how much it meant to him that
I had taken the time to visit western China. He was so chatty that at first I
wondered whether he was filibustering—deliberately squandering the 45 min-

utes we had scheduled for our meeting so that he would not have to discuss the thornier issues of U.S.-China economic relations. Instead, he extended our meeting to 90 minutes, and it was one of the best interchanges I had had with him.

"Were you uncomfortable at the high altitude?" he asked of my trip to Qinghai, adding that he always took a little time to adjust when he visited there. I said that I spent a lot of time in the mountains in Colorado, so the altitude had not affected me.

I moved straight into the issues on my mind. I emphasized to Hu that as the world's two largest consumers of energy, the U.S. and China had to exert joint leadership on the issue of climate change. I noted that I had used some of my short time in Beijing to see State Forestry administrator Jia Zhibang to encourage him to take action against illegal logging.

I then turned our discussion to a more sensitive subject. I told the president that in the wake of recent product safety problems, some U.S. companies had begun to advertise their products as "China-free." His country's reputation with U.S. consumers had deteriorated since the pet-food scandal had erupted in March. In June, Chinese toothpaste containing an antifreeze ingredient had been yanked from U.S. shelves (the same ingredient had been mistakenly added to cold medicine in Panama and caused more than 100 deaths there). There were reports of toys made with lead paint—including some sold by U.S. toy giant Mattel—as well as seafood raised with restricted antibiotics and sold in the U.S. The news within China wasn't any better: on July 10 the country had executed the former chief of its State Food and Drug Administration, Zheng Xiaoyu, for corruption.

Hu responded by telling me that he had put Wu Yi personally in charge of a new leadership group to deal with these safety issues. The problem was difficult to fix, stemming as it did from a complex combination of corruption, counterfeiting, lack of transparency, and ineffective regulation and supervision. But with her long experience in promoting Chinese exports and her well-deserved reputation for being able to get things done, the vice premier was a logical choice for the job.

It was a measure of how much my trip to Qinghai had caught the attention of the Chinese that the subject came up eight months later when

I was in China again. This time I was visiting with Premier Wen Jiabao, an engineer and geologist by training who had taken a lead in examining the social impact of the country's breakneck growth. We had a broad agenda, touching on a number of important economic and financial issues, so I was surprised when he suddenly raised his arm to cut me off while I was speaking.

"My staff told me you picked up beer cans on the shore of Qinghai Lake," Wen noted. "It is clear that you care about China. The situation we are facing is very grim."

As he spoke his face glowed with appreciation, and his eyes moistened. I knew that Wen cared deeply about his country's troubled environment. China had created a national task force on climate change, and Wen had urged local governments to push harder to reduce energy consumption and greenhouse gas emissions. Still, I took little comfort from these efforts. Talk is cheap the world over, and actions are what matters. The Chinese were sincere and understood the climate problem, but confronting it was not something that Wen was able to do, nor was it the government's top priority then.

The trip to Beijing was notable for another reason. About two weeks before I had left Washington, Representative Barney Frank called to ask my help for one of his Massachusetts constituents. Yang Jianli, a Chinese pro-democracy activist who had become a legal permanent resident of the U.S.—his wife and two children were U.S. citizens—was being prevented by the authorities from leaving China.

Born in the coastal province of Shandong in 1963, Yang had been a promising Party member before he left for the U.S. in the 1980s to pursue a doctorate in mathematics at the University of California, Berkeley. His fellow Chinese students selected him to fly home in 1989 to join the Tiananmen Square protests. He escaped the government crackdown and returned to the States, where he earned a second doctorate, in political economy, from Harvard. Though banned from returning, Yang flew back in 2002, using a friend's passport, to observe labor unrest in northern China. Authorities arrested him when he tried to board a domestic flight, and he was held incommunicado for more than a year. By the time he was sentenced to five years in prison for espionage, he'd already spent two years in confinement. In prison he suffered harsh physical treatment that he said included electric shocks and beatings.

In 2005, to try to secure his release, Yang's father traveled from his home in Maryland to China, only to die there. A year later, authorities offered to free the dissident and let him return to the U.S., but Yang insisted on visiting his father's grave first. He was released from prison in April 2007, but without a passport or other legal papers, he was unable to leave the country. Condi Rice and other high-level U.S. officials had tried to obtain his release without success. The United Nations had issued a resolution that Yang was being held in violation of international law.

Yang's wife had asked Barney Frank, whose congressional district she lived in, to put pressure on the Chinese government to give her husband a passport so he could return home. Barney turned to me—the Massachusetts Democrat and I had developed a mutual trust and respect while working together to reform Fannie Mae and Freddie Mac, the struggling government-sponsored mortgage giants. I promised to see what could be done. I admire people who sacrifice their freedom and comfort to help their countrymen, and, based on what Barney had told me, I wanted to help Yang. When I inquired, I found that the issue was so sensitive in Beijing that Yang's only hope for getting a passport was if I discussed the matter personally—and very quietly—with the Chinese. We decided to include it among the issues I would emphasize on my July trip.

Sandy Randt, our ambassador to China, was skeptical that I'd have any success. "We've already tried really hard," he told me.

"Watch," I said. "You can't come in the meeting with me, but I'm going to get this done."

I had decided that, rather than going directly to President Hu and putting him on the spot, I would approach Wu Yi and let her do the rest. After formal meetings with her and a number of ministers, I took Wu Yi aside. Normally, we would be accompanied by Taiya Smith and Wu Yi's assistant, but given the sensitivity of Yang's situation, I arranged to see the vice premier alone—with only our translators in attendance. I explained to Wu Yi that it was in China's interest to release Yang because I'd been asked to do so by Barney Frank, who was head of the House Financial Services Committee and one of the most important leaders in the newly elected Democratic majority of Congress. I reminded her of the possibility of currency legislation and said that Yang's release was important to me. I promised that we would not make a big deal about this. We didn't want publicity; we just wanted him back.

"Let me look into it," Wu Yi said. She needed to consult with other officials.

I did not raise the issue of Yang Jianli in my meetings with Hu or Wen. But on the day I was leaving Beijing to return to Washington, Wu Yi pulled me aside and told me that if I could ensure that Yang would leave China immediately on receiving a passport, her government would issue it. She asked that I keep the news quiet until Yang had reached the U.S. I returned home on August 1, 2007, and waited until I had confirmation from the Chinese that Yang was on the plane. Then I called Barney on New York's Fire Island, where he was enjoying the weekend. I told him the news, emphasizing that we had to keep mum to the press about the activist's release. Yang arrived on August 18.

The Yang Jianli episode was a good example of how the SED gave me access to Chinese leaders and the ability to talk about issues that to some might have fallen far outside the dialogue's economic umbrella. No question, I defined "economic" very broadly when it came to the SED, and some people at the State Department are still a little bit angry about it. Not Condi Rice, however; she understood and supported what we were trying to do. And, more important, so did President Bush, who made the SED a centerpiece of his China policy.

The president knew that it was crucial for the U.S. to have a constructive relationship with China—that it paid to work constantly to increase incentives for mutual cooperation and reduce the likelihood for conflict. He was among the first world leaders to announce that he would attend the Beijing Olympics, knowing how important that decision was to China. Yet he never wavered in his conviction that the U.S. needed to be strong in Asia: economically, diplomatically, and militarily. He knew we needed to stand up for human rights and religious freedom. But he recognized the critical importance of the U.S.-Chinese economic relationship, and he supported our trade with China even when it was politically inconvenient to do so.

CHAPTER THIRTEEN

Hammering Out a New Framework

In August 2007, a few days after returning from my meetings with President Hu in China, I traveled to the American West on a relationship-building trip of another sort. My destination was Billings, Montana, whose dramatic mountain ranges and sweeping blue sky bore a notable resemblance to the high plateau surrounding Qinghai Lake. I was to meet with Democrat Max Baucus, chairman of the Senate Finance Committee, at his invitation.

The soft-spoken, silver-haired senator was home for the late-summer recess, and I hoped that by meeting with him on his turf I could ward off the anti–Chinese currency legislation that he had drafted along with New York Democrat Chuck Schumer, Iowa Republican Chuck Grassley, and South Carolina Republican Lindsey Graham. Their bill sharpened the U.S. response to currency manipulators, allowing the government to impose restrictions ranging from initiating World Trade Organization consultations, which could open a path to International Monetary Fund penalties, to imposing steep antidumping duties on the imports of offending countries. It had been introduced in June, and the markup passed out of Senate Finance in late July.

I did not want this bill to get to the Senate floor, because it would surely pass. If it did, President Bush would use his veto, but his action would likely get overridden. I was beginning to worry that unlike some legislators who did not really want to vote on anti-China legislation, Schumer and Graham sincerely wanted to pass the bill. I hoped that during my visit to Billings I could persuade Baucus not to let the genie out of the bottle.

The Baucus-Grassley-Schumer-Graham bill was one of four—two

each in the House and Senate—that had been introduced in 2007 to punish countries that manipulated their currencies to gain an unfair competitive advantage. A second Senate bill, introduced by Banking, Housing, and Urban Affairs Committee head Chris Dodd and ranking Republican Richard Shelby, proposed to eliminate the need to prove that a country intentionally manipulated its currency before the U.S. was required to take action. The clear target in all of the legislation was China. Both Senate bills allowed a presidential waiver on national security or economic grounds, which gave an administration some leeway. But the two House bills were tougher. One did not allow the president to waive the sanctions and gave the Commerce Department the ability to impose duties on imports of goods that had benefited from an artificially weakened exchange rate.

I was encouraged to make the trip to Montana by Kevin Fromer, assistant secretary of Treasury for legislative affairs, and Ambassador Alan Holmer, SED special envoy, who were working on the Hill to keep the anti-China bills from becoming law. Why travel all the way to Montana when I could have called on the senator at his Capitol Hill office? The answer is simple: people appreciate special efforts. I had never before made a pilgrimage to visit any member of Congress in his home district, and I would not make another one, but I knew that if I visited Max Baucus during summer recess, outside of the glare and pressure of the capital, I would strengthen our working relationship, and I just might influence his thinking. And, no small thing, Baucus was up for reelection in November 2008, a Democrat running in a red state. It couldn't hurt for President Bush's Treasury secretary to make a special trip to see him.

I wanted the senator to know I valued his opinion and to make clear my stance: the markets were shaky, and the last thing we needed was a trade war sparked by protectionist legislation. Baucus, a onetime SEC lawyer, understood my arguments well, but his constituents, a mix of ranchers, small-business owners, and Westerners with strong independent streaks, were mostly concerned about jobs in Montana.

I made my points at a steakhouse dinner with Max my first night there (the steak was a helluva lot tastier than the yak knuckle I'd feasted on the week before). The next day we made the rounds together: a joint interview with the *Billings Gazette*; a hardhat-and-goggles tour of a Billings factory floor; and a town hall meeting with the senator's constituents. Max didn't make any promises, but I knew he understood trade issues well; in the early 1990s he had brought the Senate's "grains caucus" together to sustain President George H. W. Bush's veto of legislation that would have overturned most favored nation status for China. I left Billings convinced that at a minimum, he wouldn't make a move on currency without first talking to me.

As I had explained to Max, I understood that Congress was responding to the frustration of Americans, but knee-jerk protectionism would be self-defeating. Legislation that made Chinese goods more expensive would only hurt American consumers, who might suddenly find products like televisions beyond their means. Moreover, China was our country's fastest-growing export market, buying products that benefited U.S. companies and their workers. Max wanted to add beef from his state to the Chinese shopping list, but China had been closed to U.S. beef since mad cow disease had been detected in a U.S. herd in December 2003. The Chinese did not respond well to public threats. They were more likely to retaliate than back down, which would hurt key export sectors such as computers, aircraft, agricultural goods, and machinery. Further legislation might trigger similar protectionist measures by other countries.

China's trade surpluses were enormous and had spiked since the country joined the WTO, but they were as troublesome for Europe and Japan as they were for us, and I didn't think we should have to bear the burden of leading the push on the currency issue. I'd been working behind the scenes for some time, pressing the International Monetary Fund to take action. As part of its mandate, the Fund monitors its members' currency policies. In June 2007 the IMF had announced that it was revising its 30-year-old framework for exchange rate surveillance, giving itself broader powers to determine what constituted currency manipulation, with a new focus on outcomes rather than intent. China had opposed this change as an infringement of its national sovereignty.

In any case, having spent my career working in capital markets and not on Capitol Hill, I saw the currency issue as something of a red herring. It might have sounded good to portray the U.S.-China economic differences in strictly us-versus-them terms, but both sides shared the blame. The central problem was one of economic imbalances. The cautious Chinese saved too much, while Americans, incentivized by the U.S. tax system and government policies, piled on debt and gorged on low-cost Chinese goods. If China hadn't provided cheap goods, we would have bought them elsewhere. But there was no question we needed to clean up our excesses, and China needed to alter aspects of its model to assure sustainable growth. The vast sums of money being accumulated by China and recirculated to the West had helped create a world strewn with the tinder of cheap money fueling speculative excesses. Our profligate ways would set it alight.

Late in August Jin Renqing resigned as China's Finance minister. The government gave no official reason, but rumors quickly circulated that he had been swept up in a sex scandal. (Later it would be reported that he had been romantically involved with a Taiwanese spy.) To be honest, we weren't going to miss Jin much; apart from an unnerving tendency to belch in meetings and fall asleep with his mouth hanging open, he had lacked influence within the government. He was replaced by Xie Xuren, director of the State Administration of Taxation, a much more likable man, who supported the SED but reflected the conservative nature of his ministry.

I had little time to savor the latest political gossip from Beijing, however. The financial crisis that would engulf the U.S. and the rest of the world had erupted. It started in France, on August 9, when the Paris-based bank BNP Paribas halted redemptions on three investment funds that held mortgage-backed bonds, citing "a complete evaporation of liquidity." Europe's credit markets tightened severely. The next day the Dow Jones Industrial Average fell almost 400 points, its second-biggest one-day drop in five years. After swelling for years, the housing bubble had burst—though the word "bubble" does not do justice to the scale and misery of the disaster that would unfold.

Problems that had originated in the subprime mortgage market spread through the housing sector to banks and other lenders, as well as to investors the world over who had bought mortgage securities. They soon affected the quasi-governmental entities Fannie Mae and Freddie Mac, which packaged and guaranteed mortgages in the U.S., as well as a variety of nonbanking institutions, from investment houses to specialized insurers active in the market. At Treasury we believed that the housing correction would likely extend into 2008. With housing and associated sectors like construction in a slump, economists began to revise downward their estimates for economic activity. Market turbulence and lower growth estimates weakened the dollar; in the 12 months through mid-November, it dropped 14 percent against the euro. Oil prices rose quickly, putting pressure on major oil importers like China. Volatility wracked the global markets.

As financial pressures intensified in the United States, I traveled in November to Cape Town, South Africa, for the gathering of finance ministers and heads of central banks from the world's leading economic powers, known as the Group of 20. The G20 was a relatively new organization, established in 1999 after the Asian financial crisis to coordinate policy responses. Like the G7, which represented the world's biggest economies, the G20 was made up of finance ministers, but it included major emerging markets countries, which had grown rapidly but had previously lacked a voice in international decision-making bodies. The G20 included the "BRIC" members—Brazil, Russia, India, and China—and countries like Saudi Arabia and Mexico as well as big Western economies like Germany and France. (In 2011 BRICS was formed, including South Africa.)

I was looking forward to a private meeting I had set up with China's top central banker, Zhou Xiaochuan, at Hôtel Le Vendôme, a lovely resort outside of Cape Town where I was staying. The month before, the Communist Party had held its once-every-five-years leadership conclave that revealed who was in, who was out, and who was rising in China's circles of power. The culmination of each Congress—this was the 17th—took place when members of the newly elected Standing Committee strode onto the giant stage in the Great Hall of the People by order of rank, one through nine. For China watchers this was an important moment. Because the country's political processes are so secretive and opaque, every public event becomes more meaningful and closely scrutinized, and few more so than this.

To no one's surprise, Hu Jintao and Wen Jiabao had retained their first and third rankings in the Party (Wu Bangguo, the head of the Standing

Committee of the National People's Congress, remained second in rank). Significantly, Xi Jinping had been promoted to the Communist Party's Standing Committee, cementing his political future. I was pleased because Xi was now clearly in line to succeed Hu as China's top leader. I believed that he would be good for both China and the U.S., because he knew that the development of free markets and the private sector were keys to China's future economic success. (He would be named vice president of the country in March 2008.)

Another rising star, Li Keqiang—a protégé of Hu Jintao's credited with turning around the northeast rust-belt province of Liaoning while he was its Party secretary—was also promoted to the Standing Committee (he would be named executive vice premier in March 2008). Also joining the all-important Standing Committee was Zhou Yongkang, the head of Public Security, who had carried my idea for the SED to China's president back in 2006.

During the weeklong Party gathering, Hu and Wen had said all the right things, pushing back against emerging protectionist tendencies and pledging to adjust the country's growth model by providing more social welfare programs, encouraging energy conservation, and strengthening environmental protections. But changes in the Standing Committee also appeared to reduce the influence of former general secretary Jiang Zemin's Shanghai faction, which favored reform, while confirming the control of Hu, a more cautious leader. We would get another glimpse at the prospects for Hu's next five years in March, when government responsibilities were shuffled. Wu Yi was retiring, and we did not know who would take her place as our interlocutor, for example.

Zhou Xiaochuan and I had breakfast on my oceanfront balcony overlooking the glittering South Atlantic. It was a beautiful morning that darkened when Zhou gave me some bad news. With U.S. markets in upheaval, he said, China was not going to move ahead with capital markets reforms as we had hoped. Though I was disappointed, I was not entirely surprised. I had been concerned that the prospects for reform might be diminishing.

We knew from many sources that antireform forces had gained traction, and the global financial turmoil had only strengthened their cause. Why imitate what was wrong in the West? Opponents of change had tapped a rich vein of paranoia and xenophobia exemplified by the extraordinary success of a book called *Currency Wars* published in China that year. The book was written by a fellow named Song Hongbin. It was an odd mix of economics and *Da Vinci Code*–style "sleuthing" that purported to show how Western nations, acting on the orders of rich private banks tied to the Rothschild family, were using the capital markets to subjugate developing nations and, specifically, to contain a rising China. No one in the West took *Currency Wars* seriously—part of the conspiracy, no doubt!—but it was hugely popular in China and was said to have a readership among the members of the State Council.

Zhou Xiaochuan was nevertheless upbeat on the path to reform in general, indicating the Chinese were likely to show more flexibility with their currency. But he noted that given the unsettled climate, it was important that the U.S. avoid anti-Chinese legislation. China-bashing was in full cry in the States: at a campaign event in mid-August, Democratic presidential candidate Chris Dodd had called on President Bush to suspend all imports of food and toys from China. I reminded Zhou Xiaochuan that President Bush opposed protectionism and retaliation, and I recounted my trip to Montana to discuss the issue with Max Baucus. I would do the best I could to stave off anti-China laws, I said.

As our meeting wound down, I turned the conversation to my concerns about Chinese bank financing for Iran. Working with Stuart Levey, Treasury's undersecretary for terrorism and financial intelligence, I had been trying to alert all major global banks to the risks of doing business in Iran. It was not illegal for foreign banks to finance legitimate business activity there, but it was dangerous to do so, because the Iranians were known to disguise their illicit activities. I had made clear we would sanction any bank aiding and abetting Iran's terrorist activities or its efforts to build nuclear weapons. The last thing the Chinese wanted was for one of their major banks to be stigmatized by a U.S. sanction that would undermine its ability to do business in the U.S. and Europe.

Zhou said, "I have looked at it carefully, and I don't believe our banks are doing any unlawful or inappropriate business with Iran."

"They should be very careful because we will be watching," I cautioned. I know he got the message.

At the Cape Town gathering, and with side trips to examine the solid economic progress under way in Ghana and Tanzania, I was reminded of how quickly China had become central to the global economy. The Chinese were everywhere in Africa, making big investments in local infrastructure and nailing down deals to secure vital resources like oil. It was good, I thought, that the G20 gave China and other emerging nations a voice—they deserved to be heard. And the G20 was much more representative of the modern world economy than the G7, which consisted of developed nations and dated back to the mid-1970s, when countries like China barely registered economically. As a result, at Cape Town, finance ministers and central bankers representing much of the global economy could examine the challenges we all confronted. It was an ideal venue for Fed chairman Ben Bernanke and me to explain our nation's problems and policy responses.

The Cape Town experience would help convince me less than a year later to recommend that President Bush take the G20 one key step further and expand it from a ministerial to a leaders' group, with heads of state from a broad range of developed and emerging countries addressing the world's issues. The idea dovetailed with one key goal of the SED: to bring China more into the global community. Though the third-biggest economy, on track to become the second-biggest, China was not adequately represented in global leaders' forums. Its views weren't being properly heard, but, just as important, it was not taking on its fair share of the responsibilities and burdens that accompanied its position in the global order.

At a minimum, we required greater international coordination, because the financial crisis was spreading. Major banks in the U.S. had announced big losses, there had been an outright run on the British bank Northern Rock, and consumer confidence was plummeting along with home sales. Inside the administration we had begun to consider stimulus spending to jump-start the languishing economy. As the problems in housing spread through the credit markets, the dollar continued to lose value, fueling protectionist sentiment in Congress. The renminbi had appreciated recently, rising a full percentage point over the course of November, but no one in Congress seemed to notice.

I warned Wu Yi on a call before SED III, scheduled for December 12 and 13, 2007, in Beijing, about the hostile mood among lawmakers. I would do all I could to steer Congress away from that. But, I added, I needed some help from her side.

"I'm trying my hardest," I said. "But I wouldn't rule out the possibility of the currency bills moving before the end of the year."

Wu Yi was agreeable on the phone, but when I had dinner with her in Beijing the night before the first session, her attitude was anything but conciliatory.

The Chinese hosted SED III at Grand Epoch City, about 30 miles outside of Beijing. This tourist attraction combined a faithful re-creation of the Forbidden City with a 27-hole golf course and was known as Top City to the Chinese. Taiya Smith and I met with Wu Yi and Zhu Guangyao at the vice premier's traditional-style quarters in the center of the complex. An odd Chinese cross between Disneyland and Colonial Williamsburg, Grand Epoch City vividly illustrated the rapid changes brought about by China's economic development. Just a few years before, I had walked through Beijing's historic alleyways. Now they and the neighborhoods they helped define had been torn down to accommodate a helter-skelter urbanization, and I was having dinner in a facsimile created for a tourist fantasy world.

Wu Yi used this intimate gathering to reverse roles and give me a hard time about our currency. The dollar's weakness was causing problems for the Chinese. Their trading partners in Europe and Japan were complaining as the already undervalued renminbi sank further against the euro and the yen. The Chinese faced sharply rising costs for imported commodities, like oil, that were priced in dollars. Wu Yi also expressed her concern for China's investments in the U.S. By December 2007 China's foreign exchange reserves had reached a stunning $1.5 trillion, up from $212 billion in the six years since it had joined the WTO. Approximately $900 billion, or 60 percent, of that was invested in U.S. government notes and bonds or in the securities of agencies like Fannie Mae and Freddie Mac, the two mortgage giants.

"You want us to move our currency, but you need to control the value of yours," she told me. "You're getting us in real trouble because you're letting the dollar fall, and the Chinese people are being hurt because they have invested in your dollars."

"We are committed to maintaining a strong dollar, but its value is determined by free markets," I responded. "We need to pursue policies to keep our economy strong. And we are doing just that."

Wu Yi then asked me for specifics on the currency adjustment we wanted. "How much would you like the renminbi to move? Give me a number."

I resisted. We both knew that the Chinese would appreciate the renminbi because they now believed that doing so was in their best interest, so there was no point in my making a suggestion. Instead, I repeated my pitch for China to embrace a market-determined currency. Until China let the market determine what the renminbi was worth, it should at least base its value more on economic reality.

"Today you are a long way from that point," I told Wu Yi. "You should move your currency a lot."

I then returned to the more important and, to my mind, higher-priority topic: Why were the Chinese backing off financial markets reform?

The next night, after a celebratory banquet, the Chinese thought it would be amusing if I played Wu Yi at Ping-Pong. I'm not good at the game, and I would have had no problem letting the vice premier beat me— no shame in that. Wendy beat me all the time. I thought the game would be good for U.S.-China relations. I started to feel the adrenaline pumping, and I was looking forward to playing her, but my staff disagreed and wouldn't let me.

"It wouldn't look good for you to be beaten by Wu Yi," said Michele Davis, Treasury's assistant secretary for public affairs and director of policy planning.

There was another reason for my staff's reluctance to have me play. Our Treasury team in Beijing included an IT specialist, Ron Lilly, a nationally ranked player in the U.S. The SED team had included Ron, who had brought his own paddles, just so we could beat the Chinese at their own game. So we suggested that instead of Wu Yi and me, we would pick a staffer from Treasury to play someone on the Chinese SED team. They nominated Zhu Guangyao, then head of the international department at the Ministry of

Finance, whom Ron proceeded to beat, albeit in a hard-fought match. The Chinese were great sports, clapping and cheering on the match, and then razzing us for months afterward for bringing in a ringer.

The Ping-Pong game gave me a chance to witness the close working relationship that had formed between the U.S. and Chinese SED teams. Their weeks-long joint preparations for each meeting created a bond of respect and trust between our officials that would prove very important as the financial crisis deepened in the year to come. The SED was characterized by intense personal interaction. Over the course of the first five SEDs, there were 30 face-to-face meetings among Chinese state leaders and U.S. officials. I spoke on the phone two dozen times with my direct counterparts; Taiya Smith and Zhu Guangyao oversaw some 200 consultations and preparatory meetings.

With SED III we were able to announce several sweeping agreements. Foremost, we reached a detailed, far-reaching accord on product safety meant to improve manufacturing standards and government oversight of eight areas that ranged from foodstuffs and animal feed to drugs and medical products, and from alcohol and tobacco to toys and electrical products. Although the problems were primarily on the Chinese side, the protocols we developed represented best practices for a modern marketplace that relied on global manufacturing networks and supply chains.

Health and Human Services Secretary Mike Leavitt was an enthusiastic participant, eager to take advantage of the SED. He built a strong relationship with his counterpart at the Chinese Ministry of Health. At the third SED Leavitt ventured a proposal that might very well have been rejected out of hand by the Chinese as offensive before we'd launched the dialogue: he asked that we be allowed to put U.S. food safety and product quality inspectors on site in China. In the negotiations that followed, China demanded reciprocity. That may have seemed ridiculous to many Americans, but fair was fair, and the fact was, China was very accommodating on this issue—at SED IV we were able to announce that U.S. FDA personnel would be in China and that Chinese inspectors would be working in the U.S. Our improved dialogue would pay off even before then: in early 2008 a blood-thinning drug containing key ingredients from China turned out to be contaminated, and our two countries' agencies worked together to quickly track down the source of the problem.

By late 2007 I started to wonder what would happen after the Bush administration left office, and I began to think about a joint U.S.-Chinese effort with even longer-term aims. The Chinese were strategic thinkers, rolling their long-term economic goals through successive five-year plans whose progress they meticulously tracked. U.S. policies often veered from election to election. What if a new president allowed the SED to be pushed aside? I concluded that it would benefit us to find some subject that addressed the shared objectives of China and the U.S. that Republicans and Democrats alike could sign on to—something that wouldn't be so easily dropped by a new administration from either party.

I wasn't the only one thinking this way; Wu Yi had suggested that we find an important subject to jointly work on for the long term. I started asking people in Washington for input. My former colleague John Thornton— who was now dividing his time between China, where he was a professor and director of the global leadership program at Tsinghua University, and the United States, where he was chairman of the Brookings Institution— pointed out that both sides could work productively on energy issues. I agreed, and thinking back to my July trip to the Qinghai-Tibetan Plateau, which had dramatically underscored the importance of collaboration by the U.S. and China to mitigate the effects of climate change, I decided that environmental and conservation issues should be part of any such discussion.

I proposed to Wu Yi that we put together a ten-year framework for our two countries to address the paramount issues of energy and the environment. She immediately said she thought it was a good idea, and we were off to the races. We announced the establishment of a working group on the Ten-Year Framework for Cooperation on Energy and Environment at SED III, and a U.S. team spent the next six months crafting with their Chinese counterparts at the National Development and Reform Commission what would be one of the most important achievements of the U.S.-China dialogue.

Given the enormity and sensitivity of issues like climate change and energy security, we would need the participation of top decision makers throughout the governments of both countries. On the U.S. side, this would mean coordinating the EPA, Commerce, State, Energy, Treasury, and later the U.S. Trade and Development Agency. The inextricable interrelationship between energy and the environment would be reflected in task forces focused on six key areas: clean water; clean air; clean and efficient transportation; clean, efficient, and secure electricity production; energy efficiency; and the conservation of forests and wetlands. Among other issues, we would explore how to reduce both countries' dependency on foreign oil and how to meet growing energy needs while providing clean air and safe water for our citizens. I hoped that our best laboratories would talk to one another and conduct joint research for everyone's benefit.

In time we would pursue together a new concept we called EcoPartnerships. Where the Ten-Year Framework addressed sweeping issues of strategic importance, the EcoPartnerships were meant to encourage innovation at the university or local level—for example, a city-to-city partnership to develop electric cars, or a utility-to-utility partnership on environmentally friendly business models. Seattle and Dalian would work together on energy-efficient ports, Wichita and Wuxi on clean water. We would unveil the program at SED V, in December 2008, with seven partnerships.

For SED III the Chinese officials had, as usual, planned lavish entertainment. Wu Yi personally oversaw the preparations, right down to the elaborate carvings made from vegetables that decorated the tables. The festivities included fireworks that were spectacular even by Chinese standards—what we in the U.S. would consider a thrilling finale exploded for an hour over Grand Epoch City. I had forgotten to bring my overcoat, and I felt my teeth chattering by the time the display got under way. As gifts for this cold-weather gathering, the Chinese had given our delegation thickly padded and belted Red Army coats with fur collars and star-stamped brass buttons. I craved the warmth but didn't dare put mine on. What a photo that would have made: the U.S. Treasury secretary dressed like a Red Army soldier! Talk about the Manchurian candidate. (I did keep the coat and wear it today when I walk in wintertime on the prairie near our Illinois home, where the only paparazzi are deer and coyotes.)

Because Wu Yi was retiring in the spring, this would be her last SED, which made the meeting bittersweet for me. Despite my initial misgivings about the vice premier, I'd grown to respect her and the efforts she'd made. There's a Chinese saying that people sometimes have to fight before they can become friends. And while I'd had my differences with Wu Yi, I came to really like her. I hope she felt as fondly about me—in any case, she gave me a beautiful gift, a bronze horse and chariot sculpture that was a miniature reproduction of a piece discovered in the mausoleum of China's first emperor; I kept it in my office at Treasury. After Wu Yi retired, I sent her a set of golf clubs, custom-sized to her small stature, hoping to give her some fun in retirement.

Though the third SED meeting produced some noteworthy policy achievements, I remember it just as much for a drama that took place away from the meeting room that few in my delegation ever knew about. We were in the midst of discussions at a long, dark wood table in a huge ballroom in the Top City hotel when Ambassador Sandy Randt, who was sitting next to me, leaned over and told me that he'd just gotten a message from the embassy that the destroyer USS *Mustin* would cross the Taiwan Strait, which China claims as its waters, that night.

A couple of weeks before, the Chinese—with no explanation but apparently miffed about planned U.S. arms sales to Taiwan and President Bush's recent public appearance with the Dalai Lama—had annoyed the U.S. Navy and Department of Defense by refusing to let the U.S. aircraft carrier *Kitty Hawk* and accompanying ships dock in Hong Kong, where thousands of airmen and sailors had planned to spend Thanksgiving with their families. The authorities relented within a day, for "humanitarian considerations only," but by then the *Kitty Hawk* had been rerouted to its home port in Japan. The *Kitty Hawk* and its five-ship support flotilla had sailed home through the Taiwan Strait, heightening tensions further.

Now there I was, hearing that a U.S. ship was going to pass through the strait again. This would not only irritate the Chinese but undermine my credibility and that of the SED itself.

"That can't happen," I whispered to Sandy.

"Hank, the decision's been made. There's nothing you can do to stop it."

"The Navy wouldn't do it if Bob Gates was over here," I said. "They wouldn't do it if Condi was over here. And they should not be doing it when I'm over here."

In fact, Defense Secretary Robert Gates had visited Beijing the month before and addressed the arms-sale issue directly, saying that the U.S. would continue to sell Taiwan weapons to defend itself. But he'd also called for better communications between the U.S. and China on other matters. As I waited impatiently for a break in the proceedings, I reflected that a U.S. destroyer crossing the Taiwan Strait the night before I was to meet with President Hu seemed inconsistent with Gates's objective.

When the break finally came, I quickly called National Security Adviser Steve Hadley. Because of the 13-hour time difference, it was the middle of the night in Washington. A groggy Hadley confirmed that the operation had been approved.

"Then I guess I'm going to need to wake the president up," I said. "Because it's not acceptable."

"Don't do that," Hadley said. "Wake Bob Gates up instead."

I knew the Defense secretary from National Security Council meetings, and I greatly respected him. But it took too much time to get through to him that night. First I had to deal with a bevy of very senior military aides, as well as officers from the Pacific Command. When one aide asked me—rather superciliously—exactly why I was making this call, I pulled rank in a way I never had before and never would again: "This is the secretary of the Treasury," I said. "Wake up Secretary Gates."

Bob eventually got on the phone to ask, sleepily, "What's this all about, Hank?"

I told him point-blank that I didn't want the Navy ship to cross the strait when I was in Beijing.

Bob quickly did what I expected him to do and what I would have done had the situation been reversed. "If this is important to you, Hank, we will call it off," he said.

I could hear murmuring among the other people on the phone—huge consternation, in fact—and decided to get off the line before there could be any debate or backsliding. I just said, "Thank you very much, I appreciate it. This is important."

I went back to the SED session and told Sandy: "It's done. The ship isn't going there."

I'll admit my nose felt a little out of joint, but I didn't make a fuss over the Navy's plans out of any exaggerated sense of self-importance. I did it because I knew as well as anyone on the U.S. side of the table that the Chinese would not view any such episode as an accident. In a culture that places such a high value on signs and symbols, everything big or small, every action and event becomes freighted with significance, a tendency that gets magnified by a cloistered decision-making process that lacks transparency. If the destroyer had passed through the Taiwan Strait while I was in Beijing, it would have been viewed not only as a rebuke of the Chinese over the *Kitty Hawk* incident but also as a denigration of the SED and of my position as the dialogue's American leader. The irony was that Gates himself was looking to improve communications with the Chinese, but the Defense Department risked undermining the important dialogue we'd been building through the SED.

When I got back to Washington, I was still quite put out, but President Bush was amused by my predictably aggressive behavior. He greeted me with a wide grin and a chuckle at a Cabinet meeting the day after my return. "Why did it take you so long to ask for Gates?" he quipped, knowing I had demanded to speak to the Defense secretary immediately. The president had a sense of humor, and he liked tough guys. Both of those characteristics would come in handy when the full force of the financial crisis descended on us.

CHAPTER FOURTEEN

A Global Reckoning

We had decided to focus the fourth meeting of the Strategic Economic Dialogue on sustainable economic growth, and when we met in June 2008, the theme could hardly have been more appropriate. Oil prices were soaring. At $138 per barrel, crude sold for twice what it had a year earlier. Rising fuel and fertilizer costs, combined with local droughts, had hiked the tab for food, especially staples, while shortages sparked deadly riots in some poor parts of the world. The price spikes reflected in part the ever-greater demands that the rapid growth of developing countries was placing on scarce natural resources. China's success alone had lifted hundreds of millions out of poverty. Now the country's challenge was to maintain that progress without upsetting its domestic stability or causing a global calamity.

By the time we gathered at the U.S. Naval Academy in Annapolis, Maryland, for SED IV, the United States was being buffeted by the deepening financial crisis that would engulf the financial world. Much has been written about this dark period in our nation's recent history. Less well known to Americans is how profoundly the crisis would shape Chinese attitudes and policies. It exposed China's overdependence on exports and confirmed the need to rebalance its economy toward domestic consumption. Measures that China would take to withstand the worst of the crisis—particularly a massive fiscal spending program—would halt needed structural reforms and leave the country with a costly legacy of bad debts that it continues to suffer from today. China would play a stalwart, responsible role in helping us contend with rapidly multiplying problems. But the nature of the relationship between our two countries began to shift noticeably as the U.S.'s troubles brought doubt and discredit to our system in some quarters and boosted China's self-confidence.

This was brought home clearly to me along the sidelines of the SED, during a break in the proceedings, when I was pulled aside by Wang Qishan, who had moved from his post as mayor of Beijing to succeed Wu Yi as my SED counterpart. Qishan, who had been named vice premier in March, wanted me to know that the financial crisis in the U.S. had affected the way he and others in the senior ranks of the Party saw us.

"You were my teacher, but now here I am in my teacher's domain, and look at your system, Hank. We aren't sure we should be learning from you anymore."

The crisis was a humbling experience, and this was one of its most humbling moments.

I'd known Wang Qishan for nearly 15 years now and had worked closely with him on several pressure-packed occasions. He'd become a friend and confidant. He was charming and cheerful, and though he could be quite diplomatic, he was generally direct and no-nonsense with me. I appreciated that quality, and his comments, earnest and animated, did not offend me in the slightest. Instead, coming from a man who had spent the past three decades pushing for reforms at home, they told me how difficult the climate for such change had become in China. The Western financial crisis had toughened internal resistance to opening the country's capital markets.

"We've made plenty of mistakes, but you can learn from them," I responded. Our problems, I said, shouldn't lead China to conclude that it didn't need to continue to develop open, competitive markets. In any case, I added, "we are determined to do what it takes to fix our markets and protect our economy."

Still, there could be little doubt our system was under great—and increasing—stress. In March the crisis had claimed its most prominent U.S. victim to date in the investment bank Bear Stearns, an outsize player in the mortgage-backed securities markets. As housing unraveled, Bear lost the confidence of the market and fell victim to an all-out run. It would have failed had the Treasury, the Federal Reserve, and the Federal Reserve Bank of New York, working together over a frenzied mid-March weekend, not found a buyer for it in JPMorgan Chase and had the Federal Reserve not provided financial assistance.

As I have related in *On the Brink*, my previously published account of the financial crisis, Bear's collapse sent a shock wave around the world. The fallout was felt deeply in China, whose state-owned investment company, CITIC Securities, had previously agreed to buy a 6 percent stake in Bear for $1 billion; it hastily retreated as Bear fell apart. Separately, China's sovereign wealth fund, China Investment Corporation (CIC), had made high-profile investments in 2007 in Blackstone Group and Morgan Stanley, giving the country's leaders a keen interest in Wall Street's imperiled health. Moreover, China was beginning to feel the reverberations of the crisis. Though the country's banks had been spared, the downdraft in global stocks had contributed to a 45 percent drop in the Shanghai Stock Exchange Composite Index since its October 2007 peak. GDP growth was moderating, and the slowdown in economic activity in the U.S. and elsewhere threatened to reduce demand for the country's vital exports.

I had gotten a taste of China's concerns firsthand in April, when I had been in Beijing to plan for SED IV. Hu Jintao, Wen Jiabao, and Wang Qishan had all peppered me with questions about the U.S. economy, the health of our banks, and their country's money-losing investments in Morgan Stanley and Blackstone. I assured them that the U.S. responses had been swift. The Federal Reserve was providing liquidity to stressed financial markets, while the $150 billion stimulus program I had negotiated with the Democratic-controlled Congress on behalf of the Bush administration would soon put money in the hands of consumers. I noted, too, that many forecasters expected the economy to rebound in the second half.

How wrong they were!

The Chinese appreciated how openly we were communicating with them. After the Bear Stearns rescue, Neel Kashkari, a senior Treasury adviser, had led a call with officials from the Chinese Ministry of Finance. We would increase the frequency and depth of contact as the crisis escalated over the coming months. The broad-based constant communications fostered by the SED, coupled with my long-standing relationships with Wang and Zhou Xiaochuan, would prove enormously valuable in helping

us manage the economic relationship with the second-biggest foreign investor in U.S. securities during this fraught period.

I had let the Chinese know during my April visit that Treasury was on
high alert for more problems. It turned out, of course, that we were right
to be vigilant, as one financial institution after another felt the wrath of
investors suddenly worried about toxic assets, weak balance sheets, and the
banks' hesitance to lend to one another. I stressed the need for more capital
and greater liquidity cushions to Wall Street and banking CEOs, repeatedly encouraging Lehman Brothers CEO Richard Fuld through the spring
and summer of 2008 to gird his firm for the tough times ahead by finding
a deep-pocketed strategic investor or, eventually, a merger partner.

Bad news accumulated. As U.S. share prices drifted down from their
record highs in October 2007, the economy continued to lose steam and unemployment climbed. At 5.6 percent in June, it was up a full percentage point
from the previous year. Though checks from the federal stimulus reached U.S.
citizens in record time, they barely covered the higher cost of gasoline.

China-bashing grew louder through the presidential primaries. In May
the Democratic rivals, Senators Hillary Clinton and Barack Obama,
endorsed legislation that would have allowed punitive duties on Chinese
goods in response to currency manipulation. I spent hours on Capitol Hill
with Al Holmer, Treasury's special envoy for China and the SED, trying
to deflect such knee-jerk protectionism. We pointed to the progress we had
made on currency valuation—the renminbi was up nearly 14 percent since
July 2005—and noted that the SED was yielding tangible results, from the
open-skies agreement to enhanced product safety, that we risked losing if
we took a punitive turn.

I had cautioned Wang Qishan shortly before his arrival in the States
in June that the mood in Congress had grown far darker and more volatile
than it had been when Wu Yi had visited the previous spring. If Democrats
pushed anti-China legislation, Republicans wouldn't vote against it.

"Anything could set off a cascade," I warned.

Still, I figured that if anybody in China had the charm to soothe irritated legislators, it was the vice premier. Wang Qishan was as different as
yin and yang from Wu Yi, a tenacious negotiator who stuck to debating
points and stayed on message. Wang Qishan held just as firmly to his coun-

try's positions, but his approach was at once expansive and subtle, intellectual but leavened by a dry sense of humor. A real people person, he welcomed almost any meeting. When asked tough questions, he relished giving as good as he got.

Wang Qishan was scheduled to meet the Capitol Hill leadership, but I'd also invited a handful of senators and members of the House to meet China's new SED leadership team for breakfast in Treasury's Cash Room. It was a magnificent, gold-trimmed palazzo-style space on the second floor of the Treasury building, where the government had once transacted such financial business as redeeming gold and silver certificates and supplying local commercial banks with coins and currency from the Treasury's vaults. Seven lawmakers attended, including Senators Norm Coleman (R-MN) and Maria Cantwell (D-WA) and House members Sandy Levin (D-MI) and Don Manzullo (R-IL). At one point, one of the lawmakers challenged the vice premier on China's lack of commitment to combating climate change.

Wang Qishan surveyed the table for a moment as if he were thinking through his response or wondering whether the guests were up to following him. Then he headed off on a lengthy discourse that touched on economics, social policy, and personal responsibility. China might have the third-biggest economy in the world, he pointed out, but it was still a poor country; by GDP per person it was ranked 125th—below Namibia. This was a standard Chinese talking point, but Wang Qishan turned it in a less familiar way.

On the one hand, he noted, some in the U.S. were criticizing China for wasting resources, damaging the environment, and contributing to global warming. On the other hand, many claimed the Chinese were hurting the U.S. by exporting too cheaply, and they were pushing China to rebalance its economy to encourage even more domestic consumption. How was China to pursue both increased consumption *and* sustainability?

"Here we are," he said. "It's a hot summer day, but it's cold in your offices because you've got the air-conditioning on. In the winter you've got the heat blasting out. For exercise you work out in air-conditioned gyms, then take hot showers, then get into air-conditioned cars. This is America! In China, we don't live that way. We can't afford to. I tell my colleagues: conservation with personal conduct! For exercise, ride your bikes to and from work."

It was quite a show. What had been meant to be a Q&A session turned into a tour de force disquisition that laid out the paradox of sustainable development for his country without a hint of the reflexive defensiveness that often colored, and weakened, Chinese arguments. I knew that Wang Qishan, as a reformer and conservationist (he had served with me on the Nature Conservancy's Asia-Pacific Council), was committed to finding solutions. In pointing out the inherent difficulties of China's situation, he was not so much lecturing U.S. lawmakers as trying to illuminate for them a thorny problem, just as he had for me a few months earlier when we met in Beijing to discuss the energy and environmental initiative of the SED.

"The world simply does not have enough resources to support another billion Chinese living the Western lifestyle," he had noted. "We have to find a new model."

I frankly thought he was right. As he spoke, I remembered that long-ago February meeting at Zhongnanhai during which I'd spied Zhu Rongji's long underwear sticking out under his pant cuffs—a precaution against the cold that our pampered leaders would never have to take.

For the June 17 and 18 SED IV, we met on the pristine grounds of the U.S. Naval Academy, which was established in 1845 where the Severn River meets the Chesapeake Bay in Annapolis, Maryland, about a half hour east of Washington. Its distance from the District was one of its attractions; we wanted to keep members of our delegation away from their offices and concentrated on SED business. But even for me, it wasn't easy to focus. A little more than a week before the meetings began, Lehman Brothers had released second-quarter earnings in a vain attempt to reassure investors. Its shares kept falling, and behind the scenes, no buyers or major strategic investors had emerged. My team at Treasury and the staff at the Fed continued to look for ways to prevent a Lehman failure. At the same time, we were becoming preoccupied with the mortgage titans Fannie Mae and Freddie Mac, which had come under intense market pressure as legislation to reform them stalled in Congress.

Just about every break was consumed with phone calls, but I made a point of not ducking out of the SED meetings and asked my fellow Cabinet members to do the same. At one point I had to negotiate with the White

House about who would attend an emergency meeting President Bush had called to deal with widespread flooding in the Midwest that demanded the administration's attention. The president's meeting was vital, but I was determined to respect the SED process as much as the Chinese did. I believed that our dedication to the SED would pay dividends.

I tried to address the fragile state of the markets head-on in my SED remarks. I explained the Bush administration's efforts to stabilize the financial system and the economy and noted that flexible, market-based prices serve as automatic stabilizers in the ups and downs of economic cycles. I also made the point that the market turmoil was no excuse for halting financial sector reform and development in China.

Most important, we signed the Ten-Year Framework for Cooperation on Energy and Environment, committing the U.S. and China to work together for the next decade on clean, sustainable energy development. The agreement, which we had begun working on during SED III, increased the likelihood that our efforts would carry over to the next administration.

Currency issues continued to give me grief. In September 2007 Dominique Strauss-Kahn, the former French Finance minister and presidential hopeful, had become head of the IMF and sought our backing to make some much-needed changes, including a plan to sell some of the Fund's gold reserves. I made clear that our support was contingent upon the IMF's citing China for currency manipulation. The undervalued renminbi was a global concern, and the IMF was the proper forum to address it. Frankly, I was also tired of the U.S.'s always having to lead on this issue.

DSK agreed that the IMF would cite China, but afterward he indulged in some backdoor maneuvering that sparked the protestations of my friend Zhou Xiaochuan, China's central bank chief. Zhou came up to me during one of the breaks in Annapolis and said, "Hank, Strauss-Kahn says he doesn't want to cite us. He wants to give us more time to make progress, but you are insisting that he act now. If the IMF acts now, it will make it harder for us to move the currency because our people will think we're bowing to outside pressure."

China was eager to avoid public criticism from a credible and independent multilateral institution, but as always, Zhou was measured and reasonable. I was a bit irritated that DSK had used me, albeit accurately, as his excuse for getting tough with China, but I didn't let on to my friend.

"The IMF needs to do its job," I told Zhou. "And if you show more flexibility with your currency, there will be no need to cite China."

Though I wished DSK had not told Zhou Xiaochuan about our agreement, I realized the Frenchman's transparency was just part of his pragmatic, straightforward nature. I always found him easy to deal with, and when he later was convinced by Zhou Xiaochuan that the Chinese needed more time, I just asked him to move as soon as reasonably possible.

As it happened, our world was about to change dramatically, and China's currency would soon become the least of our worries.

The financial crisis had deeply wounded Fannie Mae and Freddie Mac. These government-sponsored enterprises, or GSEs, owned or guaranteed $4.4 trillion in U.S. mortgages, including a big chunk of subprime loans. They were bloated, undercapitalized, poorly managed—and politically all but untouchable. Because they had been established and were regulated by the U.S. government, many investors assumed their securities were backed by the full faith and credit of the United States. They were not. Fannie and Freddie were shareholder-owned private corporations, but their perceived government backing gave them access to cheap funding and led them to take on enormous risk. I'd come to the Treasury Department determined to reform this untenable business model, which privatized profit while socializing risk. But lawmakers resisted changes; the two companies had wrapped themselves in the "American dream of home ownership" and were past masters of public relations and lobbying.

By early July Fannie Mae and Freddie Mac had come under intense pressure. We had to ensure that they got through the mortgage crisis without triggering a full-scale financial panic that could spread quickly across our borders. Many of the GSEs' biggest investors were foreign central banks. Of the $5.4 trillion in Fannie and Freddie securities outstanding, $1.7 trillion was held by foreigners.

On July 7 speculation that the two GSEs needed up to $75 billion in capital spurred investors to flee the stocks. Shares plunged again on July 9. Hoping to calm the markets, I stood on the steps of the Treasury Department on July 13 and announced that I would ask Congress to give me temporary emergency authority to increase Fannie's and Freddie's lines of credit with the Treasury and to allow us to buy equity in the GSEs if I deemed it necessary.

Two days later I was in the hot seat on Capitol Hill as members of the Senate Banking Committee pounded me over my request. I had to perform a delicate balancing act: convince skeptical lawmakers that the situation with Fannie and Freddie was so dire that it warranted government intervention without panicking nervous investors about the fragility of those institutions. Reaching for what I hoped would be a helpful analogy, I used words that made sense to me at the time but would come back to bite me.

"If you've got a squirt gun in your pocket, you may have to take it out," I said. "If you've got a bazooka and people know you've got it, you may not have to take it out."

Anyone listening to the rancorous Banking Committee response would have assumed that the GSEs, and their investors, might be abandoned by fed-up lawmakers. Worried foreign governments began calling for guidance, and I summoned David McCormick, the department's undersecretary for international affairs, to my office. A West Point graduate who had served in the first Gulf War, Dave had worked at the White House as deputy national security adviser for international economic affairs. I admired and trusted him and knew he could help me with a touchy undertaking.

We put together a list of the top 15 holders of GSE debt, and I asked Dave to work with me to reassure major foreign investors about our commitment to the agencies. This group included finance ministers and central bankers from countries like Brazil, Russia, Japan, and Kuwait. I would talk with finance ministers and central bank governors as needed, while Dave communicated with a range of government officials in many nations. One of the most important of Dave's group was Madam Hu Xiaolian, administrator of China's State Administration of Foreign Exchange, the investing arm of the central bank, which oversaw $1.8 trillion in foreign reserves. Just under $1.1 trillion were in U.S. Treasuries and agency paper. It was crucial that the countries hold on to their positions and not sell into an already weak market.

"Make sure they understand what we're doing," I said. "Let them know that, as much as possible, our government will stand behind Fannie and Freddie. Give them some confidence."

Dave kept in constant touch with the investors. He quickly discovered that although the technocrats in the ministries and central banks understood that the GSE paper they owned was only implicitly backed by the U.S. government, their bosses believed they owned the equivalent of Treasury bonds, but with higher yields. In some cases, these bosses didn't fully understand the difference between equity and debt, so when they saw the terrible headlines about GSE shares, they thought their investments were in trouble and pressured the technocrats to reduce their positions.

I called many government officials, including Wang Qishan and Zhou Xiaochuan, to reassure them.

"We're watching this carefully," Wang said. "We want to make sure you are going to protect our financial interests."

I tried to explain the contentious congressional debate to my Chinese friend. "This is political theater," I told him. "In the U.S. we always do what we need to do, and I am confident Congress is going to support Fannie and Freddie."

I only wish I'd been as confident as I sounded.

Congress finally granted Treasury 18-month emergency authority on July 30. In the first week of August, Fannie and Freddie announced awful second-quarter earnings. Combined, they had lost more than $3 billion. The calls with foreign investors became more frequent and urgent.

I decided that we had to be as open as possible in explaining the situation. David Loevinger, minister counselor for financial affairs at the U.S. Embassy in Beijing and Treasury's senior representative in China, launched a series of weekly conference calls with staffers from Treasury—and sometimes the Fed and the SEC—to post Chinese officials on any developments. The Chinese asked very pointed questions focused on protecting their assets. How could we make sure they weren't at risk? The Chinese assured us that they would not sell, but they would also not start buying again until they saw others buying as well.

On August 7 I flew to Beijing with my family for the Olympic Games, a commitment I'd made a year before that fortunately fit into a brief hiatus while the regulators evaluated the financial condition of Fannie and Freddie. Though the crisis at home was much on my mind and I had a number of official meetings, this was technically a vacation with Wendy, our children, Merritt and Amanda, and their families. I was not a part of the presidential delegation.

When we reached our hotel, the Westin Beijing Chaoyang, we found that Wendy and I had been given a suite, while Amanda, her husband, Josh, and our 14-month-old granddaughter, Willa, had been assigned to a smaller room. At Wendy's suggestion we decided, much to the consternation of the hotel's front desk, to switch rooms to give the kids more space. I didn't see what the fuss was at first, and then it dawned on me. I may have been on vacation, but to the Chinese it was business as usual, and our original room was no doubt equipped with listening devices. Once we switched, it was too late to bug our new room, because my Secret Service detachment was standing guard all of the time. Wendy and I had a good laugh at the thought of the Chinese listening to Amanda reading *Goodnight Moon* to Willa.

Wendy, the family, and I had fun watching the Olympic Games and seeing the sights—even though I gouged my head at the Great Wall when I neglected to duck for a too-low ceiling in one of the guard towers. I bled so heavily (and yelled so loudly) that the Chinese still remind me about it. But the whole time—watching the U.S. men's basketball team beat China, practicing tai chi in a park with my wife and the kids, giving interviews to the American press—I worried about the situation back home and found it increasingly hard to sleep. Just before I had left Washington, Ben Bernanke told me that his people at the Fed had found some troubling things as they inspected the GSEs' books. Ben said the review was only in the preliminary stage, and he didn't want to spoil my trip, but of course he had. I was itching to know more, but I didn't want to call him up and ask for the gory details, fearing the worst and not wanting the Chinese, listening in, to learn how bad the situation was.

While in Beijing, I received some disturbing news: I was told that Russian officials had made a top-level approach to the Chinese with the suggestion that together they might sell some of their GSE securities to force the U.S. to use its emergency authorities to support the companies. I didn't know how serious the Russians were about their proposal, which could have hurt the GSEs and the capital markets, but the thought that they might test us added to the restlessness of my sleepless nights. The Chinese had declined to go along with the plan and would show admirable resolve in cooperating with our government and in maintaining their holdings of U.S. securities throughout the crisis.

Most days I exercised in a nearby park, and one morning, I was walking briskly, mulling things over, when I stopped and pulled aside Taiya Smith. She was in Beijing negotiating with her Chinese counterparts for the December SED. "I've been thinking about Fannie and Freddie and the financial markets back home," I said. "As much as it kills me, I have to honestly say I'm not going to be able to focus on the SED. I need you to run the show and only come and get me if you've got a big problem."

I had complete confidence in Taiya, whose bright smile belied a steely determination and resourcefulness. She had worked as special assistant to Deputy Secretary of State Robert Zoellick as his policy adviser for Africa, Europe, and political/military affairs. She had been the State Department's point person on Darfur before that. I trusted her judgment and her ability to read the Chinese. Her job as SED coordinator could be painful and thankless: she had to organize the efforts of the entire U.S. government, managing Cabinet-level egos and occasionally explaining why some people's pet projects were not big priorities. She had to overcome similar challenges in China, where teamwork did not come naturally. In between SED sessions Taiya and her team spent weeks in China going back and forth among different Chinese ministries that didn't naturally work together. I kidded Taiya that she was not only running our interagency operations but those of the Chinese as well.

I returned to a full-blown crisis in Washington on August 15. That weekend, in an article titled "The Endgame Nears for Fannie and Freddie," *Barron's* predicted that the U.S. government would take over the GSEs and wipe out common shareholders. Their shares subsequently plunged to 18-year lows that Monday. The report was prescient. Examiners from the Federal Reserve and the Office of the Comptroller of the Currency, aided by outside advisers, had found huge unrecognized losses and poor-quality capital on the GSE books. With no access to the markets, the companies were doomed, and we had no choice but to take control of them, something I had not anticipated weeks earlier.

On Saturday, September 6, I took the unpleasant but necessary step of seizing Fannie and Freddie, replacing their CEOs, and putting them in conservatorship under the Federal Housing Finance Agency. The government would provide up to $100 billion to each company to backstop any capital shortfalls, and Treasury would set up new secured lending facilities for both agencies. Common shareholders would be hard-hit by the rescue, but bondholders were protected.

The following day, Sunday, I announced the actions publicly, taking care to explain why what we had done with these enormous but—to most Americans—obscure institutions was so important. I described conservatorship as a temporary "time-out" while the government decided what further steps to take. The failures of these companies, I said, would have affected "the ability of Americans to get home loans, auto loans, and other consumer credit and business finance...and would be harmful to economic growth and job creation."

I believed then—and continue to believe today—that the failure of the GSEs would have led to a global financial meltdown.

Later that day I got on the phone to walk Zhou Xiaochuan and Wang Qishan through our decision. From the start of the crisis, we had decided to be frank about any problems, and they had trusted us and helped to steady markets at a fraught time.

"I think we've put out the fire," I told Wang Qishan. "I believe this will stop the panic."

He assured me that the Chinese would continue to hold their positions and congratulated me on our moves, but he cautioned me: "I know you think this will end all of your problems, but it may not be over yet."

As we spoke, I reflected on how much Wang and I had reversed roles from a decade before, when Guangdong Enterprises ran aground. Like the GSEs, though on a smaller scale, Guangdong Enterprises had embraced an unsustainable business model in which investors thought they had Chinese government guarantees when they did not. In passing, I reminded the vice premier that Steve Shafran, who had led the Guangdong restructuring, was now a critical member of the team advising me at Treasury. Wang respected Steve enormously for his work and never failed to ask after him.

"Your investments are in good hands," I told Wang.

When I look back on that gloomy summer and fall, I recall few bright moments. One came in late August, as we prepared to seize control of the two GSEs, when Chinese activist Yang Jianli came to see me at Treasury with his wife and two young children. He wanted to thank me personally for helping to secure his release from China and return to the U.S. a year before. Though barred from China, he had remained active in human rights efforts, leading the Foundation for China in the 21st Century, a prodemocracy group he'd founded in California in 1990.

I didn't go into a lot of detail about my efforts on his behalf, simply crediting the SED for providing me with a vehicle for pressing for his release.

However, it turned out he had heard plenty—not about my jobs at Goldman Sachs or Treasury but about my work in conservation.

"I read about what you were doing in Yunnan when I was in prison," he said.

And in a gesture that struck me profoundly, Yang made a point of thanking me not just for his release but for the work we had been doing with the environment. Here was a prominent dissident thanking me for the same things, and in much the same way, as had the very leaders he protested against. His words drove home to me yet again how important it was to find common ground and identify issues that mattered to the Chinese. Showing my genuine concern for China, the well-being of its environment and its citizens, had made a big difference to people in very different walks of life there.

To my discomfort, markets weakened further even after we seized Fannie and Freddie. Unable to find new capital or a strategic partner, Lehman Brothers deteriorated sharply as nervous creditors cut their dealings with the strapped institution. Finally, after an emergency meeting in New York of the world's leading investment banks failed to devise a rescue, the storied bank, whose roots stretched back to 1847, filed for bankruptcy. Try as we could, without a buyer or a capital partner, we could find no government authority that would allow us to save an insolvent investment bank. That same weekend we learned that another major investment bank, Merrill Lynch, was also faltering. Worse, the gigantic insurer American International Group was in dire straits, weighed down by credit default swaps tied to bad mortgage investments.

Lehman's fall set off a near panic, and financial shares—led by AIG's—plunged on Monday, September 15. (Fortunately, Bank of America had agreed to acquire Merrill, averting an even bigger disaster than Lehman.) Funding sources began to dry up, hurting banks and big companies alike. Major industrial companies like Procter & Gamble and Coca-Cola began to have trouble selling commercial paper. Often bought by money funds looking for a little extra yield compared with government bills, commercial paper was a crucial short-term financing source for many companies.

A nonstop series of explosions kept detonating within the larger unfolding disaster. On Tuesday, September 16, we learned that AIG would need an $85 billion Fed loan *that day* to avoid bankruptcy. Lehman's assets had been frozen in London, causing hedge funds to pull back from dealing with even apparently healthy investment banks. A riled-up John Mack called me to report that short sellers were attacking Morgan Stanley, where he was chairman and CEO. A respected name and a stout balance sheet were no longer enough. Mack was desperate to raise capital for his firm, and he logically thought of China Investment Corporation, which managed a part of China's foreign reserves and had purchased 9.9 percent of Morgan Stanley in December 2007, after the Wall Street firm had posted its first quarterly loss ever. John knew I was close to Wang Qishan and asked me to see if I could talk to him and get the Chinese to increase their investment.

"All the signals we get are that they'd like some reassurance and encouragement from you," the Morgan Stanley CEO said.

I promised to do what I could.

The interconnectedness of markets caused problems to spread rapidly from one sector to another. The trouble with money market funds began when a few funds were hurt by their holdings in now worthless Lehman paper. Fear that they would "break the buck," or fail to pay investors 100 cents on the dollar, triggered a deluge of redemptions. This shrank their coffers, reducing the money available to invest in the commercial paper market, which soon froze up. Spooked investors shifted to safe Treasuries, creating such demand that banks and investors soon refused to lend government bonds to one another, slamming shut the doors of another crucial venue for short-term funds, the so-called Treasury repurchase market. Only an emergency guarantee the Treasury Department devised for the money market funds would prevent a catastrophic run that could take down industrial companies of all sizes and quickly spread the crisis from Wall Street to Main Street.

As all of this was unspooling, Dave McCormick rushed into my office to declare, "I've got really bad news. The Chinese are moving their money."

After one of the big money funds, the Reserve Primary Fund, had broken the buck, Dave had begun hearing from Wall Street sources that nervous Chinese banks were withdrawing large sums from the money market. We'd heard, too, that the Chinese were pulling back on secured overnight lending, afraid of counterparty risk. And they had begun shortening the maturities of their GSE holdings.

We didn't know quite what to make of this, though the implications were ominous, since the Chinese were such big investors. In my chats with Wang Qishan, he had emphasized that while China would not purchase more U.S. government and agency paper, it would also not be a seller. I asked Dave to find out what was going on. He called Chinese leaders, including Zhou Xiaochuan and Finance Minister Xie Xuren.

"You may not be giving the advice that they sell," he told Zhou, "but somewhere in the bureaucracy these decisions are being made."

Zhou said he was unaware of what Dave was describing but promised to find out. True to his word, Zhou called the next day to confirm the substance of the reports we'd gotten, but he assured Dave that none of the sales had been coordinated.

"People are making what they think are smart choices," Zhou said. "We're going to give some guidance particularly about the overnight lending and the pullback from the Reserve Fund."

Shortly afterward, nervous Chinese institutions reversed course. The irony was that Chinese banks were supposed to make independent decisions: that was what the reform and restructuring process had been about, after all. We didn't expect Zhou Xiaochuan to prevent the banks from taking measures to protect themselves, but he could point out the dangerous consequences of their actions. The truth was that the Chinese banks remained very much under the thumb of the State Council. Though they had public shareholders, they were owned by the state, and their CEOs ultimately took their orders from the government. As a result, the "guidance" given by the Chinese government stemmed some of the panic in the markets. And the financial world ought to be grateful for that.

On the evening of September 19, John Mack called me again to report that he had not made much progress with China Investment Corporation.

"The Chinese need to know that the U.S. government thinks it is important to find a solution," he said.

"I'll talk to Wang Qishan," I told him, adding that I was prepared to ask President Bush to contact President Hu if it would help. Morgan Stanley was much bigger than Lehman, and its failure would have brought down other institutions and might have caused the collapse of our entire financial system, triggering another Great Depression.

The next day I alerted the president to be ready in case he was needed to speak to President Hu. That would happen only if CIC appeared more interested in increasing its stake in Morgan Stanley. The approach would have to be careful and indirect, because the president couldn't very well ask a foreign government to invest in a U.S. company. But President Bush could thank Hu for his country's cooperation in helping us deal with problems in the capital markets to signal how important Morgan Stanley was to the financial system. My staff would make it clear to Hu's people that the thank-you concerned Morgan Stanley. President Bush asked me to work with National Security Adviser Steve Hadley on this.

That night I spoke to Wang Qishan. After the disagreement over the joint venture investment bank formed by Morgan Stanley and China Construction Bank in the 1990s, he and John Mack had become good friends, and he had a high regard for Morgan Stanley. But friendship went only so far. I concluded as we spoke that the Chinese were not quite as enthusiastic about investing as John Mack had hoped. As a matter of fact, Wang didn't seem very interested at all. It was clear he was concerned with the safety of any investment the Chinese might make. And because I couldn't give him the assurances I knew he was looking for, I moved on to the next topic. I knew there would be no need for President Bush to talk to Hu.

I wasn't surprised because I understood the Chinese concerns. They didn't want to lose any more money on Morgan Stanley. The stakes were simply too high. Our troubles had given new energy to Chinese opponents of reform, who were denouncing the U.S. and stoking nationalist sentiments. The government had been taking a public relations beating for months over its money-losing investments in Blackstone and Morgan Stanley, which were tracked meticulously every day by an army of online bloggers. If China had suffered losses on its vast holdings of Fannie or Freddie securities, there could have been a huge political problem and a loss of confidence in the government.

Morgan Stanley would end up finding a partner in a Japanese firm, Mitsubishi UFJ—which agreed to invest after some encouragement and assurances from the Treasury Department—and I certainly don't blame China for not wanting to risk putting good money after bad. Overall, its leaders were very supportive, despite frightening headlines, breathtaking market plunges, and the outright failures of major institutions. It was, as I've said, in their interest to stay the course. Though unnerved, they held firm—just as they had during the Asian financial crisis, when it was their region on the brink of collapse. Now it was the U.S. and Europe that were faltering, and China's strength of purpose and resolve would play a big role in helping the West survive and emerge from the worst of the crisis.

In my view, the relationships I had built in China, at Goldman and through the painstaking efforts of the SED, had paid off. True, I can't draw a straight line from the personal trust and frequent informal communications fostered by the SED discussions to China's restraint during the financial crisis, but there's not a doubt in my mind that there *was* a connection. This achievement may have fallen outside the list of deliverables, but its importance during a dire period for the United States is impossible to overstate.

Meanwhile, it had become clear to anyone with eyes to see that we were not going to be able to keep holding the financial system together with ad hoc measures. We would have to ask Congress to grant us extraordinary powers to deal with the worst American economic catastrophe since the Great Depression. This conclusion led us, in consultation with Congress, to craft the $700 billion Troubled Assets Relief Program, which authorized the government to buy toxic assets from financial institutions to help clean up their balance sheets.

As I remember only too well, the passage of TARP was a nail-biter; the

House of Representatives rejected it initially, triggering a week of market chaos. TARP's eventual passage—on Friday, October 3—failed to steady the markets, in part because the pervasive, global nature of the problems was becoming clearer. The following Monday, Asian, European, and U.S. shares plunged as investors worried that a squabbling Europe would be unable to fix its banks and that TARP might not be enough. The situation had worsened significantly during the two weeks we had been working with Congress to get TARP authority, and we realized that TARP's asset-buying program would not be enough. We needed something that would work more quickly to restore confidence in the markets and be more powerful. My team at Treasury began to work on a sweeping plan to inject equity and recapitalize more than 700 banks.

British prime minister Gordon Brown, whose government would unveil an $875 billion bank bailout of its own, suggested to President Bush that he call a meeting of the G20 leaders. Inside the administration we debated the merits of the idea. Though I was concerned that such a gathering could lead to a political brouhaha that might destabilize markets further, we needed a global approach to a global problem, and I advocated holding a meeting as soon as possible after the U.S. presidential election on November 4.

First, we wanted to make sure we had a productive meeting of the G7 finance ministers, who were to gather on Friday, October 10, during the annual World Bank/IMF meeting. The usual G7 format was highly scripted, with ministers reciting talking points to one another and then the group releasing highly technical communiqués understandable only to a small group of insiders and members of the press. This time we needed to come together in a serious, substantive way to communicate our resolve to the public and the markets. We got off to a bumpy start as one central banker after another rose to blame the U.S. for the global mess, tracing their countries' problems to Lehman's collapse. In truth, Europe's overleveraged and undercapitalized banks had been on the road to disaster long before Lehman fell. Still, the venting helped. In the end, the group issued a strong, clear communiqué, long on substance and short on jargon, committing us all to decisive action in dealing with the crisis.

The outcome inspired the White House to press ahead with a global leaders' summit. I pushed for inviting the G20, as did a number of the president's advisers—including chief of staff Josh Bolten, National Security

Adviser Steve Hadley, and Dan Price, who wore two hats as deputy national security adviser for international economic affairs and assistant to the president for international economic affairs. The G20's Finance ministers and central bankers met regularly, but its heads of state had never convened. I thought that should change; taken together, emerging G20 powerhouses like Brazil, India, and China represented not just the present but also the future.

Not everyone was enthusiastic. Some in the U.S. government felt 20 countries was too many to be effective and that the participation of countries like Argentina, with its populist president, Cristina Fernández de Kirchner, who we believed had a history of taking irrational, irresponsible, and anti-U.S. economic positions, might undermine the group's effectiveness. But we all saw eye to eye on one thing: if the Chinese were willing to exert a leadership role at the G20—and if the biggest developed nation and the biggest developing nation were in agreement on the issues—the G20 would be a success. Before moving ahead with our plans for the gathering, President Bush authorized me to call Wang Qishan and get a quick answer from President Hu.

We knew there was a very small risk of being rebuffed—the Chinese were still smarting over a U.S. decision to sell $6 billion in arms to Taiwan in early October—but we got a strong yes within 24 hours from an eager Hu. The Chinese leader surely realized that this emergency gathering would be an ideal showcase for China in its new role as a global power. With the Chinese on board, President Bush decided to move forward with the G20 leaders' summit.

With the exception of Gordon Brown, the Europeans resisted a group that size, fearing their influence would be diluted. In a concession, we agreed to invite Spain and the Netherlands, which belonged to neither the G8 (the G7 plus Russia) nor the G20. After much back-and-forth, a summit of G20 leaders was scheduled for November 14–15 in Washington. Dave McCormick worked with Dan Price to coordinate the effort.

China also was beginning to feel its share of pain. Its equity and real estate markets were off sharply, while export and investment growth were declining. On November 9, less than a week before the G20 leaders were to arrive in Washington, the PRC announced a large $586 billion two-year stimulus program, chiefly to build infrastructure. It was the biggest such plan the country had ever attempted. The government also eased credit and would encourage a massive $1 trillion–plus lending campaign by state-owned banks the following year. How ironic, I thought, that the very banks whose weakness had endangered China five years before were now helping to pull the country's economy—and the world's—out of the ditch.

On November 15 the G20's leaders gathered in Washington at the Great Hall of the National Building Museum, a vast space with soaring Corinthian columns that had originally been designed to house the Civil War pension bureau. An enormous square table had been set up in the hall to accommodate the large group. As I surveyed the room, I saw a vivid illustration of how the order of things was changing—for the better. Joining such European leaders as French president Nicolas Sarkozy, Germany's Angela Merkel, and Italy's Silvio Berlusconi were China's Hu Jintao, Brazilian president Luiz Inácio Lula da Silva, and Indian prime minister Manmohan Singh.

As Hu's eagerness to attend had demonstrated, China was stepping up as a major participant in the global community. This was not the scenario I had hoped for—China's emergence on the international stage being driven by a global financial disaster centered in the U.S. and Europe—but the Chinese, too, had a stake in global economic stability, and I was glad to see them playing a leading role in working to restore confidence.

During a break in the proceedings, I had an opportunity to visit briefly with Hu Jintao and Wang Qishan. We talked for a bit, and Hu said, "I bet you're glad we didn't move the currency faster than we did. I hope you now understand why. Some of the things you wanted us to do would have been dangerous. Now we're stable and can stimulate the economy, and that's helping us and the whole world."

I thanked President Hu and told him I thought the steps China had taken to begin reforming its currency had been beneficial. "It's important that you keep your economy growing," I said, adding, "but I believe that it is your fiscal spending, and not your currency policies, that has bolstered this growth."

Throughout the meeting the Chinese were accommodating on just about everything, with one notable exception: they didn't want the final communiqué to use the word "imbalances," which they viewed as short-hand for China's oversaving and the U.S.'s overborrowing. The subject had been a thorny issue for years. Citing imbalances as a cause of financial excesses leading to the crisis was the same, to the Chinese, as faulting them for something that was our doing. I had always held that imbalances worked both ways: the U.S.'s huge debts and low savings were as much a cause of the parlous state of the global economy as China's excessive savings. But the Chinese were very sensitive to any hint of blame, and Wang Qishan had cautioned me about publicly addressing the subject of China's imbalances in connection to the financial crisis.

"If you talk about this, it looks like you're pointing the finger at us," he said. "And we haven't pointed the finger at you."

Going into the G20, I'd been concerned that our efforts to deal with the financial crisis might get bogged down in petty protectionism and recrimination. But I could not have been more wrong. The developed economies apologized for their role in the current disaster, but instead of blaming the freewheeling Western financial system, the smaller economies expressed concern about overreaction. All the countries rejected protectionism and agreed that reforms would only be successful with a commitment to free-market principles. The communiqué the group released affirmed that the 20 nations would implement reforms to strengthen the global financial system and noted the importance of international cooperation.

Three weeks after the G20 leaders' summit, in early December, I flew to Beijing for what would be my last SED meeting. When the group reconvened in July 2009, president-elect Barack Obama's new team would be in place. The U.S. government transition, truly a marvel of our democracy, was under way, but markets remained tense, and we were still contending with an unrelenting series of crises. General Motors and Chrysler were teetering on the verge of failure (and would require a government loan from TARP funds to be saved). In late November we had had to rescue U.S. banking giant Citigroup with a combination of capital injections and guarantees. Citi was the largest U.S. bank, with assets of $2 trillion—and another $1.2 trillion assets off balance sheet, half of which were related to mortgages. It had begun to wobble under the weight of toxic assets and speculative attacks in the stock market. We were forced to act to prevent its failing, which would have had catastrophic consequences.

Given these persistent problems, Vice President Dick Cheney suggested that I stay home. "The president is relying on you to protect our financial system and economy," he told me on the sidelines of our weekly Wednesday lunch with the Bush administration's economic team. "This is equivalent to leaving the country at a time of war."

I argued that it would look worse if I didn't make the trip. The markets would surely see my cancellation as a sign that the situation in the U.S. was truly disastrous. "If I don't go to Beijing, or if I call off the SED, everybody will really think we're in deep trouble," I said.

The vice president was a low-key guy, and he didn't push the issue, but I could tell he was uncomfortable with my leaving the country. Despite his strong conservative principles, he never wavered in his support for TARP or any of the ugly capital markets interventions we were forced to make during the financial crisis. He was also supportive of the SED and our two-way economic relationship with the Chinese.

SED V brought home to me the value of two and a half years of effort, as issues our teams had been diligently working on bore fruit: the U.S. affirmed that it welcomed investment from China. We made sure to emphasize the link between foreign direct investment and well-paying American jobs. We didn't want anyone thinking we were trying to sell precious U.S. assets to the Chinese—or to anyone—at fire-sale prices. Our analysis showed that foreign investment had led to 5 million U.S. jobs; these paid, on average, 30 percent more than the going rate nationally.

At SED V we also signed the EcoPartnerships agreement as part of the Ten-Year Framework, ensuring that local institutions would work together to address environmental issues. We built upon the successes of past SEDs by organizing technical training to promote food and product safety and improving our ability to jointly deal with emergencies. To critics of the SED, some of these achievements—from increasing and expediting the number of Chinese tourists visiting the U.S. to agreeing to work together to combat illegal logging—might have seemed less than spectacular. But there were hundreds of them, they added up to a lot of progress, and they would not have been achieved without the SED. I saw each one as a brick in a strong structure that we were building—a structure that would withstand the winds of future tensions and crises.

At the first SED, back in December 2006, Wu Yi had used her opening speech to underscore the extent to which Americans failed to understand China. In her view, China was a developing country not respected by the world powers, which failed to treat it as a strategic partner. Now, two years later, our countries were committed to working hard together. There was plenty we disagreed about, but we both valued the dialogue that allowed us to defuse crises and make progress on those areas where we could agree.

In my first days as Treasury secretary, we had drawn up plans for the SED with three overarching goals: to advance the economic relationship between the U.S. and China, to help bring about market reforms in China, and to encourage its emergence as a responsible global citizen. Our economic relationship with China was now on a stronger footing, buttressed by joint efforts to achieve environmentally sustainable economic growth. We had not gotten the market reforms we wanted—as I write this, China still hasn't lifted its cap on foreign investment in its financial companies, though I believe our work in this area will bear fruit—but we had won a broader latitude for U.S. firms to operate in China as well as a stronger renminbi, without destructive U.S. protectionist legislation. Finally, elevating the status of the G20 had provided the Chinese an opportunity to play a responsible leadership role in supporting the economic system from which they had benefited so much. Over time, I hoped, they would learn to do just that, because their commitment to solving problems is crucial to global stability.

As a young investment banker, I learned that the key to success was building relationships, between you and your client, between your firm and his or hers. As Treasury secretary, I had worked to build lasting relationships, this time between countries. Personalities came and went—I wouldn't be Treasury secretary much longer, and the Chinese leadership would also change. But with the SED we had created a forum for relations between our countries that would carry on after us. Indeed, the Obama administration would embrace the SED approach, while broadening it to include foreign policy and national security as the renamed Strategic and Economic Dialogue. In November 2014, building on the platform of the Ten-Year Framework, the U.S. and China reached a breakthrough agreement to limit greenhouse gas emissions, fulfilling my vision of increased collaboration to combat climate change.

I learned something else as a young investment banker: never take no for an answer. You almost never got what you asked for the first time around, especially with new clients. You had to work hard to understand their needs and frame your proposals to appeal to their best interests. Then you had to push and push, and keep asking for the same thing. With enough time and effort, the answer might just change to yes. I certainly employed that approach in China. How many times did I hear "no" or "not yet" or "not so fast" in response to my requests for the Chinese to open their markets or move their currency? Even when we didn't get the answer we wanted, we managed to wedge the door open a little further, and the next time we'd push a little more. In a country where so many people weighed in on so many issues, we were, at a minimum, helping them build a consensus for change.

As was the custom, after the rest of the U.S. delegation had met with President Hu in a formal setting, I shared a private chat with him. The Chinese leader and I sat side by side on a cushioned bench in a screened alcove behind the elaborate meeting room in the Great Hall of the People. I let him know that I remained concerned about problems in the U.S. economy, and I reminded him that the new administration would be feeling its way for a while and not to expect too much too soon.

"There's still significant anti-China sentiment in the U.S.," I noted, cautioning him that U.S.-Chinese relations would suffer if his country stopped or slowed down reform. I urged him to stay committed to the kind of engagement with the world he had demonstrated during the G20.

This was my closing official advice to China's president, and his final words to me as Treasury secretary were meant to be reassuring.

"We may not go as fast as you like," Hu said. "But the direction is always going to be forward. Our reform process is irreversible."

I certainly hoped so. In a short while I would leave Treasury, just as I had left Goldman Sachs, behind me. I had no idea what I would do next, but even as Hu spoke I knew that one way or another, I would continue to push my Chinese friends to speed up their reforms, for the simple reason that doing so would be good for China, good for the U.S., and good for the world.

PART THREE

Building Bridges

CHAPTER FIFTEEN

Darkness at Noon

I'm no fan of Beijing in the late fall or winter, but I'd never found the city as dreary and unpleasant as I did the first week of December 2011. I was there to host a conference on urban sustainability for the Paulson Institute, my newly created nonprofit organization, and not long after I'd arrived, the Chinese capital was blanketed by smog so thick and murky that airport runways were closed and hundreds of flights were canceled or diverted. Some of our later arrivals wound up being sent to Inner Mongolia.

During a break for lunch, I left our hotel to do a photo op with Los Angeles mayor Antonio Villaraigosa, one of our featured speakers, for an all-electric car that combined a Chinese-made battery and body with a proprietary drivetrain installed in L.A. I had been indoors all morning, and, boy, was I shocked to step outside. It was just after noon, but it was so dark and gloomy it might as well have been dusk. Office towers just across the street were as dim as shadows. My eyes stung and began to water.

We posed beside the Coda Automotive car with company CEO Phil Murtaugh. Then Antonio slid behind the wheel for more photos. On the spur of the moment, he slipped the car in gear and off we sped, soundlessly, down the crowded side street. Phil had taken the back seat. I rode shotgun. Even inside the car I could almost taste the grit in the acrid air. Antonio flicked on our headlights. In the blur of oncoming beams, my mind flashed to scenes from old black-and-white movies depicting the fogs of Victorian London. Beijing couldn't get cars like this on its roads fast enough, I thought.

We hadn't driven far before Antonio realized he had no idea where the street was going or how we'd get back if we went any farther. So he spun us through a quick U-turn that might well have been illegal.

"I've lived in L.A. all my life," Antonio told me. "But I've never seen smog like this."

For good reason, too: the air in L.A., the most polluted big city in the U.S., is positively pristine compared with that of Beijing, where smoke from coal-burning power plants, factories, and home furnaces mixes with exhaust from the world's fastest-growing fleet of cars and trucks in an ever more toxic combination. On average, the Chinese capital's air contains nearly seven times as many fine particulates as does the L.A. area's. Measuring no more than 2.5 microns in diameter—or PM 2.5—these microscopic bits of matter can infiltrate the body's tissues and are among the deadly by-products of internal combustion.

The day of our drive, Monday, December 5, 2011, ranked among the worst in memory. I'd have said "on record," but the Chinese government didn't release such information back then. Beijingers relied on hourly Twitter posts from the U.S. Embassy, which recorded the city's air quality through instruments on its roof. That day registered 416 on the PM 2.5 scale—deep into what the U.S. Environmental Protection Agency labels "hazardous" air quality (any measurement over 300) and nearly 17 times the World Health Organization standard for healthy air. The day before had been worse, exceeding 500. When a reading had gone that high the previous year, it had carried the label "crazy bad." The embassy quickly dropped that mischievous term, but its tweets about air quality had registered with beleaguered city residents and helped to fuel an outcry from local environmental activists, journalists, real estate developers, and concerned parents that upset China's leadership and eventually caused it to take action.

Foul air is just the most visible of the many daunting challenges China's government must address as it confronts the increasingly dark side of its extraordinary economic success. Pell-mell growth combined with a legacy of poor planning, gross energy inefficiency, inadequate regulation, and lax enforcement have ravaged China's cities and countryside. Groundwater in the arid northern half of the country—always scarce—is now all but depleted. Rivers and lakes are polluted, some so badly they are not fit to use for irrigation, much less drinking. Indeed, some 300 million Chinese do not have ready access to potable water. In many places the soil has been contaminated by industrial by-products, harming crops, livestock, and the people who eat them. Reports of rice laced with cadmium abound. In 2013 thousands of dead pigs were found floating in the Huangpu River and its tributaries, threatening Shanghai's water supply. Hundreds of so-called cancer villages have been identified whose residents suffer unusually high rates of the same cancers; the villages are usually located near polluted water or concentrations of industry.

The environmental crisis is only part of the unhappy story. The country's wealth has not been shared anywhere near equally. Corruption is widespread, and China suffers a wide gap between rich and poor, with glaring regional disparities. Its riches are concentrated in the eastern coastal cities and provinces. Rural areas, the west and the country's interior, lag badly. China's cities teem with hundreds of millions of people who—thanks to an outmoded system of residential permits—live all but illegally as second-class citizens in a land whose newfound prosperity they have labored to create.

The threats to the health, happiness, and economic well-being of China's citizens pose a serious risk of unrest. Polls show growing unhappiness among the people about corruption, the environment, and the confiscation of land by public officials to promote development. According to a 2013 survey by China Merchants Bank and the U.S. consulting firm Bain & Company, three-fifths of wealthy mainland Chinese—defined as those with investable assets of at least $1.6 million—were looking to leave the country or had already left. One-third had invested abroad, twice the level of two years before. Nationally, so-called mass incidents, a catchall phrase for protests and civil disturbances, have soared in the past decade. Complaints about environmental damage or the illegal seizure of farmland constitute the two biggest sources of local protests. The paradox, painfully obvious to the Chinese leadership, is that the very prosperity that has ensured the legitimacy of the ruling Communist Party now threatens to undermine it.

As the country's leaders also know, these pressures will only intensify. For all its success, China remains relatively poor. It may boast the second-biggest economy in the world, but measured by GDP per capita, it ranks just 80th, a notch above war-ravaged Iraq at 81st. Hundreds of millions of citizens have climbed out of poverty into a nascent middle class, but tens of millions more barely scrape by. Raising their standard of living, without a drastic change in China's growth model, will only put more pressure on the environment, exacerbate inequality, and boost the country's ravenous demand for resources—all with potentially dire consequences for China and the world.

Meantime, the country's economic engine has slowed. The double-digit average annual growth of the past 30 years fell to 7.4 percent in 2014. That's a giddy pace for the rest of the world, but it marked China's worst performance since 1999, in the aftermath of the Asian financial crisis. The slowdown was partly intentional. The government resisted the big stimulus measures it had used in 2008 and 2009 to goose growth rates. The leadership wants to wean the economy off its overreliance on exports and infrastructure-driven government investment and shift instead toward increased domestic consumption and the creation of a thriving service sector. It is banking on continued rapid urbanization to help accomplish this: since 1978, an estimated 300 million have made the trip from farm to city, and another 300 million are expected to relocate by 2030.

This coming wave of migration may well be one of the most important events shaping economic and environmental outcomes in China and throughout the world in coming years. To achieve the modernization it seeks, China needs a new urbanization model that is economically sound, socially just, and ecologically sustainable.

When I left Treasury and returned to private life in 2009, I had no set idea of what I would do next, which was just as well, because I was pretty exhausted and plenty miserable. Though grateful to have more time with my family, I was as unhappy then as I'd ever been. Even favorite pastimes that I looked forward to all year, like saltwater fly-fishing for tarpon and bonefish, left me unsatisfied. I had lost my sense of joy—and purpose.

Looking back, I'd say there were several reasons for this. For one, I took personally the continued suffering of so many Americans who, in the midst of the worst economic downturn in decades, suddenly found themselves jobless, homeless, and running out of hope. I was frustrated by my inability to do anything to help now that I was out of office. I believed I had done my best to prevent the 2008 financial crisis from turning into another Great Depression, but the withering criticism we received from the press—and some in the Obama White House—stung me deeply. (I still remember one set of polls that showed that more people favored torture than TARP!) I spent months huddled with my lawyers: complying with subpoenas, being deposed, testifying before Congress. As the Treasury secretary who had been forced to use extraordinary authorities in novel and unpopular ways, I knew it was only natural that my actions would be investigated and that I should be expected to explain them. But it's one thing to understand that in theory; it's another to have to live through it.

I didn't pretend to think that we in the Bush administration, working closely with Ben Bernanke and Tim Geithner at the Federal Reserve, had done everything right. But we had done our best, and under excruciating conditions we got the major decisions right. When we made mistakes, we corrected them quickly and prevented far worse from happening. I was proud of that record—and remain so. I began a memoir, *On the Brink*, to record the challenges we had encountered and how we dealt with them. I believed it was important to never forget the lessons we learned during the financial crisis.

Writing is said to be therapeutic for some authors. I'd like to meet one or two of them. It sure wasn't for me. Writing *On the Brink*, I found myself reliving the most harrowing moments of the crisis—complete with sleepless nights. The strain wore on my family. As a matter of fact, when I later told Wendy that I was thinking about writing another book—this one—she said simply: "Fine. And I'm going to start dating again."

After *On the Brink* was published, Wendy and I left Washington, D.C., and returned to Barrington, Illinois, our home just outside of Chicago, where we had lived before I'd moved to New York in 1994 to help run Goldman Sachs. I took a long, deep breath and began to focus on what I would do next. I had not given much thought to this—at Treasury, there had been no time. When I'd left Goldman, I knew that I would be leaving Wall Street for good. I'd loved working with both smart colleagues and demanding clients to solve complex problems, but I was ready to try my hand at something new. Wendy and I intended to devote much of our time and effort, and most of our money, to the cause of conservation. We briefly considered starting our own NGO but concluded we could be more effective partnering with established organizations. I declined offers to join the boards of directors of many public companies and nonprofits. The hands-on work of business and conservation fascinates me. Board meetings do not.

However, one thing had remained clear in my mind—I wanted to stay involved with China in a meaningful way. Toward the end of 2009, I received a call from an old friend, Zhou Wenzhong, the outgoing Chinese ambassador to the U.S. He would soon take a position as secretary general of the Boao Forum for Asia, which had been established by the Chinese as an Asian counterpart to the famed World Economic Forum in Davos. Zhou invited me to become the first U.S. trustee, and I accepted.

The forum held in Hainan in April 2010 took me back to China for the first time since I'd left Treasury 15 months before. I brought with me copies of the just-released Chinese version of *On the Brink* and made stops in Shanghai and Beijing to see a number of old friends, including current and former leaders like Jiang Zemin, Zhu Rongji, Xi Jinping, Wang Qishan, and Zhou Xiaochuan. These meetings, in which I was peppered with questions about the Obama administration and U.S.-China relations, helped galvanize my thinking. All my life I've gravitated toward big challenges, and, as my conversations with China's leaders reminded me, there were few things more important to America than getting our dealings with China right.

I was struck by a newfound sense of confidence, verging on triumphalism, among many of the Chinese I saw and spoke with. To an extent, this attitude was well earned. The West was reeling, but China's economy appeared strong; growth rates that had dipped to 6.2 percent in the first quarter of 2009 had roared back to reach 8.7 percent for the full year. Meantime, the U.S. economy had shrunk by 2.4 percent, while the Eurozone had contracted by 4.1 percent. A decade before, China's banks had been near collapse. Now they were well capitalized and thriving while many of their Western counterparts were being bailed out. Some on our shores were penning paeans to the state-directed market socialism of the Chinese economic model.

Yet I felt—as did many of my reformist friends in China—that such hosannas were misguided. If anything, the global financial crisis had laid bare China's flaws: its export businesses had collapsed as markets dried up in slump-ridden Europe and the States. China's economy was booming again, but that was thanks to massive government stimulus spending that, I feared, would lead to harmful distortions and more corruption. Crucially, major economic reforms remained stalled. Without further market-oriented initiatives, I doubted China would be able to successfully rebalance its economy. All of this made me wary, especially since—given China's seemingly unbridled self-confidence—I could see hints of future tensions with the U.S.

Some months later Chinese president Hu Jintao was scheduled to come to the States. With the assistance of my former colleagues Deborah Lehr and Taiya Smith, I offered some advice to Chinese ambassador Zhang Yesui. Among other things, I strongly encouraged an official visit to Chicago, which Hu made in January 2011. After a dinner for the Chinese leader hosted by Mayor Richard Daley, I accompanied the Chinese delegation back to the Mandarin Hotel, where I reminisced with Wang Qishan. I left his room with a clear understanding that the Chinese leaders very much wanted me to find a platform that would allow me to make a real difference in improving U.S.-China relations.

"You will always be welcomed and listened to in China," Wang Qishan assured me. "You know how to get things done."

I began kicking ideas back and forth with Deborah Lehr, in much the same way that four and a half years earlier the two of us had brainstormed the creation of the Strategic Economic Dialogue. Out of this several-month process came the Paulson Institute, a nonprofit that was to be funded initially only by me. It was officially established in June 2011 with a mission of promoting sustainable economic growth and a cleaner environment by facilitating greater cooperation between the U.S. and China. We laid down several clear goals: to encourage energy efficiency and better environmental practices, to increase cross-border investment leading to the creation of jobs, and to promote responsible executive leadership and best business practices on issues of international concern.

Today the Institute has a staff of 30 professionals in the U.S. and China engaged in thought leadership and advocacy, and we are working on several major programs to achieve our goals. Our programs—in urbanization, global leadership, climate change and air quality, conservation, and cross-border investment—have spurred a variety of initiatives, from courses for Chinese mayors on urban sustainability to a plan to map the biodiversity of China's coastal wetlands as a first step toward devising a strategy for their preservation. PI publishes the research and policy prescriptions of scholars and experts from around the world on timely issues of global importance. Topics have ranged from the environmental lending standards of China's development banks to the reform of China's state-owned enterprises.

From the beginning, I wanted the Institute to have intellectual rigor, and we were fortunate to be able to find a home at the University of Chicago, whose dynamic president, Robert Zimmer, has been developing programs to apply his institution's brainpower to solving pressing problems in the U.S. and abroad. I accepted an appointment as a distinguished senior fellow at the Harris School of Public Policy Studies, and the Institute was set up as an independent center affiliated with the university. All the same, I didn't want the Institute to be like other think tanks that only commission studies or publish reports. I wanted to get things done. In fact, I was inclined to call the institute a "do tank."

That was my plan, anyway, until I visited my former boss John Whitehead in New York. John, who passed away in February 2015, was a man of great wisdom, stature, and gravitas. He had run Goldman Sachs and then served as U.S. deputy secretary of State and overseen numerous philanthropic and civic projects, including the Lower Manhattan Development Corporation after 9/11. I described my plans for the institute and explained my aversion to the term "think tank."

"Words matter," John counseled me. "If you call it just a 'do tank,' people will say, 'There Hank goes again, acting without thinking.' Why not call it a 'think and do tank'?"

I got the point. A few weeks later I flew to Beijing for our first conference on urban sustainability, and that was exactly how I described the institute to Li Keqiang, who was then executive vice premier in charge of the economy. Li broke into a broad smile when I said we were a "think and do tank." He noted that his favorite Chinese proverb was "*zhixing heyi*," which he explained meant "uniting knowledge and action." Then in his own calligraphy he wrote the Chinese characters for the proverb, which we use on our website and letterhead in China.

Since the dawn of civilization, people have moved from farms to cities in search of better lives. Cities are richer. Their residents produce more and consume more than their country cousins do. In economic terms, urbanization increases productivity and incomes as labor is reallocated from lower-value-added traditional agriculture to higher-value-added manufacturing and service sectors. At the same time, cities generate new sources of domestic demand—for housing, public works like roads and sewers, services like education and health care, and big-ticket consumer products like cars and home appliances. Combining greater productivity and higher demand creates a virtuous cycle that generates jobs. Industrialization and urbanization, not surprisingly, have long gone hand in hand.

The extraordinary recent growth of China—throughout its history a land of poor farmers ruled by a small, educated elite—has been accompanied by a migration of people to cities on a scale and at a speed unlike anything mankind has ever before seen. The estimated 300 million Chinese who have made the journey in the past 30 years is the equivalent of having relocated nearly the entire population of the United States over that time.

This migration was initially inadvertent, the result of the stunning success of rural reforms, which dramatically increased agricultural production and created huge pools of surplus farm labor. Some peasants joined fledgling township and village enterprises; millions more streamed to the special economic zones and revitalized cities along the coast in search of newly available jobs—on factory assembly lines, on construction sites, on street corners selling steamed breakfast buns or Gucci knockoffs. The flow increased as the economy grew. The floodgates opened after China entered the WTO and became the world's factory floor. As recently as 1978, at the start of Deng Xiaoping's Reform and Opening Up, 80 percent of China's people tilled the land. Now slightly more than half live in cities.

All over China, villages have become towns, towns have become cities, and cities have built up and out to become ever bigger and more sprawling megalopolises, changing the face of the country in stunning, rapid fashion. For decades my hometown, Chicago, laid claim to being the fastest-growing city in history. From just over 112,000 residents on the eve of the Civil War in 1860, it had mushroomed to 1.1 million by the time of the World's Columbian Exposition of 1893, when it first bared its big shoulders to the world. Yet Chicago's breathtaking growth pales before that of Shenzhen, a rural community of 321,000 in 1980 that today teems with 10.6 million permanent residents. Today China has 174 cities with over 1 million people; the U.S. has nine.

As China's economy soared, so did its skylines. Six of the world's 15 tallest buildings are in mainland China (the U.S. has three). Sixty-two of the tallest skyscrapers under way are being built there, including eight of the top ten. When I first visited Shanghai in 1992, the tallest building in town was the brand-new 48-story Portman Ritz-Carlton Hotel, which reached 541 feet. Since then, no fewer than 96 new buildings have topped that height; 15 more are under construction. In seemingly every corner of the country, office towers, hotels, factories, shopping centers, and residential housing have been thrown up posthaste. From a start in 2011, the government is in the midst of putting up 36 million units of affordable housing by 2015. At an average of about three people per household, that's enough to shelter nearly the entire population of the Philippines, the world's 12th most populated country.

All manner of public infrastructure has been built to serve and link these cities. China had next to no modern motorways at the start of Reform and Opening Up in 1978; by 2013 the country's National Trunk Highway System had just under 53,000 miles of road and was expected to exceed 67,000 miles by 2015. It surpassed the U.S.'s iconic 47,000-mile interstate system in 2011. Since construction started in 2006, China has built nearly 7,000 miles of high-speed rail, used by almost 2 million people per day. The U.S. has no dedicated high-speed rail line, and the first one likely to be built, in California, won't be finished until 2028. (China should have 11,000 miles by 2020.) The list goes on: China had 77 civilian airports in 1980; it has 182 today, and the current five-year plan calls for building 82 more by 2015. China expects to have subway systems in 40 cities in 2020, up from 21 today; 15 cities in the U.S. now have metro systems.

In the process, China has created tens of millions of jobs—in construction, in the factories and office buildings being built, and in the services needed to support the workers, from food supply to janitorial work to financial advice. This development has come as a result of policies and incentives that favored growth at any price. Now the Chinese are seeing the true cost of that growth and its insatiable demands on the country's limited resources and those of the world.

China's mind-set of unrestrained development has altered public and private life in profound ways, warping incentives and distorting market mechanisms. Public officials from the lowest village leader up through provincial governors have been rewarded with promotions and, all too frequently, personal enrichment for promoting growth. It's no wonder that in addition to so many worthy public works and stunning architectural breakthroughs, China has produced so many white-elephant projects. Among these are China's so-called ghost cities, sprawling developments that are all but unoccupied; the most notorious may be the Kangbashi New Area, outside the old city of Ordos in Inner Mongolia. Built to house 1 million people beginning in 2003, it had a population in 2014 that was estimated to range from 20,000 to 70,000.

Meantime, Chinese society has steadily become more unequal, approaching levels seen in countries like Nigeria, Brazil, and South Africa and unsettling the Chinese leadership. In 2005, then president Hu Jintao advocated the creation of a "socialist harmonious society" that would shift the Party's focus from pressing for growth to addressing festering social concerns. Nonetheless, big state initiatives in areas like clean energy development were overwhelmed by the social and environmental stresses of continued growth and industrialization. Hu's harmonious society was further away than ever when he left office in 2013, bequeathing his successors an even bigger cleanup.

"To modernize, we have to take the path of urbanization," Li Keqiang told me on another visit, a year later. "But the path is so difficult that we feel like we're walking on a tightrope."

It was December 2012, and I was in Beijing for the Paulson Institute's second annual conference on urbanization. Li had been named the second-highest-ranking member of the Party a few weeks before, though he would not be installed as premier until March 2013. We were speaking about the need to balance the continued rapid pace of urbanization with ensuring food security, protecting the environment, and conserving the country's limited resources.

"It's like an acrobat walking with a bamboo stick for balance," Li told me. He stretched his hands wide apart in front of him as if holding an imaginary pole and swayed a little for emphasis. "The acrobat has to be careful. He takes one small step after another. He has to keep going forward, he can't go backward. If he stops, he'll fall off."

Few leaders are more familiar with this high-wire act than Li, who wrote his Ph.D. dissertation on coordinating rural industrialization and urban development. Like many of China's leaders, he favors conservative dark suits and sports pomaded jet-black hair, but in person the 59-year-old Li comes across as anything but a dour apparatchik. Smart, charming, with a flair for the spontaneous, he's a shrewd politician who rose through the Communist Youth League and Party ranks as one of former president Hu Jintao's protégés.

We were chatting in the Purple Light Pavilion in Zhongnanhai, the Chinese leadership compound where I had talked with Zhu Rongji the week after Deng's death nearly 16 years before. Bright, late fall sunlight streamed through translucent white curtains, silhouetting the delicate teapots and vases arrayed on shelves in front of the room's large windows. Li leaned back in his doily-covered red armchair, self-assured, relaxed, and modest as he spoke.

Like so many in the leadership who endured the deprivations of the Cultural Revolution, Li knows firsthand how starkly different life is in China's cities and in its countryside. He grew up in Anhui Province in central China, where his father was a local Communist Party official in the capital, Hefei. After graduating from high school in 1974, he was sent to work on a farm less than 100 miles away. He joined the Party two years later and served as head of a village Party committee. During the day he moderated local disputes and chased pigs from fields; late at night he read through crates of books. The hard work paid off when China's nationwide entrance exams to universities resumed and he placed into the law department at Peking University, one of China's best schools. Along the way, he helped to translate an English textbook on due process into Chinese.

After graduating in 1982, Li turned down a coveted opportunity to study abroad, choosing to head the university's chapter of the Communist Youth League, where Hu Jintao was among his first bosses. The pair worked closely together until Hu was sent to the poor southwestern province of Guizhou. Li married the daughter of a senior official of the youth league and, while working his way up, completed his doctorate in economics in 1994. Four years later Li was dispatched to serve as acting governor in Henan, a backward, crowded province of 93 million people in central China. In his six years there he helped steer the province's national GDP ranking from 28th to 18th among China's 31 provinces, directly administered municipalities, and autonomous regions. But Li was dogged by a series of crises ranging from an HIV outbreak traced to tainted serum at local plasma clinics and blood banks to a rash of fatal fires that briefly earned him the nickname Three Fires Li.

In 2004 Li was named Party secretary of Liaoning Province in China's rust-belt northeast. He began to revitalize the province, coupling market incentives with bank loans and central government funds. Among his projects, he built new housing for 1.2 million people and masterminded the "Five Points to One Line" project, which expanded five ports along the Bohai Sea and linked them through a new coastal highway. In the 2007–2008 leadership transition, Li was picked for the CPC's all-powerful Standing Committee and named executive vice premier.

Given responsibility for economic management and reform, Li has emphasized the importance of urbanization for China. In a speech to Party leaders in 2010, Li made the case that expansion of cities would not only drive growth but that it could also help alleviate inequality and create an income distribution in China that was "olive shaped," with more people in the middle class than at either extreme of very wealthy or poor.

The gap between urban and rural areas is stark. City dwellers are four times as productive as their rural counterparts; they earn three times as much and consume three to four times as much.

"The discrepancies are large, but it also means the potential is large," Li told me that afternoon. "We've come to a consensus: urbanization has the greatest potential for boosting China's future domestic demand."

Indeed, that's the premise of urbanization: reducing the income gap by bringing farmers to the city, improving their lot, and increasing domestic consumption. But there's also a nettlesome income gap inside the cities, where hundreds of millions of migrants live in a legal netherworld, tolerated as cheap labor but denied the richer benefits available to native city dwellers. This state of affairs traces to China's creaky household registration system, or *hukou*, which started in the 1950s as a way to keep farmers in the countryside to assure sufficient grain production as the country industrialized rapidly. As in the Soviet Union, Chinese government planners classified citizens as rural or urban workers and tied employment rights and social benefits to their official classification and place of residence. Hukou holders in cities received such benefits as housing, education, health care, and pensions; those in the countryside got to live on and use the land belonging to their collectives. The system effectively restricted worker movement, as it was nearly impossible for farmers to obtain urban permits, and without these they wouldn't have a place to stay or food to eat in the city, much less any of the other benefits that came with official city residence.

The success of Reform and Opening Up changed the dynamic. The business boom created cash-paying jobs that made it possible to survive in cities without an urban hukou. Officials, eager to promote growth, turned a blind eye to the farmers who poured in. Conditions were often miserable: migrants labored in stultifying or dangerous jobs and lived in packed unisex dorms in the burgeoning cities. Once a year, at Chinese New Year, they took overcrowded trains home, lugging cheap nylon bags full of gifts for the children they had left behind to be raised by their grandparents. (Today it is estimated that there are more than 60 million of these "left behind" children being raised apart from their parents.)

Even so, the opportunities were so much greater than in the countryside that farmers came in waves. Today the so-called floating population of migrant workers accounts for one-third or more of the populations of Beijing, Guangzhou, and other big cities. On its own, the pool of migrants nationally would rank among the five most populous countries in the world. This cheap and diligent labor force helped build today's China. But migrants who come to cities for a piece of this prosperity don't have a fair shot at it. They earn on average less than two-thirds of what urban hukou holders do. After they pay for their rent and food and send money back home, they've got little left to spend—or save.

In our conversation Li noted that the urbanization rate in China, officially over 50 percent, is closer to 35 percent if only those with an urban hukou are counted. In other words, in a population of some 1.35 billion people, more than 200 million migrant workers live in cities without urban residence permits. That means that nearly a third of those living in cities are excluded from enjoying the full benefits of their country's great success. This is a recipe for potential unrest.

Changing the household residency system is a crucial step that makes sense as a matter of economic wisdom and social justice. As full-fledged urban citizens, migrants would be able to build better lives for themselves and their children. China would benefit from the boost in consumption and from the free movement of labor that hukou reform would bring about. For this to happen, China will need to make it easier for migrants to obtain social services, like pensions and health care, as they move about. It will also need to take steps to reinforce the finances of its urban areas.

China would also do well to address property rights: unlike in the U.S., the state owns all the land. Since the late 1990s, city dwellers have been permitted to own their apartments (the land beneath buildings is leased from the state), but farmers are allowed only so-called land-use rights to work and live on land that is owned by local agricultural collectives and held in the state's name. Many city residents have made a killing as property values soared in recent years. Not so farmers, who can't sell or mortgage their land rights. Financially strapped cities, which can't afford to pay pension and health care benefits to armies of migrants, would be more welcoming if the farmers could turn the land they live on into capital to provide them with financial security.

The Chinese leadership is trying to make it easier for rural residents to apply for urban permits and to sell or lease out their land rights. In July 2014 the government put out guidelines for reform that would begin to ease the hukou rules. The aim is to completely lift restrictions in townships and small cities, relax them in medium-size cities, and improve the prospects for large cities, while strictly controlling the population of the biggest cities. As much as it aims to encourage continued urbanization, the government does not want migrants flocking to megalopolises like Beijing and Shanghai. The catch, of course, is that these are often the very places, with their seemingly boundless opportunities, that migrants most prefer.

Though the proposed changes are cautious in nature, the need to reform is clear. If China doesn't integrate its migrants into the urban economy, it risks creating a permanent, and restive, urban underclass living in the kind of baleful slums that plague cities elsewhere in the developing world and that China has mercifully avoided so far. That will not only be a human tragedy and a severe drag on growth, but it will also be a ticking time bomb for the government.

"The difference in standard of living between urban residents with registration permits and those without is very large," Li told me. "This is a very unstable situation."

CHAPTER SIXTEEN

Skylines and Shorelines

I got a firsthand look at one of the front lines of China's changing cities when I flew to Chongqing in December 2011 as part of our inaugural urbanization conference. I had no idea at the time just how lively things in that hilly city in southwest China would soon become.

Located on the Yangtze River at the upper end of the Three Gorges Reservoir, Chongqing is so big, and its position as the gateway to the country's vast poor hinterland so strategic, that it is one of only four municipalities that report, like provinces, directly to the central government. (The other three are Beijing, Shanghai, and Tianjin.) More than 33 million people are spread over Chongqing's nearly 32,000 square miles of farms, forests, villages, and larger urban areas: think of South Carolina but with seven times the population. Chongqing city proper accounts for some 7 million people; altogether more than 40 percent of the municipality's population lives in towns and cities. Officials aim to increase the urbanization rate to 70 percent by 2020.

When I visited, the city was in the midst of a noisy Maoist revival led by my old sparring partner from the SED, Bo Xilai. He had been moved from the Commerce Ministry to become Party boss of Chongqing in 2007, a promotion that secured him a seat on the 25-member Politburo. A charismatic populist in a country where other leaders were reluctant to stand out, he took his case directly to the people, gaining a huge following in his city and throughout China in what amounted to an unprecedented public campaign to be selected for the Communist Party's Standing Committee. He famously held mass meetings in which crowds of hundreds of thousands sang "red songs" from the days of the Cultural Revolution—a spectacle that attracted curious foreign dignitaries as well as some of China's top leaders. Bo aggressively pursued Mao-like leftist policies in a bid to win grassroots support and cultivate a national image as an unconventional leader of the people.

And Chongqing was prospering, racking up impressive growth numbers. Local GDP jumped by 16.5 percent in 2011, the highest of any province in China, and 7 percentage points above the national average. Fostering such rapid growth was the time-honored path to advancement for officials in the Communist Party, and Bo appeared determined to leverage the "Chongqing model" to the pinnacle of power. Combining a popular appeal with ruthless politics, he led a brutal, high-profile crackdown on so-called gangsters that critics charged was meant more to eliminate potential rivals than to impose law and order. Purging private entrepreneurs while expanding the power of the state sector, Bo had emerged, in the view of some admiring Chinese scholars, as the strongest leader to champion an autocratic model of state capitalism in the nation.

To be sure, Chongqing's resurgence had begun before Bo began singing songs and knocking heads. Its mayor, Huang Qifan, a protégé of former premier Zhu Rongji, had earlier paired central government money with innovative policies to achieve growth rates well above the national average. Huang had arrived as vice mayor in 2001, shortly after the city began to receive billions of dollars to serve as the "dragon head" of the central government's Go West investment plan that was meant to help the poor interior catch up with the booming coastal regions. He cleaned up state-owned enterprises and invested in modern infrastructure to attract business and industry from China and abroad. Chongqing built dozens of new bridges, more than tripled the length of its streets and roads, began operating the first section of a planned 18-line subway system, and constructed a trunk rail line to connect the city to Europe.

I caught up with Mayor Huang for lunch before the Chongqing leg of our urbanization conference got under way at the InterContinental Hotel. Inside, a gaily decorated Christmas tree worthy of a place in Rockefeller Center soared in the high, arching lobby.

"Chongqing is what Shenzhen was in the 1980s, and what Pudong was in the 1990s," Huang declared, citing two urban areas that had been at the cutting edge of innovative growth.

Amiable and incisive, he was eager to detail the city's successes, as well as to discuss broader economic issues. Christmas carols played in a loop on the sound system as we shared a traditional Italian meal in a restaurant in the hotel's basement. I chuckled to myself thinking I had come to Chongqing wondering if I would get to hear any of Mao's favorite revolutionary anthems, only to listen to Bing Crosby crooning "White Christmas."

Huang had been born in Zhejiang Province in 1952 and began working in 1968 at a Shanghai coking plant. He joined the Communist Party in March 1976 and rose through the ranks in Shanghai. He eventually played a big role in turning Zhu Rongji's vision of a new financial center for China into the stunning Pudong New District, where he served as deputy director in the mid-1990s. He subsequently became deputy secretary general of the Shanghai municipal government and was responsible for, among other things, attracting investment to the city.

The mayor had taken a page from Guangdong's playbook and set up industrial zones to attract multinationals. Nearly half of the Fortune Global 500 companies had set up manufacturing operation there, and exports were doubling every year. Roughly half of Chongqing's output was industrial; a third came from finance, trade, and logistics. In 2011 Chongqing produced more than a tenth of the world's laptops. Two years later it was up to a quarter of global production, with Hewlett-Packard, Lenovo, Acer, Asustek, Sony, and Toshiba all ensconced there.

Huang expressed concern that family incomes in China were declining as a share of GDP, a development that would hinder the increase in consumption. He saw income inequality and the inequitable distribution of wealth as threats to sustainable development.

"We are working on narrowing the gap between the rich and the poor," he said.

As one way of doing that, Chongqing was experimenting with programs to bring farmers into the city. The key was for new arrivals to pay their way and not become burdens on the government. Other cities had imposed conditions, such as requiring applicants for urban residency permits to immediately give up their rural hukou, which kept down the number of permits granted. Chongqing allowed farmers who obtained urban residency permits to retain rights to their land for three years. Chongqing also made it easier for farmers to lease out and trade their rights to farms, forest lands, and residential plots; they could even use these rights to obtain mortgages to buy homes in the city.

Altogether, Chongqing planned to convert 10 million farmers from rural to urban permits by 2020. By the end of 2011, when we spoke, some 3 million were said to have taken up the offer. Among other big cities experimenting with such reforms, only Chengdu, the capital city of neighboring Sichuan Province, had seen similar results: 2 million migrants had switched their residences. Cities like Shanghai and Guangzhou, with much stricter criteria, have seen far fewer conversions.

Newcomers to the city need jobs and homes, so Chongqing had cleared away miles of shantytowns and was in the process of building 500,000 units of subsidized housing—enough for 2 million people. The city had thrown its weight behind a program to back microbusinesses with a combination of tax breaks, direct subsidies, and bank loans. In 2011, the city seeded 50,000 small enterprises with the aim of creating 400,000 new jobs. The plan was to generate 1.6 million jobs over the next five years.

Like his mentor, Zhu Rongji, Huang is a pragmatic man, not an ideologue. He may be directing billions in subsidies toward housing and business start-ups, but he's got an eye for other approaches as well. During lunch, we got to talking about the U.S. economy and its issues, from slow growth and unemployment levels to the fiscal cliff that was then so much in the news. He surprised me with his solution.

"My preferred model," he said, "is the supply-side approach that Reagan used in the 1980s—with tax cuts."

That afternoon I drove off to another part of town to see Bo Xilai. He greeted me warmly in a graceful building he identified as having once been used by the Nationalist government of Chiang Kai-shek, which relocated to Chongqing during the war against Japan. The marble hallways were lined with historic black-and-white photos, including some of Deng Xiaoping, who after the revolution had been named the first secretary of the Southwest Bureau, which included Chongqing. There was also a famous picture of the meeting in Chongqing between Mao Zedong and Chiang Kai-shek after the defeat of the Japanese.

Bo eschewed the traditional Chinese ceremonial horseshoe, and we faced each other across a wide polished wood table, in a grand meeting room, on whose high walls I could make out bas-relief scenes of local attractions. He was well briefed, brimming with pertinent facts, and as feisty and competitive as ever. When L.A. mayor Antonio Villaraigosa, who was in our delegation, noted that his city had planted 100,000 trees in the past three years, Bo was quick to point out that Chongqing had planted 1.5 billion in that time.

"In the past Chongqing was a cement forest," he declared. "Now it's a real forest."

He recited many of the same statistics I'd heard from Mayor Huang and reminded me of the close ties the U.S. had had in the past with Chongqing, when it was Chiang Kai-shek's wartime capital, the U.S. had its embassy there, and brave American pilots flew the Hump route over the Himalayas to supply China with food and war matériel.

But as always, Bo was talking his own book. "It is my wish," he said, "that you encourage American companies to come to Chongqing."

I explained that I was no longer an investment banker and that the Paulson Institute was, in any case, a not-for-profit organization.

But he kept returning to this theme. "You can use your influence to get companies to come to Chongqing," he insisted. "Together we can do matchmaking activities!"

When I peppered him with questions about the government's current five-year plan and the push toward more domestic-led growth—would it really happen?—he deflected me with more statistics to illustrate the virtues of the city.

"My questions are for China," I said. "Not just Chongqing."

"If you want to know about China, you will have to ask Premier Wen Jiabao," he said. "I'm narrow-minded. I just focus on Chongqing."

Of course, his focus was on something more distant and enticing than his city—the walled compound of Zhongnanhai and the ultimate seat of power. It was a vintage Bo performance: he was the master of all he surveyed, in complete control, casually interrupting his translator to improve a turn of phrase. I can recall nothing now in his manner that hinted at the trouble that was soon to come. Quite the opposite. He made a point of extolling the "magical strengths" that had made Chongqing a "breeding ground for future leaders."

In retrospect, I see there were omens. Originally, Huang Qifan had been scheduled to attend our urbanization conference in Beijing, but just before it was to start, he had suddenly withdrawn. We'd subsequently heard that a team from the Central Commission for Discipline Inspection, the Communist Party arm that investigates corruption and wrongdoing, had been dispatched to Chongqing to look into some irregularities. A little while before our meeting with Bo, the *Wall Street Journal* had run a story about the lifestyles of China's princelings, the sons and daughters of high-ranking Party members. The piece had focused on Bo's son, Bo Guagua, who had attended Harrow, the elite boarding school in the U.K., then went on to Oxford and Harvard, drove a flashy red Ferrari, and had allegedly escorted the daughter of former U.S. ambassador Jon Huntsman to a popular Beijing bar.

The article had caught my attention, not so much for the sensational reporting—I assumed the *Journal* had solid substantiation—but for the timing. I thought it a prelude to jockeying for the Standing Committee. I'd seen enough stories in my day to wonder if someone weren't trying to damage Bo. But I also assumed Bo was powerful enough to prevail over whoever might be out to get him.

I sure got that wrong. Two months after our meeting, Bo's charmed life began to unravel. The first sign came in early February 2012, when the Chongqing police chief, who had been Bo's trusted protégé, was abruptly removed from his post. A few days later he fled 200 miles to seek refuge in the U.S. Consulate in Chengdu. Huang Qifan led a large convoy of police vehicles to Chengdu to try to retrieve the police chief, who agreed to exit the consulate, where he'd sought asylum and holed up overnight. He was whisked away, but not to Chongqing. Instead, he turned himself over to the Beijing authorities and to what was described as "vacation-style medical treatment." The subsequent investigation into the incident would bring Bo down.

Bo was deposed as Chongqing Party chief in March 2012. The following month his wife, Gu Kailai, was placed under investigation for the death in November 2011 of a British businessman who had worked closely with Bo's family. A steady drip of lurid details emerged through news accounts and leaks in the state-run and foreign media—and were quickly disseminated on China's hyperactive social media. It emerged that the police chief, formerly Bo's chief enforcer, had fallen out with his boss after telling him of a corruption investigation into Bo's family. The *New York Times* would report that Bo had set up a wiretapping operation that had listened into a call involving President Hu Jintao. This was soap opera elevated to the level of national security, complete with money, sex, murder, police chases, and political intrigue, a sensational tale right out of *House of Cards*, an American TV show that had lately become a favorite of many Chinese leaders.

For a time it was thought that Mayor Huang might be tarnished by his association with Bo. But in the fall of 2012 Huang was promoted to the Central Committee of the Communist Party. He remains mayor, pushing forward Chongqing's experiments. Bo, on the other hand, was systematically stripped of authority, expelled from the Communist Party, put on trial, and is now serving a life sentence for corruption and abuse of power. His wife was convicted of intentional homicide and given a suspended death sentence.

Integrating hundreds of millions of migrants into cities like Chongqing won't be cheap: the government pegs the cost at close to $6.8 trillion over the next 20 years. The big question is, who will foot the bill for the new roads, bridges, rail lines, sewers, housing, and electricity that will be needed, as well as for the social services programs like pensions, schools, insurance, health care, and prescription drug schemes that must be expanded? The cities and provinces are saddled with debt and lack the ability to increase their revenues without major reforms. The central government has little inclination to take on such a gigantic burden, although it has pledged to increase outlays to local governments.

In theory, urbanization helps pay its own way by boosting economic growth, as new urban workers produce more, consume more, and pay more taxes. But this will take time to develop, and China's tax collection system is porous. Meanwhile, China's local authorities will almost certainly continue to suffer from strained finances, partly as a result of nationwide reforms undertaken by Zhu Rongji in the mid-1990s. To shore up weak central government fiscal policies, he centralized tax collection and introduced a new value-added tax that today accounts for perhaps 60 percent of fiscal revenues. A share of the tax receipts was sent back to the provinces, but the sums fell increasingly short as local governments were required to take on more responsibilities for services that were previously provided by state-owned companies under China's old "work unit," or *danwei*, system.

Even today local officials have few ways to raise revenues to cover these unfunded policy mandates. They do not have budget accountability, they lack the independent power to impose new taxes, and they were not, until 2014, allowed to issue municipal bonds. As a result, they have resorted frequently to seizing and selling land, a practice that on average funds one-third—and in some cases nearly one-half—of local budgets. More recently, they have turned to opaque short-term borrowing arrangements in a shadow banking market that is hard for regulators to monitor.

These approaches are fundamentally unsound. Seizing farmers' land fuels widespread protests, threatens the nation's supply of productive farmland, and encourages urban sprawl. Cities become less livable, less efficient, and, ultimately, less sustainable. Not infrequently, too, the process lines the pockets of corrupt officials.

Begun decades ago as a practical adaptation to revenue constraints, so-called local government financing vehicles (LGFVs) are also risky. Cities have used them to take on much bigger debt loads in recent years. According to China's National Audit Office, local governments had racked up about $2.9 trillion in borrowings and guarantees by the end of June 2013, a nearly 70 percent jump from 2010, adding to a national debt load that has worried many financial experts.

Chongqing offers a prime example of aggressive local government borrowing and spending. Its growth in recent years has been exceptional, helped by generous infusions of cash from the central government and far-sighted policy choices. But Chongqing has also employed aggressive land sales tactics and built up massive debts through off-balance-sheet vehicles. Today Chongqing is among the most heavily indebted municipalities in

China. According to government audits, Chongqing was among the top three of China's provinces and regions when ranked both by total debt as a portion of local gross domestic product and as a portion of fiscal income. Chongqing's borrowing accelerated after Bo Xilai arrived in 2007 and ramped up spending in his doomed effort to make a showing that would elevate him to the highest reaches of power in the country. The *Wall Street Journal* calculated that Chongqing's use of LGFVs more than doubled, to some $55 billion, between 2007 and 2011.

The problem with China's borrowing isn't just the sheer amount, but the opaque nature of both the debt and how the proceeds have been spent. Poor decisions and bad management have led to overbuilding, property bubbles, and an impending environmental disaster. So the leadership is taking steps to give local governments the necessary fiscal tools to better manage their finances. In early 2014 Beijing authorized a pilot program that would allow ten local governments to sell bonds directly to the public, with the cities and provinces taking direct responsibility for repayment. Guangdong, so often a pioneer in reform, led the way in June 2014, selling more than $2 billion of bonds. That August lawmakers passed amendments to the budget law to allow local governments to sell bonds to finance public projects (bonds to finance day-to-day expenditures will still be banned).

These are important developments, but in my judgment China won't have a healthy municipal bond market until local officials gain additional sources of reliable revenues and are able to provide a clear accounting to investors and to Beijing. China should ultimately give provinces and cities independent power to tax, and it should introduce property taxes in more cities and provinces and experiment with taxing commercial real estate on an annual basis instead of the current practice of imposing levies on transactions. Once Beijing ensures they can handle the responsibility, local leaders should be given full control of their budgets and begin producing and publishing transparent financial statements, the sine qua non for prudent fiscal management and a sound bond market.

These changes require national fiscal and tax reform and an overhaul of the system of sharing revenues between Beijing and the cities and provinces. But they would provide localities with more consistent revenues, while reassuring Beijing that it will not have to be the permanent guarantor for bad decisions made at the local level. Taken together, these measures would decrease the reliance on dangerous off-balance-sheet financing vehicles, reduce land seizures, curb urban sprawl, and make it easier for cities to become more energy efficient and people friendly. In February 2014 Finance Minister Lou Jiwei told me that tax reforms were proving to be more complicated, and would thus take longer, than budget reforms. But he and his colleagues are focused on both sets of reforms. Lou said, for example, that expansion of the property tax was a big part of the government's thinking.

The good news is that these changes are under way: in June 2014 the Politburo said it aimed to have a new round of fiscal and tax reforms done by 2016 and to establish a modern fiscal system by 2020. The liberalization of municipal bond underwriting in August 2014 was part of a series of amendments to the budget law that included requiring local governments to do more long-range planning and to use accrual accounting.

That China's cities have become so unworkable is deeply ironic, because the Chinese were ahead of their time in designing livable urban areas. Advocates of sustainable development today emphasize the importance of building mixed-use neighborhoods that bring together in close proximity housing, work, education, recreation, and shopping. They press for zoning that promotes dense grids of streets and small blocks, rather than huge boulevards and superblocks, and that creates green spaces to improve air quality and give residents spots to gather. The architects of ancient Beijing might as well have inked the site plans of these so-called New Urbanists: the blocks of courtyard houses that they laid out along hutong alleys did not just house people, they provided places to shop and go to school; they were near where people worked; and their courtyards served as oases in which families could relax.

All of this began to change in 1949 when China's new Communist rulers cleared space in the old city for the factories and bureaucrats of a centrally planned economy, demolishing ancient city walls and uprooting hutongs. Their embrace of monumentality culminated in a series of big projects completed for the tenth anniversary of the People's Republic in 1959 that included the immense, Soviet-style Great Hall of the People set next to a vastly expanded Tiananmen Square. Chang'an Avenue, the city's traditional east-west axis, was stretched almost beyond recognition: from 50 feet in width and 2.5 miles in length in 1949, it is today 260 feet wide, or nearly the length of a U.S. football field, and runs 24 miles end to end.

When I first arrived in Beijing in the early 1990s, there were still many vestiges of the Mao era. Citizens rode bikes or took buses. Many of the cars on the avenues were army jeeps, police cars, or the black sedans with the white license plates of officials. "It's gray. It's dirty. It's crowded," Wendy wrote in her journal after a visit to the capital in 1994. "But it is vibrant. The streets are alive with workers, vendors, students, shoppers, and, above all, cyclists." While I worked, Wendy took off by herself to explore the hutongs. She wandered, fascinated, through narrow passages, filled with playing children and suffused with the smells of cooking, that separated the houses.

It's easy to wax nostalgic, but in truth the old neighborhoods had become badly neglected. Many courtyard houses lacked plumbing, modern kitchens, and sanitation, and they were bitterly cold in the winter. When migrants poured in, the living spaces became overrun and unsafe.

Beijing clearly had to make changes, but it made choices that destroyed much of the city's rich heritage and rent its social fabric. Blending the architectural megalomania of Soviet Russia with soul-deadening modernism, Chinese planners threw up massive office and residential towers isolated from one another in superblocks a quarter of a mile long and separated by broad arterial boulevards, which were linked by ever more distant ring roads. Beijing is now working on the seventh ring road—a nearly 600-mile-long extravaganza that will wend its way through neighboring Hebei Province to encompass an area the size of Indiana. A belated start on adequate mass transit left residents stuck with crowded and intolerably long commutes. We made similar choices in the United States, particularly in the development of our Sunbelt after World War II, but we had more time and more space to deal with the consequences—and far fewer people.

All over China, cities followed Beijing's lead. Seemingly every local official wanted a replica of Tiananmen Square and a municipal government headquarters that looked like the Great Hall of the People. Mayors and governors get promoted for pleasing their Party bosses and spurring growth, their cities make money by selling land rights to developers, and developers want to complete their work quickly, all of which leads to cookie-cutter projects thrown up hastily and often shoddily and cut off from commercial activity by wide roads.

In effect, China's planners chose to build a façade of false efficiencies and were left with sprawl, congestion, and pollution. The country is trying to undo the damage. It has spent tens of billions of dollars to clean the air—with little effect. Before the 2008 Olympics, Beijing shut or moved to Hebei more than 200 smoke-belching factories, including one of the country's biggest steel producers, which was located just 10 miles from Tiananmen on Chang'an Avenue. Officials installed scrubbers in factories within city limits and banned the burning of coal for heating. Beijing simultaneously embarked on a massive build-out of modern mass transit systems. Today, all over the country, the construction of subways, monorails, bus rapid transit lines, and high-speed rail lines is in full swing.

Yet for all these efforts, it's hard to escape the conclusion that, for now at least, China is losing a race against time and its own growing prosperity. As bad as the pollution was the week we held our first conference on urban sustainability, it has only gotten worse. In January 2013 the U.S. Embassy's rooftop instruments measured PM 2.5 levels of 886, far more toxic than the PM 2.5 levels of 416 we had contended with that week in 2011. In the wake of that "airpocalypse," as pundits called it, the government subsequently pledged to spend $280 billion to combat smog in Beijing over five years.

One big reason for the pollution is that China's rising middle class is putting cars on the road at a pace the world has never before seen. Beijing had a million cars in the late 1990s, 3 million cars during the 2008 Olympics, and 5 million by February 2012. The city instituted a monthly lottery in January 2011 to limit the number of licenses granted; by 2014 it was allowing only 150,000 new licenses per year. But the roads remain impossibly clogged with the world's worst traffic jams: one infamous snarl near Beijing in 2010 backed cars up for 62 miles and lasted 11 days. More highways aren't the solution—they just invite more cars.

Other cities are following Beijing's lead in restricting ownership—commercially minded Shanghai has resorted to auctioning off new licenses—but it's a tough battle. Autos are a huge business for China, employing millions. China overtook the U.S. as the world's biggest market for new auto sales in 2009, and it was selling 15.5 million passenger cars (and a further 4 million buses and trucks) by 2012. That's more cars than the country owned in 1999. China now has about one car for every 11 citizens, and some experts expect that rate to triple in the next few years. Imagine what China's traffic jams and air quality will be like then!

Finding a better way forward isn't easy even for cities whose leaders are deeply committed to sustainable growth. I saw this in Changsha, the bustling capital of south-central Hunan Province, where Zhang Jianfei, who was named mayor in 2008, made great efforts to clean up his city and save energy. Zhang, a rising star in the Chinese system, holds a Ph.D. in civil engineering from the University of California, Berkeley. Before this appointment, he worked in the traffic and transport division of the World Bank's China desk and in China's Ministry of Transportation. In 2013 he was promoted to vice governor of Hunan.

Changsha is tackling big and small projects with zeal. It has more than doubled its raw sewage treatment rate to 97 percent. It became the first municipal government in China to set up a waste collection system in each of the hundreds of villages and towns under its jurisdiction; households pay a fee for waste collection but get a discount if they recycle. "I'm an environmentalist from Beijing," Zhang said. "When I wash vegetables, the first round of water, we dump. But the second round, the third round, we save it for flushing. Why not?"

A Communist stronghold in the early years of the Party, Changsha was the city where Hunan native Mao Zedong first plotted revolution. Today it's a bustling transportation hub and inland port, with vibrant agricultural markets and a thriving manufacturing base. It's home to dynamic private sector companies like Zoomlion Heavy Industry Science & Technology Development Company and Sany Heavy Industry Company—two major heavy-equipment makers—and to Broad Group, the central-air-conditioning manufacturer whose flamboyant chairman, Zhang Yue, made waves when he announced his controversial and still-unrealized plan to build the world's tallest building, Sky City, in Changsha, employing modular construction techniques he's developed.

The vanguard of a province that grew on average at a stunning

14.6 percent annually for the previous decade, Changsha was a city literally in upheaval in 2013. Everywhere you looked you could see giant cranes bobbing and dipping on rising rooftops, the skeletons of the buildings below wrapped in green construction nets and encased in bamboo scaffolding. There was a very good reason for this activity. From a population of 3.7 million, Changsha expected to grow to 8 million residents by 2020. It anticipated spending $134 billion over the next decade to build new housing, widen roads, install sewer and water mains, and lay in gas and electric lines. It opened its first subway lines, with 19 stations, in 2014.

But despite Mayor Zhang's best intentions, there was no effective zoning or control over the types of buildings being built. City planners were tearing down old neighborhoods that, while in need of an upgrade, were far more people friendly and ecologically sound than what's replacing them.

Downtown on a cool, dim day in February 2013, the old and new neighborhoods stood out in vivid contrast. In the middle of an intersection filled with earthmoving equipment, work crews were digging a pit for one of the city's new subway lines. West of the intersection you could see a narrow street lined by four-story apartment buildings, with vendors selling fruits and meats from little shops and street carts. Some of the buildings were marked to be razed, others were in the process of being torn down or were already rubble. On the sidewalks, men sat on low stools playing cards, while packs of children meandered home from school.

On the opposite side of the intersection, stretching into the distance, a broad avenue loomed, flanked by brand-new 30-story residential towers, with no pedestrians in sight. These new buildings brought much-needed improvements. Their apartments were more suited to modern living—with bathrooms, kitchens, and separate bedrooms. But the overall approach to urban design was badly flawed.

At Mayor Zhang's invitation, a team from the Paulson Institute led by Deborah Lehr—working with Peter Calthorpe of the Energy Foundation, a group of energy and urban planning experts—spent time in Changsha advising city leaders. They introduced the officials to a rapid assessment tool developed by McKinsey for the Inter-American Development Bank and adapted by us for China. The tool provides a snapshot of how well a city is performing in areas ranging from water use to carbon footprint to population density to pollution. It's meant to help a city prioritize its needs. The PI team also sought to demonstrate how even minor modifications could make a huge difference in sustainability, whether that meant building more small cross streets to supplement those wide boulevards or putting more people on public transit and bikes than in cars and thus cutting air pollution and carbon emissions.

Rethinking development will be a challenge for Changsha. Like all Chinese cities, it is working from a detailed urban plan that took years to shepherd through the various agencies and departments of government. Modifying the plan would require holding up construction, but with migrants pouring in, the city can ill afford to stand still. Adjusting the official mind-set is even harder, despite city leaders who understand the importance of new approaches. Until cities—and their mayors—are truly judged on more than economic growth, it will be hard for places like Changsha to introduce the sustainable practices necessary to bring about positive change.

The Paulson Institute also did an assessment in Baoding, a municipality of some 11 million people about 100 miles southwest of Beijing in Hebei Province, that illustrates the difficult trade-offs of dealing with China's environmental problems. Baoding ranked as China's most polluted city for air quality in 2014, according to the Ministry of Environmental Protection, yet it is the leading manufacturing base for renewable energy equipment in the world. It is home to Yingli Green Energy Holding Company, the world's second-biggest solar panel maker, and scores of similar companies. Wrapped around Beijing like a horse collar, Hebei is a heavily industrialized coal-mining and iron-making center of China; it contains seven of the country's ten most polluted cities. Geography is one reason: Much of Hebei lies on the fertile North China Plain, wedged between mountains to the north and west and the Bohai Sea to the east. Frequent temperature inversions in winter trap smog for days at a time.

Beginning a decade ago Baoding aggressively pushed policies that favor makers of renewable energy equipment like wind turbines and solar panels. With backing from the central government, it became the country's industrial base for the renewable energy sector. It was selected in 2010 to be one of eight pilot cities charged with demonstrating different ways to achieve low-carbon growth while meeting stringent carbon emissions targets.

Baoding's initial push into alternative energy was a great success. From 2005 to 2008 the number of renewable energy companies more than tripled to 200, revenues shot up fivefold to $3.5 billion, and 13,500 jobs were created. The United Nations named Baoding the world's first "carbon-positive" city, noting that its products, when installed, would save more carbon over their lifetimes than Baoding itself would emit. Then the global financial crisis hit, China flooded markets with its renewable wares, causing prices to tank, and the U.S. and the European Union slapped tariffs on China's solar panel exports. Local industry reeled; many of the biggest players, including Yingli, reported quarterly losses in 2012. Before long the city's chief taxpayer was Great Wall Motors Company, China's biggest SUV producer and a local stalwart since its 1984 founding.

As it looks to triple its urban center to 3 million residents, Baoding is developing in the all-too-familiar auto-centric way of other cities in China, with superblocks of huge apartment buildings interspersed along huge boulevards. Though many buildings are equipped with solar panels or wind turbines, Baoding relies on traditional sources—coal and natural gas—for most of its power.

Getting its ongoing urbanization right is critical for Baoding, which stands to benefit from Xi Jinping's ambitious plans to knit the 130 million people of Beijing, Tianjin, and Hebei Province into one massive economic zone that will require local leaders to coordinate far better. The central government is planning to relocate a number of administrative or back-office functions to Baoding to relieve congestion in the capital and perhaps improve the economy in the outlying areas. With the proposed Beijing-Tianjin-Hebei megalopolis—or Jing-Jin-Ji, as it's popularly known, after the Chinese names of these cities—Xi Jinping sees a regional approach to solving problems as one of his legacies. As he told me simply in July 2014, "This was my own personal initiative."

Jing-Jin-Ji is meant to be a model of sustainable development. The region's rancid air shows the need for better coordination. The pollution is the nasty by-product of Beijing's cars, Hebei's coal-fired factories, and

Tianjin's chemical plants, but the three local governments have pursued competing growth policies. When Beijing's air became all but unbreathable for days on end in the winter of 2013, the central government called on Hebei and other provinces to shut down factories. Doing that, of course, hurts those areas in the pocketbook, and their officials naturally resist. Development in the region has been uneven, with Beijingers enjoying a per capita income 2.5 times that of those who live in Hebei.

When he sought our help in 2012, Baoding mayor Ma Yufeng was eager to use the Institute's assessment tool, but local bureau heads were reluctant to share information that might reflect poorly on them. The Paulson Institute had to persuade traditionally uncooperative ministries to work together. Fortunately, we have, in the China Center for International Economic Exchanges (CCIEE), headed by my friend former vice premier Zeng Peiyan, a sophisticated partner that has frequently bridged the gap between "foreigners" and "locals." Zeng played a crucial role in helping to plan and promote China's extraordinary urbanization.

Baoding would certainly benefit from innovative thinking around water. As our assessment tool confirmed, the city maintains a strong conservation effort. But it suffers from a severe water shortage, like all of arid northern China. For Baoding the shortfall is particularly harsh, because it is home to Baiyangdian, a network of 143 lakes that constitutes northern China's biggest body of freshwater and serves as the main source of water for Beijing. Baiyangdian has been steadily shrinking and becoming more polluted under the pressure of drought, development, and the demands for more water from Beijing heading into the 2008 Olympics. Water had to be diverted from the Yellow River in 2006 and 2008 to save the wetlands and with them the livelihoods of the people who live along its shores, including the local fishermen famed for using hand-reared cormorants to catch fish. Baoding stands to benefit from the completion of China's massive and controversial South-North Water Transfer Project, which will bring water from the Yangtze River Basin to Beijing and other cities of the North China Plain. The first phase of the central-line operation began delivering water to Hebei in mid-December 2014.

Baiyangdian's plight is hardly unique—for China or, for that matter, the world. From tidal mudflats on the coast to freshwater lakes and marshes,

China's vital wetlands are fast disappearing. They are being drained and paved over for urban and industrial development, silted in by deforestation, deprived of water by upstream dams, or filled in to expand agricultural acreage. Between 1994 and 2010, roughly one-third of the original intertidal area of Bohai Bay, which borders Hebei, was lost.

The rapid loss of these vital areas is one reason wetlands conservation is so important to Wendy and me. Wetlands are a crucial part of our planet's life support. They protect against storms and help control flooding. Among the most diverse and productive ecosystems on earth, coastal wetlands serve as nurseries for many marine animals, including the fish, shellfish, and crustaceans that we take for granted. The biomass in these rich habitats functions as an important carbon sink. The mixture of mud, sand, and sediments on these flats acts as a filter that purifies water and helps clean the air. As President Xi Jinping commented to me in a meeting in April 2013, "We have to build more wetlands, which will be the kidneys of planet Earth."

Wendy and I are avid birders, and there are few better places than wetlands to observe the drama and diversity of creation. Wetlands serve as crucial pit stops for migrating species to find refuge, rest, and replenishment on their epic journeys between their breeding and wintering grounds. But as these habitats are lost, so, too, are the shorebirds, whose numbers are declining at shocking rates. Many global species that were thriving not many years ago today face extinction. The threat is greater in Asia than anywhere else.

Thankfully, more and more Chinese from all walks of life are becoming concerned about the environment. Protests are increasingly common, as seen in 2014's demonstrations against plans to build a petrochemical plant in Guangdong that would manufacture paraxylene, a potentially hazardous chemical used in polyester fabrics and plastic bottles, and against the construction of a waste incinerator in the city of Hangzhou. Ordinary citizens are taking to the streets to demand protection for their health and safety.

You see the newfound concern of the Chinese in other ways. Even as bird populations have come under increasing threats, for example, the number of bird-watchers in China has grown exponentially. That's a healthy development, because birders make dedicated conservationists.

I met one of this new breed of Chinese birders at the BirdLife International Congress, which Wendy and I attended in Ottawa, Canada, in June 2013. Tina Lin was all of 12, still in grade school, charming and serious and barely able to see over the podium as she gave a talk in impeccable English on ways to connect the world's youth to nature.

Tina comes from Fuzhou, a city of 2.9 million in southeastern China whose warm and rainy climate produces some of the world's best oolong tea. She had discovered birding through a local program and had become something of a celebrity in bird-watching circles for having spotted eight endangered spoon-billed sandpipers.

"I hope we can set up more nature reserves to protect the habitat for birds," she told me when we shared a stage in Ottawa. "People can stop catching or killing birds."

Wendy and I made plans to bird with Tina and her mother when we were in China at the end of the year. We had a specific place in mind: Beidagang, a coastal wetland located in Tianjin municipality, which contains China's fourth-biggest city and is a bustling industrial center some 80 miles southeast of Beijing. Tianjin abuts Bohai Bay, the westernmost part of the Yellow Sea, and was once replete with tidal flats that teemed with marine and bird life. As these wetlands have been lost to development, bird populations have been decimated.

Beidagang itself is a tidal oasis in the midst of the heavily industrial Binhai New Area district. The wetlands border a massive oil field and are surrounded by refineries, nuclear power plants, and other monuments of heavy industry. They support more than 200 species of migratory birds, from rare oriental white storks and great pelicans to small coots and bean geese, but the reserve was under intense pressure from developers and local profiteers and, according to reports, suffered from mismanagement. We had heard that fishermen, looking to maximize their daily catch, had poisoned some white storks, which can eat five pounds of fish a day, to maximize their daily catch; that water levels were being pumped artificially high to drive away wading birds and increase the value of fishing rights; and that, in some places, the rich soil was being dredged and sold.

Wetlands preservation in China is a top priority for the Paulson Institute, and we outlined two key objectives to that end. One was to identify and map the most ecologically important wetlands so that the Chinese authorities would have the best scientific information available when they made decisions about reclaiming land for development. Our idea was to submit this blueprint to the Chinese government by the end of 2014, along with recommendations for improvements to wetlands management policy based on international best practices. Then, we hoped, the government could incorporate the suggestions into the 13th five-year plan, which will run from 2016 to 2020.

Our second goal was to work with local officials to select one or two sites to protect and manage in a way that could serve as models for other preservation efforts. We hoped to make Beidagang one of these. Our initial approaches were turned aside, but I had the good fortune to be seated next to the Tianjin mayor, Huang Xingguo, at a small dinner in Chicago at the home of businessman Tom Pritzker, a longtime friend and China hand. Huang and I hit it off, and he agreed to try to find ways to work together.

Our timing was good. Xi Jinping was pressing governors and mayors to emphasize environmental protection, not just GDP growth. Though we still encountered obstacles as lower-level Tianjin officials tried to interest us in other sites, we arranged a visit to Beidagang. On a bright, windy day in November 2013, Tina and her mom joined Wendy and me in a motorcade of at least a half-dozen cars filled with government officials. Also on board were Taiya Smith, who was now working with the Institute; Rose Niu, who had joined as our chief conservation officer; and Cynthia Zeltwanger, the Paulson Institute's newly hired executive director.

Before long we realized we were headed in the wrong direction. The officials were evidently trying to take us somewhere else. We got the procession to halt on the shoulder of a busy highway, and after a heated conversation we persuaded our hosts that the only wetland we had any interest in visiting was Beidagang—not the site they had decided to take us to. It's possible that local officials truly did not understand our desire to see the reserve, but it was just as likely they did not want us to catch a glimpse of any of the untoward activities that we'd heard were taking such a toll there.

We arrived so late that I could stay only briefly before I had to leave to join the mayor for lunch. Still, we were able to get a look at oriental white storks, and I saw how spectacular Beidagang could be. Wendy, Tina, and her mother remained behind with local guides and academics while I headed to town. At lunch I relayed my concerns about Beidagang to Mayor Huang, who pledged an immediate review of the procedures and regulations governing the refuge. When I returned home, I wrote to assure him that the Paulson Institute would work with Tianjin to help provide expertise and some funds to restore, protect, and manage the refuge in a world-class fashion. He has said he would like to adopt best conservation management practices and ultimately turn the Beidagang wetland reserve into a national ecological park. The Paulson Institute is helping Tianjin and the State Forestry Administration work toward this objective by developing a master plan for the reserve.

What does the future hold for Beidagang and other coastal wetlands in China—and around the world? We are close to a tipping point, but there's still time, if we act decisively, to preserve remaining wetland habitats. I've been impressed to see Xi Jinping's sense of urgency in tackling environmental problems, as well as the growing commitment of enlightened leaders like Tianjin mayor Huang. I've seen how the efforts of forward-thinking leaders can make a difference. In 1983 officials in Hong Kong wisely brought in the World Wildlife Fund to help secure the Mai Po wetlands along the northern shore of Hong Kong's Northwest New Territories. Today they're part of a 2,700-hectare patch, or more than 10 square miles, of protected coastal wetlands and tidal mudflats that include the Futian National Nature Reserve on the Shenzhen side of Deep Bay, which lies between the Hong Kong SAR and China. The cooperation between Hong Kong and Shenzhen has been exemplary and farsighted. It ought to be maintained—and copied—by cities throughout China and around the world.

I think often of the bright morning in April 2011 when I went with Wendy to Mai Po. We hadn't been there in a decade, and I was eager to see the shorebirds. It was the height of the spring migration, and while the tide spooled in, we watched from a concealed blind as flock after flock vectored in, changing direction sharply and frequently in perfect synchronization, before landing on the mudflats, which were crawling with bivalves, worms, and crabs.

We saw several species for the first time, including a handful of young black-faced spoonbills, a spectacular large wading bird that breeds on the west coast of Korea. (It favors the demilitarized zone between North and South Korea because of the lack of human activity there.) About 400 of these birds, one-quarter of the world's surviving population, had wintered in Mai Po that year. We also saw a flock of bar-tailed godwits, famed for making the avian world's longest uninterrupted flights—more than 8,000 miles from their summer breeding grounds in Alaska and Arctic Russia to their wintering grounds in Australia and New Zealand.

As I watched these amazing birds, it occurred to me that they and their ancestors had been making their incredible journeys with no regard to boundaries or borders or any considerations of man for countless millennia—since long before our own ancestors first walked the earth, much less built the cities that were now threatening the birds' very existence. The thought was deeply humbling, and my mind turned to those stirring words from Psalm 104: "O Lord, how manifold are thy works! In wisdom hast thou made them all: the earth is full of thy riches." Extinction is a profoundly moral issue. There is no going back from it. We forget, at times, and at our peril, that we are not the sum of all of creation.

We bear a great responsibility as the first generation to understand the environmental consequences of climate change and the destruction of our natural ecosystems. We are the first with the science and the tools to address these threats by adopting sustainable practices. I'm not one to preach, but it seems to me that with such knowledge and understanding comes an obligation to act. For my part, watching the birds that day in Mai Po reinforced my determination to make conservation a key part of what we would do in the Paulson Institute. It is already the primary focus of Bobolink, our charitable foundation, which Wendy runs.

China faces tough, paradoxical choices. Its new model of growth requires more domestic consumption, a change that will be driven in good measure by continued urbanization. But boosting consumption can bring its own risks as the demand for energy and resources grows. As Wang Qishan once put it to me: "If everyone in the world, including big countries like China, India, and Indonesia, wants to live like Americans, four earths won't be enough."

I believe that it will become increasingly obvious that climate change poses the biggest environmental and economic risk to the world. We can avoid the worst outcomes only if China acts soon to curb its alarming emissions growth. Already it accounts for over 28 percent of global carbon emissions, or more than twice the level of the U.S. China takes climate change seriously and is committed to addressing it. But it sees dealing with its air pollution problem as a higher, more immediate priority. Fortunately, many of the steps to clean the air and increase energy efficiency will also reduce carbon emissions.

In September 2014 we decided to add ten new members to the Paulson Institute's Beijing office to allow us to play a small role in working to solve this monumental problem for China and the world. At the request of the Chinese government and our partner CCIEE, the initial efforts of our Climate Change and Air Quality Program will be focused on tackling the air pollution mess in the Jing-Jin-Ji region.

China is trying to craft a new approach that will allow it to grow in a cleaner, more sustainable way. In the current five-year plan, which began in 2011, the government has committed to spending hundreds of billions of dollars on, among other things, reducing sulfur emissions, building water treatment plants, and investing in clean sources of energy. After experiencing some of the dirtiest air on record in the winter of 2012–2013, the government unveiled a $280 billion plan to combat severe air pollution. In March 2014 Premier Li Keqiang famously declared war on pollution.

Beijing is not just throwing money and words at the problem. As part of its broader efforts to rebalance the economy, it is shifting growth away from traditional heavy industry and fixed asset investment toward the services sector and prioritizing seven so-called strategic emerging industries: energy-efficient and environmental technologies, next-generation information technology, biotechnology, advanced equipment manufacture, new energy, new materials, and new-energy vehicles.

Ambitious goals in the current five-year plan could make China a leader in clean technology and energy efficiency. The cost of clean technologies has dropped, not least because of massive Chinese investment in areas like solar and wind turbines. Technologies to reduce certain air pollutants by more than 90 percent, such as sulfur scrubbers for coal plants, have been commercialized throughout the world. By adopting existing technologies, and commercializing emerging ones, China has the potential to accelerate through the dirty stages of development and clean up its environment faster than many other developing countries.

Technology solutions are important, but China must also fundamentally change its energy structure and move away from coal, which accounts for nearly 70 percent of its primary energy mix. This figure isn't expected to drop much in the near term because so much new power is coming onstream to meet relentlessly growing demand. Each year through 2030 China is expected to add the equivalent of the United Kingdom's total power capacity, according to Bloomberg New Energy Finance estimates. In the meantime, the country can do a lot to clean its air and curb the growth of carbon emissions. Making prices more market based would eliminate huge subsidies for carbon-based fuel, for example. And the government can promulgate and enforce regulations that increase efficiency for new and existing buildings and motor vehicles.

Meantime, nongovernmental initiatives can also help make a difference. Let me give you one example from the Paulson Institute's latest program. The U.S.-China CEO Council for Sustainable Urbanization teams U.S. and Chinese companies to advance practical urbanization solutions through joint projects, case studies, research, and advocacy. About 40 percent of all greenhouse gases globally come from buildings, and half of the buildings under construction in the world are in China. Under the CEO Council's auspices, Honeywell International and China's state grid have been testing automated demand response (ADR) technology through a smart grid pilot project for buildings in the city of Tianjin. ADR technology tracks and controls energy use in individual buildings and provides immediate feedback that allows operators to adjust and fine-tune heating, cooling, and lighting usage, leading to cost savings and energy efficiencies. The Tianjin project has seen savings of approximately 15 percent in industrial buildings and 20 percent in commercial buildings. A second pilot project is now being launched in Shanghai.

For now, China has embraced an "all of the above" energy strategy that also employs wind, solar, biomass, natural gas, and nuclear. And the country is looking to significantly boost natural gas as a bridge fuel to a cleaner future. Natural gas isn't carbon neutral, but it is much cleaner than coal. The major state oil companies are deeply involved in producing shale gas, hoping for the kind of boom that has transformed the U.S. energy landscape. Sixty percent of Sinopec's exploration budget is now earmarked for natural gas, for example, up from 40 percent five years ago.

Since 2012 the government has announced carbon-trading pilots in seven provinces and cities, aiming to create a credible cap-and-trade program. All of this is having an effect: China leads the world in investment in, and installed capacity for, renewable energy. The country appears on track to meet its 2015 goal of having nonfossil fuels account for 11.4 percent of its energy mix, and it is working to phase in cleaner fuel targets for the five-year plan cycle that starts in 2016.

The Party is beginning to add quality of life considerations to its political platform. In his first speech as president, Xi announced the concept of "Beautiful China," which emphasized not just ecological beauty but also the importance of the environment in achieving a higher standard of living. Environmental considerations have been added to official performance evaluations. President Xi has said officials will be liable for environmental problems in cities and regions they have governed even after they have moved to new positions. In July 2014 Xi's chief economic aide, Liu He, raised the stakes when he told me bluntly that governors who did not take action would be removed from office. Nonetheless, it will take great political will not to revert to a growth-at-all-costs mentality during periods when the economy slows down.

China's willingness to be a laboratory for innovation should be a source of help. A defining feature of the country's nearly four decades of economic reforms has been a willingness to embrace pilot schemes and experiment with technologies that may be too expensive for other countries. China's considerable market power allows it to drive down prices and commercialize any advances quickly. It may not yet be pioneering and inventing cutting-edge technologies, but it has proven adept at adapting existing ones to its needs and spreading them rapidly in its huge market.

China's efforts are as important to the world as they are to the Chinese. Those magnificent shorebirds, traversing the globe, remind us how small and interconnected our world is. What happens in Bohai Bay does not stay in Bohai Bay—literally. A 2014 National Academy of Sciences study found evidence that up to one-quarter of the sulfate pollution on the West Coast of the U.S. can be linked to air pollution caused by Chinese manufacturers and borne east by the winds blowing across the Pacific Ocean. From the perspective of climate change, a ton of carbon produced in China is no different from a ton produced in America.

Balancing economic development with energy security, while transitioning to a cleaner and more efficient energy system, is a monumental challenge. China's needs dwarf those of every other country and will require ingenuity and technologies suited to its conditions and unparalleled scale.

CHAPTER SEVENTEEN

BIT by BIT

That China's new leadership would be keen to press ahead with economic reform became clear to me when I caught up with Wang Qishan in early July 2012 in Beijing. It was a fraught time for the country, and I hadn't been sure he would be able to see me. Hu Jintao was stepping down as China's top leader in the fall, and it was certain that Xi Jinping would succeed him as Party general secretary and president of China and that Li Keqiang would likely be named premier and rank number two in the Party. Beyond that, much was uncertain: how many members the Standing Committee would have, who they would be, what portfolios of duties they might be assigned. Reports of unusually intense behind-the-scenes maneuvering played out against the still-unresolved fate of Bo Xilai, whose actions had precipitated the most serious political crisis to hit China in decades.

The scandal riveted the Chinese public much the way Watergate had preoccupied U.S. citizens nearly 40 years before. As Bo was systematically stripped of power, and his wife scheduled for a murder trial in August, it became clearer every day that the press was not, in its heated coverage, reporting rumors but leaks from well-placed sources. The government appeared to be preparing the public for the cashiering of a high-profile, controversial figure, whose popularity with some of the masses was matched by the loathing and distrust of many of his fellow leaders. Bo's fall laid bare in lurid detail an unseemly intersection of privilege, power, and corruption at the highest levels. Ordinary citizens and political leaders alike understood that the rot that was being exposed at the heart of the system threatened the Communist Party's legitimacy and authority.

Under the circumstances, I wouldn't have blamed Wang Qishan, who was in the running for a more powerful role, one iota for laying low. But he invited me in for a visit, and I met with him at Zhongnanhai on a rare clear and sunny afternoon. Wang Qishan was as confident and relaxed as ever, padding around the soft carpets of the Purple Light Pavilion in cloth slippers.

We were meeting informally, but Qishan had more in mind than a social call. After a few pleasantries, he asked me where I thought the U.S. stood on a Bilateral Investment Treaty (BIT). He had given the matter some thought and had decided it was time to really get behind renewed talks.

This was welcome news. I'd long been a big advocate of BITs, which are agreements that protect investments by foreign nationals in other countries. They do this through legally binding rules that guarantee investors that their investments will be treated on a par with those of locals. BITs vary from country to country but typically allow investors to pursue claims for redress through binding and neutral international arbitration rather than local courts.

The U.S. had been discussing a BIT with China off and on since the 1980s with little to show for it. BITs were politically unpopular in some quarters in the States. Job losses had hit American workers hard, a subject of concern to many, including me. A number of legislators believed—erroneously—that a BIT might lead to jobs being shipped overseas. In fact, more jobs were lost to productivity gains from technological advances than to offshoring. For their part, the Chinese objected to key elements of the U.S. approach, in particular the requirement that our investors be given broad market access. Put simply, we wanted our citizens and companies not only to have their investments protected after they were made but also to have the same rights as locals to choose what sectors to invest in and to decide how much they wanted to own and in what form.

Wang Qishan and I had agreed to restart the talks when we were counterparts at the SED, but the financial crisis put nonpressing issues like the BIT on a back burner. Then the Obama administration suspended negotiations while it revised terms of the U.S. model for BITs. Shortly after the completion of this review—which, among other things, strengthened labor and environmental protections—our two countries had announced plans to resume talks. That was barely two months before I had come to Beijing.

"I've made up my mind to give the BIT a push," Wang Qishan confided.

As I listened to Wang Qishan, I wondered about his timing. In a few months he would likely be leaving his post after nearly five years as vice premier in charge of finance and as the main economic principal for China at the Strategic and Economic Dialogue (S&ED), the Obama administration's version of the SED. The U.S. presidential election campaign was heating up, and with it, calls by some to get tougher with the Chinese.

"There's no way a deal can get done now," I said. "They're focused on the election back home."

"Hank," he responded with a smile, "I'm not negotiating timing with you. I just want you to listen."

So I did—carefully—as Wang Qishan spent the rest of the meeting examining in his methodical way the issues that separated our sides. He had concluded that the two countries' differences could be bridged. As he spoke, I realized that of course he had known as well as I did that nothing was going to happen right away. But Wang Qishan does not say or do things lightly. He was signaling what to expect when Xi Jinping took charge: China's newfound interest wasn't a pro forma gesture. Xi wanted to negotiate a BIT and use it to jump-start broader economic reforms that had languished in recent years.

Wang Qishan knew, too, that I would bring this message home with me. Several weeks later I was visiting Treasury Secretary Tim Geithner in his office—and sinking into what had once been my favorite overstuffed chair—when we got to talking about my meeting with Wang Qishan. Tim agreed that Wang certainly knew that there was no chance of anything moving on the BIT with the elections looming, but that he was, in the very best Chinese tradition, seeking to build support for a future treaty.

Through the fall, during their leadership transition, the Chinese were quiet, and I found only tepid interest on the U.S. side—the administration had more immediate economic priorities. The lull was soon over. In April 2013 I was back again in Beijing, having dinner with Wang Qishan. He had been elevated to the Standing Committee and given the crucial task of running the Party's Central Commission for Discipline Inspection. In this role he had been put in charge of Xi Jinping's widespread crackdown on corruption. He no longer had direct responsibility over the economy—that lay with Premier Li Keqiang and Vice Premier Wang Yang. But he was close to Xi and stayed on top of economic reform initiatives.

"The Paulson Institute should do some work on the BIT," Qishan recommended. "This is important to President Xi."

I received the same message from everyone I saw that week. It was such a typically Chinese phenomenon. An issue will lie dormant, or be put on simmer, for weeks, months, even years, as the Chinese study, debate, test, and build consensus around it behind the scenes. Then, suddenly, they will embrace it wholeheartedly and drive home their message with great clarity and urgency.

The surge in interest made sense in a practical way, as well. Senior Party assignments had been made in November, two months later than expected—a testament, I surmised, to the difficult internal politics following Bo Xilai's fall. Government appointments had followed in March 2013. Xi's administration was taking shape, and his people were eager to get going. Xi would have the advantage of working with a smaller, seven-person Standing Committee, whose interests were more closely aligned. The nine-member Standing Committee that Hu Jintao had presided over had had conflicting power bases and different agendas.

The Chinese had good reasons to want a BIT. Since 2008 China's big companies had become more active abroad. They were looking to buy assets and set up operations, not just export goods, and they wanted protection for their investments. The Chinese were also concerned about being left on the sidelines as a new regional free-trade agreement, the Trans-Pacific Partnership, took shape. This pact was being hammered out by many of the major countries of the Pacific Rim—the U.S., Australia, New Zealand, Canada, Mexico, Japan, Brunei, Malaysia, Vietnam, Singapore, Chile, and Peru. Under Hu, Beijing had been implacably hostile to the TPP, fearing that the partnership might be used to counter China's own rapidly growing trade in Asia.

Most of all, Xi Jinping and his leadership team were committed to reform, and like some of their predecessors, they saw the opportunity to use an international agreement to help overcome domestic resistance to change. As one senior Chinese leader told me, "When reform encounters obstacles and can't be pushed further, we need some external forces [to help]."

In the 1990s Jiang Zemin and Zhu Rongji had leveraged negotiations on World Trade Organization membership to open domestic markets wider, and they had used the prospect of stock listings on Western exchanges to break the iron rice bowl and begin to restructure the country's lumbering state-owned enterprises. The U.S.-model BIT, which promotes market-oriented policies, transparency, and adherence to the rule of law, offered reformers a valuable tool.

Wang Yang, Qishan's able successor at the S&ED, told me when we met, "We're ready to be more proactive and open in future discussions."

Neither he nor any of the Chinese tipped their hand, but it was clear China would need to offer greater market access to U.S. investors for a deal to work. Opening additional sectors and relaxing other investment restrictions would remove some protections enjoyed by China's state-owned enterprises, boosting the country's private sector and attracting foreign companies. The increased competition would make China's domestic markets more efficient and deliver better products and services to the country's consumers, helping to stoke demand. Our companies would enjoy wider opportunities in China, while at home we would attract Chinese investment. It would be a victory for both sides.

I did my best to encourage new talks, emphasizing to Obama administration officials how serious the Chinese were. I drove home this point in separate calls to Jack Lew, the new Treasury secretary, and Mike Froman, who oversaw trade and investment issues for the White House and would soon be named U.S. Trade representative. "You want the Chinese to reform. The BIT will get you that, if structured and negotiated properly," I said. "I would have loved to have had this opportunity when I was Treasury secretary."

I put my pen to work, publishing op-eds in the *Financial Times* and the *Wall Street Journal*. The Paulson Institute also released a policy paper, written by my former Bush administration colleague Dan Price, explaining the benefits of a BIT for the U.S. economy. I was pleased when in July Jack

Lew announced at the press conference following the latest S&ED that the U.S. and China had agreed to start negotiations on a BIT that would include, as he put it, "all stages of investment and all sectors."

It marked the first time China had agreed to negotiations on the principle of broad market access for the U.S. Crucially, the Chinese indicated they were willing to create a so-called negative list that would name the specific sectors where investment was banned; all other sectors would be open to investment. That was a big improvement over the prevailing policy, which required permission to invest even in sectors that were not officially proscribed.

Obviously, the U.S. would want to negotiate hard to make sure that the negative list wasn't too long—but the key was the Chinese willingness to change the principle of their approach in a fundamental way. They were making a huge concession that demonstrated the urgency of reform and their commitment to it. It was up to us not to miss the opportunity.

Why the renewed urgency for reform? There's a simple reason: for all that China has accomplished, its leaders know only too well how far they still have to go. Shortly after he took power, Xi Jinping unveiled his "Chinese Dream," a vision of national rejuvenation that calls upon the Chinese people to strive to restore their country to its rightful, historical place in the front ranks of the world's civilizations. Xi's dream isn't just a tonic for boosting morale and forging national unity at a time when many Chinese, tired of pollution, corruption, and extreme gaps in wealth, are questioning their country's direction. It also embraces an ambitious set of goals.

As Xi reminded me when we met in April 2013, shortly after he assumed the presidency, China aims to be a "moderately prosperous society" by 2020 and a fully modernized "affluent and prosperous" nation by 2049, the 100th anniversary of the founding of the People's Republic. In other words, now that China has pulled itself out of poverty and into the ranks of lower-middle-income countries, it is determined to climb to the high-income bracket and take its place alongside countries like the U.S., Germany, and the U.K.

Few countries have ever fulfilled such lofty ambitions. For perspective, in 1960 the World Bank classified 101 countries as middle income.

In the five decades since, just 13 of these countries have been able to move up to high-income status. The biggest by far was Japan. Even today those 13 countries combined have only 300 million people; in 1960 they had about 190 million, roughly one-seventh of China's current population. The countries that did not advance got caught in the "middle-income trap," a phrase economists use to describe what happens to developing countries that make it to the middle-income range only to watch as their relative cost advantages erode before they are able to compete effectively with developed countries on innovation and higher-quality services and manufacturing. The bottom falls out of their once-booming growth rates, and they can no longer climb the wealth ladder.

China stands at a crucial juncture. The country's nearly four-decades-old growth model has run its course, a victim of a sharp, cyclical downturn and structural flaws laid bare by the 2008 global financial crisis. China's dependence on exports exposed it unduly to global economic fluctuations. It was hit hard by weak growth and slack demand in the key markets of the U.S., Europe, and Japan. Prosperity has led to rising wages and production costs, as well as a stronger currency, all of which have dented competitiveness. Meantime, the other driver of Chinese growth, investment spending, has also begun to show its limitations. Excessive fixed-asset investments by the government and state-owned enterprises have led to poor rates of return on many projects, outright waste of resources on others, and severe excess capacity across a range of industries, from shipbuilding and steel to cement making and solar panel manufacturing.

The days of double-digit growth are gone. After peaking at 14.2 percent in 2007, China grew 7.7 percent in 2012 and 2013, but fell to 7.4 percent in 2014, the lowest level in 24 years. It missed the government's projection (7.5 percent) for the first time since the Asian financial crisis of 1998, and experts foresee continued declines. Higher-quality growth that may be slower but can be sustained over the long haul is the Xi administration's goal as it seeks to rebalance the economy. But achieving this won't be easy, because even the lower growth of the past few years rests on a shaky foundation fueled by an investment binge paid for by an ominous run-up in municipal debt.

China's leaders are wisely trying to accelerate this growth, shifting to increased domestic consumption, high-end manufacturing, and higher-value service industries. Consumption is growing faster in China than in any other major economy—albeit from a low base—but this won't happen overnight. China will need investment and will continue to depend on its export might for years to come even as it places more emphasis on domestic demand. Moreover, people aren't just going to suddenly start consuming more. It will take time, structural reforms, and more education for China to develop its service sector and create better, higher-paying jobs. Urbanization can be a driver of this kind of growth, but the key, as the Chinese know, is to free up the private sector. Although it operates at a competitive disadvantage to the favored state-sponsored sector, private enterprise accounts for 90 percent of new jobs, 65 percent of patented inventions, and 80 percent of technological innovation in China, according to a paper authored by Liu He, chief economic adviser to Xi Jinping.

"Frankly speaking, when all these farmers move to the urban areas, the SOEs alone won't be able to provide jobs for them," Li Keqiang observed in December 2012. "It's the private sector, not the public sector, that will shoulder the employment burden."

How far and how fast to change has been a source of often-pitched debate since the launch of Reform and Opening Up. China's leaders have sought to balance the benefits of a booming economy ever more integrated into the global system with their desire to remain loyal to core socialist beliefs. Good arguments can be put forward for different roles for the state depending on a country's level of economic development and the needs and preferences of the people. But I can think of no model that has ever proven consistently successful in which the government makes business decisions for individual companies. State planning and good business management just don't mix very well.

In the 1990s Premier Zhu Rongji decided to restructure the country's hapless state-owned enterprises. Though they were the backbone of the economy that they dominated, he knew that they held back long-term growth. Pervasive and deeply ingrained inefficiencies choked performance and stifled innovation, and their monopoly status in many industries stymied competition. These dinosaurs of the old statist economy were grossly mismanaged and suffered from such primitive accounting and disclosure that it was almost impossible to calculate their financial losses. But their losses were real—and massive—and threatened to bring down the giant state banks whose government-mandated loans kept the SOEs on life support.

Zhu began the painful overhaul in part by dangling the carrot of WTO entry as a way to force reluctant Party members to accept necessary and required changes. Then the iron rice bowl was broken and tens of millions of workers jettisoned as companies were closed, combined, or reorganized. Local governments shut or sold more than 100,000 small SOEs, from fertilizer plants and local steel mills to township-village enterprises that had sprung up to make light-manufactured goods like buttons and combs. Some 500 of the biggest industrial enterprises under central government control were separated from the ministries that oversaw them and reconfigured into 196 monoliths that were placed under the management of the State-owned Assets Supervision and Administration Commission, or SASAC, which was created for this purpose in 2003. (The big state-owned commercial banks were managed separately.) The number of centrally controlled SOEs was subsequently reduced through mergers and consolidation to 113 in 2014.

Zhu Rongji's reforms paid off handsomely. Many SOEs became leaner, profitable, better run, and particularly for those that listed overseas, somewhat more transparent, with better governance. Once China joined the WTO, the benefits of the hard-won reforms poured in. Productivity surged. China became a manufacturing and exporting powerhouse and in the process rapidly amassed the world's largest stockpile of foreign exchange reserves.

But after Zhu left office in 2003, the pace of change slowed. Reformers ran into increased opposition, and Zhu's program to force the SOEs to be run more commercially and to face greater competition stalled. President Hu Jintao spoke favorably of reform but signaled a shift in priorities away from breakneck growth and toward the creation of a "harmonious society" to cope with social tensions rising from such things as illegal land seizures for development and the increasingly overt corruption of officials. Resurgent leftists pointed to the glaring gap between rich and poor to argue for a return to orthodox socialism.

The SOEs themselves stood out among the forces most resistant to change. Newly profitable, they began to wield more power and influence. They used their muscle to resist new measures that would have taken away the subsidies they still enjoyed or increased the competition they faced. The SOEs had plenty of supporters in government for whom the state-owned companies were tempting honey pots as well as powerful tools for implementing policy goals. With the 2008 financial crisis, any remaining momentum for reform wilted. Local governments and SOEs were pressed to build new infrastructure throughout the country. And the big state banks reverted to old-fashioned policy lending at the behest of the government. Beijing announced a massive $586 billion stimulus in November 2008, and the following year new bank loans nearly doubled, to $1.4 trillion, to fund projects meant to fight the downturn, as export markets dried up.

Zhu Rongji and the country's leadership had never intended to get rid entirely of SOEs. They are fundamental to the Chinese conception of a socialist market economy. He also understood that given their abject condition, it would take years, and a series of stages, for them to become efficient businesses that could spark the economy and compete globally. And I believe that he wanted to level the playing field they competed on.

Nearly two decades after Zhu began his restructuring, SOEs may be better managed and much more profitable, but they remain inefficient and highly subsidized monopolies—or oligopolies—that hinder China's long-term economic development by hogging resources and squandering capital, restricting competition, and limiting the opportunities for private sector companies. There is no shortage of countries that promote national champions and protect certain favored companies and industries, but none does so to the same extent, or in quite the same way, as China. As Andrew Batson, the director of China research at GaveKal Dragonomics, notes in a 2014 paper for the Paulson Institute, China's stated goal has been to create national champions in strategic areas critical to national security, to improve global competitiveness, and to boost technological progress at home. In 2006, he writes, the government revealed a list of sectors that SOEs must dominate, including defense, electricity, oil and petrochemicals, telecommunications, coal, aviation, and shipping. Beijing also wanted to maintain a strong presence in "pillar industries" like equipment manufacturing, automaking, electronics, construction, steel, nonferrous metals, chemicals, surveying, and scientific research.

Even after shutting more than 100,000 SOEs, perhaps another 100,000 or more remain. No one seems to know the exact number, but they operate in areas far afield from these strategic and pillar industries. In his piece for the Institute, Batson notes that roughly half of all SOE assets are in non-strategic sectors like restaurants, retailing, and low-end manufacturing. In recent years, they have branched out even more. Many SOEs have become active in the shadow banking market, lending surplus funds to borrowers who can't get loans from state banks.

While expanding, SOEs used their influence with policymakers and regulators to keep Chinese private companies from entering even those state-dominated sectors that Beijing had ostensibly opened to them. This "glass door" barrier rankled private companies and is bad practice.

"In recent years the situation has gotten worse for the private sector," the CEO of one of China's biggest private companies explained to me in 2013. "The SOEs had no boundaries. There was no sector where they would not go. On paper there are regulations that are supposed to make things fairer for the private sector, but in practice there are areas that are untouchable."

Although many SOEs have become profitable—some hugely so—their profits can be deceiving. For one thing, even poorly run companies could make money as China embarked on a windfall growth spurt after joining the WTO in 2001. More fundamentally, SOE profitability did not increase because of productivity gains or technological innovation, but thanks to continued government largesse. SOEs didn't have to pay for land, they enjoyed substantial tax breaks, and they received subsidies for inputs ranging from oil to glass to their use of utilities. They raised capital easily and cheaply because of their government ties, and they received low-cost loans from China's big state-owned banks. These benefits added up in a hurry. Unirule Institute of Economics, an influential Beijing think tank, calculated that if SOEs had to pay full freight for their land, loans, and utilities, from 2001 to 2008 their average return on equity would have been a negative 6.29 percent.

Moreover, many of the biggest SOEs continue to enjoy monopoly or oligopoly status, protected from domestic and foreign competition.

For all these advantages, SOEs have actually become less profitable since 2007. In his Paulson Institute paper, Batson writes that the return on assets for industrial SOEs, around 6.7 percent in 2007, dropped to 3.6 percent in 2009 and has since recovered to about 4.5 percent. Some of the decline can be attributed to the difficult operating environment, but not all. Non-state-owned companies posted returns of about 8 percent in 2007; these now run above 9 percent, twice the level of the SOEs, Batson shows. The dip in SOE earnings, I imagine, reflects the downside of being so tied to the state's apron strings. SOEs are routinely directed by officials at national and local levels to fund infrastructure and other projects that may be politically sensible but economically irrational. For example, CNOOC, China's offshore oil giant, was tasked with helping to construct the high-speed rail line between Beijing and Tianjin. The line, begun in 2005, was finished in 2008, in time for the Beijing Olympics. The train is a marvel of engineering and recorded the fastest-ever time for intercity travel. It's a great boon for the country but far removed from CNOOC's mission of developing offshore oil resources and unlikely to ever pay its way.

Though dominant at home, China's state-owned enterprises do not rank among the world's strongest or most highly regarded businesses. Some are listed among the biggest global companies by size, but they don't boast many top brands outside of their country, and their top executives are not well known abroad.

There's a very good reason for this. Industry and brand leaders must be competitive, market-driven companies that innovate and respond to the demands of their customers and shareholders. But China's SOEs remain under the thumb of Party and state. Their activities are tied to specific targets and guidelines laid out in the nation's five-year plans, and that leaves them little flexibility as market and competitive conditions change. The key to success in any modern business is to select a strong and commercially minded CEO who enjoys full operational autonomy and accountability as well as the ability to pick the members of a management team and to motivate them with long-term, market-based compensation schemes; help develop their management skills; and advance their careers. The most important of these functions lie outside the control of the SOEs. Their boards of directors don't choose their own companies' CEOs; the Communist Party does. And the CEOs have limited ability to promote and direct their people. That work is done by the Central Organization Department, the Party's powerful personnel arm.

The secretive yet all powerful Organization Department appoints the top management of the SOEs, acting through SASAC, which controls the boards of directors of listed companies and their holding companies. The Organization Department oversees the training, selection, career management, and even the retirements of all ranking officials in the Party—in government administration, in the SOEs, in the military, and even in the areas of arts, sports, and education. It is responsible for the appointments of all but the highest-ranking members of the Party, determining which officials should be promoted among posts in the central government bureaucracy, and in the provinces.

At times, the Party operates in seemingly arbitrary ways that defy modern notions of how businesses should be run. In 2004, for example, the Party required the chairmen of China's three leading telecom companies to swap jobs as easily as if they were playing musical chairs. Imagine for a moment the CEOs of Verizon, AT&T, and Sprint engaging in a party game like this with the U.S. secretary of Commerce calling the tune! And the Organization Department can act without notifying a company's board or stock market authorities. Consider the 2011 job switch of Fu Chengyu, the maverick oil executive then running CNOOC. One evening Fu received a phone call informing him that he was to report the next morning at Sinopec headquarters to start his first day as its new chairman (his predecessor would move to Fujian Province as acting governor). When Fu protested that he wanted to give his board the courtesy of notifying them before the public announcement, he was told that it was too late to do so. He managed to reach an accommodation that allowed him to stay as titular chair of CNOOC until he was replaced so that the board could go through the formal processes of ratifying the selection of his successor. Meantime, Fu had already started at Sinopec. He was permitted to bring only his driver with him. His personal assistant joined a few months later. After that, no one else; it wasn't in the Party's plan.

In essence, members of the Party work first and foremost for the Party: that's where their allegiances and career prospects lie. The Organization Department says it conducts a rigorous selection process as it promotes and transfers officials, and its approach does develop some well-rounded and skillful political leaders with management capabilities and a breadth of experience who compare favorably with their counterparts elsewhere in the world. But when it comes to individual companies, the Party's system of cadre selection and promotion, heavily based on political considerations and personal ties, can, with some notable exceptions, produce unfortunate results. Ill-qualified bureaucrats often end up running important state-owned companies, undermining their professional culture and commercial performance. The CEOs of the 53 biggest central state-owned companies are further compromised by the fact that they serve either as alternate members of the Central Committee of the Party or as members of the Central Commission for Discipline Inspection.

Zhu Rongji was acutely aware of the shortage of top-notch managers and championed a break from the outdated cadre selection system. He attempted to attract talent from outside the SOE sector and even from outside China. Two decades later, however, political patronage, not meritocracy, remains one of the main factors in senior appointments for SOEs. This impedes China's ability to attract and retain the best managerial talent to run the most important companies.

Many SOEs have sold shares in the past two decades. That has helped them become increasingly better run and more transparent. But the IPOs have not affected the control that the Party ultimately exerts. China structured the offerings in unique fashion, keeping 100 percent ownership of a holding company that often retained the company's least appealing assets and selling a small interest in a publicly listed subsidiary to the public. The listed companies kept the most attractive assets and were modeled after global industry leaders. They have boards with independent directors to represent the new shareholders. They adhere to international accounting standards and make full disclosure of their business dealings. In contrast, the holding companies disclose little. Some have boards with no outside directors. Many have no boards at all, only Party committees that make the ultimate decisions for all subsidiaries, including the listed companies.

This two-tier board structure reflected the pragmatism of Zhu Rongji. He knew the market would not have accepted an IPO from, say, a Petro-China with a million redundant workers on its payroll. But had the leadership chosen to fire or transition these workers to the private sector before completing its IPO, the process would have been delayed for years. So the workers were "left behind" at CNPC, the parent. This approach was possible because overseas investors were eager to buy into a booming economy. I believe that Zhu saw this approach as a first step in a reform process, not as the final structure.

China's leaders want SOEs to compete globally. But for that to happen, they will need to make big changes in the way they are set up, beginning with the selection of senior managers and the lines of control and reporting relationships at the top. Otherwise SOEs won't stand a chance against the world's leading companies, which are constantly refining and remaking themselves, thanks to corporate governance structures that allow them to be nimble.

That's what I told a gathering of CEOs and Party leaders in Shanghai in July 2012. "Excellence, efficiency, and industry leadership will only be achieved," I said, "when CEOs are chosen, evaluated, and compensated on their abilities to run commercial enterprises and their companies compete with the private sector without subsidies or special benefits."

I was speaking at the China Executive Leadership Academy Pudong (CELAP), one of five national-level Party schools operated around the country by the Communist Party, whose members are required to undergo periodic training. I had been invited to organize a seminar on global leadership there by Li Yuanchao, who was then head of the Central Organization Department, which oversees CELAP, and has since become China's vice president. China has many of the world's biggest companies—73 of the Fortune Global 500 was the statistic he cited—but relatively little in the way of a global footprint. Li asked pointedly if I would recruit top Western CEOs to explain how to build a leading enterprise and make acquisitions overseas. "We've been trying to help them figure out how to go global," he told me, "especially in America."

I agreed to lend a hand, believing that one of the most important economic developments over the next 25 years will be the emergence of Chinese companies in the global marketplace. I was keen to help them adopt better governance and business practices as they learned to operate overseas. I assembled a group of distinguished executives to make presentations and field questions for two days. They included Bob McDonald of Procter & Gamble; Daniel Vasella of Novartis International; Andrew Liveris of Dow Chemical; Lee Scott, the retired CEO of Wal-Mart; Indra Nooyi of PepsiCo; Larry Fink of BlackRock; Paul Achleitner of Deutsche Bank; and Martin Sorrell of WPP.

I arrived in Pudong to address a room packed with representatives of China's top companies. I had thought that as Treasury secretary I had some power to summon the good and the great, but that was nothing compared with the Party's ability to convene. In just three months Li had assembled 92 Chinese CEOs—including 20 from the private sector—for what he described in his "welcome comrades and friends" opening speech as a "voluntary" get-together.

Among them were Fu Chengyu of Sinopec, Zhang Ruimin of Haier Group, and Shu Yinbiao of the State Grid Corporation of China, the biggest electric utility in the world. I knew quite a few of them already, leaders like Jiang Jianqing of the Industrial and Commercial Bank of China, Xiao Gang of Bank of China, Wang Xiaochu of China Telecom, and Liang Wengen of Sany, the heavy-equipment maker. Nearly all were dressed in dark slacks and white short-sleeved shirts; all had name cards that identified them by their Party, not job, titles.

It was a microcosm of China at its best: these executives were talented and ambitious, educated and tough-minded. I was struck by their focus and energy. I've been to a good number of meetings of high-level American CEOs where half of the attendees thumbed away on their smartphones, paying no attention. But this group was tuned in, taking notes and asking tough questions. After Deutsche Bank chairman Paul Achleitner spoke, ICBC's Jiang turned to Paul's days on the supervisory board of Allianz to ask: "You bought Dresdner Bank. Why did the acquisition screw up? Was it the macro environment, or was it that an insurance company can't manage a bank?"

The CEOs were hungry for specific advice that could help them run their businesses better. During a break, several of the SOE heads approached me to say how much they agreed with me, and spoke about their difficulties reconciling the conflicting demands of their shareholders and the state.

That night at dinner Liu Deshu, chairman of Sinochem Corporation, the giant petrochemical company, observed, "There is great ambiguity. Do we report to SASAC, our public shareholders, or the 1.3 billion Chinese people? If everybody is the shareholder, no one is the shareholder."

The next day I mentioned Liu's comment to Fu Chengyu over lunch. Fu offered a pragmatic view, saying that helping the government helped his company, because ultimately the government would pour in resources to support its policies. "I tell shareholders there's no conflict between serving them and the government," he said. "Any time there's a government strategy, it means there's a tremendous market."

Fu is not a prototypical SOE chief. For one thing, he likes to stir things up. An early advocate of international expansion, Fu made a bold, headline-grabbing $18.5 billion bid in 2005 for Unocal that was withdrawn in the face of fierce political opposition in the States. Undaunted, he invested billions in U.S. oil and shale leases, and shortly after joining Sinopec launched an ultimately unsuccessful bid for China Gas Holdings, the first hostile bid by an SOE for a private company in China. An oil maverick, Fu rose through the ranks of China's oil industry, beginning at CNOOC, where he worked on offshore drilling ventures with foreign companies in the early 1980s. Fu holds a master's in petroleum engineering from the University of Southern California, where he sits on the board of trustees.

As head of an SOE, Fu has a three-part job: make money, restructure the company, and ensure social stability. The last obligation remains enormous. Sinopec is still paying hundreds of thousands of employees who don't work but were brought back onto the company payroll after the restructurings of the late 1990s. Because the central government hasn't figured out how to build and fund an adequate national safety net, SOEs are still footing the bill for their laid-off workers. Sinopec and other SOEs benefit from subsidies and preferments, but they are burdened by social obligations and political controls.

Dow Chemical's Andrew Liveris was very blunt with his advice. His company has a big business in China, including his leading research lab.

He said, "Exit businesses where you can't win. You don't need subsidies. Leave the shackles of the SOEs behind."

At the end of Liveris's presentation, Fu asked a question. "Our system is not suitable for globalization. We can't hire and keep people from abroad. We have to create value, but at the same time, we have to deal with the people we have and can't just lay them off. We cannot just jump from the current situation to the future. What are your recommendations?"

I could tell from the way he phrased his question it was intended as much for Li Yuanchao's ear as for Andrew's. I looked over to Li, who was sitting in the front row, smiling and nodding.

During a break I took a quick tour of CELAP's magnificent facility, which sits on a 102-acre campus. Its gleaming main building was designed to recall, with its red roof and glass tower, a Chinese scholar's table, traditionally made of redwood with a holder for ink brushes. The building is sleek, ultramodern, at once traditional and forward-looking—exactly the image the Party is keen to project.

It holds facilities for training cadres in, among other things, urban planning and dealing with the media. We stopped at the crisis management center, where a group of officials from Hebei Province sat before large-screen televisions, working on an exercise that simulated the aftermath of an earthquake, complete with sirens, dazed victims, and importuning reporters.

There was a media center where cadres could receive training on how to give interviews, how to make speeches, even how to dress. There was a prep room where officials participating in mock interviews could first be made up and have their hair touched up. In one room, the comfy furnishings were configured to resemble the set of a morning talk show; another room, complete with host's desk, was ready for a late-night chat.

In the press conference room, the director of media training, who was showing me around, put me through an impromptu grilling under bright lights. Without missing a beat, he transformed himself from a pleasant tour guide into a fierce interrogator, focusing on the toughest, most politically sensitive topics: "Mr. Paulson, what do you think about China's efforts to protect its territorial rights in the South China Sea?" I had to laugh— I knew there weren't many government officials in China who would be subjected to questions like that anytime soon from the Chinese press. But the Party was preparing the CEOs of its state companies to deal with the Western press as they went global.

I couldn't help but be impressed by the magnitude of the effort being made and expenses being incurred to invest in China's upcoming leaders. But I was struck by the paradox the Party faces. For all its efforts, what the Party must do, if it truly wants SOEs to evolve into global leaders, is the hardest thing yet. It has to find a way to set them free.

CHAPTER EIGHTEEN

The $10 Trillion Reboot

"Speaking about 'reform' in China is not an empty slogan but rather an enterprise," President Xi Jinping assured me during a wide-ranging talk in July 2014. "In our system of [Leninist] democratic centralism, I myself have to take responsibility for this."

We were meeting at the Great Hall of the People in the vast, gilt-edged Fujian Room, the president's preferred place to welcome foreign guests. Xi had served for more than a decade as a senior official in Fujian, eventually rising to governor, before moving to Zhejiang in 2002. The ornate room was also said to have been a favorite of Mao Zedong's.

We were discussing progress on the ambitious goals for economic reform that had been unveiled at the Third Plenary Session of the 18th Party Central Committee the preceding November. Dating back to 1978 when Deng Xiaoping launched Reform and Opening Up, the Third Plenum of new Party congresses has become known as an occasion for China's leaders to reveal their bold visions and plans. Xi had more than lived up to that tradition, laying out the most sweeping economic and institutional reform agenda since the heyday of Jiang Zemin and Zhu Rongji in the 1990s. The Party, among other things, had declared for the first time that the state should no longer take on the primary responsibility for allocating economic resources. This would be a function of the markets, which would have a "decisive role" going forward.

As Xi had told a study session of the Politburo in May: "The relationship between the government and the market is the core issue for our economic reforms."

I wouldn't fault a longtime China watcher for being skeptical—Beijing spent much of the decade before Xi took power talking a good game about reform but not getting much done. This leadership group is different, I believe. Xi Jinping and his team are not just thinkers—or talkers—but doers, pragmatists ready to use persuasion and power politics to achieve their goals. They understand the difficulty of their task and how much is at risk: changing the underlying model in an economy of China's size and ever-increasing complexity is a challenge in sequencing, execution, and implementation of almost unimaginable scope. It requires determination and the ability to demand, and incentivize, top-to-bottom cooperation in a diffuse political system that often shrugs off directives from on high. Even to a leader with the skills and fortitude of Xi Jinping, obstacles in the form of entrenched interests, ideological opposition, and bureaucratic inertia are formidable. State-owned enterprises don't want to lose their advantages, domestic businesses demand protection from international competition, and some of China's think tanks, as well as the restive left wing of the Party—emboldened by the West's stumbles since the global financial crisis—are pushing for greater socialist orthodoxy.

Xi was keen to let me know his administration was not sitting on its hands. After the Third Plenum it had undertaken more than 300 reform measures, he told me. "For each of them we have a timetable," he said. "We intend to achieve nearly all by 2017, and all of them by 2020. And 80 of them are to be completed this year alone."

Recognizing the strength of resistance and the weakness of some of the ministers and regulators responsible for implementation, Xi has created a small group in the Party to direct the design and execution of the reform process outside of normal government channels. Unlike previous general secretaries who for the most part did not take an active lead in economic policy, Xi is assuming a very public role—and putting his personal credibility on the line—by chairing the so-called Central Leading Group for Deepening Reform Comprehensively, whose members include Premier Li Keqiang and other seniormost Party and State Council leaders. Xi's chief economic strategist, Liu He, is director of the group's staff. An able and experienced reformer, Liu also heads the general office of the Central Leading Group for Financial and Economic Affairs, a post similar to that of the director of the National Economic Council at the White House.

Xi has embarked on a high-profile, far-reaching crackdown on corruption that also serves a useful purpose in weakening any resistance to reform. Garish displays by corrupt officials of ill-gotten wealth don't just alienate the citizenry and lead to disaffection and unrest, they attest to a pervasive and enervating institutional rot. That is deeply troubling to Xi because he sees the Party as the only force in China capable of carrying reform forward. His anticorruption campaign is meant to burnish Party credibility and strengthen ties with ordinary citizens. But it is also a tool to bring Party members in line behind his plans.

Xi is giving his administration until 2020 to implement some of the most fundamental changes, while looking to achieve small but significant victories to establish momentum. The government's first priority has been to cut through red tape, eliminating unnecessary approvals and delegating certain authorities from Beijing to local governments or to the markets. The economy has simply become too big and complex to be managed by blizzards of overlapping and sometimes conflicting orders issued from a maze of bureaucratic offices in Beijing. Indeed, Xi's economic changes are accompanied by an equally ambitious government modernization agenda. Unless China improves its governance and builds the institutions and the processes necessary to manage such a sprawling nation, Xi's economic reforms will falter, if not fail.

"Reform for us is a very complicated, systematic engineering process," Premier Li Keqiang told me on the eve of the Third Plenum, while we met in Zhongnanhai, the leadership compound. "We have to remove all those unreasonable and irrational shackles and constraints in Chinese society so as to unleash the creativity of the market." Among other things, he said, Beijing was asking local governments "not to charge so many irregular fees or fines, so as to create a level playing field for the market players."

In a speech he gave by teleconference to Party officials throughout the country in May 2013, the premier sounded like a Chinese version of Ronald Reagan inveighing against the growth in federal regulations. "I read an investigative report which says that to get a project started, an enterprise must go through 27 departments and more than 50 links, which will take as long as six to ten months," Li said. "Some items that require review and approval are really perplexing; for instance...verification of some fishing vessels' names."

The goal, he had said, was to create a system where "access is easy, but oversight is tight." New companies should be able to enter the market more freely, allowing the private sector to play a larger role in growth and job creation. But once these new companies were operating they would have to abide by more stringent and well-enforced standards.

"To expand employment, very little can be achieved by purely relying on the large enterprises and state-owned units," Li said in his speech. "We must vigorously develop medium-size, small, and mini enterprises and an economy with diversified ownerships."

Li told me in November that the government had pledged to reduce its vast number of administrative approvals by a third over its first five-year term and had already eliminated 300. This is the right direction to head in. The government has been an overly heavy-handed and intrusive player in the economy, but it has not been nearly as involved as it should be in other areas—such as in setting and enforcing regulations that protect public health and safety. Adjusting this balance is a critical element of revamping China's economy and further embracing markets. Even as the state plays less of a role in resource and labor allocation, it must take on greater responsibility in the funding and delivery of social services, such as medical benefits and pensions, that have traditionally been handled by SOEs. Other functions, like environmental regulations, zoning laws, and building codes, have also been neglected. They may have been overlooked in part because SOEs were hogging so much of the country's resources. In short, the Chinese state should drastically redefine its approach from the command and control system of the central planning era to focus primarily on providing public goods and services such as a social safety net, rule of law, fair competition, and environmental safeguards.

Those looking for the dismantling or privatization of the state sector may have been disappointed by the Third Plenum, which, as a matter of course, endorsed state ownership as a central pillar of the economy. Given the Party's commitment to a Chinese form of socialism and its desire to keep a whip hand on strategic sectors, its approach is not surprising. China's SOEs aren't going to disappear anytime soon, especially those on the commanding heights of the economy. The task for the government is to reduce their number, diminish their roles, expose them to competition, and eliminate the favoritism they enjoy. This will allow them to operate on a more commercial basis and create space for the private sector to flourish. It will also enable them to operate more successfully on the global stage. China's SOEs will be accepted as acquirers of foreign businesses and become market leaders outside of China only when they are seen to be truly commercial enterprises competing on a level playing field.

The Third Plenum made clear that reform would be anchored in a more market-driven allocation of resources and pricing of economic inputs. Pricing reforms for such factors as oil, natural gas, and electricity will allow the economy to function more efficiently. They will also reduce the subsidies the SOEs have long enjoyed. This marks an important shift away from the legacy of a planned economy. So, too, does the government's commitment to liberalizing interest rates, which will benefit Chinese households by giving them a higher return on their savings, reducing the effective subsidy to SOEs, and freeing up sorely needed credit for the private sector. The government has also decided to force higher dividends out of SOEs—as much as 30 percent of earnings annually by 2020. Currently, they pay a range from 0 percent (for SOEs like China Grain Reserves Corporation and China National Cotton Reserves Corporation) to 25 percent (China National Tobacco Corporation). Most will pay at least 10 percent in 2014. As a practical matter, many SOEs are not in good enough shape financially to pay dividends, but the principle is important.

The Third Plenum stressed the importance of defining areas of the economy where nonstate ownership should be encouraged, and the government says it will move to reduce the number of areas where SOEs hold monopolies. As one small step, China will move toward "mixed ownership" in certain industries like electric power generation, water supply, oil refining, and even railroads. Pursuing this policy will involve selling IPO shares in certain discrete businesses within SOEs or increasing the private sector ownership of the SOEs to apply shareholder scrutiny and pressure on them to operate more commercially. Oil giant Sinopec, for example, is selling a 30 percent stake in its gas station assets to private investors, and a number of provinces have announced that they will sell stakes in locally owned SOEs.

The reform blueprint foresees giving private sector firms more market access in finance and in education, health care, accounting, logistics, air travel, and e-commerce to promote the services sector and provide jobs for future workers. The most committed reformers would like to allow foreign firms to compete as well, but there is wider opposition to that, which is one reason it's important for the U.S. to push for a Bilateral Investment Treaty with China. In 2014, in fact, many foreign companies began to complain that they were increasingly being subjected to zealous regulatory investigations that featured hefty fines and "dawn raids" for data. It's unclear whether these were the result of active targeting or of China's implementing new antimonopoly laws in a harsh and heavy-handed manner. In either event, Western firms were finding it suddenly harder, not easier, to get business done in a China undergoing economic reform.

Actions the government can take to promote competition and stimulate private sector activity include reducing the number of centrally owned and controlled SOEs by limiting them to fewer "strategic" enterprises in fewer industries. The vast majority, if not all, of the 100,000 or so SOEs that are owned and controlled by local governments should be privatized. The most inefficient entities will need to be shut down. Others should be restructured, merged, or sold. This process should help cities and provinces pay down the mountains of debt they have accumulated.

Unlike other major world economies, China lacks a regulatory framework to encourage competition and guard against monopolies or oligopolies in the industries dominated by SOEs. In practice, regulation of Chinese SOEs has meant imposing administrative and legal barriers to limit private sector competition. That needs to change, starting with the establishment of independent regulators. SOEs should not be able to referee the game they're playing.

Shifting the control of hiring, firing, and promotion of senior executives from the Party to the boards of SOEs will help ensure they are operated commercially. The government also needs to better manage the complex ownership stakes of the SOEs. It's not uncommon for multiple agencies to own pieces of the same SOE and for SOEs to own pieces of one another. Ideally, all of these stakes should be held by a single entity, and they should be recorded for accounting purposes at market value, not book value, as under current practice. The performance of these holdings ought to be measured and transparently reported. The state should monetize these shares, maintaining control of those enterprises where state control is deemed important. As more shares are sold and dividends are collected, the proceeds could be used for social welfare needs.

The government has been taking some steps in the right direction. In mid-July 2014 the State-owned Assets Supervision and Administration Commission (SASAC) announced that half a dozen companies had been selected to participate in three pilot programs. Details were sketchy, but one pilot would advance a plan for mixed ownership in two centrally owned SOEs, China National Building Materials Group and China National Pharmaceutical Group Corporation. Both of these companies, along with two others, Xinxing Cathay International Group and China Energy Conservation and Environmental Protection Group, would also participate in a second pilot in which the boards of directors, not SASAC, would be allowed to hire senior managers and decide on criteria for evaluating performance, among other things. In a third pilot two SOEs would become investment companies and assume the responsibility for the state's ownership stakes in other SOEs. The idea would be to separate SASAC's regulatory function from its role as a shareholder.

"SOE reform is very important but very tough because of existing interest group resistance," Liu He told me during a long talk we had in his offices across the street from Zhongnanhai on my visit to China in July 2014. "Right now, reforms are not going very fast. But the speed doesn't worry me. The credibility and quality of reform measures are what worry me."

Getting the reforms, and their sequencing, right is important. Xi's administration is focusing first on tax and fiscal policy, which makes plenty of sense. Doing so will put pressure on local governments to stop taking on so much debt. It should also accelerate the reform of the SOEs, which will be forced to run more commercially to enhance performance, to pay dividends, and to sell shares to produce revenues for government funding needs. Political pressure will drive reform rather than resist it.

But all this takes time, and Liu is perhaps a little more patient than I might be in his shoes. I am concerned that the longer it takes to correct some of the fundamental flaws in China's economy, the more difficult it will be to successfully make the transition to a sustainable economic model without a hard economic landing along the way.

As important as it is to reform state-owned enterprises, the most immediate and important action China can take to speed its transition to a domestic demand–led economic model is to modernize its still-stunted financial sector. China's lack of robust, diversified capital markets limits options for companies raising funds and gives investors few good choices. Liberalizing banking and capital markets activities—and promoting full-throttled competition among domestic and foreign firms—would accelerate economic activity by channeling credit to its best uses and encouraging job-creating innovation. It would reinforce the country's efforts to strengthen its social safety net, freeing citizens to spend more of their money.

Zhu Rongji's recapitalization and restructuring plan in the late 1990s staved off a disastrous banking collapse and produced much stronger institutions with far better loan quality and stronger capital bases. Today China's four leading state-owned banks rank among the ten biggest in the world by tier-1 capital—the primary measure of financial strength—and they are hugely profitable: number-one-ranked ICBC earned about $43 billion in 2013, nearly twice the income of Wells Fargo & Company, the most profitable U.S. bank.

But the state banks continue to play far too central a role in the economy because alternatives remain underdeveloped. Equity markets are volatile and undependable sources of capital, and stocks trade more on government policy choices than on corporate fundamentals. The domestic bond market, though growing rapidly, remains undersized and inefficient. Most debt securities are issued by government entities or SOEs and are bought and held by the banks.

Altogether, China's commercial banks supply about 80 percent of corporate finance needs or more than twice the level in the U.S. They lend primarily to local government borrowers and SOEs. Because the government set lending rates until 2013, private sector loans were difficult for banks to price for risk, so few were made, leaving China's small and medium-size enterprises scrambling for funds through unofficial channels. Loan rate restrictions were coupled to a ceiling on deposit rates, which was still in place at year-end 2014. The arrangement enabled banks to lock in handsome spreads and pad their profits, and it coddled poor-performing SOEs. But it hampered the private sector and hurt ordinary savers, who had to choose among bank accounts earning less than inflation, shares in a Wild West stock market, or illiquid property in an overheated real estate market. In essence, savers subsidized banks, which passed the subsidies on to the state-run companies. This makes little sense.

Like other SOEs, the big banks can't be said to act fully as commercial enterprises, since they frequently function as agents of the Party and the government. To combat the effects of the financial crisis, they opened their lending spigots; bank assets more than tripled to $25.9 trillion in the six years leading up to the end of March 2014. The credit binge helped to stabilize the economy but led to severe overcapacity in many industries and a rash of infrastructure projects that won't repay their debts for years, if ever.

Also fueling an increase in credit is a rapidly expanding shadow banking market, which sprang up to meet the demands of investors hungry for higher yields and willing to purchase risky and complex products from less-regulated vehicles like trust companies. Trusts are nonbank financial institutions with broad-based businesses ranging from corporate lending and project financing to commercial real estate investment and wealth management for institutions and high-net-worth individuals. While regulated by the China Banking Regulatory Commission, they face fewer restrictions and enjoy more operational autonomy than deposit-taking banks. So-called wealth management products offered by trusts and other entities often promise returns significantly higher than regulated rates on bank deposits. The money is then lent—often through special-purpose financing vehicles—to a variety of borrowers, from strapped local governments to hard-pressed private sector companies. In this opaque, complex market, the trusts sometimes have ties to the big banks, which use the off-balance-sheet vehicles to dodge regulatory restrictions. Complicating the picture further, some SOEs, with easy access to state banks, turn around and relend their borrowed funds to private sector companies at higher rates.

Investors' hunger for yield has also attracted a new wave of innovative competitors. Among these are e-commerce giant Alibaba Group Holding, social networking and web portal powerhouse Tencent, and China's dominant search engine, Baidu. All have begun offering high-yielding money market funds online and finding many takers. Alipay, the third-party online payment provider that Alibaba has spun off into a separate company, led the way into the market in June 2013 and had pulled in a reported $93 billion in funds by the following May. Alibaba executive chairman and founder Jack Ma told me in April 2014 that more than 80 million investors had made deposits, often in the $300 to $400 range. The company combines these into pools of $1.5 million or more and auctions them to the banks, which are forced to pay higher yields or lose deposits.

"Regulators have been talking about reforming the banks for years, but nothing has happened. Now private sector competition will actually force reform on them!" says Ma, who sees the banks as easy targets. "They have grown fat and lazy making the easy money by taking 80 percent of the industry's profit and serving only 20 percent of the customers."

The insurgents' bold entry is an important development that has literally given the big banks a run for their money and increased pressure on the government to liberalize interest rates. It's reminiscent of the transformational wave that swept U.S. finance in the late 1970s, when money market funds and other players began selling higher-yield alternatives to the then fixed-rate offerings at banks and thrifts. That movement—a response to a macroeconomic shift as energy prices soared and inflation shot past the rate banks offered—helped speed the pace of banking deregulation, but the disintermediation of deposits shook up the banking industry. China's deposit market disruption is full of promise, but it must be handled carefully—with transparency and appropriate regulatory oversight to minimize systemic risk. Regulators need to make sure that this process doesn't move so quickly that it destabilizes the banks, and investors need to understand that the new money market funds are investment products that may carry a greater risk of loss.

Slowing economic growth and rapidly rising debt levels are rarely a happy combination, and China's borrowing spree seems certain to lead to trouble. Warning signs popped up in 2013, when interbank lending rates soared in June and December, prompting fears of an incipient cash crunch. In January 2014 a high-yielding trust product, distributed by ICBC, narrowly avoided defaulting on some $469 million of obligations. Then in March a Shanghai-based solar cell maker became the first Chinese company to default on domestically sold notes. The total amount of debt in China's economy climbed from 130 percent of GDP at the end of 2008 to 206 percent of GDP at the end of June 2014, a dangerously high level for an emerging economy. (The U.S. total debt to GDP ratio at the end of the second quarter in 2014 was roughly 102 percent.) Equally concerning: China's debt has been growing much faster than its GDP, a clear recipe for trouble.

These developments have raised the concern of international financial authorities. The IMF urged China in April 2014 to rein in credit growth, which it said posed a risk to the global economy. Two months later, at a *Wall Street Journal* forum, World Bank chief economist Kaushik Basu cautioned that China might face a financial "adjustment" similar to what the U.S. went through in 2008, because of its "bloated finances."

Frankly, it's not a question of if, but when, China's financial system, particularly the trust companies, will face a reckoning and have to contend with a wave of credit losses and debt restructurings. The commercial banks will also have to deal with a higher level of bad debts. That's the inevitable outcome of economic growth that is too dependent on debt-financed fixed investment in infrastructure, real estate, and manufacturing. The issue is how big the losses will be and whether the resulting disruption in the financial market can be kept from spilling over into the broader economy.

It is impossible to predict with any certainty the timing or the severity or even the immediate cause of a financial crisis. Credit bubbles inflate and pop in every economy. In the U.S. we have had them every eight to ten years or so. In China a likely trigger for a crisis might be a significant broad-based decline in real estate. It has been red-hot for years, and collateralizes much of the nation's rapidly increasing debt.

There are no easy answers. Faced with big losses, the central government will have to step in to protect the banks and stand behind local government debts. That is an unpleasant necessity. The key is to fix the structural flaws in the underlying economy and stave off financial system excesses from becoming so big they threaten the real economy. The Chinese government's economic reform plan is meant to do just that, but it will take time to adjust the distorted relationships that hold among the government, the SOEs, and the banks. And a flawed system of municipal finance that leaves mayors and governors dependent on land sales and opaque off-balance-sheet mechanisms to fund infrastructure won't be mended overnight. Under the strong direction of Finance Minister Lou Jiwei, Xi's government is working on a wide range of fixes, beginning with national fiscal and tax reform, but they will take years to implement.

The good news is that China has the financial capacity to deal with near-term problems—even if, as is likely, any loan losses substantially exceed those of the banking crisis of the late 1990s. China's economy is much bigger and more diverse than it was back then, when the government had to recapitalize the banking system. China has deep pockets—close to $4 trillion in foreign exchange reserves—and its banks are much more profitable and better capitalized. Nor does anyone doubt that China has the legal authorities and the political will to bail out failing financial institutions. The country's leaders know the risks they face, and their senior financial team, led by central bank chief Zhou Xiaochuan, is capable and experienced. Having dealt with the problems of the 1990s, they're likely to manage any future upheaval skillfully if they are given the leeway to do so by the top political leaders.

Nonetheless, if my career in finance has taught me anything, it is that even good regulations and regulators can't be relied on by themselves to prevent problems in the financial system. It takes market discipline that can only come through the vigilance of all participants—customers, creditors, counterparties, shareholders, and management—and their belief that they will suffer the economic consequences of a failed institution. One of the biggest problems in China's banking system is the moral hazard created by the expectation that the government will always step in to prop up a failed institution and assume its losses.

In a country like China with diffuse decision making, it is especially important to have clear lines of authority so decisions can be made expeditiously and consistently to bolster market confidence. If the government is to discourage bad behavior on the part of market participants counting on a government bailout, it is crucial to decide clearly and decisively which institutions are systemically important and need to be supported and which creditors and investors should share in the losses. The many financial institutions that aren't systemically important should not be propped up by the government. They should be allowed to fail.

The current tumult has given financial system reform some momentum. Since Xi took office a raft of measures have been announced. The question, as always in China, is how effectively these will be put into practice. In July 2013 the government began allowing banks to set their own lending rates, and in 2014 Zhou Xiaochuan said he expected deposit rate reform to come within two years. The government is readying a first-ever deposit insurance scheme that will give savers protection in the new deregulated environment; draft regulations for the insurance plan were released in late November 2014. The government is also encouraging the creation of privately owned banks. By early 2014 the government had approved the applications of five private banks in a pilot program.

China is also taking steps to reduce its reliance on banks and strengthen its capital markets. The equity market needs higher-quality issuers and better financial disclosure. Headed since 2013 by former Bank of China chairman Xiao Gang, the China Securities Regulatory Commission plans to move in this direction by changing the rules governing IPO listings to a U.S.-style registration system that will assure that the market, not the government, allocates capital. In the new approach—submitted in draft form to the State Council in late 2014—companies would file applications for public offerings that are reviewed by regulators, who check to see that all financial and disclosure requirements are met. Currently, companies undergo a review in which the CSRC itself decides whether they should be allowed to list. The change should speed up the IPO process and make the allocation of capital more efficient, remove the bias toward SOEs, and open up more sources of funds for companies. By the end of November 2014, nearly 600 companies were in various stages of the pipeline awaiting approval. The government was also preparing to allow companies to sell preferred shares.

The corporate bond market should be much deeper and more liquid—as it is in every other large, healthy economy. This will only be possible when China liberalizes bank interest rates and develops a yield curve, which will require extending the maturity on government bonds out to 30 years. China will also need stronger credit rating agencies and high-quality institutional investors to buy the bonds. A broad-based, liquid corporate bond market will reduce the credit risk concentrated in the banking system and give companies and investors a wider range of funding and investment options.

If China wants to make the renminbi a reserve currency, it will need to make good on its pledge to move toward a fully convertible currency and to open its capital account and allow China's companies, state-owned and private, to benefit from the free flow of funds across the country's borders. Toward that end, China has increased in stages the amount the currency can move in a given day, and it has experimented with programs that encourage more cross-border renminbi capital flows.

Strong, commercially minded banks and competitive capital markets go hand in hand with an open capital account and a market-determined currency. As with other SOEs, China's big banks lack truly accountable corporate boards and make too many decisions driven by government policy or under pressure from powerful Party leaders who appoint their CEOs. Beijing needs to free the banks from state control and noncommercial directives. Unless the government eases its grip, the banks will not be able to compete effectively at home or abroad; pressed to do the government's bidding, they will generate a larger number of bad loans and be more susceptible to corrupt practices.

In 2003 the government set up Central Huijin to hold its investments in state banks. Huijin subsequently moved from under the strict oversight of the central bank to the Ministry of Finance and took responsibility for the government's ownership positions in many more financial institutions, including small, nonsystemically important banks, securities firms, and life insurance companies. These have been held in a nontransparent way that hides underperformance and can mask wrongdoing. Financial performance and governance should be transparent, and systemically important banks should be subjected to more rigorous regulatory scrutiny and oversight. Huijin also takes on debt, which it uses to recapitalize banks, rather than have them issue new equity on their own. This is an imprudent practice that effectively injects double leverage into an already overleveraged system.

If China wants to have a world-class financial system, it should also allow more diversified ownership. The experiment with privately owned banks is a start. The government should also permit foreign financial institutions to compete on an equal basis with domestic institutions. It makes sense to empower the world's leading commercial banks, securities houses, and money management firms to operate freely in China, creating innovative investment products and opening up opportunities for the country's citizens to build their wealth.

In early 2014 China nearly doubled the amount all foreigners combined can own of Chinese stocks to $150 billion, and it has increased the total amount that foreign investors can take in any company to 30 percent from 20 percent (a single foreign investor is still limited to owning up to 10 percent of a China-listed company's shares). In 2012 it increased the amount foreign partners can own in joint venture securities firms from 33 percent to 49 percent. But these are small steps. It needs to remove the ownership caps on joint ventures entirely if it wants to benefit from the world-class firms operating in its markets.

In September 2013 China launched the Shanghai Free Trade Zone (FTZ), setting up an area separate from the rest of China's economy where regulators could experiment with liberalizing finance and other service sector activities like health care and hospitality. Inside this walled-off zone, foreign investors would in theory face fewer restrictions on investing in Chinese securities, and domestic firms would have more options when investing and borrowing from overseas. It is still early days, but it has been encouraging to see that China has begun by deciding on a negative-list approach for foreign investment in the zone. The key question will be how policies affecting the zone link up to policies affecting the broader national economy. If Chinese leaders follow through on their commitment, the Shanghai FTZ pilot will succeed and be expanded to other regions. As former vice premier Zeng Peiyan told me on a visit to Chicago in October 2013, "the significance is not in the zone itself but in the signal of reform."

By the time Deng's market-oriented reforms began to breathe life into a moribund economy nearly four decades ago, the private sector had been all but eradicated. Today it's commonly thought to account for perhaps 60 percent of China's $10 trillion GDP. That's enough to rank, on its own, as the second-biggest economy in the world, trailing only the U.S.

Even more startling than the numbers themselves is that they came about despite the lingering constraints of a statist economy that restricted where China's fledgling entrepreneurs could operate, limited their access to credit and capital, and stacked the competition against them. Through hard work, ingenuity, and opportunism, these enterprising men and women literally helped build a new country from the ground up, creating great fortunes for themselves, jobs for China's workers, and wealth for the country. They are, in essence, the ultimate engines of reform.

China now has more billionaires than any country save the U.S.—152 in all, according to *Forbes*'s 2014 list, up from 122 in 2013 and 95 in 2012. They run the gamut from real estate developers to technology pioneers. Almost by definition all are self-made—there was no wealth to inherit in 1978—and they embody the qualities of luck and pluck extolled in America by author Horatio Alger, Jr., during the Gilded Age at the end of the 19th century. Like the U.S. back then, China could do a much better job of sharing these newly created riches. But imagine where the country might be today had its entrepreneurs not had to contend with all of the obstacles thrown in their way.

I've had the good fortune to know many of these extraordinary individuals. I have advised some and partnered with others (especially on conservation work). I've had the pleasure of watching a few who worked with me at Goldman Sachs do quite well on their own. Indeed, my first trip to China for Goldman Sachs was organized by an exceptional young Beijing native who had grown up dirt-poor and labored in a Hong Kong sweatshop before finding her way to the U.K. and earning a master's in development economics from Cambridge University. Today Zhang Xin, her husband, Pan Shiyi, and their company, Soho China, are household names in China and rank among the country's biggest and most ambitious property developers.

"Our differentiating advantage has been our ability to bring best practices to the industry and access to the capital markets and the best architects worldwide," she told me. Increasingly, her name is becoming well known outside of China. In New York recently, she and her husband teamed with another private investor to buy 40 percent of the landmark GM Building—as a personal investment.

Entrepreneurialism is much the same the world over: identify an opportunity, design a solution, and find a way to market it. That's much easier said than done, of course, because of all of the risks and obstacles involved. Zhang and Pan spotted a need for better-quality housing and office space as the pace of urbanization picked up and city dwellers got wealthier. And they took the risks to meet those needs.

"Look where the problems are," Alibaba founder Jack Ma told me not long ago. "That's where you will find opportunities for innovation."

A onetime English teacher, Jack has improbably become China's best-known Internet pioneer. In the late 1990s he took note of his country's poor supply and distribution infrastructure, and in 1999, as China's economy began to take off, he launched a B2B network to connect domestic manufacturers with foreign buyers online. Alibaba would go on to link domestic buyers with sellers and launch the fabulously successful Taobao, an online consumer-to-consumer market. Ma subsequently created China's biggest online payments service and is now making waves in online finance. In September 2014 Alibaba raised $25 billion in the world's biggest-ever IPO, topping the previous record of $22.1 billion set by Agricultural Bank of China in its 2010 debut. Two months later Alibaba boasted $280 billion in market capitalization, second only to Google among Internet companies, and bigger than U.S. commerce giants Amazon and eBay combined.

Alibaba's business moves were hardly sui generis: eBay preceded Taobao, PayPal came before Alipay, and online banking has been standard in the West for years. But in each case, Ma made key changes for the local market; he wisely designed a trustworthy online payments system, for example, because many Chinese don't have credit cards. In China, necessity has been the mother of adaptation.

Ma's is just one of China's spectacular success stories. As he prepared for his company's IPO, Alibaba found itself dueling on multiple fronts with another remarkable entrepreneurial company, Tencent Holdings, which was co-founded in 1998 by Shenzhen native Ma Huateng, or Pony Ma, as he is known. Pony turned an Israeli technology into an instant messaging service called QQ that swept the country in the late 1990s and laid the foundation for an online gaming, e-commerce, and social media empire that includes the immensely popular WeChat, a multimedia suite of communications services for smartphones that claims nearly 470 million users in China. With a market capitalization of about $150 billion in November 2014, Tencent was the fifth-biggest Internet company in the world, ranking behind Google, Alibaba, Facebook, and Amazon. It was roughly twice the size of Baidu and eBay. Tencent has relentlessly extended its mobile and online platforms to include banking and e-commerce services. Alibaba in turn has pushed into social media to compete with WeChat.

Tencent has steadily developed an overseas presence, establishing an outpost in Silicon Valley to be close to the innovative spirit of the area. WeChat has perhaps another 100 million registered users internationally. As Pony told me during a wide-ranging conversation in December 2011 in Hong Kong, "We want to expand outside of China, because we see the Internet as fundamentally a global business." Tencent went public in Hong Kong in 2004 and shortly afterward brought in Martin Lau as chief strategy and investment officer. Martin, who was one of the team of Goldman Sachs bankers who led the company's successful IPO, became president in 2006.

China's private companies are far more welcome in foreign countries than its SOEs are. Lenovo, the world's largest seller of personal computers, is a case in point. Founding chairman Liu Chuanzhi got his initial capitalization from the state-run Chinese Academy of Sciences, but Lenovo, by design, has been run from the start as an independent company and makes its own decisions about finances, operations, and hiring and firing personnel. In 2005 it bought IBM's PC business, and today it maintains dual headquarters in Beijing and North Carolina. It purchased IBM's server business in 2014. That same year it acquired Motorola Mobility, giving it a line of mobile devices, like smart phones, powered by the Android operating system.

Lenovo, originally known as Legend, got its first big break as a business when it came up with a circuit card that enabled PCs to process Chinese characters. The fledgling company's creativity was not restricted to designing products. In the late 1980s, as inflation soared, the company invested in a pig farm to make sure workers could afford to eat enough protein. It took ingenuity not only to attract customers and grow revenues but also to survive in a rapidly transforming economy where the rules weren't fixed or clear, where government intrusion was inevitable, and where the biggest competitor was often the state.

Unsurprisingly, many of these entrepreneurs display exuberant, idiosyncratic styles that reflect their mold-breaking personalities. The office of Huang Nubo, the onetime Party propagandist turned real estate developer who famously bid on huge tracts of land in Iceland and Norway's Spitsbergen Island, is something of a menagerie, for example. In a hallway leading to his office in the Xizhimen district just northwest of central Beijing, perhaps 20 pairs of hiking boots are displayed alongside ropes, axes, and other equipment of this mountain-climbing enthusiast. Inside, two spider monkeys scamper along ropes in their cages, and a half-dozen gray cats prowl about, while Huang feeds walnuts to his two pet macaws and a cockatoo. Several small sharks swim in a tank. "Entrepreneurs," Huang once said to me, "should have the shark spirit."

The campus of Broad Group in Changsha was designed to reflect Zhang Yue's eclectic influences and his passion for the environment. It encompasses a sprawling organic garden that provides up to half of the food consumed by his workers, and the grounds are dotted with dozens of statues of inspirational figures, from Confucius and the poet Li Bai to Coco Chanel and Jack Welch. There are likenesses of environmentalist Rachel Carson, Sir Isaac Newton with an apple about to fall on his head, and Winston Churchill flashing a V for Victory sign. One company building is modeled after the palace at Versailles, another after an Egyptian pyramid.

Zhang Yue and his brother started Broad Air in 1988 to manufacture central-air-conditioning systems based on nonelectric absorption chillers for industrial or commercial use. They adapted existing technology, patenting an arrangement of copper pipes inside the chillers, and sold the energy-saving devices in China and around the world. Powered by gas and waste energy, the coolers hold a particular appeal in developing countries with unsteady electricity supplies, but some companies in more developed countries have also gravitated to the technology owing to its quality and energy-efficiency performance. Every nonelectric cooler comes with 25 years of free real-time monitoring. On a visit to the company in the spring of 2012, I watched as technicians in Broad Air's space-age control room checked on the performance of its units in locations as diverse as the Adolfo Suárez Madrid–Barajas Airport in Spain; Qualcomm headquarters in San Diego, California; and Fort Stewart, the U.S. Army base in Georgia.

Zhang says that 80 percent of his clients are repeaters. "If you bring long-term benefits for your clients, they will choose you."

An artist who began his career as an interior decorator, Zhang is a passionate environmentalist who gave up his private jet to limit carbon emissions and distributes a pamphlet entitled "Life Attitude of an Earth Citizen" with 22 rules for an environmentally responsible person to live by. He has guided the company into several new lines of business. Broad Air now sells devices to measure air quality, as well as air purification devices, more than 200 of which are said to be in use in the Zhongnanhai leadership compound. More recently, Zhang launched a subsidiary to construct prefabricated, energy-efficient, environmentally friendly buildings.

Companies like these are the future for China. They are big job creators and are expanding internationally—clear goals for the country. The companies are beginning to stake a claim for Chinese innovation as well. It's an area where China should have vast potential to become a global leader. China has 2 million university graduates in engineering and sciences, and its top graduates are smart. They are joined in the workforce by tens of thousands of young men and women who have attended the finest universities and graduate schools outside of the country. In recent years China has upgraded its technological capabilities in a range of industries, notably consumer electronics, personal computers, construction machinery, mining, clean tech, steel, and telecom equipment. And it will continue to do so thanks to high levels of government R&D spending, the sheer number of very able, highly educated professionals coming into the workforce, and the ingenuity of China's entrepreneurs. In his talk at CELAP, the Party leadership school in Pudong, Andrew Liveris noted that Dow's facility in Shanghai, where 500 scientists and engineers work in more than 80 labs, was the company's most patent-productive operation in the world.

But overall, China falls short of its potential. Chinese manufacturing exports still concentrate on low-end assembly products, and China is known more as a clever copycat than as an innovator. Poor protection of intellectual property, rampant piracy, and a school system that remains too focused on rote learning have all played a part in hobbling the country's development. Overregulation and excessive state interference in the economy have encouraged rent seeking and corruption and have limited the development of a vibrant venture capital and private equity industry that could play a positive role in promoting innovation and entrepreneurship.

Xi Jinping and his fellow leaders have set out to change this with their ambitious plans for economic and institutional reform. "Thirty-five years back, most of the peasants in China were simply illiterate. By removing the shackles and obstacles on them, they were free to do the things they liked. In just a matter of two to three years, the farmers managed to solve the problem of food self-sufficiency," Premier Li Keqiang told me in November 2013. "China's reform has entered a new phase, and I believe the same rule applies: all we have to do is remove those shackles and obstacles and make sure that people unleash their creativity."

Li is absolutely right. The best course for China is to continue to free up its markets, to promote a vibrant domestic private sector, and to allow foreign firms to do business unhindered. The success of China's reforms will be determined by how fast and to what extent the country rolls back subsidies and regulatory advantages for state-owned enterprises, opens key industries like energy and finance to the private sector, and fosters competition from foreign companies.

Encouraging the private sector to work its magic and transform important parts of the economy long closed to it could provide the boost China needs now. But as well intentioned as China's leaders may be, I am mindful of the magnitude of the economic challenge they confront and the slow progress of reform to date. I remain cautiously optimistic, however, because I know how seriously Xi wants to change things, and I have learned over my years in dealing with the Chinese never to underestimate their capacity to get difficult things done.

CHAPTER NINETEEN

The Party Line

I have talked a lot about reform in this book, but not much about political reform, even though that is what probably comes to mind first for many American readers. Inside China there are big, even pitched public policy debates about economic and social issues, but the fundamental nature of the political system is not open to discussion. Despite the many meetings I've had with President Xi Jinping and my two decades of experience dealing with China, I can't tell you how a one-party system with an authoritarian government might evolve in such a complex country. I don't know what Xi's long-term agenda may be, but I can tell you that it doesn't involve Western-style multiparty electoral democracy. His chief political concern is to maintain the primacy and power of the Communist Party by cleansing, strengthening, and revitalizing it. Those hoping for signs of Western-style democratic initiatives are certain to be disappointed.

"The very essence of 'socialism with Chinese characteristics' is the leadership of the Chinese Communist Party. And this makes China quite different from the United States and other countries that believe that we should have a multiparty system," Xi told me in July 2014. "Because we have one-party rule, we need to be a good party. So we have three tasks: self-improvement, self-purification, and self-regulation."

Xi's stance is as much pragmatic as ideological. He sees the Party as the only institution with the strength and organization to carry out his ambitious plans to reform the economy, modernize the government, and rebuild

China's power and international standing; political pluralism, to him, is a threat to those objectives.

Residents of Hong Kong got a taste of Xi's views on representative democracy in August 2014 when the Standing Committee of the National People's Congress ruled that candidates for the post of chief executive of the Hong Kong SAR would be limited to those nominated by the territory's 1,200-member election committee, which is widely viewed as pro-Beijing. Many in Hong Kong interpret the commitment to universal suffrage laid out in the Basic Law that governs the territory under the Chinese as a promise of popular democracy. They had hoped that the election process would be much more open, with anyone who met certain basic criteria eligible to run, not just those approved by an elite body chosen by Beijing. The decision of the NPC led to weeks of protests by students and other activists beginning in late September. Beijing stood firmly behind its decision and in support of the initial hard line taken by the Hong Kong authorities.

To be sure, Xi has proposed some welcome changes in China's social policies. The Third Plenum in November 2013 promised, for example, greater freedom of movement through a relaxation of restrictions on residency permits, the effective end of the one-child policy, and the elimination of forced labor camps for reeducation. China's citizens are also likely to benefit from broad efforts to improve governance, increase efficiency of government institutions, and professionalize the legal system, providing greater consistency in the application of law—all of which are essential to a smoothly functioning market economy.

But the leadership's overwhelming priority is tackling the daunting set of economic and social challenges it inherited. Xi must reengineer a vulnerable economy, clean up the toxic mess the country has made of its environment, and take on widespread corruption and gaping disparities in wealth and income. Far-reaching plans laid out at the Third Plenum for the most sweeping economic policy changes in two decades are by no means guaranteed to succeed.

China's problems have cost the Party much credibility, and Xi's fierce anticorruption campaign is meant to bolster confidence in the Party's judgment and actions in all aspects of policy and rebuild its standing with the

Chinese people, who have complained bitterly on social media and in the streets about the lavish spending of officials and the unfair way the fruits of success have been divvied up. Corruption and unequal access to opportunity have alienated wide swaths of the public, and Xi portrays the fight against it in stark, existential terms for the Communist Party of China.

"Winning or losing public support is an issue that concerns the CPC's survival or extinction," he said in a June 2013 speech.

Documents coming out of the Third Plenum stressed Communist Party ideals and values, and in an echo of an earlier era, officials throughout the country were required to write self-criticisms and perform public confessions. These exercises are meant not only to quash illicit activity but to advance the "mass line," the Party doctrine that directs members to work foremost for the interests of the people. In all my years of traveling in China, I have never heard the role of the Party raised so often, or discussed so openly, by so many government officials as I have in my most recent meetings. When we met in July 2014, for example, Xi talked about the role of the Party in Chinese society for more than a third of our time together.

Xi's throwback approach has unsettled many, but putting officials in the dock has boosted his popularity while striking fear in the hearts of Party cadres. Xi has sought to address the aspirations and frustrations of all citizens—not just Party members—with his vision of a "Chinese Dream" and his focus on fixing the daily problems people care most about: pollution, property rights, food safety, corruption. His cause has been helped by an unexpected personal charisma that comes through in the easy, shirt-sleeved informality he has shown—taking an ostensibly impromptu stroll in a Beijing alleyway or stopping at a shop, patiently waiting in line to pay for steamed buns, then eating them while locals snapped pictures with him. We are used to such displays from U.S. politicians, but in China Xi's gestures are mostly a radical and refreshing departure and have won him much admiration among the people.

But Xi has also flexed raw political muscle, consolidating power quickly, and now stands as China's strongest senior leader since Deng Xiaoping. After securing a smaller Standing Committee of seven mostly like-minded members, he took direct charge of many elements of China's decision-making process. Xi assumed personal control of economic reform, chairing a newly formed small committee to coordinate policy formulation and implementation. He created a powerful new council to oversee matters of state and internal security; his Central National Security Commission is something of a cross between our own National Security Council and the Department of Homeland Security. Crucially, he grasped the reins of the military right away; when Hu Jintao succeeded Jiang Zemin as Party general secretary, he had had to wait two years to assume the chairmanship of the Central Military Commission.

Xi's blend of power politics and personal appeal has not been all smiles and selfies. He has presided over an ideological hardening that has focused on the supposedly pernicious influence of Western political and philosophical values. That, in turn, has led to a stifling of liberal voices and increasing pressure on some collaborations between Chinese and Western institutions.

Xi has cracked down on dissent and restrained press freedom, making life much more difficult for foreign news organizations, especially those that have reported on the riches amassed by senior officials and their families. He has clamped down on China's small army of prominent bloggers, micro-bloggers, and online commentators on *weibo*, the country's wildly popular social media platforms, which have emerged as alternatives to state control of information. Human rights issues, including the treatment of dissidents, continue to draw the attention and criticism of activists inside and outside of China. But the country's leaders show no sign of adjusting the hard line against those they see as undermining the authority of the Party.

Tightening political restrictions and consolidating the role of the Party while loosening controls on much of the economy and giving greater rein to the market might seem counterintuitive to many Westerners who, like me, believe that economic freedoms and global integration should go hand in hand with more political openness. But to Xi, who believes that a strong Party is essential to China's future, it is perfectly logical. Two years into his expected ten-year run as general secretary, Xi appears to enjoy broad public backing, but he has put his personal credibility and political capital clearly on the line. Xi must show that his economic reforms can work and deliver tangible benefits for ordinary people. That's one reason he is placing such a pragmatic emphasis on improving the efficiency of government so that it can solve problems. Declaring war on pollution, as the leadership has done, won't amount to a hill of beans if the government can't do the hard day-to-day work of cleaning the air and guaranteeing safe drinking water.

"Up until now we have enjoyed the support of the Chinese people," Xi told me in July 2014, during a chat at the Great Hall of the People. "A key part of that is to improve their lives. Deng Xiaoping said, 'Poverty is not socialism,' and 'We should allow some to get rich first' and then allow them to help others do so. But aside from enlarging the pie, we are also focused on how to distribute the pie so that every member of society will feel that the system is just and fair."

China has become too big and complex to be run without modern institutions that have the ability and manpower to implement and enforce policies, to cut and serve the pie, that is. Since Reform and Opening Up began in 1978, China has often made changes in an ad hoc way—"crossing the river while feeling the stones," in Deng Xiaoping's memorable phrase. But that strategy, while brilliantly successful for a country just starting to modernize, can fall short in an advanced economy that is increasingly integrated into the global system. Xi aims to adapt Deng's approach by making direction from above clearer and firmer. Since Deng, China has been guided by four "modernizations"—of industry, agriculture, national security, and science. Beginning in mid-2014 Xi also called for modernizing governance systems and capacity. He means to strengthen government institutions, cut red tape, design and implement better mechanisms for regulation and oversight, and create more effective incentives for officials. The leadership also intends to realign the distribution of power between Beijing and the provinces—centralizing and enhancing such functions as enforcing national environmental laws while devolving other responsibilities to the regions, including, for example, the power to collect new local taxes, such as on property.

Unlike other regimes throughout the world that no doubt shared a similar determination to be all-enduring but have since crumbled, China's leaders have so far been adept at maintaining power with an array of carrots and sticks. They have closely monitored and quickly suppressed dissent;

not for nothing does China employ the world's biggest and most powerful domestic security force. But its leaders have also anticipated and responded to many of the needs, problems, and demands of their people. And the Party has also proven to be adaptable, morphing over the years from a revolutionary organization to an establishment party of elites that since 2001 has welcomed once-reviled private sector businessmen into its ranks. It has shed its ideological debt to Marxism in favor of a form of socialism that includes many familiar features of Western capitalism. But the Party holds to its Leninist principles as the vanguard that leads the people through its domination of political and social life and its command of a large, committed cadre of nearly 87 million members in 2014.

The Communist Party is the alpha and omega of political, economic, and social life in China. The Party runs the country, controlling the government, appointing its leaders, and making all the key decisions. It directs the military and paramilitary, the police and various other state and public security operations, as well as local watchdog groups. All are run by loyal Party members and charged with protecting and defending the Party. The Party places its members in positions of authority at every level in government agencies, military and police organs, and state-owned enterprises, as well as in areas like schools, universities, and other social groups. There are even Party cells in private companies. Party committees enforce discipline on their members, communicate the Party line, and function as the Party's eyes and ears.

The Chinese Constitution, written by the Party, effectively guarantees it a monopoly of power. The Chinese system embraces an extralegal role for the Party, which is chiefly subject to its own disciplinary rules and procedures. Members who commit crimes or otherwise misbehave are generally disciplined by the Party before they are turned over to the state legal system, which is in any case also staffed chiefly by Party members.

Altogether, the Party aims to influence if not dominate all organized activity in almost every sphere of life—political parties, businesses, labor unions, universities, sports, and arts. Even religions are licensed or monitored by the Party.

There *is* life beyond the Party—citizens can make many personal economic decisions. They can find and quit jobs, travel at home and abroad, and decide about marriage and whether and when to have what was, until recently, their one permitted child. But certain options don't exist. Workers can't just start labor unions: there is one Party-sanctioned umbrella federation of unions. Nor can citizens launch a new political party. There are eight in addition to the CPC, but they are submissive junior partners of a "united front" coalition led by the Communist Party, and their policies do not challenge the Party's line.

The Party has permitted few challenges to its authority to last long. The last major challenge came with the student-led demonstrations in Tiananmen Square in 1989. Then, gatherings initially meant to commemorate the death of the liberal former general secretary Hu Yaobang broadened into protests about inflation, job prospects, and corruption, amid demands for democratic freedoms. The episode ended in a harsh crackdown. Beijing's actions drew shock and condemnation and led to sanctions from the West. Economic reform ground to a halt.

China might have chosen subsequently to go in a much different direction than it did, reversing economic reforms and turning in on itself. And, stung by the reaction from the West, it did pull back for a time, while an intense internal struggle played out over the way forward. But in the end, China chose to double down on its efforts to modernize. This decision was the work of an undaunted Deng Xiaoping, whose 1992 Southern Tour had included visits to the pacesetting special economic zones in Shenzhen and Zhuhai and served to reignite reform; led China to embrace Western investment, technology, and economic ideas as never before; and put the country on its path to stunning economic growth.

The Party was, however, determined to retain its hold on power. It sought to expunge the national memory of the "June 4th incident"—it remains a forbidden topic of discussion—and arrived at a tacit understanding with the people: it would deliver prosperity but expected no political challenge in return. The political system would tolerate limited forms of economic and social protest, but its central features were not going to change.

President Xi has inherited a China where patience has begun to wear thin. It's a fraught moment, but it's worth comparing China's situation to that of another onetime Communist giant, Russia. The Tiananmen crackdown came on the heels of a landmark moment in Chinese history, the visit of Mikhail Gorbachev, then general secretary of the Soviet Communist Party, to Beijing in mid-May 1989. He had come to renew Sino-Soviet relations—after nearly three decades of hostility. Not long after the Soviet leader's visit, the Berlin Wall came down and Gorbachev fell victim to a short-lived coup that ended with the rise of Boris Yeltsin, the dissolution of the Soviet empire, and the twilight of its Communist Party.

There was a point at which many analysts felt Chinese Communism might follow the same trajectory. But China had something Russia did not: effective economic reforms that led to increasing prosperity for its people and a resolute leader in Deng Xiaoping, who unleashed the power of markets. Gorbachev tried to introduce political reforms, even as Soviet Russia's economy spiraled down. Shortly afterward, Russia's political and economic system collapsed of its own weight.

The Chinese have studied and debated the dissolution of the Soviet Union in great depth. Was the cause the effort to launch political reforms before economic reforms had succeeded? Insufficient control of the military? A weak leader at the top? This topic will be debated for a long time. But one thing is certain: no one in the leadership, not Xi, certainly, wants to be the Chinese Gorbachev.

Corruption breeds where power meets opportunity. In China, ironically, a big opportunity came with Reform and Opening Up. Government institutions, as well as social and legal structures, were either not in place or could not keep pace with the schemes and stratagems devised by just about everyone as they tried to navigate an economy that was being reinvented on the fly and creating new opportunities for people to generate enormous wealth and for poorly paid officials to line their pockets. Ordinary citizens and officials alike operated in gray, and black, areas with unclear rules and weak government enforcement of the law. Some of this activity, though officially unapproved, was implicitly accepted and even encouraged as new economic policies were tested. Other activity was blatantly corrupt.

Seemingly everything in China occurs on an outsize scale, including corruption. Graft, bribery, and even outright theft of state-owned assets are rampant, infecting massive projects and ordinary daily transactions alike. The lack of transparency means it's hard to get a handle on the actual size of China's problem, but it's big by any standard. According to public reports, a study whose results appeared for just one day in 2011 on the website of the Bank of China indicated that some $120 billion in ill-gotten gains had been spirited out of the country by fleeing officials from 1995 to 2008. That's just the money that left. Estimates of the total annual theft range from 3 percent of GDP (Carnegie Endowment for International Peace) to 5 percent (Center for Strategic and International Studies). That's hundreds of billions of dollars each year.

However much, it is money stolen from the state, and thus from the pockets of the people, that could have been used far more productively to fund inadequate education, health care, or pension programs rather than wasted by rogue officials on fancy art, Ferraris, or beachfront property in Australia. Indeed, it is the blatant displays of ill-gotten gains and in-your-face extravagances—officials with nominally low salaries sporting $10,000 watches or their children driving $250,000 cars—that have enraged the public, damaged the Party's credibility, and hurt China.

From the start of his administration, Xi vowed to pursue high- and low-ranking officials alike, or "the tigers and flies," as he put it. He couldn't have picked a more effective person for the job than Wang Qishan, who enjoys a spotless reputation and who knows how to get a tough job done.

Together they have made good on Xi's vows, increasing the resources and strengthening the mission of the Central Commission for Discipline Inspection, the fearsome arm of the Party headed by Wang Qishan that investigates wrongdoing among its members. They have extended the discipline commission's reach to enable it to probe suspected misconduct overseas, lengthened the statute of limitations for crimes in order to pursue retired officials, and introduced new investigative technologies. The secretive commission even launched a website to encourage reporting of abuses; it received more than 24,000 reports in its first month, September 2013. Aware of the importance of public support, Wang Qishan has charted a sophisticated communications strategy that's kept the campaign in the public eye. Seemingly every day another dramatic story breaks about officials nailed for corrupt activities. A crucial internal change has enhanced the commission's effectiveness: any investigation conducted at the provincial or municipal levels must now also be reported directly to headquarters in Beijing, reducing the ability of local officials to influence the probes.

Wang Qishan's investigative teams have systematically scoured the ranks of the central government, the provinces, the military, big state-owned companies, regulators, the media, universities, and research institutes to weed out corrupt officials and uproot patronage networks. Industry sectors that Xi has marked for reform—energy, electric utilities, telecom, media, and finance—have been particularly scrutinized. Xi is, at least in part, focused on the companies in this core group to break their hold on the system and weaken opposition to his reform program—and power.

The number of investigations and prosecutions for corruption jumped 13 percent to 182,000 in 2013, Xi's first year in power. And anticorruption fighters have gone after higher-ranking officials than ever before. By mid-2014, according to the *Financial Times*, 49 officials of ministerial rank or higher had been publicly charged with corruption since the end of 2012.

The crackdown has reached to the very summit of power. In June 2014 retired general Xu Caihou, a former vice chairman of the Central Military Commission and member of the Politburo, was expelled from the Party and his case handed to prosecutors for investigation of bribe taking (he subsequently admitted his guilt). The following month Zhou Yongkang, China's former head of internal security and onetime member of the Party's Standing Committee, the country's highest decision-making body, was formally placed under investigation for possible disciplinary infractions. In December 2014 Zhou was expelled from the Party and arrested on charges of corruption, leaking state secrets, and adultery.

The probes have riveted the public. Dozens of Zhou's associates, including family members, former oil industry executives, and officials who served with him when he was Party secretary of Sichuan, had been detained, investigated, or charged through 2014. Several held ministerial-level rankings in the government.

Among the most prominent was Jiang Jiemin, the former chairman of PetroChina, who had so ably managed the company's 2000 IPO. He was named in March 2013 to run the State-owned Assets Supervision and Administration Commission (SASAC), which oversees SOEs. Less than six months later, he had been removed from office, detained, and placed under investigation. By midyear 2014 he had been kicked out of the Party and his case handed over to criminal prosecutors.

The prosecution of Bo Xilai, which Xi inherited, exposed corruption and sleaze at the highest levels, but the investigation of Zhou Yongkang and his family appears to be of yet another order of magnitude. Altogether, an estimated $14.5 billion in family-related assets were reported by Reuters to have been seized as investigators rooted through his network. I first met Zhou when he was head of China National Petroleum Corporation before the PetroChina IPO in the late 1990s and watched as he gained power over the years. He is the highest-ranking member of the Party to be brought down principally by corruption charges since the founding of the state in 1949.

When Xi kicked off his mass-line campaign in June 2013, he took aim at "decadence" and "undesirable work styles" as well. There was to be no more outrageous and uncouth behavior from officials, no more mistresses or lavish banquets. Set speeches and reading from scripts would be frowned upon. Hard liquor was banned from banquets, and officials were told to restrict themselves to "four dishes and one soup," to cease using government cars for personal purposes, and to stop giving gifts at state expense.

The campaign was also a tool to drive reform. Xi himself took charge of the mass line in Beijing's neighboring province of Hebei, using it to advance such objectives as cutting back overcapacity in the steel, iron, coal, and cement industries and to reduce the amount of air pollution blowing into the capital.

"The mass line is misunderstood in the West but hugely popular with the people," Wang Qishan explained to me when we met for dinner with our wives in November 2013. The campaign was meant, he said, to restore order and discipline within the Party. "There is no chance for economic reform without this."

Wang Qishan and I spoke again about the fight against corruption a few months later, in February 2014. I'd arrived early at Zhongnanhai because of light traffic, a Beijing rarity brought about by the fact that the air quality was so bad—PM 2.5 levels topping 500—that people were advised not to drive. Rather than stroll the grounds, I waited in the car until Wang Qishan could see us.

In private Wang Qishan often uses a medical analogy to discuss how to deal with the disease of corruption. It can be done surgically, with clear problem areas cut out; by using a targeted approach along the lines of Western drug therapies; or holistically, treating the entire system to eradicate the root cause, as in traditional Chinese medicine. All of these methods are being used. Xi is wielding a scalpel—and sometimes an ax—to arrest, prosecute, and remove corrupt officials while employing self-criticisms, austerity, and other elements of the mass line to force Party members to clean up their behavior. His approach is terrifying people in business, government, and throughout all institutions in society.

But it will take years, perhaps decades, to create a culture that discourages corruption in the first place. Wang Qishan said China will need to develop in its officials a "power of belief" in serving the people. Then the Party will have to establish systems and institutions to support that culture and put in place the right incentives to promote positive behavior. Included among these would be requiring financial disclosure, increasing government salaries, establishing clear lines of authority and reporting, eliminating the government's role in certain approvals and licenses, and reducing special benefits for officials.

"Corruption has always existed, like crime, but the scale can be changed," Wang told me. "We need to create a situation where it is the rare person who is corrupt. Punishing some officials now will hopefully set an example and deter others later. Doing so builds credibility with the people. In the long term, we have to create a system where officials have no interest in corruption."

Shaping the proper environment isn't only the work of the Party and government. Wang Qishan cited the role some in the public and media were playing in highlighting corrupt practices. Once "Netizens" started reporting and posting pictures online of officials wearing expensive wristwatches, many officials stopped wearing them entirely, he noted. One provincial official, who had earned the nickname Brother Wristwatch, was eventually sentenced to 14 years in jail for corruption.

Then Wang showed me his own watch, which he said he had bought years before. I didn't recognize the brand, but it sure looked like it cost even less than my Timex Ironman, which he pointed at with a smile. He said he changed the battery every year, the band every two years, and had replaced the crystal three times.

"You're setting a great example," I said. "I can never figure out how to change the battery, so when it goes, I just buy a new watch."

Individually, Chinese people are no more corruptible than anyone else on earth. The Party and high-level government leaders I've known best and worked the closest with—Zhu Rongji, Hu Jintao, Xi Jinping, Wang Qishan, Wu Yi, and Zhou Xiaochuan—have been able, ambitious, incredibly hardworking men and women focused not on personal gain but on solving the nation's problems and improving the lives of the people. Zhu is a paragon of ethics who insisted on the highest standards and understood the importance of appearances. When I began assembling the advisory board for the Tsinghua School of Executive Management in 1999, he made it clear that he never wanted me to discuss fundraising with him or to solicit contributions in his name. Others at Tsinghua emphasized that the board's purpose was to provide counsel and advice, not to raise money. International advisory board members could donate if they wished, but it was not a requirement. As it happened, one board member from the West wanted, with the best of intentions, to contribute but had the bad judgment to hand a check to Zhu at the board's very first meeting. Instead of a thank-you, he received a stern rebuke, and the check was returned.

When Zhu Rongji restructured state-owned enterprises in the late 1990s, he wanted to avoid a repeat of the Russian experience in which a few privileged businessmen became billionaire oligarchs by buying state-owned assets cheaply as they were privatized. Instead, the Chinese state kept ownership and control of key industries as shares were sold to the public and non-Chinese strategic investors. Nonetheless, in time, a group of princelings—children and relatives of Party leaders—became very wealthy.

China is not unique in this respect, of course. From old world Europe to many developing countries, success and fortune often skew toward members of prominent, well-connected families who treat state assets as private fiefdoms. Chinese familial ties are particularly strong. Who you know matters as nowhere else, and networks of relationships, known as guanxi, help Chinese of all walks of life get things done. The scions of China's top officials, and especially those descended from revolutionary leaders, occupy the apex of these complex relationship and power networks in a state that, until recently, controlled all assets. While many have profited from illicit activity, others have traded on their names and connections, receiving attractive opportunities from would-be partners in the expectation their dealings would receive special treatment from government officials and regulators. This is a subtler form of corruption—sophisticated cronyism in the place of outright theft. Without a legal system that ensures openness and due diligence, it is difficult for the public to know where the boundary lies between outright illegal acts and unseemly activity.

At the same time, I have been stunned and disappointed to see a number of Chinese officials and executives whom I knew detained and in some cases convicted of corrupt activities. Without excusing the individual choices these officials made, I believe that the great driver of illicit activity is a flawed system that concentrates too much power in the hands of the Party and state, and leaves too wide a gap between the law and its enforcement. While the state continues to play such a big role in the economy, corruption will fester in government overregulation, in the labyrinthine approval process for business ventures and investment projects, and in a lack of openness and accountability. State officials are paid minimal salaries but given vast influence over multi-billion-dollar decisions, from granting licenses to authorizing business transactions. That's an open invitation to graft, kickbacks, bribes, and pay-to-play schemes. The situation is exacerbated by the fact that the government participates in business. And as long as the Party operates outside of the jurisdiction of the legal system, it will be difficult for the public to have confidence in the decisions of the courts.

It is all too easy to mistake China for a monolithic, centralized state. The reality is quite different. Decisions made at the top are frequently muddled by diffuse, uneven execution down below, as provincial, county, municipal, township, and village officials interpret and apply the Party's orders. They do this in a variety of ways: some imaginative, some not; many well thought through, others breathtakingly unsophisticated. The tension is captured by a timeless Chinese phrase: "Policies from above, counterpolicies from below."

Consider the contrast between Chongqing and Guangdong a few years back. While leading his Mao-inspired mass rallies, Bo Xilai appeared to run Chongqing with an iron fist, taking a tough law-and-order-first stance, promoting state-owned companies and a leftist ideology. In Guangdong, Wang Yang stoked his province's historical entrepreneurialism and accommodated a wider role for citizens. When his "Happy Guangdong" saw violent protests erupt in late 2011 in a village called Wukan over complaints about irregular land sales, Wang took a patient, conciliatory approach in public, resolving the crisis peacefully, in part by co-opting local inhabitants.

"In the past, the policy was to suppress any type of dissent," he told me in April 2012, just a few months after the protests had captured national and international attention. We were meeting in the magnificent quarters of the former British consulate on leafy Shamian Island, the site of the old colonial concessions in Guangzhou, and discussing a range of topics when we touched on the subject of Wukan.

"The government has realized that if people's demands are reasonable and legitimate, even if they take a confrontational approach, you have to be tolerant. Only by doing this can the government ensure that they are not on the opposite side of the people," he went on to say. He added that, of course, there would be times the government would decide the people's demands were not reasonable.

Wang was subsequently named one of four vice premiers in the Chinese government transition in 2013 and is the chief economic representative for the Chinese side of the Strategic and Economic Dialogue with the U.S. He is a worthy successor to his predecessor, Wang Qishan, and the U.S. and China are both fortunate to have such an able and intuitive man in that critical role.

Provinces implementing policies differently can be a good thing; officials can learn from one another's successes—and failures. But it can lead to ineffective government and make it more difficult to maintain national standards or ensure the consistent implementation of Beijing's policies. And the power of local Party organizations can impede oversight and effective enforcement of laws and standards, since, too often, local branches of national ministries and agencies report to municipal and provincial authorities, without adequate oversight from Beijing.

The reliance on the Party to make key decisions has left the state without the modern institutions and systems it needs to govern in many areas. Environmental protection is a good example of how current governmental institutions and arrangements fall short. Nowhere are the challenges that Xi faces more stark. The Ministry of Environmental Protection (MEP) was created in 2008 to succeed the State Environmental Protection Agency and is responsible for implementing the laws handed down by the National People's Congress.

Unfortunately, the laws are often vague and require additional guidance for implementation. Under China's legal system, the country's procuratorate, which is responsible for investigation and prosecution, provides this guidance, but provinces and even municipalities can adjust it for their own "unique" circumstances. MEP has branches in provinces and major cities, but in practice these report directly to the governors or mayors and only indirectly to Beijing. This structure spawns confusion, political interference, and inconsistent enforcement. It can be unclear who has the responsibility and authority to mete out punishments—officials at all levels of MEP can theoretically weigh in on fines. Even when decisions to act are reached, they are subject to the whims of the courts, which fall under the control of the Party, whose representatives may be reluctant to close factories or punish polluters if doing so might reduce economic activity in their jurisdiction. MEP also appears to be underresourced. It reportedly has only about 3,000 employees and a budget of $643 million. By contrast, the U.S. Environmental Protection Agency has 15,521 employees and a budget of $7.9 billion.

The Ministry of Environmental Protection isn't alone in struggling to meet its mission. China's bureaucracies tend to be bottom-heavy and weighted toward local and provincial branches. Minister of Finance Lou Jiwei estimates that only 6 percent of China's public servants work at the central level, compared with 12 percent in the U.S. and 14 percent in

France. Until March 2013 the China Food and Drug Administration had only about three dozen people in its central-level office; subsequently several hundred staffers were added, but the agency continues to lack its own enforcement power and relies on local officials. I cannot think of two areas of more immediate concern for China than food safety and the environment. They are flash points of tension and conflict, but the government institutions charged with dealing with these issues remain overmatched.

China has made progress in putting better laws on its books. But the laws are not being uniformly or consistently enforced, and the courts remain under the thumb of the Party. "We know there should be protections, but we leave it to the local government," one ranking official told me. "Can you imagine that a local court or prosecutor under the jurisdiction of a provincial Party secretary would bring a lawsuit against the Party secretary or the governor?"

President Xi Jinping is eager to restore confidence in the legal system both to soothe an irritated citizenry and to ensure the success of his reforms. The protection of private property and the enforcement of contracts are crucial to the exercise of economic freedom. Without them, entrepreneurship cannot flourish, and economic vitality will decline. In an early speech as general secretary that he gave at a study session of the Politburo, Xi championed what he calls the rule of law—which is certainly different from our understanding of this principle—emphasizing the need for judges and prosecutors to be independent and for the Party to act with restraint on judicial proceedings.

Beijing is taking steps to reduce the control of local Party branches over the courts and their judgments and to limit their ability to decide individual cases. The Third Plenum called for more open trials, where decisions are made based on evidence presented in courtrooms and not in back rooms. The Party followed up on these advances by focusing its Fourth Plenum in October 2014 on the importance of the law. Documents coming out of this meeting talked of setting up circuit courts, which would effectively curtail interference by local Party leaders in judicial decisions; they stressed that officials would be evaluated on their effectiveness in implementing the law and pledged greater transparency and accountability in government.

The appointment of Zhou Qiang to head the Supreme People's Court is another positive sign. A well-trained lawyer and former Hunan Party secretary, he is a reformer determined to professionalize the judicial system. That's no small order, given that for years many of China's judges had scant legal training; they were drawn from a pool of retired military officers or recent law school graduates with little experience. Zhou's predecessor as president of the court had no formal legal background. Beginning in 2014, all Supreme People's Court decisions and those of 14 eastern and central provinces were made available online to the public; all courts in the country were to follow within three years. Pilot programs to establish circuit courts, and courts with jurisdiction across different regions, were in the works by year-end 2014 as part of the effort to reduce meddling by local officials in judicial proceedings.

Xi's judicial reforms should professionalize, modernize, and improve the current system, and, one hopes, instill a greater reliance on transparency and consistency, but no judge or prosecutor in China will be truly independent as long as the legal system isn't independent of the Party. And there is no plan to change that in a fundamental way any time soon. The Fourth Plenum asserted that the Party remains in charge of the legal system, making clear that "Party leadership and the socialist rule of law are identical."

Traditionally, the Communist Party has wanted Chinese people to look to it for their needs and was openly hostile to nonaffiliated entities like private foundations or not-for-profit organizations. But the government is becoming more receptive to philanthropic causes and charitable giving and has allowed new opportunities for people to participate in the social sphere through organizations that are not technically under Party control.

Some nongovernmental organizations that provide social services for sanctioned causes have become acceptable. Indeed, they are even seen as bolstering the state or supplementing its capacity. The devastating 2008 Sichuan earthquake, which left nearly 90,000 killed or missing and 4.8 million homeless, marked a turning point. Through September 2009, private donors in China had given $10.6 billion of charitable relief aid to help victims, with an additional $1.1 billion coming from abroad. The high-profile philanthropic work of Peng Liyuan, China's first lady, underscores this change. Peng has worked on global health and education initiatives, and in 2012 she joined with Microsoft founder Bill Gates in a widely publicized antismoking campaign in China.

I sense, too, that many people are searching for something more meaningful than getting rich or blindly obeying Party dictates. NGOs are increasing in numbers, and a new breed of Chinese philanthropist is setting up charitable organizations. Religion is practiced more widely and openly than before. There has been a strong revival of interest in Buddhism, Taoism, and Confucianism, and many are embracing traditional Chinese values.

I don't want to overstate the extent of this phenomenon. Many restrictions remain in place. Churches are required to register with the government and are closely watched. Christianity is also growing rapidly—there may be 50 million to 100 million Christians today—especially in underground churches that operate without the official sanction of the state. But government approval can carry onerous conditions: the Chinese Patriotic Catholic Association is not permitted to recognize the authority of the Vatican, which is unacceptable to Rome. Unsanctioned church gatherings are not always tolerated, and there are hard limits on what is allowed. The Falun Gong religious and spiritual group remains harshly proscribed, for example, and the repercussions for crossing the line of what's politically "acceptable" can be severe.

Still, I've seen in my work in conservation tentative stirrings of civil society. It's not the kind of autonomous activity that we know in the West, but it's a step in that direction. Currently, restrictive policies limit the registration and development of nonprofit organizations that are not affiliated with the government, and outdated tax laws and regulations diminish their appeal to potential donors. China's leadership is debating what statutory changes to make. As the country has gotten richer, a growing number of entrepreneurs and businessmen have set up charitable foundations. There are roughly 3,700 private and public charitable foundations in China today; 15 years ago there were 400. The potential for giving is huge; in 2012 Chinese donors gave $13 billion, or under 0.2 percent of GDP, compared with $300 billion, or 2 percent of GDP, in the U.S.

Private funding, and a more accepting Party, have given a boost to nongovernmental organizations. The first environmental NGO, Friends of Nature, was registered in 1994; there were 508 officially registered NGOs with 2,000 full-time employees active in environmental causes in China by 2008. In the U.S. there are 20,000 environmental NGOs with 100,000 full-time employees.

At the same time, there has been a decided chill of late. Some Western NGOs and academic institutions are finding that the Chinese think tanks, universities, and NGOs with which they traditionally worked have become more cautious about collaborating. This newfound hesitancy seems to be related to pressure from an increasingly hardline Communist Party. A number of international NGOs are playing a valuable role in China, and it is hard to imagine that they won't continue to be welcome. But their activities will be watched more closely, and foreign NGOs that the Chinese suspect might have an agenda that conflicts with the Party's won't be allowed in.

China's new philanthropists are a diverse lot. Take Niu Gensheng, who is thought to have established the first private foundation with personal funds. He has irrevocably committed nearly all of his $500 million net worth to it after his death and that of his wife and two children. Niu's personal odyssey is remarkable. Born in 1958, he was sold to a foster family for $8 shortly after birth because his parents were too poor to raise him. He spent much of his childhood in an orphanage. He started out in 1982 as a bottle washer, moved up the ranks, and had accumulated enough capital and contacts by 1999 to launch Mengniu Dairy Company, which shortly became a leading supplier of milk and a top dairy producer in China. He began working with his lawyers in 2002 to design a tax-efficient way to set up a private charity with governance modeled, to the extent possible, after the Rockefeller Foundation. Mengniu Dairy went public in 2004 in Hong Kong. The Lao Niu Foundation has supported about a hundred different projects, for a total of almost $50 million, including a major reforestation project with the Nature Conservancy in Inner Mongolia. Niu is also partnering on a wetlands conservation initiative with the Paulson Institute.

Another of our partners in conservation is Cao Dewang, a philanthropic pioneer and the founder of Fuyao Glass Corporation. Cao told me when I visited Fujian in April 2014 that his philosophy is to "help the Chinese people without regard to self-interest or business interest." Early on he conducted his philanthropy in a gray area because it was not officially allowed. In 2010 he established the Heren Charity Foundation, named for his father, with a donation of 3.5 billion yuan (or roughly $520 million) of Fuyao stock. Since his was the first stock donation to a private foundation, it took three years to get the necessary approvals. Five different ministries published a joint ruling to make this and other similar donations possible in the future. Including this contribution, Cao says his giving now totals almost $1 billion. The Paulson Institute will be partnering with Heren on conservation projects in Fujian, including working with the provincial government to make Wuyishan Mountain a national park.

I have been particularly gratified to see the Nature Conservancy flourish under the leadership of some of the nation's leading entrepreneurs and budding philanthropists. In the late 1990s, when I began my work in China with TNC, it was supported primarily by U.S. and overseas Chinese donors. The organization has now formed its own board inside China and is funded completely locally. The board envisions a chapter in every Chinese province, and its members frequently visit TNC projects around the world to understand how volunteer leaders helped make them possible. My old Goldman colleague Fred Hu and my friend Edward Tian were instrumental in the establishment of the TNC China Board and served as its founding co-chairmen. The current chairman is Alibaba's Jack Ma.

There is another, darker side of China today—and one that I think is ultimately self-defeating. When it comes to freedom of speech, freedom of the press, and expressions of dissent, Xi Jinping's new administration is proving to be even more restrictive than its predecessor's. The great public square of our time, the Internet, has been walled off, heavily monitored, and routinely censored in China for years. The new leadership has added a stern campaign against "rumor mongering" on social media. For Americans, who take for granted rights of personal expression, this can be disquieting.

After stories began appearing in the Western press in 2012 alleging that certain government leaders' families had amassed fortunes in unseemly ways, the government responded by blocking the websites of the *New York Times* and Bloomberg, which had done the investigative work. When the stories continued, the government came down hard, delaying visa renewals, which could have led to the expulsions of more than two dozen U.S. journalists. But that was nothing compared with the broader crackdown on the Internet and social media, as the government stepped up censorship and monitoring and set out to make examples of certain opinion leaders on weibo—the so-called Big Vs, or verified users with millions of followers. In a fiery August 2013 speech, Xi directed the Party to maintain "a strong army to seize the ground of new media." Detentions and arrests followed, according to public reports.

The government has long held a formal monopoly on information, a major pillar of its political power. Domestic media outlets have, with rare, brave exceptions, shown little editorial independence; even those that are not explicitly owned or informally affiliated with the state generally engage in a protective self-censorship. The advent of the Internet threatened that stranglehold on information, and the leadership, predictably, tried to control it. Beginning more than a decade ago, it erected the so-called Great Firewall of China, using blocks and filters to prevent unfettered access to thousands of Internet sites throughout the world. Popular Western services like Twitter, Facebook, and YouTube have been banned; others, like Google, have withdrawn from the country altogether. Scaling the wall to obtain unsanitized information is possible but inconvenient, and many Chinese don't bother to try, even as they have become the world's heaviest Internet users, with some 618 million online by year-end 2013. The government employs swarms of cybercops to patrol the Web and social media, tracking trending topics, and monitoring and censoring content. In 2013 the *South China Morning Post*, citing a report in the *Beijing News*, said the government paid 2 million people to act as "Internet opinion analysts," a term that can embrace censors, fake commentators, and other monitors.

The government worries that the opinions of commentators and online activists can be viewed and spread rapidly. Some celebrity bloggers have tens of millions of followers, while the *People's Daily*, the official organ of the Party, has a circulation of just 3 million to 4 million. Coupled to the public's distrust of official news sources, social media can become a threat to the state's ability to influence and shape the national narrative. Nonetheless, the government seems to allow people to post with a fair degree of freedom in areas that are not political, though it's not always clear where the line is drawn. Commentary directed against the government or Party or its leaders will likely draw scrutiny, but so, too, do many efforts to assemble even small groups. In a study published in *Science* magazine in 2014 by Harvard University, researchers indicated that Chinese censors were more likely, for example, to delete discussions of mass protests and other forms of collective actions than posts that criticized senior leaders and the government for their policies. Allowing the latter could be seen as a way to get a read on popular opinion.

Technological advances like social media have concerned China's leaders for some time. The first microblogs, known in Chinese as weibo, were shut down by the government just two years after being launched in 2007. Two years later weibo started back up, and their popularity exploded, with Sina and Tencent the most dominant operators. Described as a cross between Twitter and Facebook, weibo allow people to upload and update information in 140-character blocks, attach music and videos, and post comments, among other things. Posts can go viral and spread rapidly among registered users, who numbered more than 600 million by year-end 2013.

The July 2011 collision of two bullet trains near Wenzhou, Zhejiang, that killed more than 40 people demonstrated weibo's power. Passengers on the trains reportedly broke the news with real-time posts to their weibo accounts. Live tweeting of the accident took off, and state media outlets quickly picked up the story, citing the microbloggers' posts. As usual, since no official response was forthcoming, the local government was blamed for clumsy stonewalling and the mishandling of rescue and recovery efforts. The incident set off a gale of unsparing accusations via weibo of government corruption, opacity, and lack of accountability. Premier Wen Jiabao personally visited the crash site to assure the public that Beijing would get to the bottom of the problems, but the leadership seemed caught off guard, and the damage to government credibility was done.

Further unsettling China's leaders, the crash occurred just seven months after the start of the Arab Spring, which had demonstrated the power of the new technology to help people organize quickly around important issues. Hu Jintao's government took steps to curtail weibo's reach; among other things, it required users to register their real names with service providers. But weibo and the Internet continued to demonstrate their influence.

Pan Shiyi, the real estate developer and husband of Zhang Xin, my old Goldman colleague, created a stir when he led a campaign to fight air pollution. At the time, he had some 7.4 million followers on Sina Weibo, and Zhang Xin had 6 million or so. (They were up to nearly 26 million in 2014.)

Pan began by posting on his weibo account the PM 2.5 readings from the U.S. Embassy Twitter feed. In November 2011 he asked his followers to vote on whether they thought the government ought to begin releasing its own PM 2.5 data within a year. Zhang Xin later told me that the Beijing environmental bureau complained about Pan's posting the U.S. number, rather than the Chinese government's PM 10 reading, which measures the concentration of larger particles that are less dangerous to health. The Beijing officials reportedly said they couldn't get the PM 2.5 measurements up that quickly. Pan's campaign drew tens of thousands of votes in days, and despite the initial bureaucratic resistance, the city began posting its own PM 2.5 readings on January 21, 2012. The country's senior leaders took a close interest; Pan was invited to advise on pollution, and one year later 73 other cities in China were publishing the data.

That was in the waning days of the Hu Jintao government. Xi Jinping has taken a tougher stance. In August 2013 leading bloggers, including Pan, were called to attend a forum on social responsibility. Later that month Charles Xue, an outspoken Chinese-American venture capitalist with 16 million fans on Sina Weibo, was arrested on charges of soliciting a prostitute. Many China-watchers saw the arrest as aimed at suppressing online dissent. Xue subsequently appeared on television in handcuffs admitting to the charge of solicitation and saying that he had been too casual with some of the information he had posted online. New rules were issued specifying that rumor mongering—defined as rumors viewed more than 5,000 times or forwarded to more than 500 people—could lead to up to three years in jail.

The government's tough-minded clampdown on social media appeared to achieve its intended effect. By the end of 2013, many weibo users had reduced the frequency of their postings, and although there's some disagreement about how to measure levels of activity and their significance, it's generally thought there was less depth of political commentary and news sharing. Some microbloggers migrated to the relative privacy of platforms like Tencent's WeChat app. WeChat is more of a person-to-person messaging and conversation tool than a Twitter-like service where hundreds of thousands of people can see messages within seconds. Although rumors and "sensitive" discussions can be just as active on WeChat, the app was less able to become a "virtual public square" and appeared safer to use—that is, until early August 2014, when the government announced a crackdown on mobile messaging services. The tough new rules banned the use of pseudonyms on public accounts and forbade account holders from posting or reposting political news unless they had licenses to do so.

China's leaders are clear-eyed about the complex economic and social challenges they face and know it will take great determination and political skill to advance their agenda. But the risks of moving too slowly or doing too little outweigh those of doing too much or going too fast. China's future, after all, is not in its hands alone. There is no benign global central planner, and the outlook for growth today is nowhere near as favorable as it was in the first 30 years of Reform and Opening Up, when the world enjoyed, on balance, a relatively high level of peace, prosperity, and stability.

Xi Jinping and Li Keqiang know this only too well: they took power just five years after the global financial crisis exposed the flaws in China's growth model. No country can defy the laws of economic gravity forever, and China inevitably will have to contend with some form of economic crisis. At the same time, China's stunning success has fed rising expectations among its people that will be increasingly difficult to meet. Xi's reform agenda is meant to give China the tools it needs to govern better, but it will take years for that to happen. What if, in the meantime, the bottom falls out of the economy, job creation slows, and people lose even more faith in the Party? A rising tide may lift all boats, but a receding tide raises voices and, sometimes, clenched fists.

Could a severe and prolonged economic downturn threaten the Party's hold on power? Some in the West think so, though I am not convinced that this is the case. In the U.S. our market economy's self-correcting mechanisms have, in all but a few instances, forced us to recognize losses, write off bad debts, and address problems before the damage spread. Even in a perfect storm like 2008, the strength of our legal and regulatory systems and the checks and balances in our democracy worked with built-in safety nets and emergency support from government and not-for-profit organizations to serve as shock absorbers that cushioned social stress and unrest. It's true that because China lacks such backstops, a decline to even 3 or 4 percent growth could prove more painful than even negative growth in developed Western economies. But China has deep financial pockets and decisive leaders who are burdened by few constraints on their ability to act quickly.

At the same time, Xi Jinping is moving in two directions that are not easily reconciled. He is attempting to radically transform the growth model of a dynamic economy before it goes off the rails, while simultaneously tightening the screws on social and political activities. He appears to be making headway in advancing economic and social reforms and in modernizing the government. But clamping down on freedom of expression runs a longer-term risk. Success in the kind of innovation-rich economy to which China aspires is driven by the spark of human ingenuity, and that thrives on free and open exchanges. The most competitive countries encourage their people to think outside the box. They don't box their people in.

Indeed, what it takes for an individual to reach his or her full potential in a market-driven economy is fundamentally at odds with an authoritarian government. You can't run a successful business and be disconnected from the world. You need to understand your customers, your competition, and all of the factors that influence your markets—political, regulatory, and economic. You need unfettered access to all information. And in a modern economy it's hard to be connected to the free flow of information in one part of your life and disconnected from it in another.

I don't believe it is sustainable for people to be encouraged to express their views on a variety of economic and business topics, but forbidden to do so publicly or in an organized fashion on many other issues. Nor is it sustainable long term for people to be encouraged to seek out the best business practices or ideas on economic reform throughout the world, yet be prevented from being open to new ideas, or to advocate for change, in other areas of their lives.

It is only natural for people to want to preserve things of value that they've built through hard work—whether it's their business, their home, or their quality of life. They will naturally employ the same skills they used to succeed in business. They will seek out relevant information, and if it isn't available, they will demand it. Is the air safe to breathe? Is the water safe to drink? They will advocate for their ideas. They will want their voices to be heard.

As people satisfy their material needs, their expectations grow. Inevitably, they want a greater say in how they are governed. The desire for freedom, for life, liberty, and the pursuit of happiness, is, I think, universal and inherent in mankind and not simply the expression of the wishes of a few thousand white men mostly of English descent who happened to found the United States more than 200 years ago. So the bargain the Chinese Communist Party made—prosperity for stability—must be recalibrated once people take that prosperity for granted.

I am not saying that China, which is such a different country, with such a different history and culture from ours, must have the same political system that we do. The U.S., after all, has evolved in a great many ways since our founding. Just so, change will come for the Chinese. Today they may be more concerned with immediate problems like clean air and water, safe food, and corrupt officials. But over time they will surely want greater personal freedom, social justice, and eventually, political participation.

Chinese leaders are pragmatic, and they closely monitor public sentiment in their efforts to maintain stability. Reforming their political system, making it more open and inclusive, is the best way to ensure that stability. Undertaking political change will be risky, but postponing it too long will eventually pose even greater risks for China and the world. In the long run, for China's great successes to be sustainable, economic freedom and prosperity must inevitably bring with them greater personal and political liberties.

CHAPTER TWENTY

The Way Forward

One crisp day in early March 2014, I found myself sitting in a sleek conference room high above Boston Harbor taking questions from a group of financial executives. These men and women worked for a range of institutions that managed well over $3 trillion of financial assets, including the personal savings and pension funds of millions of Americans. They were keen to learn as much as they could about the Chinese economy. Was it about to hit the wall? Was I worried about a real estate bubble? How fragile was the country's financial system? Was the government serious about dealing with China's environmental problems? One fellow had a more personal question for me.

"Hank," he said. "You're a real patriot. Why are you helping China?"

The question pulled me up short. Three years before, when I first began planning to write this book, I don't think I would have been asked anything like that at a meeting of sophisticated financiers. They would have accepted that helping China to reform its economy, open its markets, protect its environment, and improve the quality of life of its people—all things I have been working on—would bring economic and strategic benefits to the U.S. as well. But that viewpoint has been changing as China has emerged as our biggest, most formidable economic competitor since the end of World War II and has started flexing its newfound military muscle in unsettling ways. As a result, many Americans, from all walks of life, have begun to view China with growing apprehension and resentment. Some would now prefer confrontation to cooperation.

I understand these sentiments. Partly they are a function of China's choices and actions, and partly they are born of frustration with the recent economic troubles of the United States. I've spent a fair number of pages explaining how China must carry out meaningful economic reforms if it expects to continue its amazing success story. These arguments make sense for China and its people. But why should an American care? Why should we root for China to succeed? Shouldn't we instead be hoping that this ungainly giant stumbles, if only to slow down its daunting economic and military growth? In coming years China's weight and influence in the world, already substantial, is likely to begin to rival our own. Why take the chance now of helping the Chinese deal with so many of their problems and challenges? Why aid a competitor?

The answer is simple: we should do so because it is more than ever in America's own self-interest that we do. To begin with, just about every major global challenge we face—from economic and environmental issues to food and energy security to nuclear proliferation and terrorism—will be easier to solve if the world's two most important economic powers can act in complementary ways. But these challenges will be almost impossible to address if the U.S. and China work at cross-purposes.

If we want to benefit from an expanding global economy, we need the most dynamic growth engines, like China's, to thrive. If we want to prevent the worst climate change outcomes and to preserve our fragile global ecosystems, we need China to solve its massive environmental problems at home and adopt better practices abroad. If we want to keep diseases from our shores, we need China and other countries to use the very best methods to prevent and halt epidemics. If we want to stem the spread of dangerous weapons to those who might harm our citizens, we need nations, including China, to work together to end illicit trafficking.

If we want all these things to happen, we must be proactive, frank, and at times forceful with the Chinese while seeking ways to cooperate, to develop complementary policies, and to work to more fully integrate them into a rules-based global order. If we attempt to exclude, ignore, or weaken China, we limit our ability to influence choices made by its leaders and risk turning the worst-case scenarios of China skeptics into a self-fulfilling reality.

At the same time, we have a real interest in seeing China do well economically, and we should want to benefit from its successes, just as it does from ours. China is America's fastest-growing export market; problems there will only hurt our companies, and our workers, and cost us jobs. Today, when all of the world's major economies are grappling with difficult structural issues, the need for stable growth can't be overstressed. Any significant economic problems in China—with its extensive linkages to other countries—will disproportionately hurt global growth.

Despite its successes and the fears of many in the U.S., China is not an unstoppable powerhouse that has invented a better economic model and will soon take over the world. Quite the contrary. Its economic system is sorely in need of a major overhaul and has few imitators. Its political system has none. Exaggerating China's strength is at least as big a risk as underestimating its potential. Either can lead to irrational responses and mistakes in the way we deal with China.

I don't say cooperation will be easy. In fact, I can guarantee that for many years to come it will only become harder. A newly confident China is here to stay, and Chinese nationalism cannot simply be wished away. As a proud China grows stronger, it will become more assertive in pursuit of what it perceives to be its interests. We can't know how these interests may change, only that they may increasingly diverge from our own. So we need to be strong, clear-eyed, and forthright in articulating our core principles to the Chinese and in sticking to them.

Since Deng Xiaoping began his transformative economic reforms in 1978, China's top leaders have maintained that the country's prosperity depends on a peaceful international environment. I see few reasons that the pursuit of peace and stability abroad should not continue to be the preferred strategy to complement China's economic and social progress at home. The Chinese are students of history, and they know that rising nations have almost always come to blows with status quo powers. If President Xi Jinping and his fellow leaders seek what they call a "new model of great power relations" with the U.S., it is because they want to be treated like a major power while avoiding conflict as they continue to modernize and grow their economy.

Xi put the case simply in July 2014. "My concern is mainly reform and related issues," he told me. "To enjoy a good environment for development in China, we also need a good external environment. So our path will be a peaceful one."

This does not mean, however, that China will not assert its interests boldly, and in ways that we may think unwise. President Xi knows every great power has fielded a strong military, and he is determined to modernize his country's armed forces. But China's foremost task is retooling its economy for the long run. Xi knows he must keep China's relationship with the U.S. on an even keel, because our cooperation, and that of the rest of the Western world, remains crucial to the success of this difficult challenge. As such, we retain great leverage; we can be helpful and exert our influence. As I explained to my colleagues in the Cabinet when we set up the Strategic Economic Dialogue, if we got the economic issues right, it would make other pressing matters easier to manage.

The Chinese may stand as our most imposing global competitors, but we of all people should not fear nor shrink from competition. We should embrace it wholeheartedly. For centuries, competition has made us stronger. Americans excel most in the face of a genuine challenge. Competition is the essence of the free market—the superior idea, product, service, or provider should win out. But the contest must be fair, the rules clear and agreed upon, and the referees impartial and consistent.

Nor does competition have to be a zero-sum game. We can find ways for both sides to advance their interests. At times, our conflicting aims will demand direct communication and skillful management to keep us on a steady course. At other times, common interests will create opportunities for us to work together or in complementary ways for our mutual advantage. The mix of cooperation and competition will be guided by decisions our leaders make, not least those that will determine our strength long into the future. I have little patience for fatalists who believe that America is in terminal decline or for triumphalists who don't recognize that the world has changed and that we must continue to adapt. We can't afford to rest on our laurels. We need to adopt domestic policies that respond to the economic and social challenges we face at home—from sky-high debt levels to widening income inequality. Given the changing international scene, we need to relentlessly prioritize so we don't dissipate our resources by wasting them where we don't have an important strategic interest or where we do not have a clear plan and the ability to achieve our objectives.

We can assume that China will do whatever it must in its own self-interest to continue to prosper and grow stronger. We should do the same. Our leaders must demonstrate the self-confidence to cooperate and compromise without the fear of looking weak and to take tough stands where they need to.

Before our rapprochement in 1972, China and the United States were implacable Cold War enemies that had fought face-to-face in Korea and indirectly in Vietnam. President Richard Nixon and his then national security adviser, Henry Kissinger, deftly took advantage of China's even greater mistrust of a common foe, the Soviet Union, to build a strategic relationship. The "three joint communiqués" subsequently agreed to by the U.S. and China normalized relations between our countries, established an important part of the U.S. framework for dealing with Beijing on the sensitive issue of Taiwan, and laid the principles for our diplomatic relationship ever since.

An implicit understanding took root over time, based on a mutual recognition that China's success was good for both countries. We supported China's development, while it aligned with us against the Soviet Union and undertook its unprecedented economic Reform and Opening Up. Through eight administrations, Republican and Democratic, the U.S. worked ever more closely with Beijing. We reaped the benefits of low-cost imports, and China made a fortune catering to Americans' seemingly bottomless appetite for consumer goods. China provided a ready source of capital, financing huge amounts of our debt and helping to keep interest rates and inflation low.

Washington's relations with Beijing had no shortage of critics, although the general consensus held that a positive relationship with China was, ultimately, good for America and for ordinary Americans. But as China's dynamic, rapidly growing economy has increasingly challenged our own, that consensus has begun to change. For many in the U.S., this shift was caused by a sense that we had been taken advantage of. Problems that were tolerated when China was smaller and less consequential—a reflexive protectionism that walled off much foreign investment, requirements that foreign companies invest through joint ventures, and demands that technology be transferred as a cost of entry—became increasingly unacceptable as China's state-owned companies grew profitable and began to compete in global markets while still receiving anticompetitive subsidies and favorable regulation.

China's success stung all the more when our economy began to reel after the global financial crisis. Popular opinion soured on both sides. A Pew Research Global Attitudes Project survey released in mid-2013 showed that Americans' approval of China had plunged 14 percentage points to 37 percent in two years. Meanwhile, negative attitudes toward the U.S. among the Chinese had climbed to 53 percent, a seven-point increase. Politicians in both countries played to these negative feelings. China-bashing became a popular American campaign tool. Chinese nationalists urged Beijing to challenge the U.S.-dominated regional order in Asia. The urge to cooperate turned into calls on both sides to confront.

Doing so, however, would be self-defeating for both sides. Americans have gained much from our country's relationship with China and stand to benefit even more if we can find new ways to work constructively with the Chinese and they with us. The country's new leaders have restarted the process of market reform. They have outlined steps to promote their private sector, open more of the economy to foreign investment, and liberalize capital markets with the aim of moving toward a market-based currency and, eventually, an open capital account. These moves will benefit China—and they will open opportunities for American farmers, workers, and businesses.

What of the complaints Americans have about China? Some, like charges of rampant intellectual property theft, are legitimate, and we should be firm and determined in pursuing remedies. Other issues, like job losses and the amount of our debt China owns, are complicated, often distorted, and based, in part, on bad math and misunderstandings of basic economics.

Americans have suffered terrible job losses in recent years. It's a problem that concerns me greatly, but the bulk of these losses come not from out-sourcing to China so much as from disruptive technological advances in automation, computing, and robotics that are making many jobs obsolete, hollowing out our middle class, and leading to increased income disparities. Regardless of how quickly the economy rebounds, we will have to deal with this troubling trend as a country. The workplace of tomorrow, from factory floor to office cubicle, will look very different from today's. This same technological transformation is affecting all major economies, including China's.

As of November 2014 the Chinese held almost $1.3 trillion, or about 10 percent, of our publicly held debt. This worries some people, but their fears are misplaced. We should be worried about the sheer size of our debt, not who our creditors are. In any case, America's biggest creditor is its own citizenry—in the form of the Federal Reserve, which owns a little less than $2.5 trillion of Treasury securities. The fact that the Chinese buy and hold U.S. debt benefits us, as their demand for our paper helps lower our funding costs. Nearly one-quarter of their foreign exchange reserves are in Treasuries, which the Chinese buy because it makes sense to own the world's safest, most liquid securities. The Chinese have been responsible investors, as I saw firsthand during the financial crisis, when they refused to panic and held their securities, despite fears about the value of their investments.

Many of the benefits we receive from our relationship with China are tied to the very thing many Americans decry the most: trade. Although the balance of trade remains overwhelmingly in China's favor, our exports are growing more rapidly than our imports. China is our second largest trading partner and our fastest-growing and third-largest export market after Canada and Mexico. In the decade between China's 2001 entry into the WTO and 2011, U.S. exports to China more than quintupled, to $104 billion. China's appetite for our goods has stayed consistently strong: in 2009, in the wake of the financial crisis, total U.S. exports fell by more than 18 percent, while exports to China dipped by less than one-half of 1 percent. In general, we export high-value-added products—machinery, aircraft, electronics, chemicals, and food—that support well-paying jobs here at home.

As U.S. investment in China has risen, so has Chinese investment in the United States, doubling to $14 billion from 2012 to 2013 as Chinese companies took stakes in, among other things, U.S. energy, agribusiness, and real estate. The amount is small compared with that of countries like Australia, Japan, and Canada, and piddling compared with what Chinese firms are capable of—and would like to do. Cross-border investment between our two countries has the potential to be an even more powerful and unifying force than trade. Americans abhor ownership of U.S. companies by any government, including our own, so there will always be some resistance to a Chinese state-owned firm acquiring a healthy American company. But investments that save or create jobs are more politically acceptable. That's particularly true if they are made by a private sector company or in the acquisition of a failing U.S. company or through a greenfield, or start-up, operation.

Wanxiang Group, China's largest auto parts maker, is one Chinese company that has made welcome inroads in the U.S. Founded in 1969 as a bicycle and tractor repair shop in Zhejiang Province by a budding entrepreneur named Lu Guanqiu and some friends, Wanxiang now has $23.5 billion in annual revenues and some 12,500 employees, just under half of whom are in the U.S., where the company owns 28 manufacturing plants in 14 states. My friend Lu was among the private sector business leaders with whom I shared dinner my first day in China as Treasury secretary in 2006.

Wanxiang's Illinois-headquartered U.S. operations are run by Lu's son-in-law, Ni Pin, a neighbor of mine, whose youngest child will start in the fall of 2015 at my alma mater, Barrington High School. Ni's two oldest children have already graduated from there; one is at the University of Chicago, the other at Northwestern University. "America is our new home," Ni told me. "And we're going to build an important business here."

In the early 1990s Ni dropped out of the University of Kentucky's Ph.D. program in economics at the behest of his father-in-law and used his teaching assistant's stipend to get Wanxiang started in the U.S. after the company had been unable to secure Chinese government approval to transfer funds here. Wanxiang acquired small U.S. auto parts suppliers and increased investments in clean energy technologies, flying under the radar until 2013, when it bought most of the assets of bankrupt battery maker A123 Systems. Some U.S. lawmakers opposed the deal, fearing the company's advanced lithium-ion battery technology might be put to military use and decrying the fact that a Chinese firm was the recipient of U.S. government subsidies. But Wanxiang won official government approval. The company made more headlines in 2014, when it dipped into bankruptcy waters again to buy Fisker Automotive, makers of the first premium hybrid electric car.

I bumped into Ni Pin in July 2014 on a flight to Detroit, where I was scheduled to hold a public forum with Michigan governor Rick Snyder about the advantages to his state of Chinese and other foreign investment. As it happened, Ni Pin and his father-in-law had an appointment with Snyder for the next day to discuss expanding operations in Michigan. Wanxiang had approved an additional $200 million investment for its battery business, a significant portion of which was earmarked for that state.

The appeal of cross-border investment to U.S. governors is clear: jobs and growth. Wanxiang figures it saved 3,500 American jobs between 2007 and 2009, buying up struggling auto parts companies. It rehired the 857 employees of A123 post bankruptcy and was looking to hire more in Michigan. The Chinese company aimed to get Fisker relaunched by late 2015 and planned to move production back to the U.S. from Finland. Altogether, Wanxiang employs about 5,500 in its U.S. automotive businesses, up from 3,000 in 2012. By 2020 it projects it might have 10,000 employees in the U.S.

State and city government leaders are on the front lines working with companies on job creation. As Governor Scott Walker of Wisconsin told me at a Paulson Institute–sponsored discussion of investment among a group of Great Lakes governors in April 2014, "We're a state of small businesses, and many, like those in our furniture industry, have been decimated by competition from China. What we need is a strategic effort to help those businesses. China is an important market for their growth, so maybe Chinese investment can be part of the solution." The Paulson Institute, through a program headed by vice chairman Evan Feigenbaum, is working with Midwestern governors to identify opportunities and investment models in sectors like agribusiness and manufacturing where Chinese capital can be leveraged with the know-how and ability to sell products in China.

For decades China was too weak or too focused on domestic problems to pursue large-scale foreign adventures. Today, with a $10 trillion economy and an imposing presence on Asian and world stages, Chinese leaders are less content to bide their time in asserting their national interest. They have built up their naval and air forces and are more willing to project their newfound power—as shown by recent territorial disputes in the East China Sea and South China Sea with our allies Japan and the Philippines. Tough talk and action are broadly popular with the Chinese public and with the Party elite.

China's muscle flexing is a dangerous phenomenon that has complicated its relations with the U.S., our Asian allies, and other countries in the region and has given more credence to the arguments of confrontationists. These territorial disputes have long and convoluted histories, and none will be easy to resolve. China's fraught relations with Japan are the most troubling. Their mutually antagonistic feelings persist 70 years after the end of World War II and make economic and political coordination much more difficult in the region. They contribute to an unhealthy dynamic as China and Japan compete to make economic and security inroads with South Korea. Meanwhile, the U.S. is trying to facilitate a strategic relationship between our allies South Korea and Japan, which have their own historical and territorial disputes.

In the most likely case, the intensity of these disputes will ebb and flow. I support U.S. policy, which is not to choose sides on the underlying merits of competing claims of sovereignty but to stand firm on such long-standing principles as freedom of navigation—for example, in the South China Sea. We should oppose the use or threat of force or other forms of coercion to settle these disputes. Such behavior would only contribute to a debilitating cycle of provocation and response that could all too easily spin out of control. All Asian countries have a lot to lose if they take their eyes off their common interests in trade, investment, and economic growth.

I believe China's objectives continue to be stability and economic development. You can't have one without the other, and both depend, ultimately, on Beijing's finding ways to ensure workable relations with its neighbors. Despite China's recent assertiveness, it is clearly not in its interest to actively seek out conflict. Deliberately seeking conflict, especially with the United States, would be stupid, and Chinese leaders did not bring their country to where it is today by being stupid. Nonetheless, they are running the risk of jeopardizing their economic interests through a military or security conflict in the region.

For their part, China's leaders believe they live in a tough neighborhood. China abuts four major powers with which it has fought wars, skirmishes, or proxy battles over the past 75 years: Japan, India, Russia, and the U.S., through our forward-deployed military presence. China has fought smaller neighbors, including Vietnam and South Korea, and it shares borders with the unstable nuclear powers of North Korea and Pakistan. Over its far western border lies Afghanistan, where instability may grow as the U.S. continues to withdraw its forces and reduces its commitment. China mistrusts the military bases and alliances that the U.S. maintains around its periphery and especially dislikes the fact that U.S. ships and aircraft operate and engage in surveillance nearby. Given all this, Americans should have no illusions that over the next decade we will face not just an assertive and nationalistic China but a more potent and capable one, fielding a modern and much larger navy, advanced weaponry, and sophisticated cyberwarfare capabilities and seeking to make its presence felt more broadly in Asia and beyond.

We need to figure out how to deal with this new force. To begin with, the U.S. must continue to invest in a state-of-the-art military capable of projecting power and bolstering deterrence. With the near certainty that budget constraints will be an ongoing reality, we must be disciplined about our defense spending, eliminating nonessential programs so that we can afford to maintain our position as the dominant military power. But to prevent security tensions from riding our relationship off the rails, it is more important than ever that we deepen our economic interactions. We should encourage other countries to do the same. The more economically interdependent China and Japan become, for example, the higher the costs of conflict will be for both countries.

It is important that we let the Chinese know how much we welcome their playing a bigger role in international governance. At the same time, we need to convince them that with increased international stature comes a greater responsibility to act in the broadest public interest. Global leaders need to be mindful of the rights and interests of other nations—regardless of their relative power.

Russia's annexation of Crimea in March 2014 and its subsequent efforts to destabilize eastern Ukraine remind us of the dangers of taking the status quo for granted and underscore the importance of strengthening U.S.-China relations. We certainly wouldn't want to face a united China-Russia strategic front that could frustrate American interests. Now, I don't think four decades of goodwill and close cooperation between the U.S. and China are about to be tossed on the ash heap of history. Nonetheless, 50 years after their dramatic rift, China's relationship with Russia is back on a stable track, buoyed by a growing bilateral trade relationship, a common mistrust of American power, and a shared embrace of a "multipolar" world that leads both countries to periodically take positions and actions at odds with our foreign policy.

Russian adventurism has been a gift to the Chinese. At a minimum it distracts U.S. policymakers by reviving European security issues that most had thought settled, tests our resolve and that of our NATO allies for the first time in more than a generation, complicates our so-called pivot to Asia, and stretches already strained resources. Faced with post-Crimea sanctions from the West, Russian leader Vladimir Putin is seeking to build even tighter links with China. In 2014 his regime struck two major long-term agreements to supply natural gas to Beijing on terms that were advantageous to the Chinese because of Russia's relative weakness. The two countries also announced their intention to pursue closer bilateral military cooperation, including joint naval exercises in the Pacific. The potential for Russian arms sales to China is another concern. Many Chinese admire Putin and respect his show of strength in annexing Crimea and in exposing the apparent weakness of the West to resist him. Nonetheless, the Chinese are long-term thinkers and aren't about to get dragged into unnecessary disputes with the U.S. and certainly not on behalf of a weaker Russia.

One fraught area where the U.S. and China must work together is cyberspace, which is vital to our economic and national security. As much as the world has benefited from becoming increasingly open and digitized, it has become that much more vulnerable to catastrophic attacks on global institutions and infrastructure like power grids, air traffic control systems, banks, water supplies, and national defense systems. But there are few rules or protocols governing behavior in cyberspace and no global enforcement mechanisms. This mix of excessive risk and minimal safeguards cries out for attention.

Concerning China, two key issues stand out for the U.S. One is a national security concern about cyber-war-making capabilities. It is only logical to expect China and other nations to develop offensive and defensive capabilities, just as we are doing. At a minimum, the U.S., China, and other major nations need to reach an agreement that imposes some restraints—perhaps through an updating of the Geneva Conventions—to protect civilian populations from the devastation that could accompany the use of cyber weapons on essential services and infrastructure. And we have a compelling interest to work with China to prevent cyberattacks from terrorist groups or rogue regimes.

The second issue is the pilfering of American companies' secrets. Just about every U.S. CEO of a global company that I know has told me of a Chinese-originated attempt—often successful—to breach his or her company's computer system. In one comically inept hack that I know of, data from a U.S. military contractor wound up in the files of a U.S. entertainment company. Companies don't want to discuss these attacks; they shun bad publicity and fear damage to shareholder value. An exception came in early August 2014 when Community Health Systems, a large hospital operation based in Franklin, Tennessee, claimed that personal data, including Social Security numbers, was stolen from 4.5 million people by hackers working out of China. U.S. companies also don't generally know much about the Chinese perpetrators. Some activity may simply be rogue behavior originating in a nation that has trouble enforcing its own laws. But there is evidence that a number of hackers have state sponsorship.

Corporate cybertheft is the most contentious and potentially destructive economic issue we face with the Chinese. It undermines our economic security, gives credence to the sense that China does not play fair, and makes it difficult to find common ground. The U.S. case against China has been set back by revelations from Edward Snowden, the fugitive former National Security Agency contractor who released top secret information detailing the U.S.'s most sensitive cyberespionage and counterterrorism programs. Among other things, Snowden revealed that the U.S. government had used U.S. technology companies—some wittingly and others not—to engage in espionage, collecting information about China and Chinese companies. The disclosures have made it more difficult for those companies in China and made it harder for the U.S. to claim the moral high ground. That said, I've heard of no evidence of U.S. companies stealing Chinese intellectual property on their own or with the help of the U.S. government. Moreover, a foreign government or concern gathering intelligence or trade secrets from U.S. companies for commercial use is different from governments spying on one another, which is a common practice. Nonetheless, the distinction between cyberespionage and cybertheft from a company for commercial use can become fuzzy.

The Snowden debacle and the massive breaching of corporate computer systems worldwide are a clear wake-up call. No nation has more to lose from corporate cybertheft than the U.S., and we need to protect ourselves. The attack on Sony Pictures Entertainment in November 2014 allegedly by the government of North Korea in an attempt to prevent the release of an unflattering movie about its leader, Kim Jong-un, certainly highlighted this threat. It is my hope that this will serve as an impetus to design tactical responses to thwart or mislead hackers, and devise better laws and enforcement. Major U.S. companies have to harden their systems to protect security and should have to report immediately to a government cybersecurity center when they are under attack. We need laws requiring them to do both.

Our government must work diligently on a multilateral basis with other major countries to establish norms and enforcement mechanisms for protecting commercial enterprises from cybertheft. This is a tall order but essential for the smooth functioning of an increasingly integrated global economic system. As we gain traction with other countries on corporate cybertheft, it should be easier to get China on board.

We should also look for ways to apply behind-the-scenes pressure by using carrots or sticks to induce China to begin working toward solutions, but here there are no easy answers. The May 2014 indictments returned by a federal grand jury in Pennsylvania against five officials of China's People's Liberation Army for computer hacking and economic espionage was an attempt to do just that. But I have my doubts about the effort. The Chinese officials won't be coming to the U.S. to stand trial, and it is not clear that the Justice Department action will have succeeded in doing anything other than making things more difficult for some U.S. companies operating in China.

Chinese president Xi Jinping likes to say that the most important bilateral relationship his country has is the one with the United States. But nothing in my conversations with him suggests that Xi confuses "important" with "easy." Or with "static." Quite the opposite, in fact.

"To keep our bilateral relationship moving in the right direction will be complex," he told me during a lengthy discussion we had in July 2014 in the Great Hall of the People. "The intensity of these differences [between our countries] will fluctuate over time, but the differences themselves will be with us for a long time. At the same time, I also believe that our mutual linkages and shared interests far outnumber our differences."

He went on to note: "There has been a pattern of suspicion leading to fear, which in turn leads to hostility. This is the kind of logic we need to prevent. We need to identify where our common interests lie."

This is easier said than done. Despite all of America's efforts to assist China's progress and to welcome it into the global economic system, many Chinese suspect that we now want to contain or thwart their rise. There is also a growing suspicion on the part of Americans that someday China might become our enemy. There is no quick remedy to this gap in understanding, because trust must be built slowly by better communication and successful cooperation.

Improving relations with the U.S. has been a long-standing focus for Xi. More than two years before our July 2014 meeting, I recall him zeroing in on this topic at a dinner he hosted for a small group of former U.S. policymakers in a private room at the Washington Marriott Wardman Park hotel during a visit to the U.S. It was February 2012, and he was vice president of China and expected to succeed Hu Jintao as Party leader in the fall. Relaxed, straightforward, and self-confident, he directed a lively give-and-take with a group that included former secretaries of State Madeleine Albright and Henry Kissinger; former national security advisers Zbigniew Brzezinski, Brent Scowcroft, and Sandy Berger; and my former Cabinet colleague and Labor secretary Elaine Chao. Xi said it was critical to find innovative, out-of-the-box approaches to improve the U.S.-China relationship as our countries and the world changed. He emphasized that it would require courage, or as he termed it, "pioneering spirit," to take actions in our mutual interest that nonetheless might prove unpopular in both countries.

The substance of China's U.S. policy under Xi hasn't changed, but the tone has become more strikingly nationalistic, with its full-throated endorsement of a "Chinese dream." Xi wants us to respect his nation's accomplishments, understand its challenges, and deal with it as an equal. For us, too, that is the best way to build a stable and strong bilateral relationship, as long as we hold firm to our core principles and China lives up to its international responsibilities in a rules-based order.

China is a relative newcomer on the contemporary international stage. As it grows and prospers, it naturally aspires to play a greater role in shaping global norms and governance rather than simply accepting rules written years ago by Western nations without China's involvement. The fact that the Chinese have not been very specific about what they want to change is a source of frustration to the U.S. but gives room to both sides to work out our differences. This would be more difficult to do if the Chinese had publicly locked themselves into proposals or policies that differed significantly from those we believe are best.

"We are ready to shoulder and uphold our international responsibilities commensurate with our capacity," Xi assured me in July 2014.

Our two countries often disagree on exactly what China's capacity is. We point to the strength of the Chinese economy; they poor-mouth their achievements by noting how far they still have to go to alleviate poverty. But we shouldn't let such disagreements spoil opportunities to make whatever changes are possible. We must push China to improve its respect for established international norms as much as we reasonably can, but we should not let our profound disagreements in areas where we don't like their choices scuttle our entire relationship. We're long past the point of being able to cut China loose.

The most likely and best reasonable case is for China to seek to adapt international rules to suit its national interest and not try to create a rival international system or throw the existing rules and institutions overboard. Beijing has done very well inside the global economic and governance system that was largely shaped by America after World War II. But we should have no illusions that China will simply accept this system in its exact form forever. Indeed, China has been testing alternatives. One example is the high-profile launch in July 2014 of the New Development Bank by China and the four other so-called BRICS countries, Brazil, Russia, India, and South Africa. Informally known as the BRICS Bank, the new organization will have authorized capital of $100 billion; it will be headquartered in Shanghai and will fund infrastructure projects in the developing world. China also pledged $41 billion to a separate $100 billion reserve contingency fund that will be available to support countries with short-term liquidity or balance of payments pressures.

The initiative comes as a response to the tardiness of reforms in areas like voting power and quota shares at institutions like the World Bank and IMF. China has been eager to increase its ownership and influence in the traditional development banks, but existing shareholders have been reluctant to decrease their stakes. The U.S. should take the lead in helping the institutions of the international system adapt to the arrival of big new players like China while retaining the stability the world counts on. We want China in the room, not outside. It's hard to communicate, much less cooperate, through closed doors.

The best way to ensure healthy competition is to find ways to turn shared interests into shared successes. Small or incremental steps, if they are concrete, can help build trust. Our countries might work jointly on humanitarian missions in the developing world or on a major environmental initiative, such as a project to generate renewable electric power in Africa. The more we promote understanding between our citizens, fashion economic and cultural linkages, and increase our interdependence—through cross-investment, tourism, academic collaboration, and educational, athletic, and cultural exchanges—the more incentive we have to avoid destructive conflicts. Much is being done below the national level: universities are partnering with Chinese institutions of higher learning, as Harvard Business School has done with Tsinghua University. U.S. mayors and governors are opening up to job-creating direct investments, perhaps the most enduring of economic links.

The U.S. and China should look for ways to build trust, transparency, and working relationships between our militaries, which are deeply suspicious of each other. We war-game conflict and view each other's actions as threatening. Talks between the two sides have proved mostly symbolic and empty. But our armed forces can build bridges by working together, and with other nations, to provide, say, disaster relief or to combat narcotics trafficking. There's more room for cooperation on "soft security" issues, where our interests clearly coincide. China is the world's number one ocean trader and shipper of seaborne cargo. Joint antipiracy operations, building on recent efforts in the Gulf of Aden, won't solve our big security differences, but they will give us some shared operational experience and a sense of common purpose.

The following are a few principles the U.S. should keep in mind in managing our relationship with China.

1. Help Those Who Help Ourselves

When the U.S. advances a constructive, affirmative economic agenda and negotiates hard for greater market liberalization and openness to competition, we help reformers, led by President Xi Jinping, achieve their economic goals—to China's benefit and our own. Today's Chinese leaders seek to use outside pressure to force domestic change: China rejoined negotiations for a Bilateral Investment Treaty with the U.S. in 2013 in part to accelerate the stalled process of reform. A successful BIT would require the Chinese to open up many more sectors of their economy to our companies. Doing so would help China shift its economy toward consumer-led growth. We would benefit from our strengths in financial services, telecommunications, accounting, health care, and consulting as those sectors opened to competition in China's vast and rapidly growing market. A successful BIT would almost certainly lead to greater Chinese investment in the U.S. and create more jobs. To this end, the Paulson Institute is partnering with the U.S.-China Business Council; the Development Reform Research Center of the State Council, a government think tank; and Goldman Sachs to provide technical training for BIT negotiations and to rally the Chinese and U.S. business sectors as well as U.S. mayors and governors in support of a "high standards" agreement.

2. Shine a Light: Nothing Good Happens in the Dark

Supporting reform in China means pushing for greater transparency and improved adherence to universal standards in the widest possible range of products and systems. Transparency is the best way to fight corruption and to strengthen the confidence of Chinese citizens—and foreign companies and investors—in their government and in the rule of law. We should encourage the Chinese to disseminate reliable, accurate information across the board—from air and water quality data and the enforcement of environmental regulations to property sales and the finances of local governments.

We should push for complementary standards—from health care to industrial products—to ensure the smooth functioning of a global economic system that relies on ever more integrated networks. Too frequently, China and other countries have promoted local standards, ostensibly on grounds of national security, but really to mask protectionism. Chinese officials have long resisted common standards in telecommunications, for example, to prop up domestic telecom companies, shortchanging the public in the process.

Cyberespionage tensions have unfortunately given added momentum to initiatives by countries to require that data collected on people and companies be stored and processed only on local servers. Balkanization of the Internet impairs the flow of cross-border data that is the lifeblood of the global economy and essential to the smooth functioning of so many industrial and service businesses. This is why the U.S. is seeking in the Trans-Pacific Partnership and in other agreements to fashion rules prohibiting data localization requirements.

3. Speak with One Voice

We need to define, prioritize, and coordinate our many issues to speak to the Chinese with one voice. Before I became Treasury secretary, the U.S. had scores of separate dialogues going with China. There was a heck of a lot of talk, but not enough was getting done. We devised the Strategic Economic Dialogue to engage China on short- and long-term matters across the government and at the right levels. This arrangement allowed us to deliver a clear, consistent message to those with direct responsibility for a particular economic issue as well as to the many others who would inevitably be involved in making any decision. It also ensured that all relevant ministries, departments, and agencies on both sides participated in the discussion and implementation of agreements.

The SED structure placed one person in charge on each side. I acted not as Treasury secretary but as President Bush's designee to coordinate discussions of a broad range of domestic and global economic issues. My counterparts, Wu Yi and then Wang Qishan, wielded authority to deal with these same issues in the context of the U.S.-China relationship. This structure enabled us to reach agreements outside all of our formal portfolios.

The Obama administration repositioned the SED as the Strategic *and* Economic Dialogue to include foreign policy and national security concerns. But the expanded scope of the dialogue, while a benefit, can complicate communication and coordination and make getting things done more difficult. Today our side is headed by Jacob Lew at Treasury and John Kerry at State. Their Chinese counterparts are Vice Premier Wang Yang and State Councilor Yang Jiechi. All four are very capable individuals, but the Chinese decision-making process functions best with one senior person in charge so that clear direction from the top can help forge consensus below. And without one go-to person for the U.S., the Chinese often wonder who speaks for our president. I can't count the number of times since leaving government that I have been asked by Chinese officials who President Obama is relying on to manage the China relationship or who the right person to talk to about a given issue is. The S&ED structure would work even better if each country designated one person to lead its side. In the U.S. that person should probably be the vice president; in China it could be the premier.

4. Find China a Better Seat at the Table

As the world's preeminent power, the U.S. must take the lead on many issues, or no other country will step in. But we can do a better job of matching means to ends—prioritizing objectives, building alliances, and picking our battles more carefully. We should want China to play a bigger, more responsible leadership role in international groups like the World Trade Organization and in supporting the global economic system that it has benefited so much from. China should act as a leader and embrace higher standards: opening its markets and reducing its greenhouse gas emissions, for example. We differ with China on just how big and how responsible its role should be. We think China's sheer size and scale—whether measured by GDP, trade, or carbon emissions—should help determine its responsibilities. China takes the view that it remains a poor country, with a low GDP per capita, and therefore deserves more leeway.

We should be pragmatic and prepared to make concessions or compromises to encourage the Chinese to take a more prominent role. This was the Bush administration's approach. In November 2008 President Bush convened world leaders to deal with the financial crisis. The severity of the challenge required the participation of more than just the developed nations of the G8. We knew that if China agreed to work with us, other developing nations would, too. We faced opposition from traditional G8 powers, but China was eager to sign on, and other countries followed: the G20 provided important support during the crisis and has become the preeminent forum for consultation and cooperation on the world's economic system.

Similarly, we overcame objections to prepare the groundwork for China to join the Inter-American Development Bank as a donor country in 2009—15 years after China had first expressed interest. Joining gave China greater legitimacy in Latin America, and I believe that having China work with the region's biggest multilateral development bank will encourage its companies to observe more stringent social and environmental safeguards in a region vital to U.S. interests.

5. Demonstrate Economic Leadership Abroad

China is steadily building linkages via trade and investment throughout the world, betting that these will increase its influence as it pursues its economic security and foreign policy ambitions. The U.S. government must step up its game and compete with China from a position of strength. We should reassert our status as a Pacific power, reinforcing our long-standing economic ties with countries in that region. Closer to home, we should build on the success of the North American Free Trade Agreement to work with reform-minded governments like those of Mexico, Colombia, Chile, and Peru to free up trade, create greater economic integration, and enhance regional stability. All except Colombia are among the 12 nations currently negotiating the Trans-Pacific Partnership (TPP) trade pact.

Nothing will get Beijing's attention and cooperation more than progress on the TPP; its appeal to Pacific Rim countries is one reason the Chinese have warmed to the prospect of negotiating a Bilateral Investment Treaty with the U.S. The TPP agreements will be difficult to complete unless the U.S. makes them a top priority on which the president is prepared to expend domestic political capital. I would hope China will one day seek to become a member of the pact, with its ambitious high standards for trade, investment, and environmental protection. China is more likely to make the reforms necessary to join the TPP when it recognizes the danger of being excluded from it.

In recent years, China has taken the initiative in the developing world, making deep investments in sub-Saharan Africa, among other areas. African countries want us to be more than a donor of aid—they want our capital and know-how. We should promote policies that make it easy for our businesses to provide both. Unlike China, our government doesn't sponsor or back the building and financing of infrastructure abroad; many developing countries want this, so it is important that the U.S. government support the multilateral development banks that finance infrastructure. We should be willing to provide them with more funding as well as creative ideas to leverage this money with private sources from the U.S. so that our multinational companies can contribute more fully to building infrastructure with the highest environmental standards and best business practices. At the same time, we should not reflexively oppose China's efforts to lead a new multinational initiative such as the fledgling Asian Infrastructure Investment Bank. We should accept the invitation to work with the bank, press for the adoption of high standards, and encourage the multilateral banks to do the same. We should also look to partner with China on some major projects in the developing world.

6. Find More Ways to Say Yes

Rather than trying to persuade the Chinese to adopt our approach to everything, we might be better off devising new policies together—or recasting older policies in new, fresh terms. The U.S. and China don't always need to do things jointly, just in mutually beneficial ways. The U.S. cannot "fix" China's growth model any more than the Chinese can "fix" our fiscal problems. But separate U.S. and Chinese efforts to reform and rebalance our respective economies would put the two countries on a more complementary footing.

The most fruitful negotiations in the SED came after we found innovative ways to collaborate on solutions to shared problems. During the scare over tainted Chinese food products in 2007, then health and human services secretary Mike Leavitt negotiated to get U.S. food safety inspectors in China by allowing the Chinese to put their own in the U.S. Mike's solution gave the Chinese a face-saving win that enabled them to continue exporting goods while helping protect our citizens from unsafe food. The Chinese were also able to improve their own inspection process by learning firsthand how we do things.

We should apply this approach to other areas. As the world's biggest users of energy and emitters of carbon, the U.S. and China ought to work to eliminate global trade barriers and tariffs on all environmental goods and services and collaborate on the next generation of clean energy products. The U.S. EPA could help the Chinese Ministry of Environmental Protection clean up China's dirty air. I also favor setting up a joint U.S.-China fund to commercialize next-generation technology in such areas as carbon capture and sequestration and energy storage.

7. Avoid Surprises but Be Alert for Breakthroughs

The Chinese are famous for rigorous scholarship. True to that heritage, they do their homework. Mao Zedong once called Deng Xiaoping a walking encyclopedia, according to Ezra Vogel's magisterial biography of Deng.

I can't recall a single Chinese business executive or government leader right up to the top who didn't come to meetings thoroughly prepared. They expect no less from us.

Combining thorough preparation with a consensus-driven system of decision making leaves the Chinese more uncomfortable than most with last-minute changes or operating on the fly, particularly in areas that involve difficult or complex issues or clear differences. And this impedes reaching a deal. It makes sense not only to avoid surprises in negotiations but also to cooperate on contingency planning for events beyond our control that could put us at odds with each other. North Korea is a case in point. We share some positions but disagree fundamentally on others. Neither country is happy that Pyongyang has nuclear weapons. Its erratic and belligerent behavior frustrates and angers the Chinese. But it's hard to imagine that Chinese strategists are enthused about the prospects of a reunited Korea allied to America with our troops stationed across from China's northeastern border. We, on the other hand, have a security treaty with South Korea and a strategic interest in its strong and stable democracy. A contingency planning discussion about North Korea that could minimize the likelihood of conflict and provide a road map for stability on the Korean peninsula would have the added virtue of building trust between the U.S. and China.

At the same time, we should always be on the lookout for openings or potential paradigm-shifting events that could lead to a breakthrough in our relations. The key is to be opportunistic, creative, and unafraid to float new ideas or to grasp unanticipated opportunities, as the Bush administration did during the financial crisis in shifting the center of global economic discussions from the G8 to the G20.

8. Act in Ways That Reflect Chinese Realities

Facts, not wishes or dreams, should direct our dealings. China is very different from the U.S., and we cannot be guided only by the understandable desire that it become more like us. We need to know as much as possible about what is going on inside China and be self-confident and realistic enough to focus on what is doable.

The diffuse, behind-the-scenes decision making of a one-party state coupled with low transparency and a lack of ordinary press freedoms makes China particularly opaque. Many of the country's leaders, like Wang Qishan, have made a study of the U.S., and some have even gone to school here—as have any number of the children of the elite. Many speak English. In general, we lack a similar familiarity with China. There are plenty of China policy wonks in the U.S., but one needs to find advisers who know what can realistically be achieved and who are nimble enough to jump on openings when political pressures, priorities, or public sentiments shift.

I have been fortunate to work with superb colleagues who truly understand China. Knowing that Chinese citizens were increasingly angry about environmental damage and that the government wanted to improve energy efficiency helped my team anticipate that China would be receptive to a proposal for the Ten-Year Framework for Cooperation on Energy and Environment, which we signed in 2008. The Obama administration similarly capitalized on China's growing environmental concerns to reach its landmark agreement on climate change with China in 2014. That agreement was closed thanks to some excellent work outside the formal S&ED structure by John Podesta, counselor to the president, as well as through the involvement of President Obama himself on the margins of the Asia-Pacific Economic Cooperation meeting in November 2014 in Beijing.

The simple truth is we will deal most effectively with China—and other nations—from strength, not weakness. For most of the post–World War II period, our strength and resolve were never in question. This is no longer the case. While the U.S. economy remains the biggest, most innovative on earth, we face two critical, defining challenges to our continued preeminence: our long-term fiscal situation is unsustainable, and our growth rate has been persistently anemic, exacerbating wealth and income disparities in our society. In the past decade we have seen just one year with a real GDP increase greater than 3 percent. We need to grow much faster to solve our fiscal problems and to create more and better-paying jobs.

Debt is our number one enemy. Our national debt now stands at just over $18 trillion, or $56,000 for every single American citizen. But when it comes to devising solutions, our government has proven to be dysfunctional, when it is not feckless. We need to make policy changes to restore our economic competitiveness or we will be far less able to lead from strength or by example. What nation will look to us as a model worth emulating? What nation will feel compelled to deal with us on our terms? I saw this up close when our economy was on the brink during the 2008 financial crisis: my views on reform didn't carry the same weight with Beijing that they once had. It is difficult to argue for market liberalization when our financial system is in disarray and our economic house is out of order.

We must restore fiscal sanity to the way we manage our affairs—and soon. The longer we delay, the greater the reckoning will be. We need to do this while maintaining a strong military presence globally. This is a difficult, complex challenge, but we must meet it: there is no historical example of a nation that ignored its fiscal difficulties and was able to maintain its status as a global power for long. In the final analysis, our self-induced weakness is more of a problem for us than is China's rise. We must take the long view and work to reinvigorate our economic prowess. We will advance our cause further and faster when we are once again comfortable projecting strength economically, militarily, and diplomatically. At the risk of sounding utterly simplistic, once we have dealt with our own problems, we will find it far easier to deal with China.

Acknowledgments

I'm glad that I didn't know at the outset that the task of writing a book about my work in China over the past two decades would prove to be such a difficult and arduous task. Had I suspected as much, I might not have written it. Fortunately, I had lots of help from many former colleagues at Goldman Sachs and at the U.S. Department of Treasury—as well as from my current colleagues at the Paulson Institute—in reconstructing events and reviewing all or parts of the manuscript for accuracy. A number of my colleagues kept and retained notes and journals—some quite comprehensive. I owe a big thank-you to Jinqing Cai, Jinyong Cai, Jiayi Chai, Chris Cole, Henry Cornell, Tim Dattels, Eileen Dillon, Mike Evans, Evan Feigenbaum, Fang Fenglei, Carol Fox, Tom Gibian, Brian Griffiths, Ben Herst, Dominic Ho, Al Holmer, Fred Hu, Eugene Huang, Liz Kolshak, Cherry Li, Jim Loi, Liu Erh Fei, Martin Lau, Deborah Lehr, Dave Loevinger, Damien Ma, Bob Moseley, Rose Niu, Jason Pau, Dan Price, John Rogers, Taiya Smith, Houze Song, Steve Shafran, John Thornton, Byron Trott, Moses Tsang, Lindsay Valdeon, Hsueh-ming Wang, Peter Wheeler, Tracy Wolstencroft, Dan Wright, Jenny Xu, Yang Jianmin, Yang Shaolin, Hugo Yon, Zheng Quan, Zhu Guangyao, and Ziwang Xu.

My talented executive assistant, Lisa Castro, has labored long hours keeping track of our many drafts and doing something no one else has been able to do so well—read the chicken scratch that I call penmanship, which she does quickly, accurately, and with equanimity.

I am most grateful for the privilege of working for President George W. Bush, for his support in establishing the Strategic Economic Dialogue and for my work in China, and for our recent conversations about China. I deeply appreciate the gracious assistance of former Chinese premier Zhu Rongji, who made available to me his notes from some of our meetings.

Many old and new Chinese friends gave their time generously, including Liu Chuanzi of Lenovo Group and John Zhao of Hony Capital; Zhang Xin and Pan Shiyi of Soho Group; Edward Tian, founder and chairman of China Broadband Capital Partners and former vice chairman and CEO of China Netcom; Cao Dewang of Fuyou Glass; Ni Pin of Wanxiang America (my neighbor in Barrington, Illinois), and his father-in-law, Lu Guanqiu of Wanxiang Group; Zhang Yue of Broad Air; Niu Gensheng of Mengniu Dairy; Jack Ma of Alibaba; and Ma Huateng (Pony Ma), co-founder of Tencent. Numerous other businessmen in China, as well as Party and government officials, generously gave me their time and patience and opened doors throughout the country.

I am particularly fortunate that I was able to persuade Michael Carroll, who collaborated with me in writing *On the Brink*, to jump into the swamp with me again to take on this project. Mike understands economic issues, has a long history of writing about them, and has learned how to work with me, which is no small feat. His insatiable intellectual curiosity led him to immerse himself in learning about China. His penchant for meticulous detail, his discipline, and his ability to organize were invaluable, as was his knack for maintaining the narrative drive in the context of complex big picture themes.

I also very much appreciate the long hours Emma Ashburn devoted to this book over an almost three-year period traveling with me, attending meetings and taking notes, and working closely with Mike Carroll to support him as a researcher and assemble the relevant facts and events of my long China career. Once again, Mike brought with him a superb team of contributors, including Riva Atlas, Will Blythe, Monica Boyer, Ruth Hamel, and Deborah McClellan. Deborah's editorial and organizational skills proved to be indispensable, to say the least.

I am also very fortunate to have an attorney, Robert Barnett of Williams and Connolly, whom I have relied on for his wise counsel since leaving government, and to have had two editors, John Brodie and Sean Desmond at Hachette, who provided clear, incisive advice.

My wife, Wendy, keeps a lively journal, and her insights and observations on our trips to China have been very helpful. A huge thanks to her for enduring my second and—I promise—final book.

Cast of Characters

Chinese Communist Party and Government

Bo Xilai: Communist Party secretary, Chongqing (2007–2012); minister of Commerce (2004–2007)

Deng Xiaoping: Paramount leader, People's Republic of China (late 1970s–1990s)

Hu Jintao: General secretary, Communist Party of China (2002–2012); president, People's Republic of China (2003–2013)

Huang Ju: Executive vice premier, People's Republic of China (2003–2007)

Huang Qifan: Mayor, Chongqing (from 2009)

Jiang Jiemin: Director, State-owned Assets Supervision and Administration Commission (2013); chairman, PetroChina Company (2007–2013) and China National Petroleum Corporation (2006–2013)

Jiang Zemin: General secretary, Communist Party of China (1989–2002); president, People's Republic of China (1993–2003)

Jin Renqing: Minister of Finance (2003–2007)

Li Keqiang: Premier, People's Republic of China (from 2013)

Li Peng: Premier, People's Republic of China (1988–1998)

Li Yuanchao: Vice president, People's Republic of China (from 2013); head, Organization Department of the Communist Party of China (2007–2012)

Liu He: Director, Office of the Central Leading Group for Financial and Economic Affairs, Communist Party of China (from 2013)

Liu Mingkang: Chairman, China Banking Regulatory Commission (2003–2011); chairman and president, Bank of China (2000–2003)

Lou Jiwei: Minister of Finance (from 2013); chairman and CEO, China Investment Corporation (2007–2013)

Mao Zedong: Chairman, Communist Party of China, and paramount leader, People's Republic of China (1949–1976)

Tung Chee-hwa (C. H. Tung): Vice chairman, Chinese People's Political Consultative Conference National Committee (from 2005); chief executive, Hong Kong Special Administrative Region (1997–2005)

Wang Qishan: Secretary, Central Commission for Discipline Inspection of the Communist Party of China (from 2012); vice premier, People's Republic of China (2008–2013)

Wang Yang: Vice premier, People's Republic of China (from 2013); Communist Party secretary, Guangdong (2007–2012)

Wen Jiabao: Premier, People's Republic of China (2003–2013)

Wu Bangguo: Chairman, National People's Congress (2003–2013)

Wu Jichuan: Minister of Information Industry (1998–2003); minister of Posts and Telecommunications (1993–1998)

Wu Yi: Vice premier, People's Republic of China (2003–2008)

Xi Jinping: General secretary, Communist Party of China (from 2012); president, People's Republic of China (from 2013)

Xiao Gang: Chairman, China Securities Regulatory Commission (from 2013); chairman, Bank of China (2003–2013)

Yang Jiechi: State councilor, People's Republic of China (from 2013); Foreign minister (2007–2013)

Zeng Peiyan: Chairman, China Center for International Economic Exchanges (from 2008); vice premier, People's Republic of China (2003–2008)

Zhou Wenzhong: Secretary general, Boao Forum for Asia (from 2010); ambassador of the People's Republic of China to the U.S. (2005–2010)

Zhou Xiaochuan: Governor, People's Bank of China (from 2002); chairman, China Securities Regulatory Commission (2000–2002)

Zhou Yongkang: Secretary, Politics and Law Commission of the Communist Party of China (2007–2012); Minister of Public Security (2002–2007)

Zhu Rongji: Premier, People's Republic of China (1998–2003); executive vice premier (1993–1998)

U.S. Government

Max Baucus: Ambassador to the People's Republic of China (from 2014); senator from Montana (1978–2014)

Ben Bernanke: Chairman of the Federal Reserve Board (2006–2014)

George W. Bush: 43rd president of the United States (2001–2009)

Barney Frank: Representative from Massachusetts (1981–2013)

Robert Gates: Secretary of Defense (2006–2011)

Timothy Geithner: Secretary of the Treasury (2009–2013)

Lindsey Graham: Senator from South Carolina (from 2003)

Charles Grassley: Senator from Iowa (from 1981)

Carlos Gutierrez: Secretary of Commerce (2005–2009)

Stephen Hadley: National security advisor (2005–2009)

Alan Holmer: Special envoy for China and the Strategic Economic Dialogue, U.S. Treasury (2007–2009)

Jacob Lew: Secretary of the Treasury (from 2013)

Barack Obama: 44th president of the United States (from 2009)

Clark "Sandy" Randt: Ambassador to the People's Republic of China (2001–2009)

Condoleezza Rice: Secretary of State (2005–2009); national security advisor (2001–2005)

Charles Schumer: Senator from New York (from 1999)

International Banking and Business

John Browne: CEO, BP (1995–2007)

Jinyong Cai: CEO, International Finance Corporation, World Bank (from 2012); CEO, Goldman Sachs Gao Hua Securities Company (2008–2012)

Cao Dewang: Founder and chairman, Fuyao Glass Corporation (from 1987)

J. Michael Evans: Vice chairman, Goldman Sachs Group, and chairman, Goldman Sachs (Asia) (2004–2013)

Fang Fenglei: Co-founding partner and chairman, Hopu Investment Management Corporation (from 2008); chairman, Goldman Sachs Gao Hua Securities Company (2004–2007)

Fu Chengyu: Chairman, China Petroleum and Chemical Corporation (from 2011); president, China National Offshore Oil Corporation (2003–2011)

Brian Griffiths: Vice chairman, Goldman Sachs International (from 1991)

Fred Hu: Founder and chairman, Primavera Capital Group (from 2010); chief China economist and chairman of the greater China group, Goldman Sachs Group (1997–2010)

Jiang Jianqing: Chairman, Industrial and Commercial Bank of China (from 2005), president (2000–2005)

Martin Lau: President, Tencent Holdings (from 2006); executive director, Asia investment banking division, and COO, Asia telecommunications, media, and technology group, Goldman Sachs Group (1998–2005)

Li Ka-shing (K. S. Li): Founder, Cheung Kong (Holdings) Limited (from 1971), and chairman, Hutchison Whampoa (from 1981)

Cherry Li: Director general of the research center, China Securities Regulatory Commission (2002–2006); chief representative, Beijing office, Goldman Sachs (from 1993)

Liu Chuanzhi: Founding chairman, Lenovo Group and Legend Holdings Corporation (from 1984)

Liu Erh Fei: Co-founder, Cindat Capital Management Limited (from 2013); head of China investment banking, Goldman Sachs Group (1992–1994)

Andrew Liveris: Chairman, president, and CEO, Dow Chemical Company (from 2006)

Lu Guanqiu: Co-founding chairman, Wanxiang Group Corporation (from 1969)

Ma Fucai: President, China National Petroleum Corporation (1998–2004); chairman of PetroChina Company (1999–2004)

Ma Huateng: Founder, chairman, and CEO, Tencent (from 1998)

Jack Ma: Founder and CEO, Alibaba (from 1999)

John Mack: Chairman, Morgan Stanley (2005–2012), CEO (2005–2010)

Ni Pin: President, Wanxiang America Corporation (from 1993)

Niu Gensheng: Founder, chairman, Mengniu Dairy Company (1999–2011)

John Rogers: Chief of staff, Goldman Sachs Group (from 2001)

Steven Shafran: CEO, AMRI Financial (from 2011); senior adviser to
the secretary of the Treasury (2008–2009); co-head, Asian principal
investing business, Goldman Sachs (1986–2001)

Peter Sutherland: Chairman, Goldman Sachs International (from 1995)

John Thornton: Chairman, Barrick Gold Corporation (from 2014);
professor and director of global leadership program, Tsinghua
University School of Economics and Management (from 2003);
president and co-COO, Goldman Sachs Group (1999–2003)

Moses Tsang: Chairman, AP Capital Holdings (from 2010); chairman,
Goldman Sachs (Asia) (1989–1994)

Hsueh-ming Wang: Chairman, BlackRock China (from 2013); managing
director, investment banking (China), Goldman Sachs (1994–2010)

Tracy Wolstencroft: CEO, Heidrick & Struggles (from 2014); head, public
sector and infrastructure banking group, Goldman Sachs (2006–2010)

Zhang Yue: Co-founder and chairman, Broad Group (from 1988)

Ziwang Xu: Founding chairman, CXC Capital (from 2008); head of China
investment banking, Goldman Sachs Group (1997–2005)

Nongovernmental Organizations, Academia, and Civil Society

Kim Clark: Dean, Harvard Business School (1995–2005)

Evan Feigenbaum: Vice chairman, Paulson Institute (from 2011)

Carol Fox: Director of Asia-Pacific program development, the Nature
Conservancy (1986–2002)

Deborah Lehr: Vice chairman, Paulson Institute (from 2011)

Warren McFarlan: Professor, Harvard Business School (from 1973)

Rose Niu: Director of conservation programs, Paulson Institute (from 2013); head of the China country program, the Nature Conservancy (1998–2010)

Wendy Paulson: Chairman, Bobolink Foundation

Taiya Smith: Senior adviser, Paulson Institute (from 2011); deputy chief of staff, U.S. Treasury, and coordinator, U.S.-China Strategic Economic Dialogue (2006–2009)

Yang Jianli: Founder and president, Initiatives for China (from 2008)

Zhao Chunjun: Dean, Tsinghua University School of Economics and Management (2001–2005), deputy dean (1987–2001)

List of Acronyms

Acronym	Full Name
ABC	Agricultural Bank of China
AMC	asset management company
BIT	Bilateral Investment Treaty
BOC	Bank of China
BOC (HK)	Bank of China (Hong Kong)
BoCom	Bank of Communications
BRICS	Brazil, Russia, India, China, South Africa
CBRC	China Banking Regulatory Commission
CCB	China Construction Bank
CCIEE	China Center for International Economic Exchanges
CELAP	China Executive Leadership Academy Pudong
CIC	China Investment Corporation
CICC	China International Capital Corporation
CNOOC	China National Offshore Oil Corporation
CNPC	China National Petroleum Corporation
CPC	Communist Party of China
CSRC	China Securities Regulatory Commission
FTZ	free-trade zone
G7	Group of Seven nations
G8	Group of Eight nations
G20	Group of Twenty nations
GDE	Guangdong Enterprises (Holdings)
GDI	Guangdong Investment Limited
GDP	gross domestic product

GITIC	Guangdong International Trust and Investment Corporation
GSE	government-sponsored enterprise
ICBC	Industrial and Commercial Bank of China
IMF	International Monetary Fund
IPO	initial public offering
ITIC	international trust and investment corporation
JV	joint venture
MEP	Ministry of Environmental Protection
MOF	Ministry of Finance
MPT	Ministry of Posts and Telecommunications
NDRC	National Development and Reform Commission
NGO	nongovernmental organization
NPC	National People's Congress
NPL	nonperforming loan
NYSE	New York Stock Exchange
PBOC	People's Bank of China
PLA	People's Liberation Army
PM	particulate matter
PRC	People's Republic of China
SAFE	State Administration of Foreign Exchange
SAR	special administrative region
SARS	severe acute respiratory syndrome
SASAC	State-owned Assets Supervision and Administration Commission
SDPC	State Development and Planning Commission
SEC	Securities and Exchange Commission
SED	Strategic Economic Dialogue
S&ED	Strategic and Economic Dialogue
SEM	School of Economics and Management at Tsinghua University
SEPA	State Environmental Protection Administration

SEZ	special economic zone
SOE	state-owned enterprise
TNC	The Nature Conservancy
TPP	Trans-Pacific Partnership
WTO	World Trade Organization

Index

A
Adams, Tim, 178
Agricultural Bank of China (ABC),
    137–139
Albright, Madeleine, 393
Alibaba Group Holding, 337, 344–345,
    370
  Alipay, 337
American International Group (AIG), 110,
    253
Arab Spring, 373
AXA, 110

B
Baidu, 337, 345
Bain & Company, 269
banking in China
  and asset management companies
      (AMC), 140–141, 163–167,
      206–212
  and banking sector restructuring,
      138–147
  and corporatization and capital
      restructuring reforms, 39, 139–140
banking institutions. see also banking
      institutions in China; Goldman
      Sachs
  Barings, 39
  Deutsche Bank, 171, 324
  Inter-American Development Bank,
      202
  Jardine Fleming, 39
  Lehman Brothers, 242
  Merrill Lynch, 39, 171, 253
  Morgan Stanley, 5, 8, 39, 45–47, 68, 71,
      77, 141, 143, 241, 253–256
  Peregrine Investments, 39

  Schroders, 39
  Wardley of HBSC, 39
  Wells Fargo & Company, 335
banking institutions in China. see also
      Chinese government, Ministry of
      Finance
  Agricultural Bank of China (ABC),
      137–139
  Bank of China (BOC), 91, 96, 99, 110,
      132, 136–153, 155, 159, 164–173,
      184, 261, 324, 344, 358
  Bank of China (Hong Kong) (BOC
      (HK)), 143–153, 160, 169
  Bank of Communications (BoCom),
      168–170
  China Banking Regulatory Commission
      (CBRC), 151, 336–337, 336–338
  China Construction Bank (CCB), 8–9,
      13–14, 45–46, 48, 61, 68, 96, 110,
      137, 140–148, 159, 164, 168–170,
      173, 255
  China International Capital Corporation
      (CICC), 5, 8, 13, 45–49, 53, 56,
      59–61, 68, 73–77, 83–84, 143–145,
      171
  China Investment Corporation (CIC),
      241, 253, 255
  China Merchants Bank, 112, 269
  Industrial and Commercial Bank of
      China (ICBC), 137, 139, 155, 157,
      159, 165–173, 324, 335, 338
  New Development Bank/BRICS Bank,
      394
  People's Construction Bank, 137
Bank of China (BOC), 91, 96, 99, 110,
      132, 136–153, 155, 159, 164–173,
      184, 261, 324, 344, 358

Bank of China (Hong Kong) (BOC (HK)),
143–153, 160, 169
Bank of Communications (BoCom),
168–170
Barings, 39
Barron's, 250
Batson, Andrew, 318–320
Baucus, Max, 202, 223–225, 229, 409
Baucus-Grassley-Schumer-Graham bill,
223–224
Bébéar, Claude, 110
Bechtel, 34
Beijing
Great Hall of the People, 4, 6, 14, 17,
119, 193, 194, 196, 199, 218, 227,
263, 292, 293, 328
ring roads, 26, 293
Tiananmen Square, 3–4, 6, 14, 18, 24,
27, 32, 138, 194, 220, 293, 356
Zhongnanhai, 3–6, 104, 125, 156, 186,
215, 244, 287, 310, 330, 360
Purple Light Pavilion, 6, 63, 278
Beijing Institute of Posts and
Telecommunications, 51
Berger, Sandy, 393
Berlusconi, Silvio, 259
Bernanke, Ben, 198, 200, 230, 249, 271,
409
Bilateral Investment Treaty (BIT),
310–327, 333, 395–396, 399
Billings Gazette, 224
Bo Guagua
son of Bo Xilai, 288
Bo Xilai, 194–195, 407
China National Offshore Oil
Corporation (CNOOC) Unocal
deal, 200–201
Chongqing Party secretary, 9, 283–284,
286–288, 291, 364
Commerce Minister, 194–196, 198, 205
corruption and abuse of power, 288–289,
309, 312, 360
Strategic Economic Dialogues (SED I and
SED II), 198, 209–210
Bobolink Foundation, 304
Bodman, Samuel, 198
Boeing, 17
Bolten, Josh, 257

Borman, Frank, 103
BP Amoco, 72, 76, 78–80, 83, 110, 113
Browne, John, 78–80, 110, 113, 409
Brzezinski, Zbigniew, 393
Bush, George H. W., 66–67, 178
Bush, George W., 178, 180–184, 186–187,
189, 192–197, 201, 203, 211–212,
222–225, 229–230, 234, 236,
238, 245, 255–258, 397–398,
405, 409
Bush, Neil, 66

C
Cai, Jinyong, 77, 79, 409
Cantwell, Maria, 243
Cao Dewang, 22, 369, 409
capitalism in China
"China model" of, xiii, 24, 90–91, 284
corruption and, 23–24, 58, 86
Western ideology of, 130, 355
Carnegie Endowment for International
Peace, 358
Center for Strategic and International
Studies, 358
Central Commission for Discipline
Inspection, 8, 48, 288, 311, 322,
358
Central Committee of the Chinese
Communist Party, 69
Central Military Commission, 353, 355
increase of military, xiv, 18
People's Liberation Army (PLA), 6, 91
Chao, Elaine, 198, 393
Chen Yun, 23
Chiang Kai-shek, 18–19, 286
China. *see also* economy of China
see also Communist Party of China
(CPC)
founding of modern-day, 15
relations with Japan, 387–388
China Banking Regulatory Commission
(CBRC), 151, 336–337, 336–338
China Center for International Economic
Exchanges (CCIEE), 299, 305
China Construction Bank (CCB), 8–9,
13–14, 45–46, 48, 61, 68, 96, 110,
137, 140–148, 159, 164, 168–170,
173, 255

China Executive Leadership Academy Pudong (CELAP), 323–326, 348

China International Capital Corporation (CICC), 5, 8, 13, 45–49, 53, 56, 59–61, 68, 73–77, 83–84, 143–145, 171

China International Trust and Investment Corporation (CITIC), 60, 88, 241

China Investment Corporation (CIC), 241, 253, 255

China Merchants Bank, 269

China National Offshore Oil Corporation (CNOOC), 70, 78, 200. *see also* Sinopec

China National Petroleum Corporation (CNPC), 66–77, 79–85, 104, 188, 323, 360. *see also* Sinopec

China Securities Regulatory Commission (CSRC), 34–36, 40–41, 91, 110, 132, 143, 145, 340

China Telecom, 6–8, 37–38, 43–56, 73–74, 78

China United Telecommunications Corporation (China Unicom), 51, 65

China Venturetech Investment Corporation (CVIC), 34–36

Chinese Constitution, 355

Chinese government. *see* Communist Party of China (CPC)

Chongqing, 9, 215, 283–291, 364

Clark, Kim, 109–110, 411

Clinton, Bill, 81, 169, 212

Clinton, Hillary, 242, 397

Coleman, Norm, 243

Communist Party of China (CPC), 4, 17, 19, 37, 81, 90, 141, 179, 350–377

　Central Commission for Discipline Inspection, 8, 48, 288, 311, 322, 358

　Central Committee of the Communist Party of China, 69

　Central Military Commission, 353, 355
　increase of military, xiv, 18
　People's Liberation Army (PLA), 6, 91

　China Executive Leadership Academy Pudong (CELAP), 323–326, 348

　Chinese Constitution, 355

15th National Congress, 43, 53

Ministry of Commerce, 48

Ministry of Environmental Protection (MEP), 365–366, 400

Ministry of Finance, 136–137, 140–141, 164, 167, 170, 172, 199, 233, 241, 341

Ministry of Posts and Telecommunications, 8, 11–13, 46, 48–56, 59, 64, 70 (*see also* state-owned enterprise (SOE))

National People's Congress (NPC), 365
　Standing Committee, 227–228, 351

Politburo Standing Committee, 8, 106, 292, 328, 359, 366

17th National Congress, 227

Standing Committee of the Chinese Communist Party, 23, 25, 95, 172, 186, 192, 194, 227, 228, 279, 283, 288, 309, 311–312, 351, 352, 359

State Council, 7, 35

State Council's Economic Reform Commission, 40

State Environmental Protection Administration (SEPA), 120, 124–126, 215, 365

State-owned Assets Supervision and Administration Commission (SASAC), 334

Third Plenary Session, 18th Party Central Committee, 328–332, 351, 366

Cornell, Henry, 16–17

Corzine, Jon, 42, 49

cyberespionage, cybertheft and cybersecurity, xii, xv, 389–391, 396
　and Geneva Conventions, 390

D

Dalai Lama, 236

da Silva, Luiz Inácio Lula, 259

Davis, Michele, 232

Deng Xiaoping, 400, 407
　death and legacy, 3–4, 11–12
　economic market "Reform and Opening Up" socialist initiatives, xiii, 3–4, 10–12, 18–24, 39, 43, 69, 86, 168, 275, 328, 343, 354, 357, 380

Deng Xiaoping, (*cont.*)
  "one country, two systems," 4, 145, 158
  Paramount leader, People's Republic of
    China, 3–4
  Southern Tour, 24, 41, 92, 356
  special economic zones (SEZs), 21, 356
Deutsche Bank, 171, 324
Deutsche Telekom IPO, 10–11, 49–50,
    53, 57
Directorate General of
    Telecommunications. *see* state-owned
    enterprise (SOE), China Telecom
Dodd, Chris, 224
Dow Jones Industrial Average, 62, 135, 226

E

economy of China, 328–349. *see also*
    capitalism in China; Strategic
    Economic Dialogue (SED)
  agricultural farming reforms, 3, 19–21,
    48, 275, 354
  downturn of, 23–25, 270, 315–318, 375
  gross domestic product (GDP), xiii, 3–4,
    18–19, 21, 25, 43, 77–78, 136,
    139–140, 162, 214, 241–243,
    269–270, 285, 302, 338, 343,
    358, 368, 398, 402, 413
  modern banking and capital markets,
    40, 191
  private sector and, 343–349
  "Reform and Opening Up" socialist
    initiatives, 3–4, 11–12, 18, 21–22,
    39, 328–332
  rise as superpower, xi–xv
  state banks and, 335–337
  and state-owned enterprise (SOE)
    reforms/initial public offerings
    (IPOs), 323–339
  urban industrial reform, 20–21, 43
environment
  State Environmental Protection
    Administration (SEPA), 120,
    124–126, 215, 365
Esquel Group, 110
Evans, J. Michael, 5, 7, 13, 15, 54, 57,
    60–64, 66, 71, 79, 84, 132–133,
    135, 150, 159–161, 171, 184, 410
Exxon, 72

F

Fang Fenglei
  Bank of China (Hong Kong)
    restructuring, 145
  China International Capital Corporation
    (CICC) CEO, 47–49
  China Telecom IPO deal, 51, 53, 56–57,
    63, 68
Feigenbaum, Evan, 386, 411
15th National Congress, 43, 53
Financial Times, 313, 359
Fisher, George, 110
Fok, Canning, 30
Forbes, 343
Fosun Group, 181
Fox, Carol, 116–117, 120–121, 126, 411
Frank, Barney, 220–221, 409
Free Trade Zone (FTZ), 342–343
Fromer, Kevin, 224
Fu Chengyu, 85, 321, 325, 409
Fujian Province, 21–22, 86, 88, 149, 179,
    321, 328
Fuld, Richard, 242
Fung, Victor, 110, 112, 122
Fuyao Glass Corporation, 22, 369–370

G

Galvin, Chris, 110
Gates, Robert, 236–237, 409
Geithner, Timothy, 271, 311, 397, 409
General Electric, 17
General Motors, 22, 260
Germany, 11, 39, 49–50, 167, 227, 314.
    see also Deutsche Telekom IPO
Gibian, Tom, 34
Goldman Sachs, 7, 39–40. *see also* Paulson,
    Henry M., Jr.
  China International Capital Corporation
    (CICC) and Bank of China (Hong
    Kong) (BOC (HK)) IPO, 5–15,
    46–51
  and China National Petroleum
    Corporation (CNPC) IPO, 70–85
  and China Telecom IPO, 43–58, 59–65
  and Guangdong Enterprises Holdings
    (GDE) and Guangdong International
    Trust and Investment Corporation
    (GITIC), 86–90, 92–103

and Hong Kong, 16–17, 21, 25–28, 29–34, 39–42, 57–65
and Industrial and Commercial Bank of China (ICBC) and Bank of China (BOC) IPO, 145–153, 157–172
initial public offering (IPO), 105–106, 120, 157, 160, 345
Goodnight Moon (Brown), 249
Gorbachev, Mikhail, 357
government-sponsored enterprise (GSE), 246–252, 254
Fannie Mae and Freddie Mac, 221, 226, 231, 244, 246
Graham, Lindsey, 189, 192, 197, 202, 223, 409
Grassley, Chuck, 202, 223, 409
Greenberg, Hank, 110
Greenpeace, 297
Griffiths, Brian, 10, 32, 37–38, 107, 410
Group of Eight nations (G8), 258, 398–401
Group of Seven nations (G7), 227, 230, 257
Group of Twenty nations (G20), 230, 257–263, 398–401
Brazil, Russia, India, China, and South Africa (BRICS), 227, 394
Gu Kailai, 195, 288–289
Guangdong, 27, 86–88, 92
Shenzen, 27, 90, 123, 356
Guangdong Enterprises Holdings (GDE), 86–88, 92–104
Guangdong International Trust and Investment Corporation (GITIC), 87, 92–93, 97–99, 101
Guangdong Investment (GDI), 102
Guangdong Province, 24, 33, 41, 55, 80, 88–103
Shenzhen, 21, 27
Guo Guangchang, 181
Gutierrez, Carlos, 186–187, 198, 200, 409

H
Hadley, Stephen, 187–188, 237, 255, 257, 409
Hangzhou Wahaha Group, 22–23, 181
Harvard Business School, 105–106, 107, 109–110, 220, 395
Heren Charity Foundation, 370
Holmer, Alan, 210, 224, 242, 409

Hong Kong
and Bank of China (Hong Kong) (BOC (HK)), 132–135, 143–153, 159–160, 169, 172
British rule and July 1, 1997, handover, 4, 29, 45, 57–58
cooperation with Shenzen, 303–304
and Goldman Sachs, 16–17, 21, 25–28, 29–36, 39–42, 57–65
investor requirements, 83–85
and market crisis/stability, 58–65, 97, 100–104
"one country, two systems," 4–5, 12
Reform and Opening Up, 11–12
Special Administrative Region, 12
special economic zone (SEZ), 21, 88–89
Hormats, Bob, 52
House of Cards, 289
Hu, Fred, 107–108, 111, 155, 157–160, 171–172, 184, 370, 410
Hu Jintao, xii, 24–25, 36, 106, 172, 178, 181–182, 187–189, 192–196, 227–228, 241, 259, 273, 277–279, 289, 309, 312, 317, 353, 362, 373, 392, 407
G20, 259–260
Party secretary of the Tibet Autonomous Region, 353
Hu Yaobang
reformist general secretary, 24, 179, 356
Huang Ju, 156, 163, 171–172, 192–193, 407
Huang Nubo, 346
Huang Qifan, 284, 288, 407
Hubbard, Al, 178
Huntsman, Jon, 288
hutong, 26, 292–293

I
IBM, 17, 346
Idei, Nobuyuki, 110
Industrial and Commercial Bank of China (ICBC), 155
Inter-American Development Bank, 202
International Monetary Fund (IMF), 59, 158, 169, 225, 245–246, 257, 338, 394. *see also* World Bank

International Trust and Investment
    Corporation (ITIC), 34, 88–89,
    92, 97–98

J
Jacobs, Irwin, 110
James, Henry, 26
Jardine Fleming, 39
Jiang Jianqing, 155, 157, 158, 164–167, 170,
    324, 410
Jiang Jiemin, 74, 84, 104, 359–360, 407
Jiang Zemin, xii, 4, 7, 17–18, 43, 172, 272,
    407
    "assets equal liabilities plus equity," 17,
      313, 328
    general secretary of the Communist
      Party of China, xii, 4, 7, 24, 228,
      353
    president, 76, 91, 124–125, 128, 151
Jiangsu Province, 55, 149
Jin Renqing, 184, 196, 198, 205, 226, 407
Johnson, Stephen, 198
Jordan, Michael, 17
JPMorgan Chase & Company, 164, 241

K
Kissinger, Henry, 51–52, 382, 393
Kitty Hawk U.S. aircraft carrier, 236
KPMG accounting firm, 54–55

L
Lambright, James, 198
Lau, Martin, 345, 410
Leavitt, Michael, 198, 212, 233, 400
legislation
    Baucus-Grassley-Schumer-Graham bill,
      223–224
    Sarbanes-Oxley Act, 148
    Schumer-Graham bill, 192, 195
    Troubled Assets Relief Program (TARP),
      256–257, 260–261, 271
Lehman Brothers, 242
Lehr, Deborah, 154–155, 184, 273, 296,
    411
Lenovo, 22, 110, 285, 345–346
Levin, Sandy, 243
Lew, Jacob (Jack), 313–314, 409
Li, Cherry, 5, 9, 40–41, 51, 410

Li, Richard, 31–32, 110
Li & Fung Manufacturing, 110, 122
Li Bai, 346
Li Ka-shing (K. S. Li), 29–34, 78, 134,
    152, 410
Li Keqiang, xii, 274, 277–279, 305, 309,
    312, 316, 329–330, 348, 374, 407
Li Peng, 7, 34–35, 36, 41, 67, 71, 119 134,
    407
Li Xiaolin
    daughter of Li Peng, 34
Li Yuanchao, 323, 326, 407
Lilly, Ron, 232
Lim, Edwin, 48–49
Liu Chuanzhi, 22, 110, 345, 410
Liu Deshu, 325
Liu Erh Fei, 40–41, 410
Liu Guoguang, 48
Liu Hongru, 35–36
Liu Mingkang (LMK), 110, 145–153, 163,
    170, 407
Liveris, Andrew, 324–326, 348, 410
Lost Horizon (Hilton), 117
Lou Jiwei, 158, 292, 365, 408
Lu Guanqiu, 181, 385, 410

M
Ma, Jack, 337, 344, 370, 406, 410
Ma Fucai, 72–73, 79, 83–84, 410
Ma Huateng (Pony Ma), 345, 410
Ma Kai, 198, 200, 209
Macau, 12, 21, 89
Mack, John, 253, 255, 410
Manzullo, Don, 243
Mao Zedong, 3, 36, 408
    Cultural Revolution and legacy, 19, 36,
      104, 136, 293, 295
    founding of the People's Republic of
      China, 18, 195
    Great Leap Forward, 19–21
    Long March, 95
    relationship with the Soviet Union,
      68–69
Marxism, 4, 40, 355
McBride, Ann, 121
McCormick, Dave, 247, 254, 258
McFarlan, Warren, 110, 112, 411
McKinsey & Company, 73, 110, 296

Mekong River, 117, 129, 216
Merkel, Angela, 259
Merrill Lynch, 39, 171, 253
Ministry of Commerce, 48
Ministry of Environmental Protection
    (MEP), 365–366, 400
Ministry of Finance, 136–137, 140–141,
    164, 167, 170, 172, 199, 233, 241,
    341
Ministry of Posts and Telecommunications,
    8, 11–13, 46, 48–56, 59, 64, 70. *see
    also* state-owned enterprise (SOE)
Moody's Investors Service, 37
Morgan Stanley, 5, 8, 39, 45–47, 68, 71, 77,
    141, 143, 241, 253–256
Moseley, Bob, 129–130
Motorola Mobility, 110, 346
Murdoch, Rupert, 31–32

N
National Development and Reform
    Commission (NDRC), 198, 200,
    234
National People's Congress (NPC), 365
    Standing Committee, 227–228, 351
The Nature Conservancy (TNC), 63,
    116–120, 129, 154, 180
nepotism and corruption, 23, 35, 359–363,
    372, 396
New Development Bank/BRICS Bank, 394
New York Times, 83, 182, 192, 289, 371
Ni Pin, 385–386, 411
9/11, 132–135
    Ground Zero, 135
1992 Olympics, 17–18
Niu, Rose, 120–121, 126–127, 154, 302, 411
Niu Gensheng, 369, 411
Niu Shaoyao, 118
Nixon, Richard, 17, 25, 105, 180, 382
Nokia, 110
nonperforming loan (NPL), 140, 152, 159,
    167
Noreddin, Alex, 135
Norton, Ed, 121, 126, 129

O
Obama, Barack, 242, 260, 397, 402, 409
Ollila, Jorma, 110

On the Brink (Paulson), 241, 271–272
Orient Overseas Container Line, 16

P
Pacific Century CyberWorks, 110
Pan Shiyi, 344, 373
Paulson, Amanda, 120, 129, 249
Paulson, Henry M., Jr.
    On the Brink, 241, 271–272
    environmentalist and conservationist,
        115–131. 301–306
    Goldman Sachs officer, xii, 4–15, 25–26,
        29–42, 120–172
    Paulson Institute, xii, 267, 273, 277,
        287, 296–299, 301–306, 312–313,
        369–370, 386–387, 395
    School of Economics and Management
        at Tsinghua University (SEM),
        106–114
    U.S. secretary of the Treasury, xii–xiii,
        67, 113–114, 177–192, 177–202,
        198, 203, 209–217, 224, 227, 229,
        232, 235–237, 240–263, 270–272,
        324, 385, 396–397
    writing, 270–272
Paulson, Merritt, 249
Paulson, Wendy. *see also* Bobolink
    Foundation
    naturalist and conservationist, 115–116,
        118, 154, 271–272, 293, 300–304,
        412
    wife of Henry M. Paulson, Jr., 45,
        63–64, 129–130
Paulson Institute
    and Bilateral Investment Treaty (BIT),
        312–313, 396
    Midwestern/Great Lakes governors'
        investment opportunities, 385–387
    partnership with U.S.–China Business
        Council and Goldman Sachs,
        395–396
    and state-owned enterprise (SOE) in
        China, 318, 320
    and urban sustainability in China, 267,
        273, 277, 287, 296–297, 299
    and wetlands preservation in China,
        301–306, 369–370
Pearson PLC, 32

People's Construction Bank, 137
People's Daily, 143, 372
People's Republic of China (PRC).
    see China; Communist Party of
    China (CPC)
Peregrine Investments, 39
PetroChina Company, 73–74, 76–85, 141,
    146, 152, 160, 164, 188, 359.
    see also Sinopec
Podesta, John, 402
Politburo Standing Committee, 8, 106,
    292, 328, 359, 366
pollution and environmental impact,
    xiii, 23, 81, 116, 123–131, 207,
    214, 243, 268, 294–308, 314,
    352–354, 360, 373, 398. *see also*
    The Nature Conservancy (TNC);
    State Environmental Protection
    Administration (SEPA)
    Ten-Year Framework for Cooperation on
    Energy and Environment, 245, 261,
    262, 402
Price, Dan, 257, 313
Purcell, Phil, 58

Q
Qualcomm, 110

R
Randt, Sandy, 189, 198, 210, 221, 236, 409
real estate
    Beijing investments, 16–17, 32–33
    Chinese economy and, 378
    Chinese governmental oversight and
        regulation, 291, 336–338
    Chinese investment in U.S., 385
    corruption and illiquidity, 38, 89, 207,
        258, 268, 336, 339
    Guangdong and Hainan
        speculative projects, 41
    Hong Kong, 102
Rice, Condoleezza, 187, 221–222, 409
rivers
    Huangpu River, 28, 206, 269
    Irrawaddy River, 117
    Mekong River, 117, 129, 216
    Salween River, 117, 118, 131

Yalu River, 25
Yangtze River, 29, 117, 119, 120, 216,
    283, 299
Yellow River, 216, 299
Yubeng River, 129, 130
RMS *Queen Elizabeth,* 16
Rockefeller, David, 169
Rogers, John, 82, 126, 132, 134, 159, 184,
    411
Royal Dutch Shell, 72
Rubin, Bob, 28

S
Sarbanes-Oxley Act, 148
Sarkozy, Nicolas, 259
Schroders, 39
Schumer, Chuck, 189, 192, 197, 202, 223,
    409
Schumer-Graham bill, 192, 195
Schwab, Susan, 186, 198
Science, 372
Scott, Lee, 110, 324
Scowcroft, Brent, 393
Securities and Exchange Commission
    (SEC), 34, 77
17th National Congress, 227
severe acute respiratory syndrome (SARS),
    154–156, 193
Shafran, Steven, 98, 252, 411
Shandong International Power
    Development Company, 36
Shantou, 21
Shelby, Richard, 224
Singh, Manmohan, 259
Sinopec
    China National Offshore Oil
        Corporation (CNOOC), 70, 78,
        200
    China National Petroleum Corporation
        (CNPC), 66–77, 79–85, 104, 188,
        323, 360
    PetroChina Company, 73–74, 76–85,
        141, 146, 152, 160, 164, 188, 359
60 Minutes, 21
Smith, Taiya, 178, 199, 208–209, 216–217,
    221, 231, 233, 250, 273, 302, 412
Snow, John, 184

Snowden, Edward, 391
Snyder, Rick, 386
SoftBank Corporation, 110
Son, Masayoshi, 110
Sony Corporation, 110
special economic zone (SEZ), 9, 27, 275
  Fujian, 86, 179
  Guangdong, 27, 86–88, 92
    Shenzen, 27, 90, 123, 356
  Hong Kong, 21, 88–89
  Macau, 21
  Shantou, 21
  Xiamen, 21
  Zhuhai, 21, 356
Standard and Poor's, 37
Standing Committee of the Chinese
    Communist Party, 23, 25, 95, 172,
    186, 192, 194, 227, 228, 279, 283,
    288, 309, 311–312, 351, 352, 359
Star TV, 30–32
  HutchVision Limited, 32
State Council, 7, 35
State Council's Economic Reform
    Commission, 40
State Development and Planning
    Commission (SDPC), 123
State Environmental Protection
    Administration (SEPA), 120,
    124–126, 215, 365
State Grid Corporation, 324
State-owned Assets Supervision and
    Administration Commission
    (SASAC), 334
state-owned enterprise (SOE), 11, 20–21,
    36–39
  China International Trust and
    Investment Corporation (CITIC),
    60, 88, 241
  China Telecom, 6–8, 37–38, 43–56,
    73–74, 78
  China United Telecommunications
    Corporation (China Unicom), 51, 65
  China Venturetech Investment
    Corporation (CVIC), 34–36
  overhaul and modernization reforms,
    6–7, 37–38, 48–49, 60, 76,
    103–105, 172, 317–319, 334–335

PetroChina Company, 323
  and profitability, 320–325
  and shadow banking market, 290, 319,
    336
Shandong International Power
    Development Company, 36
Sinopec
  China National Offshore Oil
    Corporation (CNOOC), 70, 78,
    200
  China National Petroleum
    Corporation (CNPC), 66–77,
    79–85, 104, 188, 323, 360
  PetroChina Company, 73–74,
    76–85, 141, 146, 152, 160, 164,
    188, 359
State Grid Corporation, 324
and telecommunications, 5–7
stock markets
  Dow Jones Industrial Average, 62, 135,
    226
  Nasdaq composite index, 122, 125–126,
    202
  New York Stock Exchange (NYSE),
    37–38, 54, 67, 86, 135, 148,
    151–152, 202
  Shanghai Stock Exchange Composite
    Index, 126, 212, 241
Strategic and Economic Dialogue (S&ED),
    311, 313, 397, 402
Strategic Economic Dialogue (SED) I, II,
    III, IV, V, 178–189, 192–212, 215,
    222, 224–226, 228, 230–238,
    239–245, 250, 252, 254, 256,
    260–262, 269, 273, 283, 310–311,
    314, 381, 397, 400
  China Energy Conservation and
    Environmental Protection Group,
    334
  China National Building Materials
    Group, 334, 374
  China National Pharmaceutical Group
    Corporation, 334
  Xinxing Cathay International Group,
    334
Sun Yat-sen (Zhongshan) University, 48
Sutherland, Peter, 10, 169, 411

T
Taiwan, 12
    special economic zones (SEZ), 21
Tencent, 99, 337, 345, 372, 374
Ten-year Framework for Cooperation on
    Energy and Environment, 245, 261,
    262, 402
Third Plenary Session, 18th Party Central
    Committee, 328–332, 351, 366
Thornton, John, 5, 13, 31–32, 59, 63, 66,
    105, 111, 126, 155, 157, 411
    China Telecom, 49–55
Tian, Edward, 122, 370
Tian Chengping, 198
Tibet, 81, 117–118, 124, 128–129, 215–218
Times Newspaper Holdings, 32
Times of London, 32
Toyota Motor Corporation, 22
Trans-Pacific Partnership (TPP), 312, 399
Troubled Assets Relief Program (TARP),
    256–257, 260–261, 271
Tsang, Moses, 26, 30, 411
Tsinghua University, 36, 108–110, 179
    School of Economics and Management
    (SEM), 105, 108, 171, 216
Tung, C. C., 120
Tung, C. H. (Tung Chee-hwa), 16–17, 32,
    120, 134, 408
Tung, C. Y., 16

U
USS *Mustin,* 236

V
Vietnam War, 25
Vogel, Ezra, 400
Volkswagen, 22

W
Wadsworth, Jack, 58
Walker, Scott, 386
Wallace, Mike, 21
Wall Street, 28, 135–136, 241–242,
    253–254, 271, 338
Wall Street Journal, 288, 291, 313
Wal-Mart Stores, 110
Wang, Hsueh-ming, 5, 13, 52, 57, 99,
    107–108, 111–112, 126, 411

Wang Qishan, 8–9, 10–11, 49, 51–52, 61,
    63, 68, 86–89, 92–104, 122, 136,
    142–143, 155–156, 240–244, 248,
    251–253–255, 258–260, 272–273,
    304, 309–311, 358–362, 364, 397,
    401, 408
Wang Xuebing, 144
Wang Yang, 312–313, 364, 408
Wanxiang Group Corporation, 181, 385–386
Wardley of HBSC, 39
WeChat, 345
weibo, 353, 371–373
Welch, Jack, 346
Wells Fargo & Company, 335
Wen Jiabao, xii, 36, 128, 148, 163, 187, 192,
    201, 219, 227, 241, 287, 372, 408
Wolstencroft, Tracy, 145–146, 150, 411
World Bank, 48–49, 77, 214, 217, 295, 314,
    338, 394
    and International Monetary Fund, 53,
    169, 257, 394
World Health Organization (WHO), 154,
    268
World Trade Organization (WTO), 44,
    155, 169, 184, 193, 212, 223, 225,
    231, 275
    General Agreement on Tariffs and Trade,
    81
    membership negotiations with China, 7,
    10, 79, 81, 155, 313, 317, 319, 384,
    397–398
Wright, Dan, 215–216
Wu Bangguo, 79, 227–228
Wu Jichuan, 13, 48, 51–54, 57, 61, 64, 408
Wu Yi, 192–194, 196–197, 199–200, 219,
    221–222, 408
    and Strategic Economic Dialogue (SED),
    202, 205–206, 208–213, 231–236,
    242, 246, 261–262, 397

X
Xi Jinping, xii, 25, 106, 159, 178–179, 189,
    195, 228, 272, 298, 300, 302–303,
    309–316, 328–329, 348, 350, 362,
    366, 370–371, 373–376, 380,
    392–393, 395, 408
Xi Zhongxun
    father of Xi Jinping, 178–179

xia hai, 21
Xiamen, 21
Xiao Gang, 155, 170, 184, 324, 340, 408
Xie Xuren, 226, 254
Xie Zhenhua, 126
Xu Caihou, 359
Xu Rongkai, 126–129
Xue, Charles, 373

Y
Yalu River, 25
Yang Jianli, 220–222, 252, 412
Yang, Marjorie, 110
Yangtze River, 29, 117, 119, 120, 216, 283, 299
Yellow River, 216, 299
Yellow Sea, 297, 301
Yubeng River, 129, 130

Z
Zeltwanger, Cynthia, 302
Zeng Peiyan, 299, 343, 408
Zhang Xin, 373
Zhang Yue, 295, 346–347, 411
Zhang Zhidong, 18
Zhao Chunjun, 111–112, 412

Zhao Ziyang, 23–24, 40, 96
Zhejiang, 55
Zhou Qiang, 366–367
Zhou Wenzhong, 189, 209, 272, 408
Zhou Xiaochuan, 68, 110–111, 125–126,
    132, 136, 140–145, 163, 170–171,
    177, 182, 198, 205, 209, 227–229,
    241, 245–248, 251, 254, 272,
    339–340, 362, 408
Zhou Yongkang, 66–72, 77, 188–189, 228,
    359–360, 408
Zhu, Levin, 143
Zhu Rongji, xii, 4, 6–14, 24, 36–37, 38–39,
    46, 60, 63–64, 68, 71–72, 75–76,
    81–82, 93, 96–96, 100–101, 103,
    104–105, 108–114, 132
    IPOs and SOEs, 43–44, 136, 322–323,
        362–363
    1993 16-point austerity plan, 7, 41,
        289–290, 313, 316–318, 328–329,
        335
Zhuhai, 21, 356
Zimmer, Robert, 274
Ziwang Xu, 71, 125–126, 145, 411
Zoellick, Robert, 250
Zong Qinghou, 22–23, 181

About the Author

Businessman, conservationist, and best-selling author Henry M. Paulson, Jr., is the founder and chairman of the Paulson Institute at the University of Chicago, a "think and do" tank that promotes sustainable economic growth and a cleaner environment through greater cooperation between the U.S. and China, a country he has visited more than one hundred times.

Paulson served under President George W. Bush as the 74th secretary of the Treasury from July 2006 to January 2009. He was the president's leading policy adviser on a broad range of domestic and international economic issues. His best-selling memoir, *On the Brink*, recounts in dramatic detail his efforts, and those of his colleagues in the Bush administration, to avert economic catastrophe during the financial crisis that engulfed the world, beginning in 2007.

Before joining the Treasury Department, Paulson had a 32-year career at Goldman Sachs, serving as chairman and chief executive officer following the firm's initial public offering in 1999. Earlier in his career, he was a staff assistant for the White House Domestic Council from 1972 to 1973 as well as a staff assistant to the assistant secretary of Defense at the Pentagon from 1970 to 1972.

A lifelong conservationist, Paulson is involved in a range of environmental initiatives, having served as chairman of the Peregrine Fund, chairman of the board of directors of the Nature Conservancy, and founder and co-chairman of its Asia-Pacific Council. In 2011 he founded and continues to co-chair the Conservancy's Latin American Conservation Council, which comprises global business and political leaders working collaboratively to address conservation issues in that region. Paulson also co-chairs the Risky Business Project, which highlights and engages U.S. business leaders on the economic risks of climate change in the U.S.

Paulson graduated from Dartmouth College in 1968 and received an MBA from Harvard University in 1970. He and his wife, Wendy, have two children and four grandchildren.